Praise for Stalin's General:

'Confident and detailed'   John Lloyd, *Financial Times*

'Although this book will naturally attract readers interested in military history, it also provides broad insights into how individuals functioned and survived under Stalin and Khrushchev. It is a skilfully written account of an extraordinary man living in extraordinary times.'   Evan Mawdsley, *BBC History Magazine*

'This book is an example of high quality biography. It is meticulously researched and objective in its judgments. It is an important contribution to understanding the Soviet psychology as well as the history of the Second World War.'
Douglas Osler, *Scotsman*

'[A] well-written and meticulously researched biography'
Richard Overy, *Literary Review*

'Roberts does a large measure of justice to Stalin's general [...] in his thoroughly researched and well-written book, which will give pleasure not only to his fellow specialists and Second World War enthusiasts but also to a wide circle of readers.'   *History Today*

'Geoffrey Roberts' fine book, *Stalin's General*, takes its place among the last, but no less valuable pieces in the jigsaw of World War Two historiography. It is a shrewd, balanced account.'
Henry Coningsby, Waterstones.com

'The most comprehensive biography of Zhukov available in English, which chronicles not only the marshal's well-known military feats but also, and very im
political intrigues and infighting t
[...] It is an informative, accessible
work, the publication of which fit
of Stalingrad.'   Seamus Martin, *l*

'Roberts is an excellent historian [...] This is a brisk, comprehensive biography.' *Herald*

'[Roberts'] book is worth particular attention [...] for its fascinating interweaving of public and private events and for the light it sheds on the changing patterns and possibilities of life among the Soviet elite.' *London Review of Books*

'[Roberts] has written in *Stalin's General* [...] the most comprehensive biography of Zhukov.' *Washington Post*

'There's no doubt that the man who comes through, bluff disciplinarian though he may have been, was undoubtedly the right man in the right place at the right time to make a substantial difference to the Soviet war effort, and thus to the whole fate of World War II. Recommended reading.' Bookgeeks.co.uk

'A welcome new biography of the ruthless Red Army general who defeated the Nazis and then spent decades alternately disgraced and rehabilitated in Soviet Russia. [...] Zhukov's relationship with Stalin emerges as a key, fascinating aspect to the story. [...] A solid, engaging life.' *Kirkus*

'Roberts makes the only English-language Zhukov biography a WWII essential.' *Booklist*

'Roberts has pored over Zhukov's personal papers, his unexpurgated memoirs and recent Russian scholarship to write a definitive account of an impressive if only intermittently sympathetic commander.' *Military History*

'With maps of the action, unpublished photos, and unprecedented access to historical documents, Roberts reveals the story of Russia's ruthless general and his subsequent fall from grace as he faced obliteration by the Soviet government he fought tirelessly to preserve.' *Daily Beast*

'To tell the General's tale Geoffrey Roberts wades through sources that are often contradictory. Accusations of enormous cruelties, mythological feats of heroism, and requisite romantic entanglements are woven through every aspect of Zhukov's life. [...] Roberts takes his task seriously and with a biographer's modesty perfectly suited to his subject's largeness. In broad, clear language aimed at history fans of all stripes, he fills pages with detailed information on the military and political aspects of the Red Army. [...] Zhukov's personality is revealed through a play-by-play account of Stalin's war with Hitler's Germany, thus offering a portrait of Stalin as well.' *Biographile*

'Roberts, who has studied and written on the Soviet experience in World War II for decades, shows his comfort with the material in his absolute control over a complex narrative. [...] This is a fine biography, wrapped well into the broader context of Zhukov's war and the Soviet system he served so loyally. The general reader can come away with a clear understanding of Zhukov's character and operating style. [...] Geoffrey Roberts has accomplished his aim, with a readable, sound, balanced portrait of a fascinating man operating on a vast scale.' *Washington Independent Review of Books*

'Roberts' book gives us a true appreciation of Russian generalship during the war' Steve Forbes, *Forbes* magazine

ALSO BY **GEOFFREY ROBERTS**

The Unholy Alliance: Stalin's Pact with Hitler

The Soviet Union and the Origins of the Second World War

The Soviet Union in World Politics, 1945–1991

Victory at Stalingrad: The Battle That Changed History

Stalin's Wars: From World War to Cold War, 1939–1953

Molotov: Stalin's Cold Warrior

STALIN'S
GENERAL
THE LIFE OF GEORGY ZHUKOV

GEOFFREY ROBERTS

This edition published in the UK in 2013 by
Icon Books Ltd, Omnibus Business Centre,
39–41 North Road, London N7 9DP
email: info@iconbooks.net
www.iconbooks.net

Previously published in the UK in 2012 by Icon Books Ltd

Published by arrangement with Random House, an imprint of
The Random House Publishing Group, a division of Random House, Inc

Sold in the UK, Europe and Asia
by Faber & Faber Ltd, Bloomsbury House,
74–77 Great Russell Street,
London WC1B 3DA or their agents

Distributed in the UK, Europe and Asia
by TBS Ltd, TBS Distribution Centre, Colchester Road,
Frating Green, Colchester CO7 7DW

Distributed in South Africa
by Book Promotions, Office B4, The District
41 Sir Lowry Road, Woodstock 7925

Distributed in Australia and New Zealand
by Allen & Unwin Pty Ltd,
PO Box 8500, 83 Alexander Street,
Crows Nest, NSW 2065

ISBN: 978-184831-517-4

Text copyright © 2012, 2013 Geoffrey Roberts
The author has asserted his moral rights.

All maps, except as noted below, copyright © 2012 by Mapping Specialists, Ltd.
Maps on pages 68, 94, 102, 146, 158, 166, 172, 174, 190, 201, 208, 217, 225 and 232
are from Stalin's Wars by Geoffrey Roberts (New Haven, Conn.
and London: Yale University Press, 2007) and are reprinted
by permission of Yale Representation, Ltd., London.

All photos, except for the photo of the statue of Georgy Zhukov,
are reprinted by permission of SCRSS, Society for Co-operation
in Russian and Soviet Studies.
Photo of the statue of Georgy Zhukov by Geoffrey Roberts.

No part of this book may be reproduced in any form, or by any means,
without prior permission in writing from the publisher.

Printed and bound in the UK by CPI Group (UK) Ltd, Croydon CR0 4YY

For Celia

PREFACE AND ACKNOWLEDGEMENTS

IF RUSSIA HAS A PRE-EMINENT HERO IT IS GEORGY ZHUKOV, THE MAN WHO beat Hitler, the peasant lad who rose from poverty to become the greatest general of the Second World War, the colourful personality who fell out with both Stalin and Khrushchev yet lived to fight another day. When Jonathan Jao of Random House suggested I write a new biography of Zhukov I was intrigued. While working on my book *Stalin's Wars* I'd formed a questioning view of Zhukov's role in the Soviet victory over Nazi Germany, not least concerning the mythology generated by his self-serving memoirs. If I had a favourite Soviet general, it would be Konstantin Rokossovsky – a rival of Zhukov's who had a very different leadership style. My working title for the new project was 'Zhukov: A Critical Biography' and the intention was to produce a warts-and-all portrait that would expose the many myths surrounding his life and career as well as capture the great drama of his military victories and defeats, and his journey on the political roller coaster. But the more I worked on his biography the more sympathetic I became to Zhukov's point of view. Empathy combined with critique, and the result is what I hope will be seen as a balanced re-appraisal that cuts through the hyperbole of the Zhukov cult while appreciating the man and his achievements in full measure.

This is not the first English-language biography of Zhukov and I have to acknowledge the groundbreaking efforts of Albert Axell, William J. Spahr, and, especially, Otto Preston Chaney. The main limitation of their work was overreliance on Zhukov's memoirs, an indispensable but problematic source. In this biography I have been able to utilise an enormous amount of new evidence from the Russian archives, including Zhukov's personal files in the Russian State Military Archive. I have also benefited from the work of many Russian scholars, especially V. A. Afanas'ev, V. Daines, A. Isaev, and V. Krasnov, who have all written valuable biographical studies focused on Zhukov's role in the Second World War. Mine, however, is a full-scale biography that gives due weight to Zhukov's early life as well as his postwar political career.

In Moscow my research was greatly facilitated by my friends in the Russian Academy of Sciences' Institute of General History, especially Oleg Rzheshevsky, Mikhail Myagkov, and Sergey Listikov. Professor Rzheshevsky was kind enough to arrange for a meeting and interview with Zhukov's eldest daughter, Era. Mr. Nikita Maximov and Alexander Pozdeev accompanied me on a fascinating visit to the Zhukov museum in the hometown that now bears his name. I do not share Boris Sokolov's hostile view of Zhukov but he was generous in advising me of the work of Irina Mastykina on Zhukov's family and private life.

Evan Mawdsley was kind enough to read the first draft and to make some valuable suggestions as well as correct mistakes. The most amusing of the latter was my conviction that Zhukov had fallen in love with a young gymnast rather than a schoolgirl (in Russian *gimnazistka*). Evan's own work on the Soviet-German war has been indispensable, as have the writings of Chris Bellamy, David Glantz, Jonathan House, and the late John Erickson. My main guides through the prewar Red Army that Zhukov served in were the works of Mary Habeck, Mark von Hagen, Shimon Naveh, Roger Reese, and David Stone.

I am grateful to Ambassador John Beyrle for finding time in his busy day to talk to me about his father, Joseph's, chance meeting with Zhukov in 1945 and for giving me the materials that enabled me to reconstruct the incident.

Opportunities to present my research on Zhukov were provided by the Society of Military History, the Irish Association for Russian and East European Studies, the Society for Co-operation in Russian and Soviet Studies in London, the Centre for Military History and Strategic Studies at Maynooth University, and the Department of Politics and International Studies at the University of Hull.

Many weeks of research in Moscow and many more months writing would not have been possible without research leave and financial support from my employer, University College Cork, Ireland.

For this book I was fortunate to have the input of not one but two brilliant editors: my partner, Celia Weston – to whom the book is dedicated – and Jonathan Jao, who gave me a master class in the writing of popular scholarly biography. I have also been privileged to have the services of my agent, Andrew Lownie, who has also encouraged me to take on the challenges of writing for a broader audience.

Finally, an acknowledgement of Nigel Hamilton's *How to Do Biography*. It was only when I read the book for a second time – after I had finished writing about Zhukov – that I realised how many of its valuable lessons I had taken to heart. But neither he nor anyone else mentioned in this preface can be blamed for any defects, which are entirely my own.

CONTENTS

———

LIST OF MAPS AND CHARTS

———

TIMELINE:
THE LIFE AND CAREER OF
GEORGY ZHUKOV

1896	*1 December:* Birth of Georgy Konstantinovich Zhukov in Strelkovka, Kaluga Province, Russia
1903	Begins elementary school
1908	Migrates to Moscow to work as a furrier
1914	*August:* Outbreak of World War One
1915	*August:* Conscripted into the tsar's army and assigned to the cavalry
1916	*October:* Wounded in action and decorated for bravery
1917	*March:* Tsar Nicholas II abdicates following military mutiny in Petrograd
	November: Bolsheviks overthrow the Provisional Government and seize power
1918	*1 October:* Joins the Red Army
1919	*March:* Becomes a candidate member of the Communist Party
	October: Wounded in action in the Russian Civil War
1920	Marries Alexandra Dievna Zuikova
	March: Enrols in Red Commanders Cavalry Course at Ryazan
	May: Becomes a full member of the Communist Party
	October: Promoted to platoon and then squadron commander
1921	Death of Zhukov's father
	March: Decorated for bravery

1922   *June:* Appointed squadron commander in the 38th Cavalry Regiment

1923   *March:* Promoted to assistant commander of the 40th Cavalry Regiment

July: Appointed commander of the 39th Buzuluk Cavalry Regiment

1924   *October:* Attends Higher Cavalry School in Leningrad

1928   Birth of daughter Era

1929   Birth of daughter Margarita

Attends Frunze Military Academy in Moscow

1930   *May:* Promoted to command of 2nd Cavalry Brigade of the 7th Samara Division

1931   *February:* Appointed assistant inspector of the cavalry

September: Japan invades Manchuria

1933   *January:* Hitler comes to power in Germany

March: Appointed commander of the 4th (Voroshilov) Cavalry Division

1935   Awarded the Order of Lenin

1937   Birth of daughter Ella

May: Arrest and execution of Marshal Tukhachevsky and start of military purges

July: Japan invades China

July: Appointed commander of the 3rd Cavalry Corps in Belorussia

1938   *March:* Transferred to the command of the 6th Cossack Corps

June: Appointed deputy commander of the Belorussian Military District

1939   *May:* Posted to the Mongolian-Manchurian border

June: Appointed commander of the 57th Special Corps at Khalkhin-Gol

July: 57th Corps reorganised into 1st Army Group with Zhukov in command

20 August: Launch of attack on Japanese forces at Khalkhin-Gol

23 August: Signature of Nazi-Soviet Pact

30 August: Made a Hero of the Soviet Union for his victory at Khalkhin-Gol

1 September: German invasion of Poland

17 September: Soviet invasion of eastern Poland

December: Soviet invasion of Finland

1940   *March:* Soviet-Finnish peace treaty

May: Appointed commander of the Kiev Special Military District

May: Restoration of the titles of general and admiral in the Soviet armed forces

2 June: First meeting with Stalin

5 June: Promoted to general of the army

22 June: France surrenders

28 June: Leads Soviet occupation of Bessarabia and North Bukovina

18 December: Hitler issues his directive on Operation Barbarossa

25 December: Delivers report, 'The Character of Contemporary Offensive Operations'

1941   *January:* Takes part in General Staff war games

14 January: Appointed chief of the General Staff

February: Elected alternate member of the Central Committee at the 18th Party conference

15 May: Draft of Soviet plan for a pre-emptive strike against Germany

22 June: German invasion of the Soviet Union

30 June: Fall of Minsk

10 July: Establishment of Stavka, campaign headquarters of the Supreme Command

29 July: Removed as chief of the General Staff and appointed to command of Reserve Front

8 August: Stalin becomes supreme commander of the Armed Forces

August: Leads counter-offensive at Yel'nya

September: Fall of Kiev and blockade of Leningrad

11 September: Appointed commander of the Leningrad Front

11 October: Appointed commander of the Western Front

5 December: Beginning of Moscow counter-offensive

1942   *January:* Launch of first Rzhev-Viazma operation

June: Germans launch southern offensive towards Baku and Stalingrad

July: Second Rzhev-Viazma operation

17 July: Beginning of the battle for Stalingrad

28 July: Stalin issues Order No. 227 – *Ni Shagu Nazad!* (Not a Step Back!)

26 August: Appointed Stalin's deputy supreme commander

November: Third Rzhev-Viazma operation (Operation Mars)

19 November: Operation Uranus – Red Army counter-offensive at Stalingrad

1943   *January:* Supervises operations to end the German blockade of Leningrad

18 January: Promoted to marshal of the Soviet Union

February: Final surrender of Germans at Stalingrad

July: Battle of Kursk

November: Liberation of Kiev

1944   Death of Zhukov's mother

June: Operation Bagration; D-Day landings in France

August: Warsaw uprising

September: Supervises Soviet invasion of Bulgaria

12 November: Appointed commander of 1st Belorussian Front

1945   *January:* Launch of Vistula-Oder operation; capture of Warsaw

18 February: Stavka halts 1st Belorussian's advance on Berlin

16 April: Launch of attack on Berlin

25 April: Soviet and American forces meet on the Elbe

30 April: Hitler commits suicide

May: Red Army captures Berlin and Zhukov accepts German surrender

30 May: Appointed commander of Soviet occupation forces in Germany

24 June: Zhukov leads Victory Parade in Red Square

July–August: Attends Potsdam conference

1946   *February:* Elected to the Supreme Soviet

22 March: Appointed commander-in-chief of Soviet ground forces

June: Dismissed as commander-in-chief of Soviet ground forces and posted to Odessa

1947   *February:* Expelled from membership of the party Central Committee

1948   *January:* Censured for extracting war booty from Germany

February: Transferred to the command of the Urals Military District

1950   Reelected to the Supreme Soviet

Meets Galina Semonova in Sverdlovsk

1952   *October:* Attends 19th Party Congress and is elected to Central Committee

1953   *March:* Returns to Moscow and appointed deputy defence minister

March: Stalin dies

June: Arrests Beria

1954   Death of Zhukov's sister, Maria

September: Oversees nuclear test and exercise at Totskoe

1955   *February:* Appointed minister of defence

May: Signing of Warsaw Pact

July: Attends Geneva summit and meets Eisenhower

1956   *February:* Elected to the Presidium at the 20th Party Congress

25 February: Khrushchev gives Secret Speech to 20th Party Congress

November: Oversees Soviet military intervention in Hungary

1957 *January–February:* Tours India and Burma

June: Leads defence of Khrushchev against attempted coup by the so-called antiparty group

June: Birth of daughter Maria

October: Central Committee dismisses Zhukov for distancing army from the party

1958 *February:* Retired from the armed forces by the Presidium

1959 Attacked at 21st Party Congress by Minister of Defence Malinovsky

1961 Attacked at 22nd Party Congress by Khrushchev

1964 *October:* Fall of Khrushchev

1965 Divorces Alexandra Dievna

1966 Marries Galina Semonova

November: Awarded fifth Order of Lenin

1967 *December:* Death of Alexandra Dievna Zuikova

1968 *January:* Suffers stroke

1969 *April:* Publication of first edition of Zhukov's memoirs

1971 *September:* Khrushchev dies

1973 *November:* Death of Galina Semonova

1974 *18 June:* Dies in the Kremlin hospital

July: Publication of the revised edition of Zhukov's memoirs

STALIN'S GENERAL

1.

SIC TRANSIT GLORIA:
THE RISES AND FALLS OF
MARSHAL GEORGY ZHUKOV

———

OF ALL THE MOMENTS OF TRIUMPH IN THE LIFE OF MARSHAL GEORGY KON-
stantinovich Zhukov nothing equalled that day in June 1945 when he
took the salute at the great Victory Parade in Red Square. Zhukov,
mounted on a magnificent white Arabian called Tspeki, rode into the
square through the Spassky Gate, the Kremlin on his right and the
famous onion domes of St. Basil's Cathedral directly ahead. As he did
so a 1,400-strong orchestra struck up Glinka's *Glory* (to the Russian
Motherland). Awaiting him were columns of combined regiments representing all the branches of the Soviet armed forces. In the middle of
the square Zhukov met Marshal K. K. Rokossovsky, who called the
parade to attention and then escorted Zhukov as he rode to each regiment and saluted them.

When the salutes were finished Zhukov joined the Soviet dictator
Joseph Stalin on the plinth above Lenin's Mausoleum and gave a
speech celebrating the Red Army's victory over Nazi Germany. The
sky was overcast and there was a drizzling rain that worsened as the
day wore on. At one point Zhukov's hat became so wet he was tempted
to remove it and wipe the visor but desisted when he saw that Stalin
was making no such move.

As a former cavalryman Zhukov relished the salute portion of the
proceedings. Giving a speech that would be seen and heard by millions of people across the world was a different matter. The idea made
him anxious and he prepared as thoroughly as he could, even

rehearsing the speech in front of his daughters Era and Ella, who were so impressed they burst into spontaneous applause. The delivery of the speech was carefully crafted, with prompts in the margin directing Zhukov to speak quietly, then louder, and when to adopt a solemn tone.

Zhukov seemed more than a little nervous but it was a commanding performance nonetheless. His delivery was halting but emphatic and reached a crescendo with his final sentence: 'Glory to our wise leader and commander – Marshal of the Soviet Union, the Great Stalin!' At that moment artillery fired a salute and the orchestra struck up the Soviet national anthem.

After his speech Zhukov reviewed the parade standing beside Stalin. Partway through there was a pause in the march while, to a roll of drumbeats, 200 captured Nazi banners were piled against the Kremlin wall, much like Marshal Kutuzov's soldiers had thrown French standards at the feet of Tsar Alexander I after their defeat of Napoleon in 1812. The parade over, the day ended with a fabulous fireworks display.[1]

Stalin's choice of Zhukov to lead the parade evoked no comment. He was, after all, Stalin's deputy supreme commander and widely regarded as the main architect of the Soviet victory over Adolf Hitler's Germany, a victory that had saved Europe as well as Russia from Nazi enslavement. Newsreel film of the parade that flashed across the world only reinforced Zhukov's status as the greatest Soviet general of the Second World War.

When the German armies invaded Soviet Russia in summer 1941 it was Zhukov who led the Red Army's first successful counter-offensive, forcing the Wehrmacht to retreat and demonstrating to the whole world that Hitler's war machine was not invincible. When Leningrad was surrounded by the Germans in September 1941 Stalin sent Zhukov to save the city from imminent capture. A month later, Stalin recalled Zhukov to Moscow and put him in command of the defence of the Soviet capital. Not only did Zhukov stop the German advance on Moscow, but in December 1941 he launched a counter-offensive that drove the Wehrmacht away from the city and ended Hitler's hope of subduing the Red Army and conquering Russia in a single Blitzkrieg campaign.

Six months later Hitler tried again to inflict a crippling blow on the Red Army, this time by launching a southern offensive designed to capture the Soviet oilfields at Baku. At the height of the German advance south Zhukov played a central role in masterminding the Soviet counter-offensive at Stalingrad in November 1942 – an encirclement operation that trapped 300,000 German troops in the city. In July 1943 he followed that dazzling success with a stunning victory in the great armoured clash at Kursk – a battle that saw the destruction of the last remaining reserves of Germany's panzer power. In November 1943 cheering crowds welcomed Zhukov as he and the future Soviet leader Nikita Khrushchev drove into the recaptured Ukrainian capital of Kiev. In June 1944 Zhukov coordinated Operation Bagration – the campaign to liberate Belorussia from German occupation. Bagration brought the Red Army to the gates of Warsaw and the capture of the Polish capital in January 1945 marked the beginning of the Vistula-Oder operation – an offensive that took Zhukov's armies through Poland, into eastern Germany, and to within striking distance of Berlin. In April 1945 Zhukov led the final Soviet assault on Berlin. The ferocious battle for the German capital cost the lives of 80,000 Soviet soldiers but by the end of April Hitler was dead and the Soviet flag flew over the ruins of the Reichstag. It was Zhukov who formally accepted Germany's unconditional surrender on 9 May 1945.

Following Zhukov's triumphant parade before the assembled legions of the Red Army, Navy, and Air Force in June 1945 he seemed destined for an equally glorious postwar career as the Soviet Union's top soldier and in March 1946 he was appointed commander-in-chief of all Soviet ground forces. However, within three months Zhukov had been sacked by Stalin and banished to the command of the Odessa Military District.

The ostensible reason for Zhukov's dismissal was that he had been disloyal and disrespectful towards Stalin and claimed too much personal credit for victory in the Great Patriotic War, as the Soviets called it. In truth, Zhukov's loyalty to Stalin was beyond question. If anyone deserved the appellation 'Stalin's General', he did. Zhukov was not slow to blow his own trumpet, at least in private, but that was characteristic of top generals the world over, including many of his colleagues in the Soviet High Command – who all voted in favour of Stalin's resolution removing him as commander-in-chief. What Stalin really objected to was Zhukov's independent streak and his tendency to tell the truth as he saw it, a quality that had served the dictator well during the war but was less commendable in peacetime when Stalin felt he needed no advice except his own. Like Zhukov, Stalin could be vain, and he was jealous of the attention lavished on his deputy during and immediately after the war, even though he had been instrumental in the creation of Zhukov's reputation as a great general. Stalin's treatment of Zhukov also sent a message to his other generals: if Zhukov, the most famous among them and the closest to Stalin, could suffer such a fate, so could any one of them if they did not behave themselves.

According to his daughter Era, Zhukov was not a man given to overt displays of emotion, even in the privacy of his family, but his demotion and exile to Odessa caused him great distress.[2] Later, he told the Soviet writer Konstantin Simonov: 'I was firmly resolved to remain myself. I understood that they were waiting for me to give up and expecting that I would not last a day as a district commander. I could not permit this to happen. Of course, fame is fame. At the same time it is a double-edged sword and sometimes cuts against you. After this blow I did everything to remain as I had been. In this I saw my inner salvation.'[3]

Zhukov's troubles were only just beginning, however. In February 1947 he was expelled from the Communist Party Central Committee on grounds that he had an 'antiparty attitude'. Zhukov was horrified and he pleaded for a private meeting with the dictator to clear his name. Stalin ignored him and the anti-Zhukov campaign continued. In June 1947 Zhukov was censured for giving the singer Lidiya Ruslanova a military medal when she had visited Berlin in August 1945. Shortly after, Ruslanova and her husband, General V. V. Krukov, were arrested and imprisoned. 'In 1947 I feared arrest every day', recalled Zhukov later, 'and I had a bag ready with my underwear in it.'[4]

The next development was even more ominous: an investigation began into the war booty Zhukov had extracted while serving in Germany. According to the report of a party commission Zhukov amassed a personal hoard of trophies, including 70 pieces of gold jewellery, 740 items of silverware, 50 rugs, 60 pictures, 3,700 metres of silk, and – presumably after casting a professional eye over them – 320 furs (he had been a furrier in his youth). Zhukov pleaded that these were gifts or paid for from his own pocket but the commission found his explanations insincere and evasive and concluded that while he did not deserve to be expelled from the party he should hand over his ill-gotten loot to the state. In January 1948 Zhukov was demoted to the command of the Urals Military District based in Sverdlovsk.[5]

Further punishment came in the form of treating Zhukov as an 'unperson'. He was written out of the history of the Great Patriotic War. Paintings of the 1945 Victory Parade omitted him. A 1948 documentary film about the battle of Moscow barely featured Zhukov. In a 1949 poster tableau depicting Stalin and his top generals plotting and planning the great counter-offensive at Stalingrad Zhukov was nowhere to be seen.

But as early as October 1949 there were signs of Zhukov's rehabilitation. That month *Pravda* carried a funeral notice of the death of Marshal F. I. Tolbukhin and Zhukov was listed among the signatories.[6] In 1950 Zhukov, along with a number of other senior officers, was re-elected to the Supreme Soviet of the USSR. In 1952 the second edition of the official *Great Soviet Encyclopedia* carried a short but favourable entry on Zhukov, stressing his important role in the realisation of Stalin's military plans during the war.[7] In October 1952 Zhukov was a delegate to the 19th Party Congress and he was restored to candidate (i.e., probationary) membership of the Central Committee. Incredibly, Zhukov believed that Stalin was preparing to appoint him minister of defence.[8]

In March 1953 Stalin died and Zhukov was a prominent member of the military guard of honour at the dictator's state funeral.[9] Zhukov's appointment as deputy minister of defence was among the first announcements made by the new, post-Stalin Soviet government. Zhukov's rehabilitation continued apace with his appointment in February 1955 as minister of defence by Khrushchev, Stalin's successor as party leader. In July 1955 Zhukov attended the great power summit in Geneva of Britain, France, the Soviet Union, and the United States – the first such gathering since the end of the war. There he met and conversed with President Dwight Eisenhower, with whom he had served in Berlin just after the war. 'Could the friendship of two old soldiers', wondered *Time* magazine, 'provide the basis for a genuine easing of tensions between the U.S. and Russia?'[10]

As minister of defence, Zhukov emerged as a prominent public figure in the Soviet Union, second only in importance to Khrushchev. In June 1957 Zhukov played a pivotal role in resisting an attempt to oust Khrushchev from the leadership by a hard-line faction led by Vyacheslav Molotov, the former foreign minister. Unfortunately for Zhukov his bravura performance in the struggle against Molotov turned him into a political threat in Khrushchev's eyes. In October 1957 Zhukov was accused of plotting to undermine the role of the Communist Party in the armed forces. Among Zhukov's most active accusers were many of the same generals and marshals he had served with during the war. Khrushchev sacked Zhukov as minister of defence and in March 1958 he was retired from the armed forces at the relatively young age of sixty-one.

During the remainder of the Khrushchev era Zhukov suffered the same fate of excision from the history books he had experienced during his years of exile under Stalin. In 1960, for example, the party began to publish a massive multivolume history of the Great Patriotic War that barely mentioned Zhukov while greatly exaggerating Khrushchev's role.[11] Another expression of Zhukov's disgrace was his isolation from the outside world. When American author Cornelius Ryan visited the USSR in 1963 to research his book on the battle of Berlin, Zhukov was the only Soviet marshal he was prohibited from seeing.[12]

Zhukov took solace in writing his memoirs. His authorial role model was Winston Churchill, whose memoir-history of the Second World War he had read when a restricted-circulation Russian translation was published in the USSR in the 1950s. Churchill's motto in composing that work was that history would bear him out – because he was going to write the history! Zhukov seems to have harboured similar sentiments and his memoirs were designed not only to present his own point of view but to answer and refute his Khrushchevite critics, even if that meant skewing the historical record in his own favour.

While Khrushchev continued to rule the Soviet Union there was no chance Zhukov's memoirs would be published. When his daughter

Ella asked him why he bothered he said he was writing for the desk drawer. In October 1964, however, Khrushchev was ousted from power and there began a process of rehabilitating Zhukov as a significant military figure. Most notably, the Soviet press began to publish Zhukov's articles again, including his accounts of the battles of Moscow, Stalingrad, Kursk, and Berlin.

Zhukov's second rehabilitation rekindled interest in him in the West, which had faded somewhat after he was ousted as defence minister. In 1969 the American journalist and historian Harrison E. Salisbury published an unauthorised translation of Zhukov's articles in a book called *Marshal Zhukov's Greatest Battles*. In his introduction to the volume Salisbury famously described Zhukov as 'the master of the art of mass warfare in the 20th century'.[13] Most reviewers agreed. John Erickson, the foremost British authority on the Red Army, writing in *The Sunday Times,* said 'the greatest soldier so far produced by the 20th century is Marshal Georgi Zhukov of the Soviet Union. On the very simplest reckoning he is the general who never lost a battle. . . . For long enough the German generals have had their say, extolling their own skills . . . now it is the turn of Marshal Zhukov, a belated appearance to be sure but the final word may be his.'[14]

When Zhukov's memoirs were published in April 1969 it was in a handsome edition with coloured maps and hundreds of photographs, including some from Zhukov's personal archive.[15] The Soviet public was wildly enthusiastic about the memoirs. The initial print run of 300,000 soon sold out and millions more sales followed, including hundreds of thousands in numerous translations. The memoirs quickly became – and remain – the single most influential personal account of the Great Patriotic War.

Zhukov's triumph in the battle for the historical memory of the Great Patriotic War was not one that he lived to savour. By the time a revised edition of his memoirs was issued in 1974 he was dead.[16] In 1968 Zhukov had suffered a severe stroke from which he never really recovered. His health problems were exacerbated by the stress of his second wife, Galina, suffering from cancer. When she died in November 1973 at the age of forty-seven, Zhukov's own health deteriorated rapidly and he passed away aged seventy-seven in the Kremlin hospital in June 1974.

Zhukov's funeral was the biggest such occasion in the Soviet Union since the death of Stalin. As Zhukov lay in state in the Central House of the Soviet army in Moscow thousands came to pay their respects. When his ashes were interred in the Kremlin wall on 21 June the chief pallbearer was party general secretary Leonid Brezhnev and at the memorial service that followed the main speaker was Minister of Defence Marshal A. A. Grechko.[17]

In Russia Zhukov was – and still is – considered not only the greatest general of the Second World War but the most talented *polkovodets* (military leader) in Russian history. In the West Zhukov's reputation is only slightly less exalted. Of course, Zhukov is not everyone's hero. Even in Russia he has his critics. There are those who consider him an egotistical brute with an inflated military reputation. According to Viktor Suvorov, a former Soviet intelligence officer, whose history books are huge bestsellers in Russia, 'all the top military leaders of the country were against Zhukov. The Generals knew, the Marshals knew, that Zhukov was vainglorious. They knew he was both a dreadful and a dull person. They knew he was rude and a usurper. They knew he was in a class of his own as a careerist. They knew he trampled over everyone in his path. They knew of his lust for power and the belief in his own infallibility.'[18]

As we shall see, Zhukov certainly was a flawed character and his fellow generals did have many negative things to say about him during the course of his career, but Suvorov accentuated only the negatives. Suvorov's critical onslaught had little impact on Zhukov's popularity in Russia. If anything, the continuing controversy only added to Zhukov's allure as a deeply flawed character of epic achievements.

One of the most common criticisms levelled against Zhukov was that he was profligate in expending the lives of the soldiers under his command and was little troubled by the human cost of his victories. Zhukov rejected this vehemently, pointing out that it was easy for armchair critics to claim in retrospect that this battle or that campaign could have been won at the cost of far fewer lives. He was, it is true, an offensive-minded general. But during the war, he learned the virtues of withdrawal and retreat. Indeed, there is plenty of evidence that Zhukov did what he could to conserve his forces and protect his troops. His preparation for battle was always meticulous, and he would garner as many resources as Stalin allowed. Certainly the troops under Zhukov's command suffered no greater casualty rates than those of other Soviet generals, including those such as Rokossovky, who had a reputation for being a more benign commander. The idea that Zhukov was personally indifferent to the fate of his troops is also mistaken. His sometimes brutal treatment of subordinates was not a matter of personal cruelty but of command style, and when frustrated and dissatisfied, most of his ire was directed at senior commanders – which may explain why some were so critical of Zhukov later.

When Zhukov published his memoirs the Russian archives were closed and little or no independent documentary evidence was available. To write his biography was perforce to gloss his officially sanctioned memoirs, and the result was a lopsided story of his life. The situation began to improve with the publication in the early 1990s of new editions of Zhukov's memoirs incorporating a large amount of material excluded by the Soviet censors in the 1960s.[19] After the end of the Soviet regime in 1991 many thousands of documents concerning Zhukov's career were published from Russian military and political archives. More recently these materials have been supplemented by direct archival access to some of Zhukov's private papers.[20] Now it is possible to render an account of his life that is grounded in the documentary evidence.

Zhukov's life consists of far more than a chronology of the battles he fought. His story reflects both the triumphs and the tragedies of the Soviet regime he served. Above all, Zhukov was a dedicated communist and a loyal servant of Stalin and the Soviet regime. While his victories over the Nazis served humanity well, they also helped to buttress and legitimate a system that was itself highly authoritarian and harshly repressive. As an ideologue as well as a soldier Zhukov accepted Soviet repression as necessary to progress the communist cause in which he believed. Had he lived to see the end of the Soviet Union it is doubtful that Zhukov would have felt the need to repudiate his beliefs or apologise for his role in saving Stalin's regime. Rather, like many of his generation, he would have argued that he was a patriot as well as a communist and that the Soviet regime – for all its faults – was the only one he could serve on behalf of his country.

Zhukov was neither the unblemished hero of legend nor the unmitigated villain depicted by his detractors. Undoubtedly, he was a great general, a man of immense military talent, and someone blessed with the strength of character necessary to fight and win savage wars. But he also made many mistakes, errors paid for with the blood of millions of people. Because he was a flawed and contradictory character it will not be possible to render a simple verdict on Zhukov's life and career. But it is those flaws and contradictions, as well as his great victories and defeats, that make Zhukov such a fascinating subject.

2.

FABLED YOUTH:
FROM PEASANT CHILDHOOD TO
COMMUNIST SOLDIER, 1896–1921

THE ACCEPTED STORY OF GEORGY ZHUKOV'S CHILDHOOD AND YOUTH READS like a rags-to-riches fairy tale. Born into a poor peasant family in rural Russia in 1896, the story goes, Zhukov was apprenticed to a furrier at the age of twelve and sent to work in Moscow. Conscripted into the tsar's army in 1915 to fight in the First World War, he was wounded and decorated for bravery. Politicised by the Russian Revolution of 1917, the young Georgy joined the Red Army and then the Communist Party and fought on the victorious Bolshevik side of the Russian Civil War. Selected for officer training, Zhukov then rose through the ranks of the Red Army to become a marshal of the Soviet Union and the most famous Soviet general of the Second World War.

There is a lot of truth in this story and Zhukov's humble origins and stratospheric rise are keys to understanding his lifelong loyalty to communism and to the Soviet system. The regime that Zhukov served all his adult life was brutal, repressive, authoritarian, and at times terroristic. Economically, it was not particularly efficient, although capable of mobilising resources effectively in emergency situations (such as wars). It was a system that consistently failed to live up to its egalitarian ideals and was ruled by a political party that rarely, if ever, enjoyed the support of a majority of the population. But compared with the old tsarist regime it offered people like Zhukov unprecedented and previously unimaginable opportunities for social mobility. With advancement came material privileges, high social status, and a strong sense of identity as a member of an elite committed to building a new socialist society. This is not to say that Zhukov's commitment to the Soviet system was merely a matter of career opportunities. For Zhukov and the many others who succeeded in becoming members of the new Soviet elite, there was no contradiction between their ideals and the perks of promotion. Both were seen as integral to progress towards a better world.

The problem with this story of Zhukov's early life is that its main source is Zhukov himself and while he did have a tough childhood by modern standards his background was not as underprivileged as the myth suggests. Because of where he was born and the connections of his family he was a relatively privileged peasant.

CHILDHOOD AND YOUTH

Zhukov's story begins on 1 December 1896, in the village of Strelkovka in the Kaluga Province about eighty miles southwest of Moscow.[1] His father, Konstantin, was a cobbler and his mother, Ustin'ya, a peasant labourer. The Zhukov family name derived from the Russian word for beetle – 'Zhuk'. In Russian slang it can also mean someone who is a bit of a rogue. For both of Zhukov's parents it was a second marriage, each having lost their previous partner to tuberculosis.[2] In his memoirs Zhukov recalled that his father and mother were quite old when they married, fifty and thirty-five, respectively. However, according to his youngest daughter, Maria, the church records (not available to Zhukov when he wrote his memoirs) show that Konstantin was forty-one and Ustin'ya twenty-six when they married in 1892.[3] But given the physical toll exacted by the harshness of peasant life in Russia it is perhaps not surprising that Zhukov remembered or imagined them to be older than they were.

Georgy was the family's second child, a sister, Maria, having been born two years earlier. When he was five his mother had a second son, Alexei, but the child did not live beyond a year. 'My sister and I, let alone Father and Mother, grieved bitterly and often went to his graveside.'[4] All three children were baptised into the Russian Orthodox Church. 'Father was by birth, upbringing and outlook an Orthodox person', claimed Zhukov's daughter Maria, 'just like his soldiers, who said with him before battle, "we go with God!" '[5] During the Second World War it was rumoured that Zhukov carried an icon in his car. However, when Zhukov's wartime driver was asked about this, he described it as nonsense: 'he was a communist . . . if there had been an icon in the car I would have known about it'.[6] His daughter's beliefs notwithstanding, there is no evidence that religious conviction played any part in Zhukov's life.

The Russia into which Zhukov was born was a vast land empire that stretched thousands of miles across ten time zones from Warsaw to Vladivostok, from the Arctic Ocean to the Caspian and Black seas. Within its borders there lived more than 100 nationalities and ethnic groups, although most of the population were Russians like Zhukov. In 1900 the population of Russia was some 140 million, the great majority of whom were peasants.

Zhukov's birthplace in Kaluga Province was located in an area called the Central Industrial Region – Moscow and its surrounding provinces. Unlike the fertile 'Black Earth' steppes of southern Russia and Ukraine the topography of the Central Industrial Region was dominated by lakes, rivers, and adjacent forests – good for hunting and fishing – which Zhukov loved – but not so conducive to agriculture. Flax and vegetables, rather than cereals, were the main crops and much of the labour was provided by peasant women like Zhukov's mother, while many peasant men in the Central Industrial Region had non-agricultural jobs and trades, often migrating to Moscow for work, where they found a city brimming with their compatriots from the countryside.

At the beginning of the twentieth century peasant life in Russia was undergoing a cultural revolution as primary education spread to the countryside. Schools were established in most villages of any size. One beneficiary was Zhukov, who took the full three-year primary education course, as opposed to the two-year course favoured by most peasants – evidence that, poor though they might be, his parents had aspirations for their son. Education as the route to personal advancement was an attitude that Zhukov retained throughout his life and passed on to his own family.

Despite having a trade Zhukov's father, Konstantin, never had much work. Consequently, Georgy's early childhood was one of grinding poverty, a common fate of Russian peasants, even those living in the relatively prosperous Central Industrial Region.

In looks Georgy took after his mother and he also inherited her great physical strength – she was apparently capable of carrying a 200-pound sack of grain some distance.[7] But emotionally he seems to have been much closer to his father, notwithstanding – or perhaps because of – Konstantin's frequent absences from home in search of work in Moscow: 'I adored Father, and he spoiled me. Still, now and again he punished me for some fault, taking it out on me with his belt and demanding an apology. I was stubborn and no matter how hard he thrashed me I bit my lips and never asked for pardon. One day he gave me such a flogging that I ran away from home and spent three days hiding in a neighbour's hemp field.'[8] Physical punishment featured also in Zhukov's life as an apprentice, and again when he joined the army, but he did not harbour resentment about his treatment. 'A difficult life is life's best school,' he told his daughter Maria many decades later.[9]

Georgy started school in 1903 at the age of seven and completed successfully the three-year elementary course. To celebrate his success his mother gave him a new shirt, while his father made him a new pair of boots. The family soon decided that Zhukov should go to Moscow to work for his mother's brother, Mikhail, as an apprentice furrier.

Moscow was only four hours from Strelkovka by train (today the journey would take a little over an hour) but to the young Georgy it was a world very different from the one he was used to. When he arrived in summer 1908 he was shocked and confused by the crowds of people, the high buildings (in the village there was nothing taller than two stories) and the frenetic pace of life. On the other hand, Moscow was a city full of people like himself: educated peasant lads with family connections in the city who worked in artisan trades as furriers, tailors, carpenters, and cobblers.

His uncle's business was in the city centre, not far from Red Square. Zhukov's working day was twelve hours, including an hour for lunch. The work was hard, and punctuated by beatings of the apprentices by the craftsmen (and women), but Georgy survived quite well, finding time to enroll in night school to continue his education. Disciplined study habits were to stay with Zhukov for the rest of his life. Zhukov was not an intellectual general. He was rather what the Soviets called a *praktik* – a practical man of action. But he was a good student of military theory, strategy, and tactics and a voracious reader of a wide range of literature. According to his daughter Ella, reading was always at the heart of the Zhukov household and by the time the marshal died he had amassed a library of 20,000 books at his dacha, his country cottage. Unfortunately, most of the collection was pulped when the dacha was repossessed by the state after his death, although a few hundred of his volumes did end up in museum collections.[10]

Georgy's partner in self-education was cousin Alexander, the boss's son. Together they studied the Russian language, maths, geography, and popular science texts. Another subject was German. Alexander was sent to Leipzig by his father to learn German to help with the business. On his periodic trips home to Moscow he found time to teach his cousin the language[11] – knowledge that Zhukov was to put to good use during his military career.

By 1914 Zhukov had finished his apprenticeship and was earning good money as a trained furrier with three young boys working under him. A photograph of him and his fellow furriers dating from this time shows affluent, smartly dressed young urbanites seemingly confident of their future. Another picture of Zhukov with Alexander similarly displays a young man who had already transcended his humble origins and successfully adapted to his new urban environment. Were it not for the outbreak of the First World War in August 1914 Zhukov no doubt would have continued his career as a furrier and ended up running his own business.

Zhukov was frank in his memoirs about his youthful lack of politics, pointing out that political apathy was common among his fellow furriers, which he attributed to the petit bourgeois individualist mentality of artisan workers, in contrast to the proletarian solidarity of the industrial working class. At the same time he claimed to have been influenced by various revolutionary ideas that were spreading in Russia under the impact of the events of the First World War and his narrative suggested a gradual conversion to communism. But aside from Zhukov's own testimony, there is no evidence of incipient class consciousness and militancy. His embrace of the communist cause was probably more hesitant than he later presented it. He did become a committed communist, but it was more by accident than design, the result less of socialist revelation than the contingencies of military and political events. The most important of these events was the First World War, which led to his military career.

TSARIST SOLDIER

The First World War broke out as a result of the July Crisis of 1914. Following the assassination of the heir to the Austro-Hungarian throne, Archduke Franz Ferdinand, by a Bosnian Serb nationalist in Sarajevo at the end of June (the Archduke's wife, Sophie, was also killed), Austria-Hungary mobilised for war against Serbia. When Austria-Hungary declared war on Serbia on 28 July Russia mobilised in support of its Balkan ally and fellow Slav state. In response to the Russian mobilisation Germany, Austria-Hungary's ally, declared war on Russia on 1 August and two days later attacked Russia's ally France. The picture was completed by a British declaration of war on Germany on 4 August in response to German violations of Belgian neutrality. Subsequently, a number of other states became involved in the war – Turkey (1914) and Bulgaria (1915) on the side of Germany and Austria-Hungary, Japan (1914), Italy (1915), and the United States (1917) on the side of Britain, France, and Russia.

From the Russian point of view they were involved in a war of national defence against the aggressors Germany and Austria-Hungary. The outbreak of war inspired a massive patriotic mobilisation in Russia – in much the same way that it did a quarter of a century later when Hitler attacked the Soviet Union. Zhukov, caught up in the patriotic fervour, was tempted to volunteer but after talking it over with another furrier from his home village, he decided to wait until his age cohort was called up. Alexander volunteered, however, and tried to persuade Georgy to follow suit.

When Zhukov was conscripted in summer 1915 he consulted with Uncle Mikhail, who told him that he could get a deferment for a year on medical grounds. When Zhukov pointed out that he was in good health and well able to serve on the front his uncle asked him whether he really wanted to be a fool like Alexander. 'I told him', recalled Zhukov, 'that it was my duty to defend the motherland.'[12]

Zhukov reported for military duty in Kaluga Province in August 1915 and was assigned to the 5th Reserve Cavalry Regiment, where he was 'very happy to serve . . . for I entertained many romantic feelings about [the cavalry]'.[13] In September Zhukov was sent with his regiment to the Kharkov province in Ukraine to join the 10th Cavalry Division. It was there that he received his cavalry training. His first horse was a shrewish dark grey mare called Chashechnaya, whom he groomed three times a day.

Zhukov completed his cavalry training by spring 1916 but was then selected for further training as a non-commissioned officer. During this course Zhukov had his first adult clash with authority, a particularly brutish NCO nicknamed 'Four-and-a-Half' because he was missing half his right-hand index finger. Four-and-a-Half picked on Zhukov and pressured him to leave the cavalry to become a clerk. Although Zhukov expected to graduate at the top of his class, a fortnight before the exams it was announced that he was being discharged for disloyalty and insubordination towards Four-and-a-Half. He thought that was the end of his cavalry career but was rescued from this fate when a fellow trainee reported the matter to the commanding officer, who decided to allow Zhukov to finish the course.

In his memoirs Zhukov looked back on his NCO training with mixed feelings. On the one hand it was good training in horsemanship, weapons use, and drill techniques. On the other hand, the 'NCO was not taught the human approach. He was expected to mould the soldier into a pliant robot. Discipline was maintained by harshness. Though regulations did not stipulate corporal punishment, it was rather common.'[14]

In August 1916 Zhukov was posted to combat duty along the River Dnestr in Moldova, at that time a province of tsarist Russia. Before he even arrived at the front Zhukov had his baptism of fire when his unit was bombed by a reconnaissance plane, killing one soldier and wounding five horses. Not long after his arrival at the front Zhukov won his first medal – the St. George Cross – for capturing a German officer. In an unpublished interview with a Soviet journalist in Berlin in 1945 Zhukov recalled that he was fascinated by intelligence work and because he knew some German he had specialised in capturing prisoners.[15] While on another reconnaissance patrol in October 1916

Zhukov was blown off his horse by a mine that badly injured his two companions. A shell-shocked Zhukov was evacuated to Kharkov in Ukraine and hospitalised. It was for this wounding that Zhukov received his second St. George Cross. He was posted back to his original unit, the 5th Reserve Cavalry Regiment, at the end of 1916. As he recalled in his memoirs: 'I had left the squadron a young soldier. I was now returning with my NCO stripes, combat experience, and two St. George Crosses.'[16]

REVOLUTION AND CIVIL WAR

Zhukov's old unit was based at Lageri near Balakleya, about eighty miles southeast of Kharkov. Here Zhukov and his fellow soldiers were soon caught up in the revolutionary events of 1917 that began with the fall of the autocratic Romanov dynasty that had ruled Russia for 400 years and culminated with the seizure of power by Lenin and the Bolsheviks. The precipitating event was the abdication of Tsar Nicholas II in March 1917 following a general strike and soldiers' mutiny in Petrograd, the Russian capital. (Petrograd was formerly St. Petersburg – a name it reverted to after the collapse of the USSR, in 1991. During Soviet times, the city was called Leningrad.)

Behind the tsar's downfall lay a rising tide of popular discontent and protest. The war had not gone well for Russia. It had suffered a series of defeats and territorial losses and incurred millions of casualties. The tsarist government had proved incapable of organising the country's war effort. There were inadequate supplies of weapons and ammunition and many of the troops' basic needs – food, clothing, and medical aid – were provided for by civic organisations. Printing money to pay for the war created rampant inflation and consequent food shortages in the cities as peasants were reluctant to part with their produce for a devaluing currency. The urban population responded with strikes and political demonstrations. In November 1915 Tsar Nicholas took over command of the armed forces and became personally identified with Russia's military defeats and its other wartime woes. Adding to his troubles was a loss of middle-class confidence in his leadership and its constant calls for the modernisation and democratisation of Russia.

Matters came to a head when strikes and demonstrations by female textile workers in Petrograd in March 1917 developed into city-wide protests. Troops were ordered to restore order and a number of demonstrators were shot. But the city's garrison soldiers then mutinied and joined the side of the protesters. Having lost control of his capital Nicholas was persuaded to resign in the national interest. He abdicated in favour of his brother, the Grand Duke Michael, who refused to take the throne. That was the end of the autocratic Romanov dynasty.

The tsarist administration was replaced by a Provisional Government of liberal, democratic, and socialist politicians whose aim was to implement urgent political, economic, and social reforms and to prepare elections to a Constituent Assembly that would agree on a new constitution for the country. These plans were thwarted, however, by the development of a situation of 'dual power' in which power and authority were shared between the Provisional Government and the representatives of Workers', Peasants', and Soldiers' Soviets – popularly elected councils that took over the running of the country at the local level. More radical than the Provisional Government, the Soviets provided fertile ground for the agitation and propaganda of the Bolsheviks and other revolutionary groups struggling for a socialist as well as a democratic regime in Russia. Led by Vladimir Ilyich Lenin, the Bolsheviks called for all power to be transferred to the Soviets and for Peace, Bread, and Land – land for the peasants, bread for the workers, and an end to Russia's participation in the war. Bolshevik policy was very popular, particularly among soldiers and the working class. Within six months they were the strongest and best-organised political party in Russia. In November 1917 the Bolsheviks staged a coup in Petrograd that overthrew the Provisional Government and proclaimed a new socialist government that would rule on behalf of the Soviets.

An important feature of these upheavals, which soon spread from Petrograd to the rest of the country, was the politicisation of the armed forces; one of the first acts of the Provisional Government was to issue a decree authorising the formation of soldiers' and sailors' committees to elect delegates to their local Soviets. Zhukov was elected chairman of his cavalry squadron's committee and a delegate to the regimental

Soviet. He later claimed to have supported the Bolshevik faction within the regiment but his election probably reflected his status and popularity as a good NCO rather than his politics. Zhukov also related how the regimental Soviet was taken over by anti-Bolshevik elements. As a result, some of the regiment's units sided with counter-revolutionary Ukrainian nationalists. His own unit was disbanded and the soldiers told to go home, while Zhukov himself had to go into hiding for several weeks to evade capture by officers serving with the Ukrainian nationalists. This seems to be the reason he did not arrive in Moscow until after the Bolsheviks seized power.

Zhukov was back in his home village of Strelkovka by the end of 1917, intending, he said in his memoirs, to have a rest before joining the Red Army, which the Bolsheviks established in January 1918. But he contracted typhus and was unable to join up for another six months. It is more likely, however, that Zhukov did what most demobbed soldiers from the former tsarist army did – he went home and waited to see what happened next.

In March 1918 the Bolsheviks signed the Brest-Litovsk Treaty with Germany, withdrawing Russia from the war. Peace came at a high price, however, and the Bolsheviks were forced to concede vast tracts of territory to the Germans. The treaty also inspired the Bolsheviks' opponents to organise an armed insurgency against Lenin's government – something they had been reluctant to do while Russia was still in the war. In response to the incipient civil war the Bolsheviks began to organise an armed force capable of defending their revolutionary seizure of power. The revolutionary militias that had brought the Bolsheviks to power were replaced with a professional army. The election of officers was abolished and a traditional command structure established. Proper rates of pay were also introduced. Most important, the Bolsheviks began to conscript former officers and NCOs of the tsarist army. In early September 1918 the Bolsheviks issued a decree ordering Zhukov's age cohort to report for military duty by the end of the month.[17]

Although he lived in the heart of Bolshevik Russia, Zhukov could have ignored the conscription decree, as many Russian peasants did. That he chose to accept conscription was in all likelihood a professional rather than a political choice: it offered him the possibility of continuing with his military career. Like many among that first generation of soldiers to serve in the Red Army, Zhukov's political convictions were the result of his military service rather than the reason he joined up.

Zhukov enrolled in the 4th Regiment of the 1st Moscow Cavalry Division of the Red Army on 1 October 1918.[18] Bolshevik Party members were the first group to be conscripted into the Red Army and Zhukov's unit had many communist cadres serving in it. In this context it is not surprising that Zhukov gravitated to the Bolsheviks and became a candidate member of the Communist Party (the Bolshevik Party's new name) in March 1919. Candidate membership provided for a probationary period during which applicants had to prove their commitment to the communist cause; Zhukov did not become a full member of the party until May 1920.[19]

In May 1919 Zhukov's division was dispatched to the southern Urals to take part in the Bolshevik campaign against Admiral Alexander Kolchak, a former tsarist commander who had seized power in Siberia and was dedicated to the overthrow of the Bolshevik government. In June Zhukov experienced his first combat as a member of the Red Army, a fierce fight with some 800 mounted Cossacks. In September Zhukov saw action again, this time at Tsaritsyn (renamed Stalingrad in 1924) in southern Russia. At the end of October Zhukov was involved in a hand-to-hand engagement that left him injured by a grenade explosion. When he was sent to a field hospital in Saratov to recover he met a young schoolgirl, Maria Volokhova. The two were inseparable for a month but the relationship ended when Maria returned to her home town of Poltava and Zhukov was sent home to Strelkovka for a further period of recuperation. This turned out to be a temporary separation and the relationship resumed three years later, notwithstanding Zhukov's marriage in the meantime to another woman. In due course Maria would bear Zhukov an illegitimate daughter, Margarita.[20]

RED COMMANDER

In January 1920 Zhukov reported for duty again but because he was not fully fit (he had been stricken by another bout of typhus, a common ailment of the time) he was assigned to the 3rd Reserve Cavalry

Division. Three months later Zhukov's career in the Red Army took a new turn when he was sent on the Red Commanders Cavalry Course at Ryazan, about 100 miles southeast of Moscow. The Red Commanders Cavalry Course was in effect a training course for junior officers but the Bolsheviks had abolished officer titles and would not reintroduce them until the 1930s. Until then the Red Army used the generic title of 'commander' to distinguish higher from lower ranks.

A number of documents relating to Zhukov's time at Ryazan provide a fascinating glimpse of his activities during this period.[21]

Zhukov had been recommended for the course by his division's party cell. He was enrolled on 15 March 1920, and placed on a preparatory course devoted to the basic education of participants. He achieved good or excellent marks in all his subjects – Russian, Arithmetic, Geography, Hygienics, Military Administration, Political Education, and Military Rules and Regulations – and quickly graduated to specialist courses in cavalry tactics, although because of his experience in the tsarist army he ended up helping to train the other cadets.

Zhukov was very active in his party cell at Ryazan, at one point becoming its secretary, but he seems to have resigned because of a controversy concerning the group's chairman, Stavenkov, who was accused of napping on duty. When the cell met to consider the case Zhukov defended Stavenkov strongly, arguing that he was a good party worker and a good commander. Zhukov opposed the proposed exclusion of Stavenkov from the cavalry course and argued instead that his accuser should be thrown out of the party cell and then out of the party altogether. Zhukov's motion was passed unanimously except for one abstention.

Zhukov's abilities were recognised, too, by his appointment to a troika overseeing sanitary conditions at the school and his membership in a mandates commission that was charged with examining the credentials of incoming trainees. Zhukov's record at the school was not exemplary, however. At the end of July 1920 he was suspended from the course for a few days following an infringement of military discipline, though for what, precisely, is unknown.

The Ryazan course ended for Zhukov in August 1920 when he and 120 other cadets were sent to join the 2nd Moscow Rifle Brigade, a composite unit of two infantry regiments and one cavalry regiment. At the end of August the brigade was sent to Krasnodar in the northern Caucasus to take part in the fight against the forces of Baron Wrangel – the leader of an anti-Bolshevik army based in the Crimea. After taking part in a few engagements Zhukov was transferred to the 1st Cavalry Regiment of the 14th Detached Cavalry Brigade, tasked with mopping up the remnants of Wrangel's forces in the vicinity of Novozherelievskaya.

By October 1920 Zhukov had been placed in charge of a platoon and he was promoted to squadron commander when the brigade was posted to Voronezh Province to put down a peasant uprising against the Bolsheviks. This uprising developed into the so-called Tambov Revolt, led by A. S. Antonov, a former commander of the local militia. It was in battles with Antonov's forces that Zhukov experienced some of the fiercest fighting of the Russian Civil War. As a result of one of these skirmishes Zhukov was awarded his first Red Army decoration – the Order of the Red Banner. According to the award citation Zhukov's squadron had 'held off an onslaught of the enemy numbering from 1500–2000 sabres for seven hours . . . on 5 March 1921 and then counter-attacking, smashed the bandits after six hand-to-hand clashes'. In his memoirs Zhukov recalled that 'in a hand-to-hand fight an Antonovite fired his sawed-off rifle at me and killed my horse. We fell, the horse pinning me down, and the next moment I would have been slashed to death but for Nochevka, the political instructor, who came to my rescue. With the swing of his sabre he killed the bandit, caught the reins of his horse, and helped me into the saddle.'[22]

By summer 1921 the Tambov Revolt had been defeated but Zhukov's unit continued to chase the remnants of Antonov's forces until nearly the end of the year. Among his companions was his young wife. According to daughter Era, Zhukov met her mother, Alexandra Dievna Zuikova (b. 1900), who was a village schoolteacher, when he transferred to Voronezh. If, as Era says, they married in 1920, it must have been a whirlwind romance, since Zhukov did not arrive in the area until October. 'The times were difficult, and,' says Era

in pursuit of the [Antonov] bands the detachment was on the move all the time. Mama joined the detachment staff and was never out of sight of the commander. Once he nearly sent her to the guardhouse for some mistake in preparing an amateur theatrical. But the difficulties and hardships of their nomadic military life did not interfere with their happiness. Both of them, I remember, loved to recall those years: how Mama would shake for hours in a light carriage, how she altered military tunics into shorts and Red Army coarse calico shirts into underwear, how she wove rope into 'sandals'.[23]

None of this featured in Zhukov's memoirs. But then apart from the account of his childhood and early youth, there was little that was truly personal in his memoirs. Once he joins the Red Army his recollections become a catalogue of his military career and service to the Soviet state. Only in passing, for example, does he mention that his father died in 1921.

Zhukov's dedication to what he saw as his sacred socialist duty as a Soviet soldier is certainly the central part of his life story but it is far from being the whole truth. Even in the regimented and repressive Soviet system citizens had personalities and private lives as well as public ones. Zhukov was no exception. Behind the stunning success of his military and political career was a driving personal ambition and strength of character that enabled him to take failure in his stride. It would be too simple to say that in the story of his childhood and youth we can discern all his personal qualities and characteristics but there are quite a few of enduring importance: equanimity in the face of hardship; dedication to study and self-education; bravery in battle; and the willingness to accept responsibility and exercise leadership.

The quintessential lesson of the young Georgy's journey through life – from childhood to adulthood, from village to city, through war and revolution, and into the Red Army and the Communist Party – was that tumultuous events and upheavals offered opportunities for advancement for those with the talent to take them. This was a pattern that was to be repeated throughout his life and career.

A SOLDIER'S LIFE:
THE EDUCATION OF
A RED COMMANDER,
1922–1938

WHEN THE RUSSIAN CIVIL WAR ENDED IN 1921 THE BULK OF THE RED ARMY was rapidly demobilised. From a force five million strong the Red Army declined to about half a million by the middle of the decade. Zhukov was among those who remained in its ranks. In his memoirs he gave no direct reason for his decision to continue in military service, but he did note a party instruction of February 1921 ordering all communists to remain in the Red Army. There were many such instructions during this period, but they did little to stem the exodus of party members from the army. Zhukov stayed in the army because it suited him. As he said himself, 'most of the men who stayed in the ranks did so because, by virtue of their inclination and ability, they had chosen to devote themselves to military service'.[1]

Although still only a junior commander when the civil war ended, Zhukov was in a strong position to make a good career for himself in the Red Army. He had served as an NCO in the tsarist army, as a junior commander in the Red Army, and both armies had decorated him for bravery. He was also relatively well educated and a graduate of the Red Commanders Cavalry Course. Above all, Zhukov was a member of the Communist Party – the most important qualification for career progress under the new Soviet regime.

Zhukov's rise through the ranks of the Red Army in the 1920s and 1930s was steady rather than spectacular. He started off in 1922 as a squadron commander and progressed to regimental and brigade commands by the end of the decade. His first higher command appointment was as an assistant to the inspector of cavalry of the Red Army in 1931. Divisional and corps commands followed and in 1938 he was made deputy commander of the Belorussian Military District, with special responsibility for training. It was not until May 1939, when Zhukov was posted to the Far East to investigate the failings of Soviet-Mongolian forces fighting a border war with Japan, that his name came to prominence.

COMMUNIST ARMY

The organisation in which Zhukov made his career was a key institution of the authoritarian and repressive Soviet socialist system. Indeed, a typical description of the young Soviet regime is that it was a form of 'militarised socialism' and was as much a product of the Russian Civil War as the revolutionary events of 1917.[2]

During the civil war millions of people had been killed or starved to death. The Bolsheviks had learned to be ruthless in pursuit of victory, using whatever level of violence was required to defend their regime. Coercion replaced persuasion as a method of political mobilisation. The Bolshevik Party (it changed its name to Communist in 1918) became even more rigidly hierarchical and authoritarian in its administration. At the height of the civil war in 1919–1920 the Bolsheviks came close to defeat as their stronghold in central and northern Russia came under siege from all sides by counter-revolutionary White armies. The Whites were aided militarily by a number of foreign governments – Britain, France, Japan, and the United States – who feared the contagion of a successful Bolshevik revolution could spread to their own countries. Hence the Bolsheviks characterised the civil war as a life-and-death struggle not only with their internal foes but with the whole capitalist world. The Bolsheviks hoped revolutionary socialist movements in other countries would come to their aid but when this did not happen they accepted that the Soviet socialist state had to coexist with capitalism, at least for a while.

Despite their civil war victory the Bolsheviks continued to fear the threat posed by a potentially lethal combination of external capitalist attack and internal subversion. War scares were common in the USSR in the 1920s and 1930s, and throughout much of the interwar period the Soviet regime was in a state of semi-mobilisation for war. In this tense context the Red Army was seen as the indispensable shield and sword protecting the revolution.

The Red Army – whose official title was the Workers' and Peasants' Red Army – was also seen as a school of socialism for the masses, a model of discipline and political commitment that would bind the population to the Soviet regime. That was the theory; in practice service in the Red Army was a brutal and brutalising experience for most of its conscripts. For career officers like Zhukov the experience was more positive. They were treated with respect and their pay and conditions were much better than those of conscripts. The high status accorded the Red Army by the regime also reinforced their faith in the Soviet system and its leadership.

At the end of the 1920s the Red Army became even more important for the regime when the country embarked upon a programme for the rapid modernisation of the Soviet Union. This programme had two main prongs. First was accelerated industrialisation and urbanisation. In 1928 the Soviets adopted the first of a series of five-year plans to radically raise industrial production and to transform the country from a largely peasant society into an advanced, industrialised state. According to official statistics industrial production increased by 850 per cent in the 1930s. The true figures were probably somewhat lower but there is no doubting the vast scale of industrialisation, which resulted in the construction of thousands of factories, the building of many new dams, canals, roads, and railways, and an increase of thirty million in the urban population. Much of the industrialisation effort was directed at the defence industry and was motivated by fear of a capitalist attack. As the Soviet leader Joseph Stalin famously put in a speech in February 1931: 'We are fifty or a hundred years behind the advanced countries. We must make good this distance in ten years. Either we do it, or they crush us.'[3]

Second there was the forced collectivisation of Soviet agriculture. The Bolsheviks were ideologically committed to a state-controlled agricultural sector but not until the late 1920s did they begin to force peasants to give up their land and become members of collective farms. By 1937 more than 90 per cent of Soviet agriculture had been collectivised. But there was considerable peasant resistance and severe disruption of agricultural production. The communist regime's response to the crisis caused by the collectivisation drive was mass executions, arrests, and deportations. The result was the deaths of millions of peasants, particularly in 1932–1933 when the brutalities of collectivisation combined with bad weather to produce a famine in Ukraine and parts of Russia. The main agencies of coercion were the Communist Party and state security agencies but the Red Army played its part, too, although there is no evidence that Zhukov took direct part in the collectivisation campaign.

When Zhukov decided to continue his military service the Red Army was a far less exalted institution than it later became. In the immediate post–civil war period chaotic demobilisation disrupted its functioning and undermined its morale. From within the Communist Party came the call to do away with a permanent army and rely instead on a part-time militia – the Bolsheviks' original idea when they seized power in 1917. In response, Red Army leaders argued that continued internal and external threats warranted retention of a professional standing army.

The outcome of the inner party debate was a compromise between the two positions – the creation of a regular army of about 500,000 plus a number of territorial divisions of mainly part-time soldiers required to serve for a couple of months each year. The regular armed forces were concentrated in border districts, while the territorial divisions were generally located in the safer interior of the country. But even the so-called regular troops were mostly two-year conscripts. The professional core of the Red Army remained quite small. Nearly all the territorial divisions were infantry, with only one territorial division among the Red Army's eleven cavalry divisions and eight cavalry brigades. The staffing, supply, and technical efficiency of cavalry units were maintained at a relatively high level of operational preparedness, putting Zhukov among the elite of the Red Army as it re-formed after the civil war. This partly explains why so many cavalry officers went on to serve at the highest rank during the Great Patriotic War.

The key figure in the post–civil war re-formation of the Red Army was its chief of staff, Mikhail V. Frunze, who also served as people's commissar for the army and navy (i.e., the defence minister). Frunze reorganised the Red Army's command structures, abolishing the system of dual military-political leadership that had developed during the civil war, under which political commissars had a veto over command decisions. In 1924 Frunze introduced one-man command – *edinonachalie* – which ended the commissars' role in military decision-making.

Zhukov served under Frunze in the 1st Moscow Cavalry Division and, like many Soviet military memoirists, spoke with great affection and admiration for Frunze's feat in re-establishing the Red Army after the civil war. Frunze died prematurely in October 1925 following an unsuccessful stomach operation but his legacy of professionalism in the new Red Army lived on. Frunze believed in iron discipline, intensive training, and the professional as well as political education of officers – tenets that Zhukov later adopted in his own command style.

Notwithstanding his fervent commitment to the communist cause, Frunze was also open to innovative thinking about military affairs, not least in relation to strategic doctrine. The Red Army that he helped re-form was an organisation in which lively debates took place about military strategy, tactics, and technology. Because the Red Army was so vital to defending the USSR it was allowed to maintain an unusually creative and dynamic environment in a Soviet system in which independent thinking was increasingly frowned upon and even the mildest critical discussion of the party line absolutely forbidden.

One reason for this peculiar combination of orthodoxy and creativity was that it suited the leadership style of the man who from the mid-1920s onward was the overwhelmingly dominant personality in the dictatorial Soviet regime – Joseph Stalin, who became general secretary of the Communist Party in 1922. When Lenin died in 1924 Stalin emerged as his successor and through a series of inner-party struggles against his political rivals he established dominance. By the end of the 1920s Stalin was well on the way to becoming the dictator of the party and of the country it ruled. One of the hallmarks of Stalin's leadership was his constant demand for new methods and new solutions to achieve prescribed goals – as long as the innovations did not question the power of the party or his own dictatorship. As both a loyal communist and a devotee, albeit a mild one, of the growing cult of Stalin's personality, Zhukov had no difficulty working in the prescribed framework, constrictive though it was at times.[4]

REGIMENTAL COMMANDER

Zhukov was appointed a squadron commander in the 38th Cavalry Regiment in June 1922, which meant he was in charge of about 100 men. In March 1923 he was promoted to assistant commander of the 40th Cavalry Regiment of the 7th Samara Cavalry Division. In July he was appointed temporary and then permanent commander of the 39th Buzuluk Cavalry Regiment in the same division. Aged twenty-six, Zhukov had reached the rank equivalent of a lieutenant colonel in a western army. He was to remain a regimental commander for the next seven years. As he said in his memoirs, it was the most formative period in his military education:

> To command a regiment was always considered a most important stage in mastering the military art. The regiment is the basic combat unit where the cooperation of all ground arms . . . is organised for combat. A regimental commander must know his own units well, and also the support units normally assigned to the regiment in combat. He must properly choose the main direction in battle and concentrate his main forces accordingly. . . . A commander who has mastered the system of controlling a regiment, and can keep it in constant combat readiness, will always be an advanced military leader at all other levels of command, both in peacetime and in war.[5]

When Zhukov took command of the 39th Buzuluk the regiment was in bad shape: it lacked combat readiness and its officers were unclear about how to go about their work in peacetime conditions.[6] Zhukov soon turned the regiment around, an achievement recognised in the higher command's review of his work for 1923: 'Theoretically and practically well-prepared. Likes and knows cavalry work. Able quickly to orient himself to the situation. Disciplined to the highest degree. In a short time has raised his regiment to the highest level. His appointment as regimental commander was entirely correct.'[7]

Judging by Zhukov's regimental edicts and reports, assiduous attention to detail in relation to training, discipline, and political instruction was the key to his success.[8] According to A. L. Kronik, who served under him in the 1920s, Zhukov was a straightforward but strict commander who was reserved in personal relations, especially with his subordinates, never indulging in over-familiarity with his men. Zhukov's attitude, noted Kronik, 'expressed his understanding of his responsibilities for his subordinates and his understanding of his role not just as their commander but as their teacher'.[9]

In October 1924 the divisional commander decided to send Zhukov on a year-long course at the Higher Cavalry School in Leningrad. The purpose of the course was to educate higher command officers in a wide range of military and political skills that they in turn could teach their subordinates when they returned to their units. 'The curriculum was packed,' Zhukov recalled. 'Besides classes, we had to do much studying at home.'[10]

Among Zhukov's classmates were two future marshals of the Soviet Union – Konstantin K. Rokossovsky and Ivan K. Bagramyan – who were both destined to play a central role in Zhukov's life and career.

Born in 1896 to a Polish father and a Russian mother, Rokossovsky was brought up near Warsaw and spoke Russian with a Polish accent. He joined the tsarist army on the outbreak of war in 1914 and served with distinction in the cavalry, rising to the rank of junior commander by 1917. When the Bolsheviks seized power Rokossovsky joined the Red Guards – the precursor to the Red Army. During the Russian Civil War Rokossovsky was wounded twice and awarded two Orders of the Red Banner. By the end of the conflict he had a reputation as an outstanding cavalry commander. His personality and leadership style was the polar opposite of Zhukov's. While Zhukov was an uncompromising, assertive commander (like General George S. Patton, for example), Rokossovsky was more courteous and intellectual (like Dwight Eisenhower) and preferred to coax rather than forcibly extract the best from his troops. Their different personalities would lead to some sharp clashes between the two during the Second World War.

Ivan Bagramyan was the son of an Armenian railway worker and one of the few non-Slavs in the Red Army ever to reach the rank of marshal. Born in 1897, he served in the tsar's army during the First World War and then as an officer in the army of an Armenian nationalist movement that arose during the chaos of the Russian Revolution and Civil War. Bagramyan joined the Red Army in 1920 but did not become a member of the Communist Party until 1939. Like Rokossovsky he had an intellectual bent and was destined to lecture in the General Staff Academy in the 1930s. His breakthrough to operational command and the highest ranks came in 1940 when he served with Zhukov in the Kiev Special Military District.

In his memoirs Rokossovsky recalled of the Cavalry School class, 'we were young and energetic and soon came together naturally in a close-knit team. We plunged into our studies with a will, especially Zhukov, who gave himself up completely to mastering the subtleties of military science. Whenever we dropped into his room he would be crawling about over a map spread on the floor. Even then there was nothing higher for him than duty.'[11] Bagramyan was even more complimentary about Zhukov: 'Among our group of students [he] was the one with the most talent. Even then he displayed not only exceptional willpower but especially original thinking. In the sphere of cavalry tactics Zhukov more than once surprised us with something unexpected. His decisions always provoked the most disputes but he was usually able to defend his view with powerful logic.'[12] While such recollections must have been influenced by retrospective knowledge there is no reason to doubt that Zhukov was a dedicated student and a talented young commander.

The curriculum included equestrian contests – vaulting, concoursing, steeplechasing, racing, and handling sabres and lances – in which Zhukov, Rokossovsky, and Bagramyan all competed. In the summer of 1925 the course switched to tactical combat training in the field, culminating in a forced march to the River Volkhov, which the participants then had to swim across with their horses. 'It is a pretty tough job to swim a river with a horse,' recalled Zhukov. 'It was not enough to be able to swim in uniform; one had also to control a swimming horse.'[13]

When the course ended Zhukov and two other colleagues decided to return to their division on horseback. The division was in Minsk in Belorussia and the distance of 963 kilometres would be a world record for a group run on horseback. The ride took just seven days, despite Zhukov's horse going lame, forcing him to dismount frequently and lead it by the bridle. When they reached Minsk the group was met by cheering crowds, commendations from the High Command, and the reward of a short leave. Zhukov went home to Strelkovka to visit his mother and sister (by this time his father was dead). When he returned to the division he learned that his regiment was to be merged with another and a new, enlarged 39th Cavalry Regiment – the Melekess-Pugachevsk – was to be formed out of the 41st and 42nd Regiments. Zhukov was given command of the new regiment and not long after was also appointed regimental commissar. Zhukov's appointment to the political as well as the military command of Melekess-Pugachevsk – the first such unified appointment in the 7th Samara Division – was consonant with the Frunze reforms and reflected the higher command's confidence in his party loyalty as well as his military competence.[14]

As well as juggling military and political responsibilities Zhukov had some personal complications to deal with. When the 7th Samara Division relocated to Minsk in autumn 1923 Zhukov resumed his relationship with Maria Volokhova, the young schoolgirl he had met while recuperating in Saratov at the end of 1919. Meanwhile, his marriage to Alexandra Dievna endured and resulted in the birth of his first daughter, Era, in 1928. Six months later, in June 1929, Maria gave birth to Zhukov's second daughter – Margarita. According to Margarita, Zhukov was a doting father who registered her birth himself. She was so named because her rosy cheeks and blue eyes reminded him of a flower. However, a stepfather raised Margarita and in the 1930s Zhukov lost touch with both her and her mother. Contact was not resumed until the stepfather was killed in action during the Second World War.[15]

At the end of 1929 Zhukov was sent to the Frunze Military Academy in Moscow to attend an advanced course for higher commanders. Once again Zhukov found himself in the distinguished company of classmates who were destined for high office during the Great Patriotic

War, including Marshal L. A. Govorov, who commanded Soviet forces during the siege of Leningrad, and Marshal F. I. Tolbukhin, a famous Soviet tank commander. The course was designed for those being groomed for command at the divisional level and higher and it laid great emphasis on the theory and practice of the conduct of battles in contemporary conditions. Zhukov's end-of-course report in spring 1930 contained an astute evaluation of the capabilities of the thirty-three-year-old commander. His knowledge of combined arms tactics was judged entirely satisfactory as was his participation in war games and group work. His familiarity with field service regulations was deemed satisfactory and his operational-tactical decision-making was commended for its clarity and, especially, its firmness. With further progress Zhukov would be able to direct the tactical preparation for battle of both regiments and divisions, wrote the assessor. The only sphere in which Zhukov fell down was his staff work, which was judged 'almost' satisfactory. 'By inclination and character he is obviously a front-line commander [and is little suited for staff work]', concluded the report.[16]

DEEP BATTLE

In common with other armies the Red Army devoted a lot of attention to learning the lessons of the First World War and to assessing the impact of modern developments in military technology – especially tanks and planes – on future warfare. The Red Army also needed to assimilate the experience of the Russian Civil War, a conflict that, in contrast to the static, positional warfare of much of World War I, had been characterised by large-scale manoeuvres and operations conducted over distances of hundreds of miles. The Red Army leadership concluded that future wars would be mechanised and would be characterised by the combined operations of tanks, artillery, aircraft, motorised infantry, and airborne troops, striking rapidly and deeply into enemy territory and defences.

By the early 1930s the Red Army had formulated and adopted the dual doctrine of 'deep battle' and 'deep operations'. Under this doctrine, successive waves of combined arms forces would penetrate the full depth of enemy defences and then exploit the breakthrough by envelopment of enemy forces from the rear. Warfare would consist of a consecutive series of such operations, utilising what the Soviets called 'operational art' – the sophisticated management of 'combined arms' – the different branches of the armed forces – in pursuit of deep battle and deep operations. The idea was similar to the German concept of Blitzkrieg being developed around the same time, i.e., breakthrough on a narrow front by concentrated columns of tanks, which would then encircle the enemy from the rear. However, the Soviets were less tank-centric than the Germans and emphasised the importance of combined arms operations in which tanks would play a supporting as well as an independent role. They were also more mindful than the Germans of the importance of coordinating and synchronising tank action with that of artillery, infantry, cavalry, and air forces.

In accordance with its new doctrine the Red Army established the world's first mechanised corps in 1932 – two formations, each consisting of several hundred tanks and armoured cars, supported by infantry, artillery, and air detachments – that would act as the central strike force of the army in the event of war. By 1936 there were four mechanised corps as well as six separate mechanised brigades, and six separate tank regiments. But it soon became apparent there were a number of practical problems with the conduct of deep battle and deep operations. How would tanks involved in deep battle strikes be refuelled and resupplied? How would slow-moving infantry and artillery keep up with fast-moving, mechanised forces? How could central command (during an era in which field communications were not very advanced) direct forces operating deep in enemy territory? The answer to these problems – on paper, at least – was to slow down the tanks so they did not outrun their supplies; speed up the infantry and artillery by motorisation; and exercise tighter, more centralised control and coordination of the combined arms.[17]

The key figure in the doctrinal and practical development of the interwar Red Army was Mikhail N. Tukhachevsky, Frunze's successor as chief of staff in the 1920s and deputy commissar for defence in the 1930s.[18] Zhukov first met Tukhachevsky during the suppression of the Tambov peasant uprising in 1921 and he greatly admired 'his versatile command of various aspects of military science. A clever, knowledgeable professional, he was splendidly conversant with both tactical and strategic problems. He well understood the role the various arms could play in a modern war and took a creative approach to all problems. . . . Tukhachevsky was an ace of military thinking, a star of the first magnitude among the great soldiers of the Red Army.'[19]

As a relatively junior officer, and one with little bent for theory or staff work, Zhukov played no discernible role in elaborating the Red Army's military doctrine. But he did absorb the ethos and methodology of deep battle and deep operations that proved to be crucial in shaping his own later practice as a general. He would later note, in particular, the influence of the Temporary Field Service Regulations of 1936, which set out the principles of the Red Army's approach to battle and operations as an offensive-oriented army that would deploy combined arms to attack the enemy in depth:

> Modern means of neutralization, primarily tanks, artillery, aviation and tank-borne infantry raids, employed on a large scale, make it possible to organise the simultaneous attack on the enemy throughout the entire depth of his positions, with the aim of isolating, completely encircling and destroying him.[20]

However, by the time these regulations were published the concepts of deep battle and deep operations were coming under increasingly critical scrutiny within the Red Army. Important to the evolution and modification of the Red Army's operational doctrine was the impact of the Spanish Civil War, which broke out in July 1936 when General Francisco Franco and an alliance of conservatives, monarchists, and fascists launched a military mutiny against the elected republican government. More than 2,000 Soviet military advisors participated in the Spanish Civil War and the USSR was the main supplier of munitions to the republican government, including large numbers of tanks. Two main lessons seemed to emerge from the Spanish conflict: tanks were vulnerable to artillery and antitank weapons, and tank units would incur large losses in open battle; and, second, that it was difficult for tanks to achieve decisive results without close infantry support. This led to an increased emphasis in Soviet doctrine on the importance of combined arms operations (as opposed to independent tank manoeuvres) and on the tank's role in infantry support. The Spanish experience also contributed to the decision in November 1939 to disband the mechanised corps and to instead group tanks in smaller formations distributed throughout the armed forces.

RISING STAR

When he finished his course at the Frunze Academy in spring 1930 Zhukov was still an obscure, middle-ranking cavalry commander, albeit one on the way up. On 17 May 1930, the commander of the Cavalry Corps, S. K. Timoshenko – a future marshal and defence commissar – wrote that during the previous seven years Zhukov had raised his regiment to the highest level of morale and military preparedness.[21] That same month Zhukov was promoted to command the 2nd Cavalry Brigade of the 7th Samara Division, which placed him in charge of the 40th as well as his old regiment, the 39th. By this time the commander of the 7th Division was Zhukov's old classmate Rokossovsky, who presumably had a hand in his appointment as brigade commander. In November 1930 Rokossovsky wrote an assessment of his new brigade commander that throws light on both Zhukov's personality and his professional abilities at this stage in his career:

> Wilful. Decisive. Has initiative and knows how to apply it to his work. Disciplined. Persistently demanding. Personally a little cold and insufficiently tactful. Has a significant streak of obstinacy. Painfully proud. In military matters well prepared. Has a great deal of practical command experience. Loves military affairs and is constantly striving for perfection. One can see scope for the further development of his abilities. Authoritative. In the current year has achieved significant results in the battle training of his brigade in drill and rifle training as well as the development of the brigade as a whole in the tactical and combat spheres. Knows and is interested in mobilisation work. Gives due attention to questions of economy of arms and horse regulations, achieving positive results. In the political sphere is well-prepared. His occupation of the post is fully justified. Could be utilised as a divisional commander or as the

commander of a mechanized unit, providing he did the appropriate course. To staff and teaching work he could not be appointed – he detests it.[22]

Shortly after this report, in February 1931, Zhukov was again promoted – this time to an assistant inspector of the cavalry.[23] The Cavalry Inspectorate was based in Moscow where Zhukov was made responsible for combat training. He was also elected secretary of his local Communist Party branch. The Inspectorate worked closely with the Combat Training section of the Defence Commissariat where Alexander M. Vasilevsky was employed. Zhukov would develop a close personal and working relationship with him during the Great Patriotic War when Vasilevsky was chief of the General Staff and Zhukov was Stalin's deputy supreme commander.

Born in 1895, Vasilevsky was the son of a Russian Orthodox priest and destined for the church until the outbreak of war in 1914 interrupted his seminary studies. Unlike most of the Red Army elite, Vasilevsky was infantry, not cavalry. During the First World War he fought on the southwest front and rose to the rank of captain. Conscripted into the Red Army he ended the civil war with the rank of deputy regimental commander. Given his education Vasilevsky tended to be posted to teaching, training, and staff jobs. But because of his 'bourgeois' background Vasilevsky was not accepted as a candidate member of the Communist Party until 1931 and a full member until 1938.

In his memoirs Vasilevsky recalled of Zhukov that his 'military talent was becoming increasingly evident with each year that passed. I recall the unanimously high opinion of his abilities among his comrades when he was commanding a cavalry division and a cavalry corps and was deputy commander of troops of the Belorussian military district.'[24]

In October 1931 Zhukov's boss at the Inspectorate, Semyon Budenny, the legendary commander of the 1st Cavalry Army during the Russian Civil War, wrote his evaluation of Zhukov, arriving at much the same conclusion as Rokossovsky. Zhukov was a 'commander with a powerful will, very demanding of himself and his subordinates . . . unnecessarily harsh and rude'. Militarily and politically, however, he was a good all-around commander, concluded Budenny, qualified to command a division or even to head up a cavalry school.[25]

Zhukov's tendency to be overly disciplinarian in command was a fault he came to admit in later years. 'I was said to have been unnecessarily exacting – but this I considered indispensable for a Bolshevik commander. Looking back, I admit that at times I was too exacting, not always sufficiently restrained and tolerant of the faults of my subordinates. . . . I could not bear to see any slackness in servicemen's work or behaviour. Some of them could not understand this, and I, for my part, was probably not tolerant enough of human frailties.'[26]

Zhukov's work in the Cavalry Inspectorate involved arranging field and staff exercises, organising war games, and convening meetings of combat training officers to exchange knowledge and experiences. He was also involved in drafting Service Regulations for the Red Army Cavalry in the early 1930s, when the cavalry was incorporating mechanised, artillery, and tank units.[27]

After two years in the Cavalry Inspectorate Zhukov was posted, in March 1933, to command the 4th (Voroshilov) Cavalry Division based in Slutsk in Belorussia. Zhukov commanded the 4th Division (which was renamed the 4th Don Cossack Division in 1936 following its transfer from the 3rd Cavalry Corps to the 6th Cossack Corps) for four years and during this time he was 'preoccupied with one thought only: to make my division the best outfit in the Red Army'. Under his command were the 19th, 20th, 21st, and 23rd Cavalry Regiments, the 4th Mounted Artillery Regiment, and the 4th Mechanised Regiment. According to Zhukov, the division was in a poor condition when he took over because it had spent the previous eighteen months building its own barracks and stables following its transfer to Belorussia from Leningrad: 'as a result a splendidly trained division was reduced to an inefficient labour force. What made matters worse was that shortage of building materials, the rainy weather, and other unfavourable factors precluded timely preparation for the winter's cold, affecting morale and combat worthiness. Discipline grew lax, and the disease incidence among horses increased.'[28] Zhukov's solution was his usual one of training and exercises followed by more training and more exercises plus a heavy dose of discipline. By 1935 Zhukov had turned the division around and both he and his unit were awarded the Order of Lenin in recognition of this achievement. The division's location in the Belorussian Military District meant that it took part in all the

major exercises conducted by the Red Army as it geared up for mechanised warfare and prepared to implement the doctrine of deep battle
and deep operations. Hence, Zhukov paid a lot of attention to his 4th
Mechanised Regiment and the activities of its tanks.

L. F. Minuk, who served as chief of staff of the 4th Cavalry Division, recalled Zhukov being an energetic, organised, and highly disciplined commander, meticulous in his attention to detail and as
demanding of himself as he was of his subordinates. Minuk fully approved of Zhukov's command style because it achieved good results
and was commensurate with the 4th Division's location in a frontier
district – which meant that in the event of war it would bear the brunt
of an enemy attack. 'If a commander loses it and hesitates in front of
me, what can we expect from him in battle?' Zhukov reportedly asked
Minuk. But Zhukov did not only criticise his commanders, says
Minuk, he corrected their mistakes and was attentive to their personal
needs as well, helping them with family and health issues, for example.
Off-duty, recalled Minuk, neither rank nor class existed for Zhukov
and he could be very sociable: 'I never noticed in him any pomposity,
arrogance or conceit but there were clear boundaries between official
and unofficial relations with subordinates.'[29]

Memoirs about Zhukov tend to be either laudatory or condemna-
tory and it is clear where Minuk's sympathies lie. But Minuk's recollections are consistent with an emerging picture of an uncompromising
but well-respected commander who could inspire affection and fear in
equal measure. Above all it is a portrait of a man driven by the desire
to succeed.

ZHUKOV'S OWN MEMOIRS say little about his personal life and concentrate almost exclusively on his military career. What knowledge we
have of his private life in the 1930s derives from the reminiscences of
Era, his eldest daughter. Apparently, Zhukov required order at home
as well as at work and did not appreciate lateness or broken promises.
Neither would he tolerate hypocrisy or dishonesty in the family. Era
remembered her father as always reading and studying – an impression confirmed by her sister Ella, born in Slutsk in 1937, who said that
books were always at the centre of the Zhukov household. Era's

memoir is most revealing about their mother, Alexandra. She was devoted to Zhukov and functioned as his aide as well as his wife, helping him, for example, to perfect his command of the Russian language during the early years of their marriage. Alexandra was a sociable woman who made friends easily, including with the wives of Zhukov's fellow officers. Era and Ella were both convinced that Zhukov was as devoted to his wife and family as they were to him.[30] Even taking into account the natural exaggerations of filial devotion, it seems clear that Zhukov could rely on a supportive family environment as he made his career in the Red Army. The two daughters' portrait also suggests that like many military men – indeed, men in general – Zhukov reserved his emotional energies and outbursts for the workplace.

In July 1937 Zhukov took another step up the promotional ladder when he was appointed commander of the 3rd Cavalry Corps in the Belorussian Military District. Then, in March 1938, he was transferred to the 6th Cossack Corps – a posting that pleased him because it contained his old command, the 4th Cavalry Division. As a corps commander, Zhukov concentrated on the combat use of cavalry within a mechanised army and on operational and strategic questions. He also sat up at nights reading the classics of Marxism-Leninism, 'by no means an easy task' he noted in his memoirs, 'especially studying Karl Marx's *Capital* and Lenin's philosophical works'![31] Then, in June 1938, he was made deputy commander of the Belorussian Military District with special responsibility for training cavalry units and tank brigades.

Zhukov's relatively rapid career progression in the 1930s took place against the background of two very important developments: the gigantic expansion of the Soviet armed forces in the 1930s and Stalin's great purge of the Red Army in 1937–1938.

Defence spending increased from 10 per cent to 25 per cent of the budget between 1932 and 1939. In the early 1930s the Red Army grew to nearly a million strong and by the end of the decade had a complement of over four million. Most of this expansion was accomplished by turning the part-time territorial divisions into regular divisions and by extending the period of conscripted service from two to three years. Between 1932 and 1937 the defence budget increased by 340 per cent in absolute terms; then between 1937 and 1940 it doubled again. By 1939 the USSR was producing more than 10,000 planes a year, nearly 3,000 tanks, more than 17,000 artillery pieces and 114,000 machine guns. As part of this expansion the pay and conditions for officers improved dramatically. Zhukov's corps commander's pay of 2,000 roubles a year in 1939 was triple what it would have been in 1934.[32]

The origins of this massive rearmament programme dated back to a war scare in 1927 when the Soviets believed the British and the Poles were plotting a combined attack. The Soviets examined their defences and found them to be highly vulnerable. That review coincided with the launch of the first five-year plan for the industrialisation of the USSR, which promised to provide the Red Army with the technical resources to build up its war machine. In 1931 Japan's invasion of the north-eastern Chinese province of Manchuria provoked further anxieties about the state of Soviet defences. The Soviets had many interests in China, not least border security, and feared the Japanese attack could develop into a wider regional conflict into which they would be drawn. Also, in January 1933 Adolf Hitler and the Nazis came to power in Germany. Anticommunism and anti-Sovietism were central to the Nazis' political identity and in *Mein Kampf* Hitler had proclaimed the goal of seeking *Lebensraum* (living space) in Russia for the German people. In response to these dire threats the Soviets spent the rest of the decade trying to build an international alliance of states to counter the Japanese and, especially, the German danger. But it was the rearmed Red Army that the Soviets primarily relied upon to protect their security.

The growth of the armed forces presented talented, professional officers such as Zhukov with unprecedented career opportunities. The status of service in the Red Army also rose, particularly for higher grade commanders. In September 1935 formal ranks were reintroduced into the Red Army at lower and mid-levels – lieutenant, senior lieutenant, captain, major, and colonel. There was still no rank of general, however, and brigade and corps commanders continued to be designated by their function (in Russian abbreviation: *Kombrig* and *Komkor*). While the Red Army had no generals it did have marshals and in November 1935 this title was bestowed on K. Voroshilov, Tukhachevsky, Budenny, the chief of staff, A. I. Yegorov, and V. K. Blukher, the commander of the Far Eastern Army.

STALINIST TERROR

Stalin's purge of the Red Army in the late 1930s was the second development to impact on Zhukov's career. This was not the first purge of the Red Army – in the 1920s and early 1930s there had been several purges of former tsarist officers and those suspected of sympathies with Stalin's great rival, Leon Trotsky, driven into exile from the USSR in 1929. However, the 1937 purge was the first to engulf the Soviet High Command itself. It began in dramatic fashion in May 1937 with the arrest of Marshal Tukhachevsky and seven other high-ranking officers on charges of treason and involvement in a conspiracy with Nazi Germany to overthrow the Soviet government. In June all the accused were tried in secret, found guilty, and shot. Verdict and sentence were announced in the Soviet press and within ten days of the trial a further 980 officers had been arrested. By the time the purge had run its course more than 34,000 officers had been dismissed from the armed forces. Among the victims was Rokossovsky, who was arrested and imprisoned in August 1937. While some 11,500 officers were eventually reinstated (among them Rokossovsky), a great number of others were either executed or died in prison. Among those who perished were three marshals (Tukhachevsky, Yegorov, and Blukher); sixteen officers of general-level rank; fifteen admirals; 264 colonels; 107 majors; and seventy-one lieutenants. The category of officer that suffered most losses, however, was that of political commissar, thousands of whom perished in the purges. As the guardians of political correctness in the armed forces it was easy to point the finger of blame against the commissars when the political loyalty of officers was called into question. The commissars were also resented by many professional military officers, some of whom took the opportunity to denounce them.

No one really knows exactly why the purge happened but it seems Stalin truly believed he was threatened by elements of the Red Army, even though there is not a single shred of evidence of disloyalty or malign intention. After the Second World War all the victims of Stalin's military purges were rehabilitated, many of them during Zhukov's stewardship of the Ministry of Defence in the mid-1950s.[33]

The armed forces were not the only targets of Stalin's ire and paranoia. Following the December 1934 assassination of Sergey Kirov, head of the Leningrad Communist Party, thousands of party members were arrested, suspected of involvement in a plot to kill Soviet leaders. In the mid-1930s there was a series of public political show trials of former leading members of the Bolshevik Party, accused of being spies, saboteurs, and plotters against Stalin. The chief defendant in absentia was Trotsky, who was assassinated in Mexico in 1940 by an agent of Stalin's. Then there was the so-called *Yezhovshchina* – named after Stalin's security chief Nikolai Yezhov – a frenzied hunt for the alleged 'enemy within' that led to mass arrests and executions of party and state officials. These events, known collectively as the Great Terror, were an intense period of political repression and officially sanctioned violence in which millions of people were arrested and hundreds of thousands executed, mostly in 1937–1938. In this context the purge of the military was relatively restrained; apart from the assault on the Higher Command it was a moderate onslaught compared with what other sections of the Soviet population suffered.[34]

What impact did these events have on Zhukov? In the version of his memoirs published in the Soviet era he noted that in 1937 there 'were unfounded arrests in the armed forces that year in contravention of socialist legality. Prominent military leaders were arrested, which, naturally, affected the development of our armed forces and their combat preparedness.'[35] In the posthumously published post-Soviet version of the memoirs there was more extensive coverage of the purges in which Zhukov named some of the prominent victims that he knew personally and described the suspicion he came under because of his connections with them. He also related how he successfully intervened in support of one of his divisional commanders who came under attack at a party meeting. The climax of Zhukov's account of the purges is a description of how he was arraigned before a meeting of leading party members of the 6th Cavalry Corps and accused of harshness and rudeness and having dubiously good relations with 'enemies of the people'. Zhukov defended himself forcefully and turned the meeting in his favour, thus escaping censure and possible exclusion from the party – the first step towards arrest.[36]

According to Era and Ella, their father expected to be arrested anytime and kept a bag ready just in case. In a 1971 interview Zhukov told the Soviet writer and journalist Konstantin Simonov:

The most difficult emotional experience in my life was con-
nected with the years 1937–1938. The necessarily fatal documents were prepared on me; apparently they were already
sufficient, someone somewhere was running with a briefcase in
which they lay. In general, the matter went like this: I would
end up the same way as had many others. . . . And then, after
all this, suddenly the call came! And I was ordered to Khalkhin-
Gol. . . . I went there happy.[37]

The problem with Zhukov's version of events is that there is no
supporting documentary evidence and only one surviving eyewitness
– himself. Zhukov's self-portrayal as a near victim of the purges seems
designed to fend off any accusations that he was a beneficiary of the
purges, even though his promotion to command the 3rd and then the
6th Corps came about precisely because the previous incumbents had
been purged. Moreover, had Zhukov actually acted as he described in
the post-Soviet version of his memoirs he would undoubtedly have
joined them. Only those who conformed and raised no fuss – the vast
majority of the armed forces, it should be said – survived the purges.
This is not to say that Zhukov was untroubled by the purges or that he
did not suffer some real scares. But it is difficult to avoid the conclusion that Zhukov, like most Soviet citizens, kept his head down, re-
pressed his doubts, and took refuge in the belief that Stalin must know
what he was doing.[38]

Equally problematic is Zhukov's claim that he only escaped the
purges because he was sent to Khalkhin-Gol in May 1939. Why would
the Soviet leadership have assigned such an important mission to him
if there were any doubts about his loyalty? Furthermore, Zhukov was
sent to Khalkhin-Gol not to fight a battle but to investigate the failings of the local military leadership during clashes with the Japanese
on the Mongolian-Manchurian border. In effect, he was sent to the
Far East to conduct a purge. Once again the harshness and repressive-
ness of the Soviet system had worked in Zhukov's favour.

4.

KHALKHIN-GOL, 1939:

THE BLOODING OF A GENERAL

ZHUKOV'S POSTING TO THE FAR EAST IN MAY 1939 CAME IN THE AFTERMATH of a series of bloody clashes between Soviet and Japanese troops along the Khalkhin-Gol River on the Mongolian-Manchurian border. His mission was to lead an inspection team to investigate the reasons for the 'unsatisfactory work' of N. V. Feklenko, commander of the 57th Special Corps, which did battle with the Japanese. Zhukov's detailed orders were set out in a directive from Defence Commissar Kliment Voroshilov dated 24 May: 'to study the work of the 57th Corps Commander and his staff in relation to battle training, what measures the Corps Commander took to support his subordinates in readying their units for action, to verify the strength and composition of the 57th's personnel, and the state and security of the Corps' arms and supplies. In the event that deficiencies in battle training are detected to take, together with the Corps Commander, immediate and decisive measures to remedy them.'[1]

Zhukov's appointment made sense given his work in the Cavalry Inspectorate in the early 1930s and his well-known prowess when it came to battle training. In the year preceding his posting to the Far East he was deputy commander of the Belorussian Military District with special responsibility for training cavalry units and tank brigades, and the General Staff's view was that armour and rapid movement would play an important role in upcoming battles with the Japanese on the flat and open terrain of Khalkhin-Gol.

On 24 May Zhukov wrote to his wife, Alexandra:

Darling Wife!

Today I was with the People's Commissar. I think it went very well. I am going on a prolonged mission. The People's Commissar said it will take about three months.

To you I have this request: firstly, don't whimper, be stoic and suffer with dignity and honesty this unpleasant separation. Take into account, my dear, that very difficult work lies ahead of me and that I, as a member of the party and as a commander in the Red Army, must do it honourably and exemplarily. You know me, I am not accustomed to carrying out my duties badly, but I need to be at ease in relation to you and our daughters. I ask you to create this calmness for me. Use all your strength, but do it. . . . In relation to me you can be a hundred per cent serene.

Your tears hurt me deeply. But I understand that it is difficult for you also.

I kiss you affectionately and lovingly. I kiss my darling daughters.

Your Zhorzh[2]

RUSSIA VERSUS JAPAN

The conflict at Khalkhin-Gol was rooted in a long history of rivalry between Russia and Japan in China.[3] For both strategic and economic reasons the two countries penetrated deeply into China in the late nineteenth century. As a result of the Sino-Japanese War of 1894–1895 Japan wrested control of Korea from the Chinese emperor. The Chinese also conceded the Liaodong Peninsula in southern Manchuria to Japan. However, Russia, supported by France and Germany, who also had extensive interests in China and were equally worried about Japan's penetration of the country, pressured the Japanese to relinquish control of Liaodong. Subsequently, the Russians moved into the peninsula and leased a naval base from the Chinese at Port Arthur (Lushan), an acquisition that gave them an all-year warm water outlet to the Pacific. To establish land communications with Port Arthur they began the construction of what became known as the Chinese Eastern Railway – a line that ran through Manchuria and linked up with Vladivostok and the Trans-Siberian Railway. They also began to encroach on Japanese economic interests in Korea. Alarmed by these developments the Japanese attempted to negotiate a deal with the Russians whereby their control of Korea was recognised in exchange for Russian hegemony in Manchuria. When these negotiations failed the Japanese launched a surprise attack on the Russian fleet at Port Arthur in February 1904.

During the Russo-Japanese War of 1904–1905 the tsar's forces suffered a series of defeats on both land and sea, including the loss of Port Arthur. Tens of thousands of casualties were incurred by both sides. Russian military setbacks contributed to the outbreak of the 1905 Revolution – a series of strikes, protests, and violent disturbances aimed at forcing Tsar Nicholas II to reform his autocratic regime. In a weak position internally as well as externally, the tsar was forced to sign the humiliating Treaty of Portsmouth with Japan in September 1905. Under the treaty the Russians were forced to withdraw from Manchuria, to accept Japan's domination of Korea, and to return to Japanese control the southern half of the island of Sakhalin, occupied by Russia since 1875. The Japanese also gained control of the southern section of the Chinese Eastern Railway.

The next clash between Russia and Japan occurred after the Bolsheviks seized power in 1917. In summer 1918, 70,000 Japanese troops supported by American, British, and French units landed in Vladivostok and linked up with the Bolsheviks' opponents in Siberia. The context of the intervention was the Soviet peace treaty with Germany in March 1918 and Russia's exit from the First World War. The ostensible purpose of the Japanese-western expeditionary force was to secure war materials supplied to their erstwhile Russian allies. In reality the expedition was part of a broader intervention in the Russian Civil War aimed at toppling the revolutionary Bolshevik regime. But when the Bolsheviks won the civil war the western forces withdrew from Siberia in April 1920. The Japanese, with ambitions to establish a permanent base in Siberia, stayed for another two years and only withdrew because of determined Soviet resistance to their continued presence.

But Japan remained entrenched in Korea, annexed by the Japanese in 1910, and in Manchuria with its Kwantung Army protecting the Japanese-controlled section of the Chinese Eastern Railway and surrounding areas. In September 1931 the Kwantung Army used the sabotage of a section of the line, supposedly by Chinese nationalist dissidents, as a pretext to invade and occupy all Manchuria. In February 1932 the Japanese established a puppet state in Manchuria called Manchukuo.

The Soviets viewed these developments with considerable alarm, fearing the revival of Japanese imperial ambitions in relation to Siberia; fears that intensified when the Japanese refused the Soviet offer of a nonaggression treaty in December 1932. Moscow responded by continuing to build up its military forces in the Soviet Far East.

The most pressing issue for Moscow was what to do with the northern sections of the Chinese Eastern Railway in Manchuria, controlled by the Soviets but located in what was now Japanese-occupied territory. This problem was resolved by selling the railway to the Japanese in March 1935. More difficult to resolve were disputes about the border between Soviet and Manchurian territory, which led to a series of frontier clashes involving Soviet and Japanese forces. Adding to the tensions in Soviet-Japanese relations was Japan's signing of the anti-Comintern pact with Nazi Germany in November 1936. Ostensibly directed against the activities of the Communist International – established by the Bolsheviks in 1919 to foment world revolution – the pact was in fact directed against the Soviet Union and contained a secret agreement that Japan and Germany would maintain a benevolent neutrality should either become involved in war with the USSR. The pact reinforced Stalin's belief that Japanese spies and saboteurs had penetrated Siberia. He responded with mass arrests of indigenous Koreans and Japanese living in the region.

In July 1937 Japan invaded northern China, quickly capturing Peking and Shanghai. During the Sino-Japanese War – seen by many historians as the opening phase of the global conflict that developed into the Second World War – the USSR became a major supplier of munitions to China. Between 1937 and 1941 the Soviet Union supplied to China 904 planes, 82 tanks, 602 tractors, 1,516 automobiles, 1,140 heavy guns, 9,720 machine guns, 50,000 rifles, 180 million cartridges,

31,600 bombs, and two million shells. Hundreds of Soviet military advisors served in China, including many pilots.[4]

A particularly thorny problem in Soviet-Japanese relations was the border between Mongolia and Manchuria. The People's Republic of Mongolia, formerly the Chinese province of Outer Mongolia, was founded as a Soviet client state in 1924. When the Japanese occupied Manchuria border disputes between Mongolia and the Manchukuo government began to accumulate. As these disputes escalated Moscow signed the Soviet-Mongolian mutual assistance treaty of March 1936, signalling its firm intention to defend Mongolia against Japanese encroachments.

The most serious incident to occur before the Khalkhin-Gol battle of 1939 was a division-strength clash in 1938 between the Soviet Far Eastern Army and the Kwantung Army at Lake Khasan on the border between Korea, Manchuria, and the USSR. After some heavy fighting the Japanese backed away from further confrontation and accepted the Soviet demarcation of the border. That the Japanese would retreat in the face of a determined stand against them was not lost on the Soviet leadership.

Despite the overall success of the Soviets there were some question marks hanging over the Red Army's performance during the Lake Khasan battle. Following an investigation the Far Eastern Army was disbanded in September 1938, its place taken by two separate army groups. The Soviets also decided to establish the 57th Special Corps specifically to be deployed in Mongolia.

The dispute at Khalkhin-Gol concerned the border between Manchuria and Mongolia. Did the frontier run along the Khalkhin-Gol River as the Japanese asserted, or was the border located somewhat east of the river as the Mongolians claimed? Given that the dispute concerned the ownership of a few square miles of inhospitable and sparsely populated terrain, it was not intrinsically important to either the Soviets or the Japanese. But the troubled history of Soviet-Japanese relations in China magnified its importance. At stake was the power relationship between Japan and the Soviet Union in the Far East and the question of who was likely to prevail in the event of a broader military conflict between the two states.

MISSION TO MONGOLIA

Zhukov arrived at the Tamtsak-Bulak HQ of the 57th Corps shortly after receiving his orders from Voroshilov on 24 May. By 30 May he and his inspection team had submitted a report to Voroshilov on an 'exceptionally disorganized battle' with the Japanese that had taken place east of the Khalkhin-Gol River on 28 and 29 May – a fight that had resulted in Soviet casualties of seventy-one dead, eighty wounded, and thirty-three missing. The disorganisation of the battle, reported Zhukov, was the result of poor tactics, ill-conceived battle management, and a failure to calculate and anticipate enemy manoeuvres.[5] On 3 June Zhukov wrote to Voroshilov that among the corps command staff only Kushchev, the chief of staff, was doing good work. As to Feklenko: 'as a Bolshevik and a person, he is good and undoubtedly committed to the cause of the party and he tries hard, but fundamentally he is badly organised and insufficiently purposeful. A fuller appraisal of Feklenko can only be given after further study of him.'[6] Also in Mongolia was the deputy chief of the Red Air Force, Y. V. Smushkevich, sent to Khalkhin-Gol with reinforcements for the air battle with the Japanese. He knew Zhukov quite well from his own time in the Belorussian Military District. On 8 June Smushkevich wrote to Voroshilov: 'I have come to the conclusion that the Corps Command and Feklenko personally have failed. . . . Without doubt, the Corps Command was not prepared or badly prepared for battle. . . . Zhukov is now imposing some order. In my view it would be advisable to retain him as Corps Commander for a while.' Voroshilov replied to Smushkevich the same day, agreeing with his analysis of the situation and informing him that Feklenko would be replaced.[7] Zhukov was appointed commander of the 57th Corps on 12 June 1939.

Zhukov threw himself into his new command with characteristic vigour and determination. One of his first actions was to propose the establishment of a system of intelligence based on agent infiltration, aerial reconnaissance, and prisoner interrogation. Without such a system, Zhukov cabled Voroshilov on 16 June, 'we do not have a full and clear view of the enemy'. Another Zhukov initiative was improved training and preparation for the forthcoming battle with the Japanese, especially the restoration of military discipline in the 57th Corps.

Battle did resume in July when the Japanese tried to dislodge the Soviets from their positions east of the Khalkhin-Gol River and to establish their own bridgehead on the west bank. During the course of fierce fighting the Red Army suffered heavy casualties. From 16 May to 25 July the 57th Corps suffered more than 5,000 casualties, mostly during the July battles. Not surprisingly, Zhukov's emphasis on discipline became even more pronounced and orders were issued that commanders and commissars would be held personally responsible for their units' conduct during battle. If they failed to carry out orders, they would be brought before military tribunals and severely punished. On 13 July Zhukov issued a decree announcing that two soldiers had been shot for cowardice. The decree, which was distributed to all soldiers in the 57th Corps, concluded with the peroration: 'To us, the sons of a 170-million-strong nation, has fallen the high honour of defending the toiling masses of the People's Republic of Mongolia from the despicable invaders. . . . I call upon you to show courage, manliness, audacity, braveness and heroism. Death to despicable cowards and traitors!'[8]

In the middle of the July battle there occurred an episode that was to have significant personal consequences for Zhukov. Deputy Defence Commissar G. I. Kulik, who was in overall charge of Soviet artillery, had arrived at Khalkhin-Gol on an inspection tour. On 13 July he ordered Zhukov to withdraw the bulk of Soviet forces east of the river to the west bank. Zhukov – as always a model of discipline – began to implement the order but when the General Staff in Moscow saw his situation reports and found out what was happening they ordered him to desist. In a conversation with Boris Shaposhnikov, the chief of the General Staff, on 14 July Zhukov explained that he was acting in accordance with Kulik's orders but that he would stop the withdrawal if so ordered. Strict instructions to that effect were cabled to Zhukov by Voroshilov that same day. Meanwhile, Kulik appealed to Moscow to support his decision but was given short shrift by Voroshilov, who ordered him not to meddle in the affairs of the 57th Corps.[9]

This incident informed an important organisational decision made in Moscow. Hitherto the 57th Corps had been formally subordinate to a Front Group of all Soviet forces in Siberia and the Far East established on 5 July 1939, and commanded by G. M. Shtern. On 19 July the 57th Corps was reorganised into the 1st Army Group and given operational independence from Shtern's Front Group. This peculiar arrangement was designed to ensure Zhukov could act without interference except for instructions coming directly from the General Staff in Moscow. It seems that Voroshilov and Shaposhnikov wanted to avoid a possible repetition of the Kulik incident during the upcoming battle. The command picture was completed on 31 July when Zhukov was formally promoted from Komdiv (divisional commander) to Komkor (corps commander) – the equivalent of a general in a western army.

BATTLE PLANNING

Shtern's Front Group continued to be involved in planning and preparations for the battle at Khalkhin-Gol and on 27 July Shtern sent Zhukov a directive asking him to submit by 31 July proposals for the destruction of the Japanese forces and their expulsion from Mongolian territory. Although Zhukov did not take credit in his memoirs for formulating the plan for the offensive of August 1939, he certainly gave the impression that he and his staff were central to its preparation – a plausible claim since he was the front-line commander and had been given operational independence by Moscow. But it was Shtern who submitted the draft plan to Moscow on 10 August and it was Shtern's chief of staff, M. A. Bogdanov, who drew up the plans for the extensive preparations for the battle.[10] Zhukov may have been the executor of the battle plan but he was not its only architect.

By far the most important aspect of the Red Army's preparations for the August offensive was the buildup of Soviet forces at Khalkhin-Gol. By the eve of the offensive the 1st Army Group included the 57th and 82nd Rifle Divisions and the 36th Motorised Rifle Division; the 6th and 8th Mongolian Cavalry Divisions; the 7th and 8th Mechanised Brigades and the 5th Machine Gun Brigade; and the 6th and 11th Tank Brigades. In all Zhukov had thirty-five rifle battalions and twenty cavalry squadrons at his disposal. In his attack on the Japanese Zhukov was able to deploy 57,000 troops, more than 500 artillery pieces, nearly 900 tanks and armoured cars, and 500 planes.

Ranged against him were twenty-five Japanese battalions and seventeen squadrons, a total of 75,000 troops with artillery and aircraft numbers equivalent to those of the Soviet, but far fewer tanks and armoured cars than Zhukov could deploy.[11]

To assemble, supply, and ready such a sizable force was a huge logistical task. The terrain was inhospitable, the roads poor, and the nearest railhead 400 miles away. According to Zhukov a round-trip to the railhead took five days and the Soviets had to use some 5,000 trucks to ship in 18,000 tons of artillery ammunition; 6,500 tons of aircraft ammunition; 15,000 tons of fuel and lubricants; 7,500 tons of solid fuel, 4,000 tons of food; and 4,000 tons of other supplies.[12]

Great attention was given to concealing Soviet offensive intentions and preparations from the Japanese – what the Soviets called *maskirovka*. Movements of supplies and troops were concealed and assault forces were deployed for attack only at the last possible moment. False radio traffic was used to indicate the Red Army was digging in for defence, not preparing an attack. A handbook entitled *What the Soviet Soldier Must Know in Defense* was distributed to troops and deliberately leaked to the Japanese. Training was carried out in secret and draft planning document distribution was restricted to the top command. A single typist was used to type out the operational directives and combat orders.[13] Zhukov also kept the Japanese guessing by continuing to launch local attacks against enemy positions. These tricks, this exercise in *maskirovka,* worked. The Kwantung Army had no idea a major Soviet attack was being prepared and when Zhukov's offensive began he achieved complete operational surprise – a major factor in the immediate and stunning success of the operation.

Zhukov issued his general directive to the 1st Army Group on the Khalkhin-Gol offensive on 17 August.[14] The attack was to begin on 20 August; its aim, stated the directive, was to encircle and destroy Japanese forces on Mongolian territory east of the Khalkhin-Gol River. For this purpose Zhukov divided his forces into three groups. The Southern Group, which constituted Zhukov's right wing, was to deliver the main blow and was to cross the Khalkhin-Gol and head towards Nomonhan, with the aim of encircling Japanese forces north of the Khailastyn-Gol (a tributary of the Khalkhin-Gol). There it would link up with Zhukov's Central and Northern Groups and destroy the encircled Japanese. The Northern Group's role was to attack the Japanese north flank at Fui Heights and to support the Central and Southern Groups' assault on enemy forces north of the Khailastyn-Gol. Most of Zhukov's armour and mechanised forces were deployed in the Northern and Southern Groups. The Central Group, consisting mainly of infantry, was to launch a frontal assault on Japanese positions north and south of the Khailastyn-Gol, in the latter case linking up with elements of the Southern Group in another encirclement manoeuvre. Zhukov's HQ was located at Hamar Daba in the central sector and immediately behind him was deployed a strong mobile reserve ready to exploit the success of the Northern and Southern Groups. (*See Map 1: The Battle of Khalkhin-Gol, 20–31 August 1939.*)

VICTORY AT KHALKHIN-GOL

The attack began in the early hours of Sunday morning, 20 August, a day chosen, according to Zhukov, because many senior Japanese officers, not expecting a Soviet offensive, had taken Sunday leave. In his memoirs Zhukov recalled:

> At 6.15 A.M. our artillery opened up for all it was worth against enemy anti-aircraft guns and machine guns. Some of our batteries lobbed smoke shells on the objectives to be bombed by our aircraft. In the area of the Khalkhin-Gol the roar of aircraft approaching combat positions grew ever more deafening. Over 150 bombers and some 100 fighters were in the air. . . . At 8.45 A.M. artillery and mortars of all calibers opened fire against enemy targets. . . . Meanwhile, our aircraft hit targets behind the lines. . . . At nine sharp, when our aircraft were strafing the enemy and bombing his artillery, red flares went up announcing the beginning of the offensive. The attacking units, covered by artillery fire, charged.[15]

The operation went more or less as planned. Soviet tanks and motorised forces quickly overran Japanese infantry and artillery positions. Soviet air forces flew hundreds of sorties and dropped 86,000 kilograms of bombs. Soviet artillery pounded Japanese positions,

MAP 1: THE BATTLE OF KHALKHIN-GOL, 20–31 AUGUST 1939

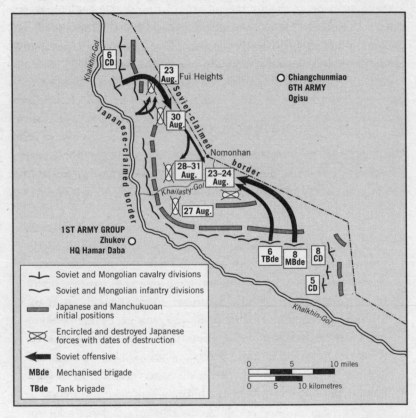

causing by far the greatest number of enemy casualties. There was a sticky moment on 24 August when the Japanese launched a counter-attack aimed at breaking the Soviet ring surrounding their forces trapped north of the Khailastyn-Gol. But Zhukov responded by committing some of his reserves, including the 6th Tank Brigade, to parry the Japanese. After three days of intense fighting the Japanese counter-attack petered out. On 27 August Zhukov issued a decree to the 1st Army Group announcing that the Japanese forces on Mongolian territory at Khalkhin-Gol had been surrounded and destroyed.[16] The battle was not over yet, however, and between 28 and 31 August some tough pockets of Japanese resistance had to be liquidated.

As early as 30 August the Soviet government was celebrating the victory at Khalkhin-Gol. A statement published in the Defence Commissariat newspaper, *Krasnaya Zvezda* (Red Star), and other Soviet newspapers, announced that Zhukov, Shtern, and thirty-one other participants in the battle had been made Heroes of the Soviet Union – the USSR's highest honour. Yet it was Shtern's name that headed the list of awards and citations, not Zhukov's:

> An outstanding commander, a talented pupil of Comrade Voroshilov, and the leader of the battle at Lake Khasan, Grigory Mikhailovich Shtern fulfilled brilliantly his military mission. One of the most notable military figures in our party and a member of its Central Committee – he is a model of a brave Bolshevik and military commander. The love and admiration evoked by the name of Hero of the Soviet Union Komkor G. K. Zhukov is well deserved. A brilliant organiser, a person of unbending willpower and boundless courage, he welded his troops together in fulfillment of the government's military mission.[17]

The published order of merit has led some to speculate that perhaps Shtern had more to do with the victory at Khalkhin-Gol than posterity has been led to believe. The explanation is probably much simpler: Shtern was the senior (and better-known) of the two officers and the writers of the government communiqué may not have been aware of the operational independence given to Zhukov by the General Staff.

Shtern did, indeed, play a central role in the preparation of the August offensive but its chief organiser and executor was Zhukov. During the battle he was left to make his own decisions, which is not surprising given the speed with which the offensive developed and succeeded in achieving its operational goals. Zhukov later claimed that on the third day of the offensive Shtern had come to him and proposed the attack should be paused for two to three days to regroup and resupply before continuing the encirclement of the Japanese. In Zhukov's telling he put it bluntly to Shtern that if he was being given advice that was one thing, but if he was being giving an order he would appeal to Moscow over Shtern's head. Needless to say, Shtern backed down and Zhukov continued with his attack.[18] Maybe some such incident did take place but more important is that the story reflects the general tensions between Zhukov and Shtern generated by the unusual command arrangements put in place by the General Staff. Zhukov was Shtern's junior and it was natural the senior officer would resent being excluded from critical command decisions. Tensions between the two men would surface again at the High Command conference in December 1940 when the lessons of Khalkhin-Gol for contemporary warfare were discussed.[19]

As the battle came to a close on 28 August Zhukov started writing a letter to his wife, which he finished on 1 September:

Hello My Darling Wife!

Greetings and all my affectionate kisses to you. I received lots of letters and telegrams from you but, forgive me, I could not reply because I was engaged in battle. Since 20.8 I have been conducting a continuous battle. Today the destruction of the Japanese Samurai will be completed. The destruction of the [enemy] army took more than 100 artillery guns and masses of machinery and equipment of all sorts. . . .

I need to tell you that the battle was fierce throughout. Naturally, as commander I had to work and not sleep. That was not too bad, as long as there was a good result. You will remember that I wrote to you from Moscow that the mission of the party had to be fulfilled with honour. I don't know how the conflict will develop. Hopefully, it will finish soon and we will see each other. I am sending this to you today by messenger. I think it will get through.

Today I received the report that I had been awarded the title of Hero of the Soviet Union. Obviously, you will know about this already. Such praise by the government, the party, and Voroshilov obliges me to try even harder to fulfill my duty to the Motherland.

Affectionately and lovingly all my kisses to you.

Until we meet again soon.
Zhorzh.[20]

Not sure that his wife received this letter, Zhukov wrote to her again in the middle of September: 'I am alive and well. You must know from the TASS report about the battle on the Mongolian-Manchurian border. Now you understand why I had to leave Smolensk so urgently. You must also know from the TASS report that the Japanese Samurai have been destroyed, in the air as well as on the land. . . . During the action I felt very good. In short, just like during the civil war.'[21]

Stiff and formal and displaying little real affection, these letters are typical of Zhukov's correspondence with his first wife. This is not so surprising given the context and conditions under which Zhukov wrote. High-ranking Soviet citizens like Zhukov were expected to have political commitments, not personal feelings, and could assume their private letters were subject to scrutiny by the security services. But their correspondence was not devoid of personal content and could reveal preferences within a prescribed framework. In Zhukov's case it is clear that he liked to be where the action was, which was to become a recurring theme of his wartime correspondence with his family.

ZHUKOV'S CANNAE

Zhukov's victory at Khalkhin-Gol has been almost universally admired as a tactical masterstroke and as a classic example of a combined arms operation that demonstrated both the power and speed of modern mechanised forces. In his monumental study of the battle Alvin D. Coox entitled his chapter on the Soviet summer offensive 'Forging a Second Cannae: Zhukov's Masterpiece, August 1939'.[22] William J. Spahr, another American military historian, agreed with this evaluation: 'Zhukov had executed a Cannae, a successful double envelopment, on the dry steppes of Mongolia on a battlefield 74 kilometres wide and 20 kilometres deep almost 2,000 years after Hannibal destroyed the Roman army of Terentius Varro'.[23] High praise, indeed, considering that Hannibal's success at Cannae is seen as one of the greatest battlefield victories in history, an example of a pincer movement encirclement that generals the world over have aspired to emulate ever since, even though the Punic Wars were eventually won by Rome not Carthage.

The battle of Khalkhin-Gol is also credited with being a key moment in Zhukov's maturation as an operational commander. According to an American biographer, Otto Preston Chaney, for example,

in this battle Zhukov's command style was revealed: personal reconnaissance, seizing the initiative, bold offensive action, innovation, skillful coordination of ground and air assets and acceptance of heavy casualties if the situation demanded it. . . . He proved calm under strong pressure, exhibiting at the same time a complete grasp of the situation. . . . He had shown himself to be a commander rigid in seeing the execution of his orders by subordinates but able to temper his rigidity with tactical flexibility when he was convinced it would achieve his goals. This ability is reflected in his superior concentration of forces, his bold and successful encirclement plan, his aggressive but resourceful reduction of the encircled enemy, and his coordination of combined-arms forces, correct combination of modern arms, and ad hoc offensive measures, resulting in a total Soviet victory.[24]

This is all true. But only up to a point. As we have seen, Zhukov was far from being the sole author of the victory at Khalkhin-Gol, which was a result of the collective effort by himself and his staff, by Shtern's Front Group, and by the General Staff in Moscow. The command traits he displayed were commendable but, surely, were those that all good generals aspire to. Moreover, it is always easier to perform well against an inferior enemy, especially when you win. Zhukov's real test as a commander was yet to come: keeping his composure in the face of massive defeats by the Germans in summer 1941, an opponent far superior to the underequipped and old-fashioned Kwantung Army.

More important was Khalkhin-Gol's personal and psychological significance for Zhukov. He had performed brilliantly and been given credit for a great victory – the Red Army's first since the civil war. It was also a victory viewed by the Soviets as suitable revenge for Russia's humiliating defeat in the 1904–1905 Russo-Japanese War. Zhukov's self-confidence and inner self-belief were immeasurably enhanced. From now on he would have peers among his fellow generals but no superiors.

A hint of the personal transformation that Zhukov experienced as a result of Khalkhin-Gol comes through in the journalist Konstantin Simonov's account of his first meeting with him. Simonov arrived at Khalkhin-Gol soon after the battle had concluded. Together with a group of Soviet journalists he went to see Zhukov in his dugout. Zhukov sat in the corner behind a small table. 'He must have only just returned from the bath', recalled Simonov, 'rosy-cheeked, sweating and without a shirt, his yellow tunic was tucked into his flannel breeches. Of low height and with his wide chest bursting through his tunic, he seemed very big and broad.' When an intelligence officer came in with a report, Zhukov looked at the officer angrily and said: 'Regarding six divisions, it is nonsense: we have established there are only two. The rest are nonsense. ' Turning to the journalists he said, 'That's how they earn their living.' When the officer asked if he could go, Zhukov told him: 'Go. Tell them over there not to fantasize. If you have blank spots be honest about them and let them remain blank spots and don't feed me nonexistent Japanese divisions in their place.' When the officer had left Zhukov repeated: 'That's how they earn their living. Intelligence officers.'[25] It is difficult to imagine the Zhukov of an earlier vintage behaving so frankly and confidently in front of an audience of journalists.

A decade later Simonov wrote a novel about Khalkhin-Gol –

Comrades in Arms – which featured an unnamed 'Commander' of the Soviet forces. Simonov always insisted this was a fictional character, but his portrait of a stern but energetic and effective commander was recognisably Zhukov.[26]

Zhukov's growing self-confidence was also reflected in a long report on Khalkhin-Gol to Shaposhnikov in November 1939. The report began with a severe critique of Feklenko and his 'criminal' failure to prepare adequately for battle with the Japanese; later in the report Feklenko was described as an 'enemy of the people'. A lot of the report was devoted to the crucial role tanks had played in defeating the Kwantung Army. But Zhukov also drew attention to some drawbacks. It was difficult to direct actions of tanks because of a lack of information and poor battlefield communications. The absence of infantry support for tanks had allowed the Japanese to withdraw in some cases. Inadequate intelligence had resulted in failure to deploy reserves to maintain the encirclement of enemy forces. Zhukov was also critical of the air force, especially during the first phase of the battle. Units had not been prepared for group battle, there was no coordination of the actions of different types of planes, and there was a failure to study enemy air tactics. These caveats notwithstanding, Zhukov's overall conclusion was very positive: 'at Khalkhin-Gol in the period 20–31 August the forces of the RKKA [Workers' and Peasants' Red Army] and the MNR [People's Republic of Mongolia] conducted the most complex of contemporary operations – and succeeded in winning a victory which, in our view, should be carefully studied by all commanders'.[27]

The political impact on the Japanese of their defeat at Khalkhin-Gol was to strengthen advocates of a 'Southern Strategy' for Japan. This held that Japan would be better advised to expand into Southeast Asia and the Pacific rather than become bogged down in a difficult war with the Soviets in Siberia. This tendency in Japanese policy was reinforced by the signature of the Nazi-Soviet pact on 23 August 1939, and the rapid emergence of a Soviet-German alliance in Europe – dashing dreams of a joint German-Japanese war against the USSR. Zhukov did not know it but he had helped set Japan down the path to the Pearl Harbor attack in December 1941. When the Nazi-Soviet pact broke down and the Germans did attack the Soviet Union in summer 1941 the Japanese reconsidered the 'Northern Strategy' – completion of the conquest of China combined with an attack on the USSR – but by this time Japan was locked into a power struggle with the Americans in the Far East and too committed to the Southern Strategy.

After the battle Zhukov moved to the Mongolian capital of Ulan Bator, where the 1st Army group was headquartered, and was joined by his family. There he languished for the next nine months. One reason for this unexpectedly long sojourn in Mongolia was that Soviet-Japanese armistice negotiations dragged on for months. A truce was agreed in September 1939 but Shtern and Zhukov were then charged with negotiating the details of the frontier with the Japanese. Not until June 1940 was agreement reached.

From Zhukov's point of view his stay in Ulan Bator was a mixed blessing. On the one hand, Europe was where the action was. In response to Hitler's invasion of Poland, Great Britain and France declared war on Germany on 3 September. The Soviets had been negotiating an anti-German triple alliance with Britain and France for several months. But Stalin was convinced that the British and French were trying to entice him into doing their fighting for them. In a stunning diplomatic manoeuvre he signed a nonaggression treaty with Hitler that kept the Soviet Union out of the war. Part of the deal was a secret agreement dividing Poland and the Baltic states of Estonia, Finland, Latvia, and Lithuania into Soviet and German spheres of influence. In accordance with this deal the Red Army joined the German attack on Poland on 17 September, recapturing western Belorussia and western Ukraine – territories lost to the Poles during the Russo-Polish War of 1919–1920. The Poles put up little resistance to the Soviet invasion but it was by far the Red Army's biggest operation since the civil war. There followed an expansion of Soviet influence in the Baltic area as Estonia, Latvia, and Lithuania succumbed to Stalin's demands for military bases.

On the other hand, being in Mongolia meant that Zhukov stayed out of the Red Army's disastrous campaign in Finland in the winter of 1939–1940. During that conflict the Red Army suffered 200,000 casualties, including nearly 50,000 dead. The so-called Winter War came to an end in March 1940 with the signature of a Soviet-Finnish peace treaty. Encouraging both sides to conclude peace was the possibility of British and French involvement in the conflict – a move that would have drawn the Germans into the Soviet-Finnish conflict and likely plunged the whole of Scandinavia into war.

The Soviets had barely digested the lessons of the Winter War when Hitler launched his Blitzkrieg invasion of Western Europe in May 1940. Within six weeks France had surrendered and Britain stood alone against Hitler. But by then Zhukov was back on the Western Front and ready to become a key figure in preparations for the coming Soviet war with Germany.

IN KIEV:

WAR GAMES AND
PREPARATIONS, 1940

ZHUKOV'S RECALL FROM THE FAR EAST IN MAY 1940 WAS PART OF A RADICAL shake-up of the Red Army after the debacle of the war with Finland.

When the Red Army invaded Finland in December 1939 Stalin and the Soviet leadership expected a quick and easy victory. The Soviets even entertained delusions that the Finnish working class would rise in revolt and welcome the Red Army as socialist liberators. Instead the Finns put up a spirited defence that won worldwide sympathy and admiration. One of the many negative political consequences suffered by the Soviets was the humiliation of being expelled from the League of Nations for aggression – a fate Nazi Germany, imperial Japan, and fascist Italy had all avoided by leaving the organisation of their own accord. In the 1930s the Soviet Union had been the foremost advocate of collective security and League action against aggression. Now it was subject to international condemnation for that very sin.

On the military front the Soviet-Finnish War had two main phases. (*See Map 2: The Soviet-Finnish War, 1939–1940.*) In December 1939 the Red Army launched a broad-front attack on Finnish defences, employing five separate armies with about 1.2 million troops, supported by 1,500 tanks and 3,000 aircraft. The main attack was on the Mannerheim Line on the Karelian Isthmus. Named after the commander-in-chief of the Finnish armed forces, this was a belt of defences, natural and constructed, that ran the entire width of the isthmus. The main assault on the Mannerheim Line was by the 7th Army under the

MAP 2: THE SOVIET-FINNISH WAR, 1939–1940

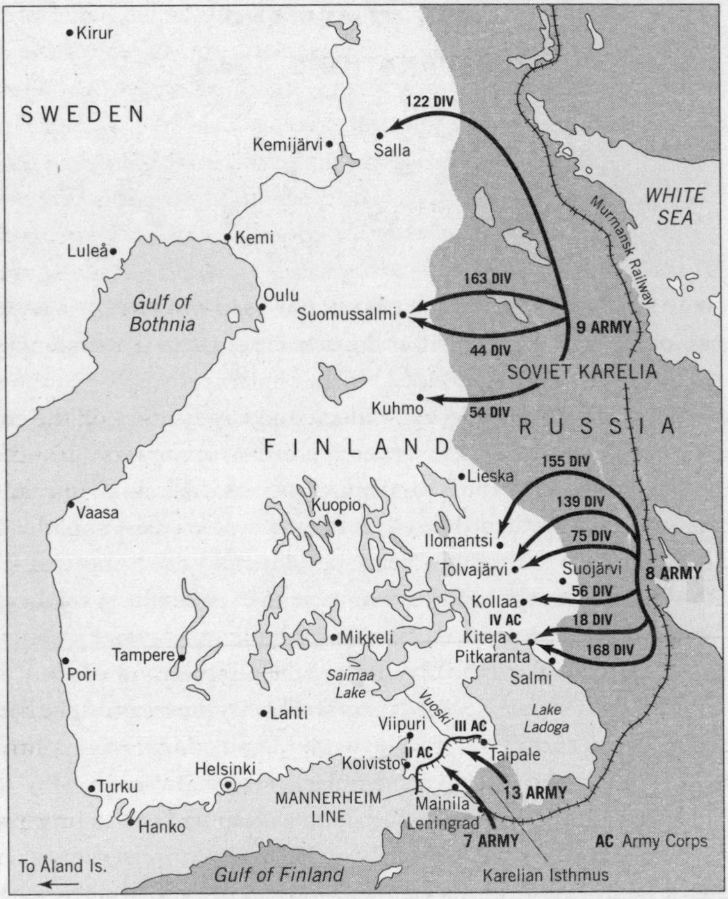

Kirur

S W E D E N

Kemijärvi • ● Salla

122 DIV

*WHITE
SEA*

Murmansk Railway

Luleå • ● Kemi

*Gulf of
Bothnia*

● Oulu

163 DIV

Suomussalmi ●

9 ARMY

44 DIV

SOVIET KARELIA

Kuhmo ●

54 DIV

R U S S I A

F I N L A N D

● Lieska

155 DIV

Kuopio ●

Vaasa •

139 DIV

Ilomantsi ●

75 DIV

Tolvajärvi ●

Suojärvi ●

8 ARMY

Kollaa ●

56 DIV

IV AC

18 DIV

Kitela ●

168 DIV

● Mikkeli

Pitkaranta ●

Salmi ●

Tampere •

*Saimaa
Lake*

Pori •

*Lake
Ladoga*

● Lahti

Viipuri •

III AC

Vuoksi

Koivisto•

II AC

Taipale ●

Turku •

Helsinki ⊙

13 ARMY

MANNERHEIM
LINE

Mainila
Leningrad

Hanko •

7 ARMY

AC Army Corps

To Åland Is.
←

Gulf of Finland

Karelian Isthmus

leadership of K. A. Meretskov, who commanded the Leningrad Military District. The Soviet aim was to breach the Mannerheim Line, occupy the town of Viipuri, and then turn west towards the Finnish capital of Helsinki. When the initial attack failed – partly because of bad weather but mainly because of the Red Army's incompetence – the Soviets regrouped, reinforced, and launched another offensive in January 1940 under the command of S. K. Timoshenko, chief of the Kiev Special Military District, who was transferred north for the duration of the campaign. Timoshenko's attack succeeded. By March 1940 the Red Army was in a position to collapse the remnants of Finnish defences and march on Helsinki. But Stalin, fearing Anglo-French intervention in the conflict, decided to negotiate a peace treaty with the Finns, signed on 12 March 1940. Under the terms of the treaty the Finns conceded Soviet territorial demands, including moving their border away from Leningrad, but retained their political independence and thereby their freedom to join the attack on Russia when Germany invaded in June 1941.

In the aftermath the Soviets conducted a post-mortem on the conflict to explain why they had suffered so many casualties (200,000, including 50,000 dead) and why it had proved difficult to subdue a small country like Finland. At a special conference of the High Command in April 1940 Stalin complained that the Red Army was still obsessed by the experience and lessons of the Russian Civil War and had failed to modernise its thinking, especially in relation to the role of artillery, tanks, planes, and rockets in contemporary warfare.[1]

After the conference a commission was established to further distil the lessons of the Finnish war. The work of this commission contributed to a series of reforms of the Soviet armed forces. In May the government restored the titles of general and admiral and in June promoted to these ranks hundreds of combat-blooded officers. Around the same time Stalin reinstated thousands of purged and disgraced officers. Among the returnees was Colonel K. K. Rokossovsky, Zhukov's classmate from the 1920s, who had been arrested and imprisoned in 1937. On 16 May 1940, training regulations were revised to provide for more realistic preparation for combat. In July the armed forces' disciplinary code was strengthened and in August unitary command (abolished during the pre-war purges) was restored at the tactical level so that field officers no longer had to agree on command decisions with a political commissar. Steps were also taken to improve propaganda work in the armed forces and to recruit more officers and men into the Communist Party.

Another stimulus to reform of the Red Army was the astounding success of Germany's Blitzkrieg invasion of Western Europe in May–June 1940. Impressed by the success of Hitler's panzer divisions, Stalin reversed the decision to abolish mechanised corps. In July 1940 a decree established nine mechanised corps, consisting of more than 1,000 tanks each, supported by motorised infantry, signal, and engineering units. Around the same time decisions were made to produce the models of many of the tanks, guns, and planes that were to become the mainstay of the Soviet armed forces during the Great Patriotic War, including the famous T-34 tank.

The key figure in these reforms was Timoshenko, who had replaced Kliment Voroshilov as defence commissar in May 1940. Indeed, the reforms are often referred to as the 'Timoshenko reforms'. Another change was a revamp of the Main Military Council – the body responsible for the overall organisation, functioning, and mobilisation of the Red Army. Stalin left the council and Timoshenko took over the chair from Voroshilov.[2]

During the war the BBC famously joked that Timoshenko had Irish roots and that his real name was Tim O'Shenko.[3] But Semyon Konstantinovich Timoshenko had, in fact, been born in the Odessa region in 1895. The same age as Zhukov, he, too, was from peasant stock and also served in the tsarist cavalry during the First World War. After the 1917 revolution he joined the Red Army and the Communist Party and during the civil war rose rapidly through the ranks to divisional commander. Timoshenko was a member of the so-called cavalry clique, a term that referred to a group of senior officers who served with Stalin during the civil war and took part in the defence of Tsaritsyn, later renamed Stalingrad. Another member of the cavalry clique was Voroshilov.[4]

After the civil war Timoshenko commanded the 3rd Cavalry Corps where among his divisional commanders was Rokossovsky and below him regimental commander Georgy Zhukov. It was Timoshenko who promoted Zhukov to brigade commander in 1930. The two men served together again from 1933 to 1935 when Timoshenko was deputy commander of the Belorussian Military District and Zhukov a divisional commander. Timoshenko's next command was as head of the Kiev Special Military District, which led the Soviet invasion of eastern Poland in September 1939. Timoshenko's handling of that operation impressed Stalin, as did his cleaning up of the Red Army's mess in Finland. That his daughter was married to Stalin's son Vasily may also have helped Timoshenko's career prospects. Timoshenko was, thus, the obvious successor to Voroshilov as defence commissar when Stalin finally lost patience with his long-time crony because of the incompetence he displayed during the Winter War.

Timoshenko's appointment as people's commissar for defence thus created a vacancy at the head of the Kiev Special Military District. And Zhukov's triumph at Khalkhin-Gol, in contrast to the dismal performance of many of his peers during the Finnish war, made him a natural successor to Timoshenko in Kiev – a district destined to be in the front line of the coming war with Germany. No doubt Zhukov's personal connection to Timoshenko helped, too.

Zhukov's recall from Mongolia in May led to his first meeting with Stalin on 2 June 1940. Stalin's habit was to rise late and work late and Zhukov saw him in his office at 11.00 P.M.[5] The meeting lasted half an hour and, according to Zhukov, the discussion centred on Khalkhin-Gol. Stalin wanted to know what Zhukov thought of the Japanese army and what difficulties he had encountered in Mongolia. In the version of his memoirs published during the Soviet era Zhukov wrote of his first impression of Stalin: 'Stalin's appearance, his soft voice, the depth and concreteness of his judgement, his knowledge of military matters, the attention with which he listened to my report – all this had impressed me deeply.' In the post-Soviet versions of his memoirs published in the 1990s there was a coda: 'if he was like this with everyone, then why was there all this talk about him being such a terrible person?'[6]

On 5 June *Pravda* announced that Zhukov had been promoted to general of the army, the next highest rank after marshal, noting in particular his effective use of tanks during the Khalkhin-Gol battle. Also promoted was Zhukov's co-commander at Khalkhin-Gol, G. M. Shtern, but only to the rank of general-colonel.[7] This was the first of a series of announcements by *Pravda* of promotions to general, including that of Rokossovsky to major general on 10 June.

IN THE KIEV SPECIAL MILITARY DISTRICT

When he arrived in Ukraine in May 1940 to take charge of the Kiev Special Military District, Zhukov seemed set for a prolonged as well as a challenging posting. The Kiev District, the largest in the Soviet Union, encompassed the reunited Ukraine and guarded a state border 500 miles long. It was one of three Special Military Districts on the USSR's western borders – the other two being the Western, with its headquarters in Minsk, and the Baltic, based in Riga. Designated 'Special' because of their importance to the defence of the Soviet Union and their readiness to undertake independent strategic operations without the need to mobilise extra reserves, each would also play an important role in the counter-invasion of enemy territory in the event of war. Because this was a time of constant reorganisation and expansion for the Red Army it is difficult to specify the precise strength of the Kiev District when Zhukov took over in mid-1940. But he certainly commanded a force consisting of multiple armies and divisions, a complement several hundred thousand strong, in addition to thousands of tanks, planes, and artillery pieces.[8]

Zhukov was happy to be posted to Ukraine; in his words, he 'regarded it as a great honour to be put in charge of the biggest military district in the country. . . . The Kiev Special Military District was a first-rate military organisation . . . the armies, formations and staff were commanded by highly capable young officers and generals.'[9]

In reality the situation in Kiev was not nearly as rosy as Zhukov remembered it. The Kiev District was beset by problems typical of the Red Army at this time: low morale, poorly trained and ill-disciplined troops, high desertion rates, defective equipment and materials, housing shortages, and, above all, too few good officers. The expansion of the district to western Ukraine following the Soviet invasion of Poland in September 1939 was additionally disruptive, as was the dispatch of some of the best divisions and units to fight in the war with Finland.[10] Such difficulties were another reason for sending to Kiev a commander whose reputation had been built on knocking units into shape by the application of unrelenting discipline and rigorous training.

Zhukov faced another pressing task when he arrived in Kiev: preparing an invasion of Romanian territory. On 26 June 1940, the Soviet government presented an ultimatum to Romania demanding the return of Bessarabia (now part of modern-day Moldova) – a disputed territory occupied by the Romanians since 1918. Stalin also demanded the Romanians cede North Bukovina, a territory with a Ukrainian population the Soviets had never claimed before. Stalin did not expect war with Romania over Bessarabia and Bukovina but as a precaution Zhukov was ordered to create a 'Southern Front' consisting of the 5th and 12th Armies from his district and a third drawn from the adjacent Odessa Military District. Before replying to the ultimatum the Romanians consulted Berlin. The Germans were not happy with the Soviet action but Hitler had conceded Bessarabia to Stalin when he signed the Nazi-Soviet pact in August 1939. The Romanians were advised to comply with the Soviet ultimatum and did so on 28 June. Zhukov's troops crossed the border that same day. Two days later the newly annexed territories were under Red Army control.[11]

Zhukov was not impressed by his troops' performance during the occupation of Bessarabia and Bukovina. On 17 July he issued a decree cataloguing a series of deficiencies, including lack of battle readiness, inadequate organisation and control over units, poor intelligence work, and poor discipline and bad behaviour towards the local population. In typical Zhukov fashion there followed detailed instructions on the training and reorganisation necessary to bring units up to scratch. Commanders who did not succeed in their tasks were threatened with punishment. Backing threats with action, he relieved several divisional commanders of their duties and court-martialled one who had lost control of his division when his soldiers ran amok in Bessarabia.[12]

Among his commanders was Rokossovsky, posted to the Kiev District to resume command of the 5th Cavalry Corps – the unit he had commanded before he was purged. But because the 5th Cavalry was still en route to the Ukraine from another posting Rokossovsky was temporarily placed under Zhukov's direct command: 'I was appointed to a team of generals working directly with the District Commander. We spent most of our time with the troops. General Zhukov's assignments were extremely interesting and I was able to assess the strong and weak points of our troops.'[13]

Another who served under Zhukov in the Kiev District was a young tank driver named Mikhail Kalashnikov. In his memoirs Kalashnikov recalled that 'we felt the will and energy of G. K. Zhukov straightaway'. Kalashnikov was working on improving the performance of Soviet tanks and a device he invented to record a tank engine's operation brought him to Zhukov's attention. Zhukov was so impressed by Kalashnikov's demonstration of the device that he decided to send him to the Tank Technical School in Kiev and then to Moscow where similar devices were being tested. This was the beginning of Kalashnikov's career as a world-famous weapons designer, most notably as the inventor of the AK-47 automatic rifle. As one biographer of Zhukov noted, 'the atmosphere of innovation that Zhukov created provided a fertile breeding ground for the future designer'.[14]

Another person who made Zhukov's acquaintance in Kiev was Nikita Khrushchev, then party secretary in Ukraine. This was the first of many occasions on which the paths of the two men intersected. At that time Khrushchev had a high opinion of Zhukov and recalled that he 'was more than satisfactory as Timoshenko's replacement'.[15]

SOVIET WAR PLANS

Another important task for Zhukov in summer 1940 was coordinating his command's contribution to the revision of the overall Soviet war plan. Seven such meta-plans were drawn up between 1928 and 1941, outlining the Red Army's grand strategy – how in general terms the Soviet Union planned to counter an enemy attack. Each one identified potential enemies, assessed the scale and possible disposition of opponents' forces, and predicted the likely avenues for an enemy invasion. The last plan to be drafted before the outbreak of the Second World War was prepared in March 1938 under the supervision of the then chief of the General Staff, Marshal Boris Shaposhnikov. A former tsarist officer, Shaposhnikov was the Red Army's intellectual guru and author of *The Brain of the Army*, a detailed study of the functioning of the Austro-Hungarian General Staff before the First World War that had served as a blueprint for the Soviet General Staff when it was formally established in 1935.[16]

Shaposhnikov's 1938 war plan identified the USSR's main enemies as Germany and its allies in Europe, and Japan in the Far East. Although the Soviet armed forces had to be prepared to fight a war on two fronts, Germany was identified as the primary threat and the west forecast as the main theatre of operations. The Germans, said Shaposhnikov, would attempt an invasion of the Soviet Union either north of the Pripyat Marshes in the direction of Minsk, Leningrad, or Moscow, or south of the marshes, with the aim of advancing on Kiev and conquering Ukraine. Which route was taken would depend on the political situation in Europe and the precise line-up against the Soviet Union of Germany and its allies in Eastern Europe (including, possibly, Poland). The document then detailed two variants of Soviet operational plans to counter a German-led invasion. If the Germans attacked in the north the Red Army would counter-attack in that sector and remain on the defensive in the south. If the Germans attacked in the south the Red Army would counter-attack there and remain on the defensive in the north. In both variants the aim was to engage and destroy the main concentrations of the enemy's armed forces.[17]

The next version of the war plan was prepared in the very different circumstances of summer 1940. Although similar in outline to the 1938 document, the 1940 version predicted the Germans would attack in the north with a thrust from East Prussia (now, after the Nazi conquest of Poland, reattached to the main body of Germany) into Lithuania, Latvia, and western Belorussia (by then all three Baltic states were part of the Soviet Union). Therefore, the plan said, the bulk of the Red Army's forces should be concentrated in the north.[18] Among the officers who worked on the plan was A. M. Vasilevsky, deputy chief of the General Staff's Operations Department, who would become Zhukov's closest colleague during the Great Patriotic War.

This version of the war plan was prepared by Shaposhnikov's staff officers before he stepped down as chief of staff in August 1940 because of ill health. He was replaced by Kiril Meretskov, the commander of the first, ill-fated attack on Finland. Further work was done on the plan and a new draft dated 18 September prepared. The

September version repeated the idea that the Germans were most likely to attack in the north but did not exclude the possibility they might concentrate their main forces in the south, thus reasserting the need for a plan with two variants of the Soviet strategic response. If the Germans concentrated in the south, the Red Army would also concentrate there and launch a counter-attack that would head for Lublin and Krakow in German-occupied Poland and then on to Breslau, in southern Germany, with the aim of cutting off Hitler from his Balkan allies and from the crucial economic resources of that region. If the Germans made their move in the north the Red Army would invade eastern Prussia.[19]

The September plan was submitted to Stalin and the Soviet leadership for discussion. Out of this consultation there came, in early October, a crucial amendment: the Red Army's main attack forces were to be concentrated in the south and tasked with an advance on Lublin, Krakow, and Breslau. The reason for this change was not specified in the memorandum that Timoshenko and Meretskov sent to Stalin.[20] There are several possible explanations. The one given by Zhukov in his memoirs was Stalin's belief that Hitler's priority would be to seize the economic and mineral resources of Ukraine and southern Russia, including the oil of the Caucasus. However, there is no direct evidence that the decision to concentrate in the south was specifically Stalin's, although he must have endorsed it. Another possibility is that when the 1940 war plan was being drawn up the Soviet leadership was obsessed with the situation in the Balkans, including Hitler's decision in August to guarantee the future security of Romania after the loss of Bessarabia. In this perspective the decision to concentrate in the south was perhaps driven more by political than strategic considerations.[21] Another intriguing suggestion comes from Marshal Matvei Zakharov in his study of the pre-war Soviet General Staff: that personal preferences and bureaucratic factors could have played a critical role. The main beneficiary of the decision to concentrate resources in the south was the Kiev District. Both Meretskov and Timoshenko were former commanders of the Kiev District. A number of the senior General Staff officers involved in drafting the war plans had also served in the Kiev District, including the highly talented General N. F. Vatutin, who was Zhukov's chief of staff before he transferred to Moscow in

July 1940.[22] Certainly, under Zhukov's leadership the Kiev District became a very active proponent of the idea that the Germans were concentrating in the southwest, and lobbied heavily for more forces to counter that development.[23]

A more radical suggestion is that Stalin and his generals chose to concentrate in the south because the Red Army was planning a pre-emptive strike against Germany and the plains of southern Poland offered an easier invasion route than the rivers, lakes, bogs, and forests of East Prussia. But the most likely explanation is the most straightforward: the Soviets expected that when war broke out the main concentration of German forces would be in the south. In the months that followed this belief dominated Soviet perceptions about the coming war with Germany – perceptions reinforced by numerous intelligence reports that the Wehrmacht's build-up along the Soviet-German frontier was concentrated in the south. This mistaken assessment reflected the effectiveness of the German disinformation campaign to cover up their real intentions – to concentrate their attack in the north, in the direction of Leningrad and along the Minsk–Smolensk–Moscow axis.

The Soviet decision to plump for a southern concentration was fateful. When the Germans attacked in June 1941 the bulk of Soviet forces and armour were located in the southwest. One should note in passing, however, that Hitler's original intention was, indeed, to concentrate the German attack along the southern axis but his generals persuaded him otherwise. Even so, it was only during the German campaign in Russia in summer 1941 that Moscow emerged as the main objective.

THE DECEMBER 1940 COMMAND CONFERENCE

At the end of September 1940 Zhukov was invited to present a paper to a forthcoming conference of higher command officers. His topic was 'The Character of Contemporary Offensive Operations' and he was ordered to submit a draft to Timoshenko by 1 November. 'Owing to the complexity of my topic and the extremely high level of the conference,' Zhukov recalled, 'I spent a whole month working on the report many hours a day. Valuable assistance was rendered to me by the District Chief of Operations, Ivan Bagramyan.'[24] Unlike Zhukov,

Bagramyan – a future marshal of the Soviet army – had studied in the General Staff Academy. According to Bagramyan, Zhukov suggested that he enlist the aid of other members of the district command. The help he received from Bagramyan and others has led some of Zhukov's critics to the uncharitable conclusion that the credit for the high quality of the paper belongs to them. But no such claim was made by Bagramyan, who wrote in his memoirs: 'Zhukov possessed not only remarkable military talent but the highest intellect and an iron will.' One trait of Zhukov's high intelligence was his ability to recognise and use the talent of officers like Bagramyan, who, far from resenting this, remained fiercely loyal to him.[25]

Zhukov had been selected to present this particular paper because he was the victor of Khalkhin-Gol and also the head of a military district that would play an essential role in the USSR's offensive war against Germany when the time came. Zhukov's main task was to evaluate the experience of German offensive operations in the west. In this respect his chief of staff, General M. A. Purkaev, was a major asset. He was fluent in German and French and had recently returned from a posting in Berlin as Soviet military attaché. Zhukov also had access to reports and articles on German operations published in a Soviet military bulletin, including translations of commentaries by foreign authors.[26]

The week-long conference took place in Moscow at the end of December 1940. In attendance were 270 high-ranking officers, including the commanders of military districts and armies and their chiefs of staff, heads of military academies, the inspectors-general of the armed forces, and numerous commanders of corps and divisions. The participants included twenty-four officers who had fought in the First World War, forty-three in the Russian Civil War, five in the Spanish Civil War, ten in the Soviet-Finnish War, and four at Khalkhin-Gol. Timoshenko opened the conference with a brief statement previewing the agenda. He was followed by Meretskov, who spoke on the General Staff's combat and command training preparations for war. Zhukov was next, followed by a paper on the battle for air superiority by General of Aviation P. V. Rychagov. General I. V. Tulenev, chief of the Moscow Military District, spoke on the character of contemporary defensive operations and General D. G. Pavlov, head of the Western

Military District, on the use of mechanised forces in offensive operations. Finally, there was a report by General A. K. Smirnov, inspector
general of the infantry, on the role of rifle divisions in offensive and
defensive battles. Each contribution was followed by extensive discussion from the floor – seventy-four speakers in all. The conference
closed with a summation by Timoshenko.[27]

Zhukov delivered his report on Christmas Day. His theme was
the lessons of contemporary wars for offensive operations. His main
conclusion was that contemporary armies now had at their disposal
forces – airpower, tanks, highly mobile artillery, and motorised infantry – that enabled them to deliver speedy and powerful offensive
blows. His most detailed example of offensive operations in contemporary warfare was the battle of Khalkhin-Gol. This operation, said
Zhukov, had been carefully prepared and characterised by close coordination of tanks, artillery, infantry, and aviation. Another example
he used was the German invasion of Western Europe, characterised by
audacious and decisive forward thrusts by tanks and mechanised
corps supported by airpower and by the independent exploitation of
breakthroughs by the same units. The speed and uninterrupted character of contemporary offensive operations was demonstrated by the
time it had taken the Germans to conquer Poland (eighteen days),
Holland, Belgium, and northern France (twenty days), and central
and southern France (eighteen days). German victories were the result, Zhukov argued, of single strategic operations being conducted
along a broad front and in several different directions. From this experience Zhukov concluded that strategic offensive operations should
be conducted along a 250 to 300-mile front and aim to penetrate 50–
100 miles. Such operations would require 85–100 rifle divisions, 4–5
mechanised corps, 2–3 cavalry corps, and 30–35 aviation divisions.
Zhukov envisaged breakthrough battles in such operations taking a
similar form to Khalkhin-Gol but on a much larger scale. Enemy main
forces would be pinned in the centre while powerful mobile forces attacked on the flanks, creating openings and encirclements that would
be exploited by strong reserves. To succeed, such operations would
need to destroy between one third and one half of the enemy's forces
in the opening phase and maintain an advance of ten to fifteen kilometres a day. 'The contemporary development of the means of struggle

– artillery, tanks, motorized forces, aviation and so on', summarised Zhukov, 'is creating a broad basis for the conduct of offensive operations and makes possible their conduct at high speed over great distances.'[28]

There were six contributors to the discussion of Zhukov's paper. Their comments were mostly technical arguments about the forces required for large-scale offensives, when and how these forces should be deployed, the timing and different phases of such operations, and the tempo of advance. The most controversial contribution came from General P. L. Romanenko, the commander of the 1st Mechanised Corps in the Leningrad Military District, who said that Zhukov's ideas reflected the thinking of 1932–1934 and did not take proper account of the experience of German operations in the West. These operations showed the need to form massive 'shock armies' of 4–5 mechanised corps, 3–4 aviation corps, 1–2 airborne divisions, and 9–12 artillery regiments. These shock armies should be involved not just in the exploitation phase of offensive operations but in the breakthrough phase as well. The most detailed commentary was made by General Shtern, perhaps stung by Zhukov's passing remark in his speech that during the first phase of operations at Khalkhin-Gol (when Shtern was in overall command) the 57th Special Corps had been ill-prepared for battle. Shtern said the experiences of World War I as well as the current war had to be taken into account. Both conflicts showed that it took a long time to prepare offensive operations, and the same applied to Khalkhin-Gol. Harking back, perhaps, to disagreements with Zhukov at Khalkhin-Gol, Shtern's most pointed comment concerned the timing of the introduction of tanks into breakthrough attacks. Zhukov favoured relatively early deployment whereas Shtern thought they should not be deployed until assault infantry and artillery had done their work, especially when faced with strong and deeply echeloned defences. During the Great Patriotic War Zhukov came around to Shtern's view and tended to delay the introduction of independent tank formations into battle until multipurpose field armies had made the necessary breakthrough. At the conference, however, Zhukov made no comment on Shtern's arguments and in his brief reply to the discussion stated there were no fundamental disagreements with his report.[29]

The companion piece to Zhukov's paper was General Pavlov's presentation on the use of mechanised forces in armoured warfare. Like Zhukov, Pavlov commanded a military district (the Western) vital to implementing Soviet plans for an offensive war against Germany. As head of the Red Army's Armour Directorate in the late 1930s, Pavlov had played an important role in developing Soviet tank doctrine. During the Finnish war Pavlov had come to doubt the value of tank units dispersed broadly throughout the army, an assessment reinforced by the successes of German panzer divisions in Western Europe. Pavlov's report reflected the new thinking of, instead, deploying massed, concentrated tank forces as an independent arm of offensive operations. Throughout Pavlov emphasised the compatibility of his comments with those of Zhukov and reiterated Zhukov's view that tanks could be used to penetrate enemy defences to their full depth (50–100 miles), destroy opponents' reserves, and achieve strategic operational success.[30]

In his concluding remarks Timoshenko strongly endorsed the offensivist thrust of the Zhukov and Pavlov papers, including their estimation of the speed and power of modern means of attack. The conference had also considered the question of defence and Timoshenko's closing speech included a whole section on this topic. He argued strongly that there was no 'crisis of contemporary defence', as some had claimed, and he contested the idea that the rapid defeat of Poland and France proved the futility of defending against modern firepower and highly mobile attackers. Effective defence was possible in modern conditions, said Timoshenko, but it had to be defence in depth with a number of zones and echelons. But Timoshenko was unequivocal in stating that 'defence is not the decisive means of defeating the enemy: only attack can achieve that in the end. Defence should only be resorted to when there is insufficient force for attack, or when it helps in the establishment of conditions necessary for the preparation of an attack.'[31]

Stalin did not attend the conference but on 2 January the most senior participants, including Timoshenko, Meretskov, Zhukov and Pavlov, gathered in his Kremlin office for a two-hour meeting to brief the dictator on its proceedings.[32] According to Zhukov the meeting had been convened unexpectedly by Stalin, who took the opportunity to complain that he had been up all night correcting Timoshenko's closing conference speech but the defence commissar had delivered it before he had a chance to send him corrections. Timoshenko pointed out that he had sent the conference timetable to Stalin as well as the draft of his speech. Stalin was not mollified, saying that he could not be expected to read everything.[33]

WAR GAMES

That same day the General Staff started the first of two war games. These were map-based exercises in which participants were allocated certain forces and resources and their moves and countermoves were assessed by an independent jury. Heading the jury were Timoshenko, Meretskov, Shaposhnikov, and other luminaries of the Soviet military establishment, while the team that drafted the games was headed by General N. F. Vatutin, the General Staff's chief of operations. The aim was to give higher commanders a chance to practice the planning and conduct of contemporary offensive and defensive operations, at least on paper.

The scenario for the first game, which ran 2–6 January, was an enemy invasion from East Prussia into Belorussia and the Baltic area. The western (i.e., German) side was played by a team headed by Zhukov, while Pavlov commanded the forces of the eastern (i.e., Soviet) side. Pavlov managed to limit enemy penetration of the border and then launched a strong counter-offensive on his left flank designed to envelop Zhukov's forces from the rear. Zhukov responded by allowing Pavlov's forces to become entangled in his fortified lines while simultaneously launching a counter-attack on his left flank in the direction of Riga. (*See Map 3: The First War Game, 2–6 January 1941.*) The second game, which ran 8–11 January, focused on the South-western theatre and featured a Soviet invasion of German-occupied Poland and an attack on Germany's allies, Romania and Hungary. For this game Zhukov and Pavlov swapped sides. Once again, Zhukov executed a successful encirclement manoeuvre that resulted in deep penetration into German-occupied Poland and the destruction of a large number of enemy divisions. (*See Map 4: The Second War Game, 8–11 January 1941.*) Neither game was played to a

MAP 3: THE FIRST WAR GAME, 2–6 JANUARY 1941

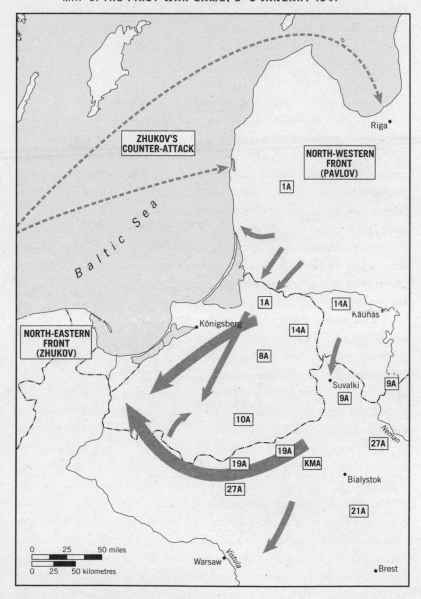

ZHUKOV'S
COUNTER-ATTACK

NORTH-WESTERN
FRONT
(PAVLOV)

Riga

Baltic Sea

1A

1A

14A

Kaunas

14A

NORTH-EASTERN
FRONT
(ZHUKOV)

Königsberg

8A

Suvalki

9A

9A

10A

Neman

19A

27A

19A

KMA

27A

Bialystok

21A

0   25   50 miles

0   25   50 kilometres

Warsaw

Vistula

Brest

MAP 4: THE SECOND WAR GAME, 8–11 JANUARY 1941

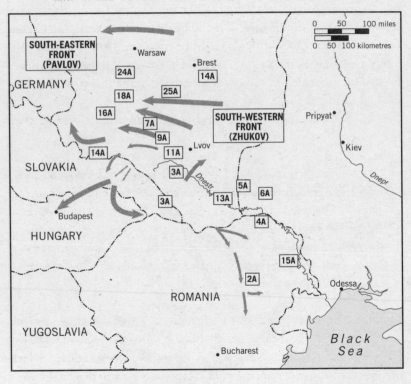

finish but the advantage clearly lay with Zhukov in both cases. One advantage that Zhukov had over Pavlov, of course, was that he had actual experience – at Khalkhin-Gol – of conducting a large-scale operation.

Three aspects of these war games and their outcome are revealing. First was the assumption that the Germans would initiate hostilities and the Soviets would counter-attack after a period of frontier battles lasting about two weeks. Second, both games confirmed the advantages conferred by a strategic counter-invasion in the south-western sector – thus reinforcing the decision of the October war plan to concentrate Soviet forces in that area of operations. Third were the projected troop losses the Red Army could be expected to incur when war broke out, estimated at 120,000 a month – a figure that proved to be a gross underestimate.[34]

Zhukov apparently remembered only the first game and recalled of it:

> Using realistic data and forces of the enemy, I developed . . . operations exactly along those lines that the Germans later unfolded. The main strikes were delivered where they later were delivered. The groupings took shape about how they later did during the war. The border configurations, the terrain, the situation – all prompted me to make just those decisions which later, in 1941, the Germans made.[35]

It must have been Zhukov's performance during the games, as well as at the conference, that persuaded Stalin to appoint him chief of the General Staff (CGS) in place of Meretskov, notwithstanding his lack of General Staff experience. Other factors working in his favour were Timoshenko's patronage and Zhukov's detailed knowledge of both the Belorussian and the Kiev Military Districts. Important, too, was Zhukov's strong commitment to the doctrine of offensive action expressed in the Soviet war plans. The Soviets intended to fight an offensive war against Germany and Zhukov was seen by Stalin as the man to orchestrate the Red Army's attacks.[36]

The decision was announced by Stalin at a meeting with Zhukov and Meretskov in his office on 14 January 1940. According to

Meretskov the Soviet dictator said: 'Comrade Timoshenko has requested the appointment of Comrade Zhukov to the post of Chief of the General Staff'. This was fine by Meretskov, who had never wanted the job anyway. When Shaposhnikov had fallen ill in summer 1940 and Meretskov was appointed to replace him, he had been told by Stalin it would be a stopgap measure until he could find someone more suitable.[37] It seems Stalin thought he had found his man in Zhukov.

Like everyone else Zhukov was in awe of Stalin, and would remain so until the day the Soviet dictator died. Even at the height of Zhukov's own fame and glory in 1945, there was never any doubt that Stalin was the dominant figure in their relationship. But that imbalance in their personal relationship did not preclude the two men from forming a creative and productive partnership – a partnership that was to lead the Red Army to the brink of complete catastrophe before leading it to the greatest victory in military history.

ARCHITECT OF DISASTER?
ZHUKOV AND 22 JUNE 1941

———

IN THE SUMMER OF 1941 THE RED ARMY ENDURED A SERIES OF DEFEATS greater than that experienced by any other army in history. Within weeks of the launch of the German invasion of Russia on 22 June 1941, the Red Army had suffered millions of casualties. Within months it had been forced to retreat to the gates of Leningrad and Moscow. By autumn 1941 Hitler's plan to conquer Russia during the course of a single Blitzkrieg campaign was poised to succeed and the existence of the Soviet Union as an independent state hung in the balance.

It is central to Zhukov's biography that when the disaster of 22 June befell the Red Army and the Soviet people he was chief of the General Staff and bore primary responsibility for planning and preparing for the expected war with Germany. At the end of July 1941 Stalin removed him from the post of CGS and put him in charge of a Reserve Front tasked to mount a counter-offensive against the Germans in the Smolensk area. In his memoirs Zhukov claimed he was removed as CGS not because of his failings in that role but because he enraged Stalin with a proposal to withdraw Soviet troops from Kiev[1] – a claim designed to distance himself from the loss of half a million troops when the Germans encircled the Ukrainian capital in September 1941. Actually, his posting to the Reserve Front was not a punishment by Stalin or even a demotion. It was an important mission, one that Zhukov relished and carried out with great success. Indeed, his Yel'nya offensive of August–September 1941 was an early turning point in the

Soviet-German war. The Red Army's first major victory over the Wehrmacht, it delayed the German advance on Moscow for a vital several weeks.

CHIEF OF THE GENERAL STAFF

Zhukov was named CGS on 14 January but did not take up the post until 1 February. He was made a deputy defence commissar as well as CGS and on 15 March was given additional responsibilities for military communications, fuel supplies, air defence, and the running of the General Staff Academy.[2] His newfound status as CGS was also recognised in his election as an alternate member of the Communist Party Central Committee (i.e., he could attend its meetings but not vote) at the 18th Party conference in February 1941. In theory the Central Committee was the highest decision-making body of the party; in practice it was dominated by Stalin and the Politburo. While Zhukov's election to the Central Committee was important to him personally as a party member, it signified little of political substance. It was, however, highly important as a symbol of the unity of the party and the military.

Now a member of the Soviet elite, Zhukov was given an apartment in an exclusive block in Granovsky Street, a quiet side street across the road from the Kremlin. Among his neighbours were Marshals Budenny and Timoshenko, while Voroshilov, the former defence commissar, lived in the building next door. This was to be the Zhukov family home for nearly twenty years, their residence surviving even Zhukov's period of exile in the provinces after the war.

Zhukov spent his first month as CGS in intensive study of the activities of the General Staff. There was much to learn and his need to master its functioning was becoming more urgent by the day. The countdown to war was well advanced and the evidence mounting that Hitler was preparing to attack.

For a time after the signature of the Nazi-Soviet pact in August 1939 it seemed the cooperation between Germany and the Soviet Union would turn into a permanent partnership. There was extensive political, economic, and military collaboration between the two states. The Soviet Union became a major supplier of raw materials to the German war economy. In return the Germans supplied machinery, manufactured goods, and armaments. Stalin supported Hitler's call for peace after the German conquest of Poland, while the Führer lent political support to the Soviets during the Winter War with Finland. German U-boats were allowed to establish a base on Soviet territory north of Murmansk. Both sides refrained from propaganda attacks on each other, in contrast with the 1930s when the Soviets had led an antifascist ideological crusade against Nazi Germany and the Nazis had identified the communists (and the Jews) as their main enemy.

Relations between Stalin and Hitler began to sour in summer 1940 when Germany conquered France. Stalin had assumed the Second World War would be a rerun of the First World War, with the Germans and the British and French bogged down in a protracted struggle in Western Europe. Now Stalin found himself faced with a partner who dominated continental Europe and threatened to overwhelm Britain, too. While Stalin was prepared to ally with Hitler, he did not trust him. In response to the magnified German threat in July 1940 the Soviets occupied the Baltic states of Estonia, Latvia, and Lithuania and expanded into Romania – the Bessarabian operation that Zhukov had been involved in when he headed the Kiev Military District. Stalin also tried to negotiate a spheres of influence deal in the Balkans with Germany and its fascist ally, Benito Mussolini's Italy. This move was rebuffed by Hitler, who extended his protection to Romania and called a halt to further Soviet territorial encroachments.

Stalin intended his actions as defensive steps and as a prelude to negotiations with the Germans about a new Nazi-Soviet pact. Hitler, however, considered Soviet actions aggressive and they prompted him to revive his plans to seek *Lebensraum* in the east – German expansion into, and the colonisation of, Russia.

The crisis in Soviet-German relations came to a head in November 1940 when Stalin sent his foreign minister, Vyacheslav Molotov, to Berlin to negotiate with Hitler. These negotiations failed when the Soviets rejected Hitler's offer of a junior partnership in the German-Italian-Japanese Axis. His offer spurned, on 18 December 1940, Hitler issued his directive on Operation Barbarossa – the code name for the invasion of Russia.[3]

Reports of a coming German attack had been trickling into

Moscow since mid-1940 from a variety of sources – military, political, and diplomatic. In early 1941, when the Germans began active preparations for invasion, the trickle of information became a stream and then a deluge. Zhukov was not privy to the full range of intelligence that crossed Stalin's desk but he was a routine recipient of information coming from the most authoritative source: Soviet military intelligence.[4]

Commonly known by its Russian acronym GRU (Glavnoe Razvedyvatel'noe Upravlenie – Main Intelligence Administration) Soviet military intelligence was a department of the General Staff. In 1941 it was headed by Deputy CGS General F. I. Golikov. Zhukov was not sent all the information generated by the activities of the GRU but he did receive the most critical intelligence and Golikov's summaries of information on the build-up of enemy forces along the Soviet frontier were of utmost importance to Soviet war planning and military preparations.

On 10 March Golikov submitted a report to Stalin, Zhukov, and Timoshenko on the strength of the German armed forces. According to Soviet estimates in September 1940 the Germans had 228 divisions including 15–17 tank divisions and 8–10 motorised divisions. Six months later the Germans had 263 divisions, including 20 tank and 20 motorised. During that same period there was significant shift of divisions (10 per cent) from Western to Eastern Europe, where 47 per cent of German strength was now concentrated. Of particular importance for the Soviets was that German forces in Eastern Europe had been repositioned and were now concentrated in the southeast (i.e., opposite Ukraine).

On 20 March Golikov presented a summary of intelligence reports that indicated a German attack on the USSR in spring 1941. Most of these reports, noted Golikov, came from Anglo-American sources and he concluded 'the most likely date for the beginning of military action against the USSR is after victory over England or after the conclusion of an honourable peace with Germany. Rumours and documentation that the war against the USSR is inevitable in the spring of this year must be considered as disinformation emanating from English or even, perhaps, German intelligence.' This report of Golikov's has been widely criticised, including by Zhukov, the suggestion being that the intelligence chief was telling Stalin what he wanted to hear. However, Golikov's subsequent summary reports presented the information on the concentration of German and allied forces along the Soviet border more dispassionately. On 4 April he reported the relocation of German troops from west to east was continuing, including the transfer of a further 6 infantry and 3 tank divisions. On 16 April he reported there were 78 German divisions in East Prussia and German-occupied Poland and noted, too, reports of the evacuation of Wehrmacht officers' families from the Warsaw area. Golikov's report of 26 April stated there were now 95–100 German divisions on the Soviet border. By 5 May this estimate had increased to 103–107 and by 15 May to 114–119, with 23–24 divisions massed against the Baltic Special Military District; 30 divisions against the Western Special Military District; and 33–36 against the Kiev Special Military District. On 31 May, Golikov reported there were 120–122 German divisions on the Soviet border and noted a significant strengthening of the Germans' right flank (opposite Ukraine) following the release of units involved in the invasion of Greece and Yugoslavia in April 1941. At the same time Golikov noted that the Germans still had 122–126 divisions deployed against the British (in all theatres, including North Africa and the Mediterranean) and speculated that they still had in mind an invasion of England.[5]

These ominous developments surprisingly were not seen as *immediately* threatening by the Soviets. The explanation for this apparent paradox is that the Soviets had begun with an exaggerated view of the overall strength of the German army, which they estimated to have reached 300 divisions by spring 1941, when the actual figure was nearer 200. From that perspective the 120 divisions the Soviets estimated to be ranged against them was neither disproportionate nor at the level to be expected on the eve of an invasion.[6]

In response to the build-up of German forces the Soviets continued with their own military preparations. One of the first General Staff documents to bear Zhukov's name was MP-41 – Mobilizatsionnyi Plan 1941. Dating from mid-February 1941, this was a plan to expand the number of troops in the Red Army from just over four million to more than eight million. Included among the 300 planned divisions would be 60 tank and 30 motorised divisions, which would be organised into 30 three-division mechanised corps. The bulk of this force (6.5 million troops) would be located in the USSR's western military districts. The mobilisation plan involved the call-up of nearly five million reservists, including 600,000 officers and 885,000 NCOs. It is not clear when the Soviets expected to complete the mobilisation, but certainly not before the end of 1941. In the event, by the time the Germans attacked in June the Red Army had its 300 divisions – including 198 rifle, 61 tank, 31 motorised, and 13 cavalry – but many of these were under-strength and total military personnel fell a million short of the target. A little under three million troops were deployed in the western districts, the bulk in the southwest where 97 divisions, including 27 tank divisions, were located.[7]

MP-41 was a plan the General Staff had been working on since summer 1940, so it is unlikely the recently appointed Zhukov had a great deal of input. Zhukov probably had more say in the revised Soviet war plan of 8 March 1941, but the changes to the existing plan – dating from October 1940 – were not extensive. The March plan estimated the Germans had 260 divisions, about 110 deployed against the Soviet Union. However, the assumption was that after the end of the war with Great Britain the Germans would be able to deploy 200 divisions against the USSR supported by 70 divisions from Romania, Hungary, and Finland. To meet an attack by this force the Soviets planned to deploy at least 250 divisions in their western districts. Crucially, the March plan, like the October plan, assumed that the main German attack would come in the south, although an attack in the north from East Prussia was not ruled out. The planned Soviet response was to be a massive counter-offensive from the Ukraine into southern Poland.[8]

It would seem that in mid-May 1941 yet another version of the Soviet war plan was prepared. However, the provenance and status of this document is complicated and controversial. Dated 15 May 1941, the document in question was handwritten by General A. M. Vasilevsky, at that time deputy chief of operations, and corrected by Vatutin, his immediate superior. It was entitled 'Considerations on the Plan for the Strategic Deployment of the Armed Forces of the Soviet Union in the Event of War with Germany and Its Allies' and signed in the name of Timoshenko and Zhukov – hence the common but inaccurate appellation 'Zhukov Plan'. In essence the May plan was the same as the October 1940 and March 1941 plans: absorb the German attack and then counter-attack in the main theatre of operations with the aim of destroying the bulk of enemy forces and fighting the war on foreign soil. (*See Map 5: The Soviet Plan for an Offensive War Against Germany, May 1941.*) But there was a new element in the May plan that has been the subject of much discussion – a proposal for a pre-emptive strike:

> Considering that Germany at the present time is holding its army, including its rear, in a state of mobilisation it has the possibility to get ahead of us in deployment and deliver a sudden attack.
>
> In order to prevent this (and to destroy the German army), I consider it necessary not to give the initiative to the German command under any circumstances, to forestall the enemy in deployment and to attack the German army at that moment when it is still at the deployment stage and has not yet managed to organise a front or coordinated the different branches of the army. The primary strategic goal of the Red Army will be to destroy the main force of the German army deploying south of Demblin. . . . The main strike of the forces of the South-Western front to be inflicted in the direction of Krakow and Katowitze, cutting off Germany from its southern allies. [There will be] a supporting strike by the left flank of the Western Front in the direction of Sedletz and Demblin with the aim of containing the Warsaw formations and helping the South-Western Front to destroy the Lublin formations of the enemy. An active defence to be conducted against Finland, East Prussia, Hungary and Rumania and preparations made for the delivery of an attack against Rumania under favourable conditions.

The document ended with a request that Stalin permit the 'timely' and 'covert' mobilisation and concentration of the High Command's reserve armies.[9]

The Red Army's offensivist doctrine and its preparations to wage an offensive war with Germany once hostilities began have misled

MAP 5: THE SOVIET PLAN FOR AN OFFENSIVE WAR
AGAINST GERMANY, MAY 1941

some historians into thinking that Stalin intended to launch a pre-emptive strike against Hitler in summer 1941. According to this view the untold story of 22 June 1941, is that the Red Army was caught unready by the German invasion not because it was surprised but because it was in the middle of its own preparations for attack. Is this May 1941 plan the smoking gun sought by the advocates of the pre-emptive strike hypothesis? One problem is that although the document was addressed to Stalin it is not clear it was ever sent to him. After the existence of the May plan became public knowledge in the early 1990s there were reports that Zhukov and Timoshenko had talked to Stalin about it, but these were all retrospective claims. The most common narrative deriving from these rather dubious post hoc claims links Vasilevsky's May redraft of the March 1941 war plan to a secret speech by Stalin to 2,000 graduates of the Red Army staff academies on 5 May 1941. By this time it was normal for every public or semi-public remark of Stalin's to be widely disseminated in the Soviet Union. On this occasion, however, there was no published text, only a short report in *Pravda* the next day under the headline 'We Must be Prepared to Deal with Any Surprises':

> In his speech, Comrade Stalin noted the profound changes that had taken place in the Red Army in the last few years, and emphasised that, on the strength of the experience of modern war, its organisation had undergone important changes, and it has been substantially re-equipped. Comrade Stalin welcomed the officers who had graduated from the military academies and wished them all success in their work.[10]

Not surprisingly rumours began to circulate about what else Stalin might have said to his graduating cadets. According to one report Stalin warned that war with Germany was definitely coming; according to another he advocated an offensive war to expand the socialist system. The version the Soviets leaked to the Germans was that Stalin talked about a new compromise with Hitler. The truth, as is usually the case, was more prosaic than any of the rumours. According to the text of Stalin's speech, which came to light in 1995, his main theme was as *Pravda* reported – the reform, reorganisation, and re-equipment of

the Red Army. However, the speech also contained a number of details about the reforms and about the Red Army's strength – not the
kind of information to put in the public domain on the eve of war.

After the graduation ceremony there was a reception in the Kremlin at which Stalin, as usual, proposed several toasts. Some of his pre-
toast remarks have been preserved for posterity. According to the
diary of Georgy Dimitrov, leader of the Communist International,
Stalin 'was in an exceptionally good mood' and said 'our policy of
peace and security is at the same time a policy of preparation for war.
There is no defence without offense. The army must be trained in a
spirit of offensive action. We must prepare for war.' Another observer
recorded Stalin saying 'good defence means attack. The offensive is
the best defence.' According to the official record Stalin also said:

> The policy of peace is a good thing. We have up to now . . .
> carried out a line [based on] defense. . . . And now, when our
> army has been reconstructed, has been amply supplied with
> equipment for modern battle, when we have become stronger,
> now it is necessary to go from defense to offense. Defending our
> country we must act offensively. From defense to go to a mili-
> tary doctrine of offensive actions. We must transform our train-
> ing, our propaganda, our agitation, our press in an offensive
> spirit. The Red Army is a modern army, and a modern army is
> an offensive army.[11]

The supposition is that having listened to Stalin's speech and toasts
Zhukov and Timoshenko decided to order a plan for a pre-emptive
strike. At this point the story of the May plan takes two forks, with
one group of historians arguing that Stalin rejected the draft and another saying that he accepted it and ordered the preparation of a pre-
emptive strike for later in the summer of 1941. We may never know
whether Stalin saw the May plan, or what he thought about it, but the
document can be taken as indicative of what Zhukov and Timoshenko
were thinking since Vasilevsky would never have prepared such a draft
without the prompting of his superiors. But, as the historian Evan
Mawdsley has argued, Zhukov and Timoshenko were probably not
thinking about an immediate pre-emptive strike, but about putting

the Red Army in a position 'to pre-empt the Germans *at a particular time in the future,* when the Germans were in the last stages of preparing an attack on the USSR, *and not before*'.[12] When that time would be, the May plan did not specify but, as we have seen, the GRU's intelligence reports indicated that the German attack was not imminent. In the meantime Zhukov and Timoshenko were concerned to speed up Soviet mobilisation plans and Vasilevsky's document may have been intended – and may have been used – to persuade Stalin to step up the pace of mobilisation. Whatever the case, nothing in particular happened as a consequence of the May plan. The steady buildup of the Red Army continued but at no stage were the High Command's reserve armies secretly mobilised in preparation for a pre-emptive strike. Among the mobilisation measures undertaken were the following:

- from February 1941 three Front (army groups) headquarters (the North-western, the Western, and the South-western) began to be formed in the Baltic, Kiev, and Western Special Military Districts
- on 8 March a decision was taken to call up 900,000 reservists
- on 13 May military districts were ordered to move 28 divisions, 9 corps headquarters, and 4 army headquarters (16th, 19th, 21st, and 22nd) from interior districts to border districts
- on 20 May border districts were asked to draw up detailed plans for the defence of state frontiers
- on 27 May border districts were ordered to build field command posts
- by early June nearly 800,000 reservists had been called up under the guise of large training exercises
- during June 38,500 men were sent to the fortified areas of the border districts
- on 12–15 June the districts were ordered to move forces to the frontier
- on 19 June, district HQs were ordered to move to new command posts. Orders were also issued to districts to camouflage targets and disperse aircraft.[13]

These measures were indeed quite extensive but, as Evan Mawds-ley also pointed out, nowhere near sufficient to deliver the pre-emptive strike projected in the May draft plan.[14]

During this period Zhukov regularly met Stalin in his Kremlin office. According to Stalin's appointments diary he saw Zhukov twenty-six times between 1 February and 21 June 1941. On all except one occasion Zhukov was accompanied by Timoshenko. One of the longest meetings (more than three hours) took place on 24 May when Zhukov and Timoshenko were joined in Stalin's office by a number of other senior military figures, including Vatutin and Pavlov, the chief of the Western Military District. It has been suggested that this was the meeting that decided on a pre-emptive strike against Germany in summer 1941, but it is much more likely to have been a discussion of ongoing mobilisation measures. Moreover, Stalin did not meet with Zhukov, Timoshenko, or any of his generals for the next ten days, hardly behaviour consistent with a momentous decision to start a war with Germany.[15]

Ultimately, there is no evidence Stalin wanted or intended to start a war with Hitler in summer 1941 (whether he might have considered the possibility in 1942 when Soviet military preparations were complete is another question). On the contrary he strove to avoid war for as long as possible – indeed, for far too long in the opinion of many military analysts, including Zhukov. Until the very last day of peace Stalin continued to believe that war could be put off for a few more months and that when the Germans did attack Soviet defences would hold, giving time to prepare for a counter-offensive.

COUNTDOWN TO WAR

While the Soviets might have been sanguine about the imminence of a German attack, throughout June the evidence accumulated that such an offensive might be coming sooner than they thought. From the western border districts came detailed intelligence on German preparations for an invasion. Of particular concern were reports that Romania and Finland were mobilising for war, too.[16] Meanwhile on the political front the Germans spurned hints that the Soviets were interested in new negotiations between the two states. These hints took the form of a statement from the official Soviet news agency, TASS, on 13 June denying rumours of an impending war between the USSR and Germany. The USSR, said TASS, was adhering to the Soviet-German non-aggression pact, as was Germany, and contrary reports were all lies and provocations. The statement denied that Germany had made any new demands on the USSR but implied that there could be nego-tiations were that to be the case. In the remaining days of peace the Soviets made a number of further conciliatory overtures to the Ger-mans, but from Berlin there came only silence.[17] On 15 June the latest GRU summary report confirmed there had been a massive transfer of German forces eastward and that the Wehrmacht now had 120–122 divisions deployed along the Soviet border, a good number of them concentrated in the southwest.[18]

In his memoirs Zhukov claimed that he and Timoshenko re-sponded to the growing danger by going to see Stalin on 14 June to urge him to alert all border forces and allow the deployment of more troops close to the border – measures that would strengthen the defen-sive cover necessary to protect a full-scale Soviet mobilisation when war came. But Stalin demurred on the grounds that such actions would be provocative and, in any case, the border forces were strong enough already. 'We left the Kremlin with a heavy heart', recalled Zhukov. 'I decided to walk a little way. My thoughts were very de-pressing. In the Alexandrov Garden beside the Kremlin wall children were romping about without a care in the world. I thought of my own little girls, and realised keenly what an immense responsibility we bore for the children, for their future, for the whole country.'[19] A touching story, except that it is doubtful any such meeting took place. According to Stalin's appointments diary Zhukov and Timoshenko saw him on 11 June and again on 18 June but not in between. There is no contemporaneous documentary evidence – as opposed to post hoc memoir claims – that Zhukov and Timoshenko, any more than Stalin, had grasped the immediacy of the German threat, at least not until the very eve of the invasion. On 19 June Zhukov ordered the HQs of the western Fronts to move to forward command posts but with a dead-line of 23 June – the day after the actual German attack.

Historical discussions of this question have focused on issues such as Stalin's failure to interpret the intelligence correctly or his strong

belief that Hitler would not attack Russia before he had finished off
Great Britain. These are valid considerations but the most important
reason for Stalin's refusal to heed warnings of an imminent German
attack was that he did not believe it mattered much if he miscalculated
and Hitler caught him by surprise.[20] Neither Stalin nor the General
Staff believed the Germans would attack with massive military force
from day one of the war. As Zhukov said in his memoirs, the Soviet
expectation was that hostilities would begin with several days of relatively minor frontier battles. During this period the two sides would
mobilise and then commit their main forces to battle. Like Stalin,
Zhukov and the Soviet General Staff fully expected their frontier defences to hold during this initial period of the war, thus buying time to
complete the mobilisation of the rest of the Red Army for the planned
counter-offensive.

On the evening of 21 June Purkaev, Zhukov's old chief of staff in
Kiev, telephoned Zhukov to say a German deserter had come forward
and warned that German troops were moving to their jumping-off
areas and that the attack would begin the next day.[21] It seems unlikely
this event alone would have provoked much anxiety; there must have
been other stimuli to provoke the actions that followed. Indeed, it is
quite possible that the prompt to action came from Stalin himself. He
was the only one who possessed the full range of intelligence, not only
from the GRU but from other intelligence agencies and from political
and diplomatic sources. It must have been clear to Stalin that an attack
was a distinct possibility, even though he might have wished otherwise. At 8.50 P.M. Zhukov and Timoshenko began an hour-and-a-half
meeting with Stalin in his Kremlin office.[22] The result was a directive
issued to the Leningrad, Baltic, Western, and Kiev Military Districts
warning that a German surprise attack was possible on 22 or 23 June.
The districts were ordered to avoid provocative actions of any kind
but to bring their forces up to a full state of combat readiness. This
directive was sent to the districts a little after midnight on 22 June.

OPERATION BARBAROSSA

The German invasion of the Soviet Union began just before dawn.
Leading the assault across a 1,000-mile front were 152 German

divisions, supported by 14 Finnish divisions in the north and 14 Romanian divisions in the south. Later, the 3.5-million-strong invasion
force would be joined by armies from Hungary and Italy, by the Spanish Blue Division, by contingents from Croatia and Slovakia, and by
volunteer units recruited from every country in Nazi-occupied Europe.

The invasion force was organised in three massed army groups:
Army Group North attacked from East Prussia and fought its way
along the Baltic coastal lands towards Leningrad; Army Group Centre advanced towards Minsk, Smolensk and Moscow; while Army
Group South headed for Ukraine and its capital, Kiev. Contrary to
Soviet expectations, the main German attack was concentrated north
of the Pripyat Marshes, in the direction of Leningrad and Moscow. The
German code name for the invasion, Barbarossa, was in honour of
Frederick I ('Red Beard'), the Holy Roman emperor who led a twelfth-
century crusade to liberate Christianity's holy places from Muslim
control. (*See Map 6: Operation Barbarossa, June–December 1941.*)

The strategic goals of the invasion had been set out by Hitler in his
directive of 18 December 1940:

> The German Wehrmacht must be prepared to defeat Soviet
> Russia in one rapid campaign. . . . The mass of the [Red] army
> stationed in Western Russia is to be destroyed in bold opera-
> tions involving deep and rapid penetrations by panzer spear-
> heads, and the withdrawal of combat-capable elements into the
> vast Russian interior is to be prevented. . . . The Operation's
> final objective is the establishment of a defensive barrier
> against Russia running along the general line of the Volga to
> Arkhangelsk.

The German intention was to employ much the same tactics as
they had in Poland and France. Concentrated columns of powerful
armoured divisions would punch their way through enemy defences
and encircle Soviet forces from the rear. The German panzers would
be followed by infantry divisions tasked to destroy encircled enemy
forces and secure captured territory.

Moreover, the Germans planned a *Vernichtungskrieg* in Russia – a
war of destruction, of extermination. Not only the Red Army but also

MAP 6: OPERATION BARBAROSSA, JUNE–DECEMBER 1941

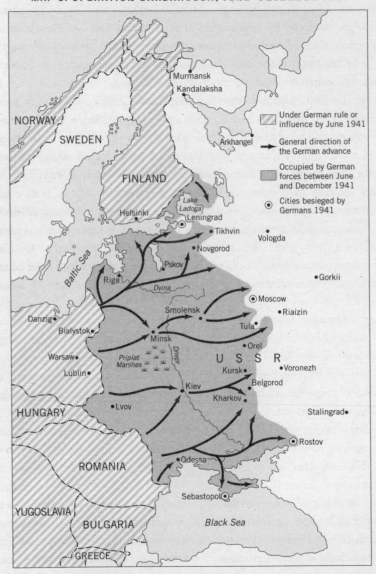

the entire Soviet communist regime was to be destroyed. According to the Nazis' anti-Semitic ideology the Soviet Union was a Judeo-Bolshevik state – a communist regime under Jewish control and influence. Nazi racist ideology also defined the Slavic peoples of Russia as an inferior race of *Untermenschen* or subhumans. Unlike the Jews the Slavs were not all slated by the Nazis for extermination or expulsion, but they were destined for servitude and slavery.

The war Hitler wanted to wage against Russia was ideological. 'The war against Russia', he told his generals in March 1941, 'cannot be conducted in a knightly fashion; the struggle is one of ideologies and racial differences and will have to be conducted with unprecedented, unmerciful and unrelenting harshness.' To this end Hitler issued decrees exempting German soldiers from punishment for any atrocities they might commit in Russia and ordering them to execute all communists on the spot. Contained in these orders was the germ of the Holocaust, which began with the German execution in 1941–1942 of more than a million Soviet Jews. They were also at the root of the savage German treatment of Soviet POWs – three million of whom died in captivity in appalling conditions of starvation, disease, and maltreatment.

As details of the invasion began to filter through to Moscow, Zhukov and Timoshenko returned to Stalin's office at 5.45 A.M. They stayed for nearly three hours and a second directive was issued at 7.15 A.M., instructing troops to destroy enemy forces that had crossed the border but not to cross the frontier themselves without special authorisation. The air force was instructed to attack enemy air and ground forces and to mount strikes on German territory to a depth of 60–100 miles but not to overfly Finland and Romania without special permission. Later that day, at 9.15 P.M., a third directive was issued stating that the main German attacks centred on the Suvalki salient on the Lithuanian border in the northwest and on the Zamost'e region south of the Pripyat Marshes. While in these areas 'the enemy has achieved considerable success . . . in the remaining sectors of the state border . . . the enemy attacks have been beaten off with heavy losses to him'. In response the North-western and Western Fronts were ordered to attack the enemy in the Suvalki region and to capture the enemy territory by 24 June. In mounting this counter-attack the Western Front was ordered to deploy two mechanised corps in a powerful counter-stroke against the flank and rear of the Germans' Suvalki grouping. In the south the South-western Front was ordered to attack, encircle, and destroy enemy forces in the Zamost'e region and then to head for Lublin – 100 kilometres west of the Soviet border – and capture the Lublin region by 24 June. In this operation five mechanised corps were to be deployed, together with the Front's entire aviation force.[23] This third directive closely resembled the scenario envisaged during the January war games and in the March and May war plans, except that the counter-offensive in the south was slightly less ambitious and was to be launched immediately rather than after a period of preparation and mobilisation.

In his memoirs Zhukov was keen to distance himself from the third directive. According to his version of events he was telephoned by Stalin at 1 P.M. on 22 June and ordered to leave straightaway for Kiev and the South-western Front to act as the representative of the High Command. 'By the end of the day I was at the Central Committee of the Ukrainian Communist Party in Kiev, where Khrushchev was waiting for me.' After he arrived at the South-western Front, says Zhukov, Vatutin rang him to tell him about the third directive and Stalin's order that his signature be affixed to it. Had it been up to him, claimed Zhukov, he would have waited until the situation was clearer before ordering counter-attacks.[24] The problem with this story is that Stalin's office diary records Zhukov, along with a number of other senior military officers, as present at a meeting from 2 to 4 P.M. It is likely that this meeting discussed not only the situation at the front but the question of implementing long-laid plans for counter-offensive action. Moreover, according to Bagramyan's memoirs, Zhukov did not arrive at the South-western Front until after the third directive had been received.[25]

Zhukov wanted to distance himself from the directive because its implementation had disastrous consequences, but given his own offensivist proclivities there is no reason to suppose he was not fully in favour of the course of action it outlined. Indeed, it is difficult to make any sense of the decision to send him – the chief of the General Staff – to Ukraine at this critical time except on the assumption that he was sent specifically to supervise the implementation of the massive counter-offensive mandated by the third directive. The General Staff had long expected Ukraine to be the main theatre of action and that was where the bulk of Soviet forces were deployed. It is likely that Zhukov himself proposed that he should go to the South-western Front – his former command – to assist in implementing plans that he himself had helped to draw up. In the event, Zhukov's sojourn in the southwest was brief. By the afternoon of 26 June he was back in Moscow and back in Stalin's office.[26]

While Zhukov was in Ukraine the South-western Front's attempted counter-offensive floundered, although the counter-attack did delay the German advance into Ukraine for a short time. This was not surprising given that the German attack on Ukraine was relatively light and the South-western Front was the strongest on the USSR's western borders, consisting of four armies, eight mechanised and seven rifle corps, and one airborne corps. The story on the Western Front, where Pavlov faced the Germans' strongest forces, was completely different. Zhukov later was highly critical of Pavlov, particularly regarding the Western Front commander's loss of control over his frontier forces. But the biggest problem Pavlov faced were the orders from the General Staff to implement the third directive, which required him to send his second-echelon forces deep into the Bialystok salient that jutted into central Poland. This exposed his forces to a massive German double-encirclement manoeuvre that closed its pincers just east of Minsk – an operation that trapped thirty Red Army divisions and resulted in the capture of 400,000 prisoners. When Minsk fell to the Germans towards the end of June, Pavlov's Western Front – the Red Army's second largest formation – effectively ceased to exist. (*See Map 7: The Border Battles, 22 June–9 July 1941.*)

It was in this context that Zhukov was urgently recalled to Moscow by Stalin. According to Zhukov, Stalin visited the Defence Commissariat twice on 29 June and 'on both occasions reacted violently to the situation that had developed on the western strategic direction'.[27] Another witness to this event was Politburo member Anastas Mikoyan, who recorded in his memoirs that when Zhukov was unable to say what casualties had been incurred Stalin turned on him: 'What is the General Staff for? What is the Chief of Staff for, if during the first days of war he loses his head, is not in communication with his forces,

MAP 7: THE BORDER BATTLES, 22 JUNE–9 JULY 1941

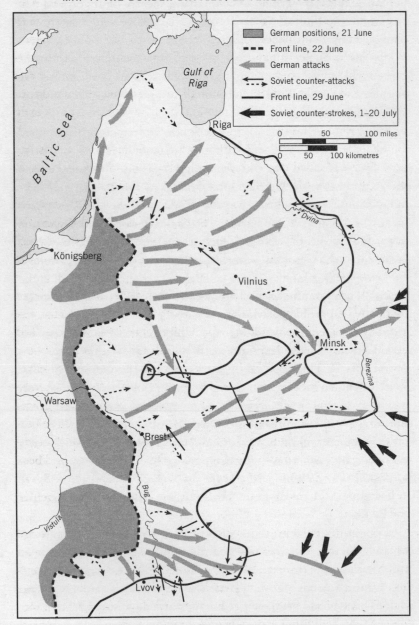

German positions, 21 June
Front line, 22 June
German attacks
Soviet counter-attacks
Front line, 29 June
Soviet counter-strokes, 1–20 July

0   50   100 miles
0 50 100 kilometres

Gulf of Riga
Riga
Baltic Sea
Dvina
Königsberg
Vilnius
Minsk
Berezina
Warsaw
Brest
Bug
Vistula
Lvov

doesn't represent anyone and doesn't command anyone?' According to Mikoyan, Zhukov 'burst into tears and ran into another room. Molotov went after him . . . 5 to 10 minutes later Molotov returned with an outwardly calm Zhukov, but there were still tears in his eyes.'[28] While it is difficult to believe Mikoyan's story, which was undoubtedly concocted as part of the Khrushchevite attack on Zhukov and was designed to discredit him personally, it does capture the tensions between Stalin and his High Command during these disastrous early days of the war.

There is also a story that after the German attack Stalin lost his head and descended into a depression, which he did not snap out of until urged to do so by his Politburo colleagues. According to Zhukov, however, 'Stalin himself was strong-willed and no coward. It was only once that I saw him somewhat depressed. That was the dawn of 22 June 1941, when his belief that war could be avoided was shattered. After 22 June 1941, and throughout the war, Stalin firmly governed the country.'[29]

On 1 July Stalin removed Pavlov as commander of the Western Front and named Timoshenko in his place.[30] Shortly after, Pavlov was arrested along with his chief of staff, his chief of communications, and other senior officers of the Western Front. Announcing the arrests in a resolution dated 16 July Stalin made it clear that he intended to deliver an object lesson for any senior officer who broke discipline.[31] When he was first arrested Pavlov was accused of involvement in an anti-Soviet conspiracy but when the military tribunal sentenced him and the others to death on 22 July it was for cowardice, panic mongering, criminal negligence, and unauthorised retreats.[32] In effect, Pavlov had been scapegoated for 22 June 1941, for the disastrous mistakes of the Soviet military-political leadership, including those of Stalin, Timoshenko, and Zhukov.

The former chief of the General Staff, Meretskov, was arrested when Pavlov was tortured into naming him as a co-conspirator in an anti-Soviet plot. However, although subjected to a severe interrogation by the security police, Meretskov was released without charge and, in September, sent to serve as a representative of the High Command in the Leningrad area, where he remained until 1945.[33] A number of high-ranking officers of the Red Air Force also fell victim to

Stalin's wrath when they were arrested and blamed for allowing the devastating attacks of the Luftwaffe on Soviet airfields on 22 June 1941. Among this group was Zhukov's old rival from Khalkhin-Gol, General Shtern, who had the misfortune to be in charge of Soviet anti-aircraft defences when the Germans invaded. Like the others, Shtern was shot without trial in October 1941.

This military purge was one of a number of measures the Soviet dictator took to bolster his regime as the Red Army's defences crumbled and it was forced to retreat deeper and deeper into the Russian interior.[34] On 30 June Stalin issued a decree establishing the State Defence Committee (in Russian: GKO – Gosudarstvennyi Komitet Oborony). Devised as a sort of war cabinet, the GKO, chaired by Stalin, was charged with directing and controlling all aspects of the Soviet war effort.

On 10 July the Stavka (headquarters) of the Main Command, established under Timoshenko's chairmanship on 23 June, was reorganised as the Stavka of the Supreme Command, with Stalin as chairman. That same day the five Fronts of the Red Army (Northern, North-western, Western, South-western, and Southern) were placed under the supervision of three multi-Front strategic Directions (*Napravlenii*). Placed in command of the three directions were the members of Stalin's cavalry clique. Marshal Voroshilov was sent to command the North-western Direction, Marshal Timoshenko to the Western Direction, and Marshal Budenny to the South-western Direction. On 19 July Stalin was named people's commissar for defence, and on 8 August he became supreme commander of the armed forces. With Stalin's appointment as supreme commander, the organisation and direction of the entire Soviet war effort had been placed under his personal control. (*See Diagram 1: The Structure of Soviet Military and Political Decision-Making During the Great Patriotic War.*)

Stalin was convinced the Red Army's initial defeats and retreats were partly the result of indiscipline, particularly among those in command positions. Stalin's solution was the same as that adopted by the Bolsheviks during the Russian Civil War: the assertion of greater political control over the armed forces. On 16 July the political propaganda directorate of the Defence Commissariat was reorganised as the Main Political Administration of the Red Army (in Russian GPU

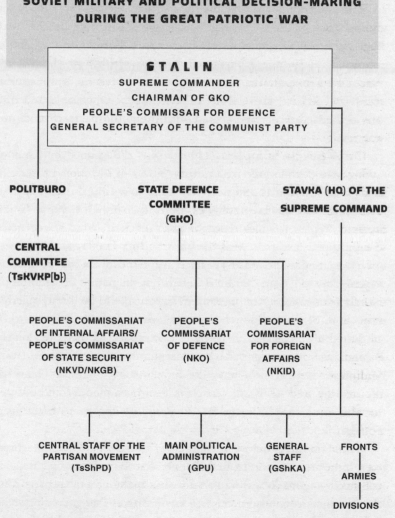

THE STRUCTURE OF SOVIET MILITARY AND POLITICAL DECISION-MAKING DURING THE GREAT PATRIOTIC WAR

STALIN
SUPREME COMMANDER
CHAIRMAN OF GKO
PEOPLE'S COMMISSAR FOR DEFENCE
GENERAL SECRETARY OF THE COMMUNIST PARTY

POLITBURO

STATE DEFENCE COMMITTEE (GKO)

STAVKA (HQ) OF THE SUPREME COMMAND

CENTRAL COMMITTEE (TsKVKP[b])

PEOPLE'S COMMISSARIAT OF INTERNAL AFFAIRS/ PEOPLE'S COMMISSARIAT OF STATE SECURITY (NKVD/NKGB)

PEOPLE'S COMMISSARIAT OF DEFENCE (NKO)

PEOPLE'S COMMISSARIAT FOR FOREIGN AFFAIRS (NKID)

CENTRAL STAFF OF THE PARTISAN MOVEMENT (TsShPD)

MAIN POLITICAL ADMINISTRATION (GPU)

GENERAL STAFF (GShKA)

FRONTS

ARMIES

DIVISIONS

– Glavnoe Politicheskoe Upravlenie RKKA). Simultaneously, the Institution of Military Commissars was reintroduced into the armed forces. This meant the reappointment of political officers, who would have the power to veto command decisions and would act as deputy commanders at every level of the armed forces. On 20 July Stalin and the new head of the GPU, General Lev Mekhlis, issued a directive to all political commissars stressing their special responsibility for maintaining discipline in the armed forces and for dealing harshly with cowards, deserters, and panic mongers. On 17 July a GKO resolution established a special department (Osobyi Otdel') of the NKVD (Narodnyi Kommissariat Vnutrennykh Del – People's Commissariat of Internal Affairs) charged with the struggle against spies and traitors in the Red Army and armed with the authority to execute any deserters on the spot.

On 16 August Stalin issued Order No. 270. Signed by Zhukov, among others, this directive to all members of the armed forces instructed that cowards and deserters were to be eliminated and that any commander displaying shyness in the face of battle was to be immediately replaced. Units finding themselves encircled were instructed to fight to the last man. Most harshly, Stalin announced that henceforth the families of cowards, deserters, and traitors would be liable to arrest. A few days later Stalin ordered that the names of senior commanders and commissars missing in action should be listed, together with those of their close relatives. The first of these lists was to be submitted to the General Staff by 8 September and thereafter on the 1st and 15th of each month. On 12 September Stalin directed front-line commanders to form 'blocking detachments' (*zagraditel'nye otriady*) to stop Red Army soldiers from fleeing to the rear and ordered them to liquidate the instigators of panic or anyone running away from battle.

With Timoshenko now in charge of the Western Direction, directives to the armed forces from the General Staff via Stavka were issued in Zhukov's name. Many had an air of unreality about them as Zhukov issued instructions for costly counterstrokes that gained little, attacks that were impossible to carry out, and advances that turned rapidly into retreats.[35] Meanwhile, the situation on the ground was going from bad to worse. By mid-July the Germans had penetrated 200–400 miles into the USSR across a broad front.

That Zhukov did not lose his composure in the face of the growing disaster is evident from the records of conversations he had with commanders at the Front[36] and, more indirectly, from the General Staff's efforts to distil the lessons of the war. On 15 July Zhukov issued a Stavka directive to all Fronts on 'the utilization of the experience of war'. The directive set out five conclusions from the experience of the war so far. First, the mechanised corps were too big and unwieldy and should be disbanded and replaced by separate tank divisions that would come under army-level command. Second, armies with a large number of divisions had proved difficult to control and should be reduced to smaller field armies with no more than five to six divisions. Third, rifle divisions had found it difficult to repulse enemy tanks in the absence of tank units of their own. The solution was to disperse small tank units throughout the infantry divisions. Fourth, the significance of cavalry had been underestimated – a conclusion that must have warmed the cockles of Zhukov's cavalryman's heart. In a situation where the front line was very long and the enemy's rear extended several hundred miles, deep cavalry raids could play an important role in attacking enemy supply lines. Finally, large air corps had proved inefficient and it would be better to organise air regiments consisting of about thirty aircraft each.[37]

While Zhukov shared the responsibility for the fundamental errors of Soviet military strategy and its consequences – above all the consequences of attempts to implement the offensivist doctrine during the early days of the war – he performed quite well as CGS, not least by keeping his head as the disaster of 22 June 1941 unfolded. Why, then, did Stalin remove him from the post at the end of July? According to Zhukov's account he was removed because he disagreed with Stalin about the evacuation of Kiev. The meeting with Stalin that led to his dismissal reportedly took place on 29 July. When Zhukov suggested the Red Army should withdraw to east of the Dnepr River and hence abandon Kiev, Stalin flew into a rage. 'How could you hit upon the idea of surrendering Kiev to the enemy?' Unable to restrain himself, says Zhukov, he retorted: 'If you think that as Chief of the General

Staff I'm only capable of talking nonsense, I've got nothing more to do here. I request to be relieved of the duties of Chief of the General Staff and sent to the front.' Stalin allegedly replied, 'if that is how you put it we'll be able to do without you'. Zhukov was sent away but was called back half an hour later and told by Stalin that he was replacing him with Shaposhnikov. When asked by Stalin where he would like to be posted Zhukov replied that he was willing to do anything, even command a division. Stalin told him not to get so excited and then appointed him to command the Reserve Front preparing an offensive in the Yel'nya area.[38]

Upon such self-serving vignettes Zhukov reinforced his reputation as a forthright commander who could tell Stalin what he did not want to hear. No doubt Zhukov often did tell Stalin what he really thought, but is this particular story true? An unpublished version of his memoirs in the Russian archives tells a different story:

> STALIN: Who do you think could organise the counteroffensive to liquidate the Yel'nya salient?
> ZHUKOV: Assign me to liquidate the Yel'nya salient and name Shaposhnikov Chief of Staff.
> STALIN: You want easier work?
> ZHUKOV: No, I don't want easier work; I want to be more useful to the country by doing work that I know better.[39]

Given Zhukov's evident desire to get directly into the fight, this is a more likely version of events. Another problem with the version of the story in Zhukov's published memoirs is that the meeting with Stalin on 29 July did not take place, at least not according to Stalin's appointments diary. Zhukov saw Stalin on 20 July and again on 5 August but not in between.[40] Furthermore, the announcement that Zhukov had been appointed commander of the Reserve Front was contained in a Stavka order dated 30 July signed by him and Stalin and Shaposhnikov's appointment as CGS was not announced officially until 10 August.[41] It would seem, then, that Zhukov's departure from the General Staff was both orderly and consensual.

Zhukov's published account was designed to distance him from any blame for the disaster of the Kiev encirclement. By early August the German Army Group South was on the approaches to Kiev and the question arose of withdrawing Soviet forces from the Ukrainian capital. Zhukov says he continued to urge Stalin to order such a withdrawal even after he ceased to be CGS, but the South-western Front command itself was against such a move and advised Stavka accordingly. On 18 August Stalin and Stavka issued a directive that Kiev must not surrender.[42] By the end of August, however, the Red Army had been forced back to a line of defence along the River Dnepr and Kiev lay exposed at the end of a long and vulnerable salient. At this point General Heinz Guderian – the famed German tank commander – and his 2nd Panzer Army was detached by Hitler from Army Group Centre and ordered south to attack the South-western Front from the rear and threaten the encirclement of Soviet forces in and around Kiev. Zhukov warned Stalin what was happening[43] but the dictator was confident that a new Front – the Briansk – commanded by General A. I. Yeremenko, would be able to deal with this threat. However, Yeremenko failed to stop Guderian and on 7 September the military council of the South-western Front requested permission to withdraw some forces to the Desna River to protect their right flank from Guderian's advance. Stalin authorised a partial withdrawal on 9 September but when he spoke the next day to General M. P. Kirponos, commander of the South-western Front, he told him, 'your proposal to withdraw forces . . . we consider dangerous. . . . Stop looking for lines of retreat and start looking for lines of resistance and only resistance.'[44] On 13 September Kirponos's chief of staff, Major-General Tupikov, submitted a report to Shaposhnikov that said complete catastrophe was only a couple of days away. Infuriated, Stalin dictated the reply himself: 'Major-General Tupikov sent a panic-ridden dispatch . . . to the General Staff. The situation, on the contrary, requires that commanders at all levels maintain an exceptionally clear head and restraint. No one must give way to panic. . . . All troops of the front must understand the need to put up a stubborn fight without looking back.'[45]

Notwithstanding Stalin's exhortations, the end came quickly. On 17 September Stavka finally authorised a withdrawal from Kiev to the eastern bank of the Dnepr.[46] But it was too little too late; the pincers of the German encirclement east of Kiev had already closed. Four

Soviet armies, forty-three divisions in all, were encircled. The South-western Front suffered some 750,000 casualties including more than 600,000 killed, captured, or missing during the battle of Kiev. Among the dead were Kirponos and Tupikov. One survivor was Bagramyan, Kirponos's chief of operations, who managed to fight his way out of the encirclement.

Had Zhukov foreseen all this at the end of July? It is doubtful. Indeed, on 28 July – the day before he was supposedly dismissed by Stalin for urging the evacuation of Kiev – Zhukov co-signed with Stalin a directive forbidding the 63 Rifle Corps from withdrawing to the east bank of the Dnepr.[47] It is also important to remember that Zhukov's harping on the Kiev debacle in his memoirs, in particular the negative role played by the local leadership, had a score-settling dimension. The political chief in Kiev was Nikita Khrushchev, who sacked him as minister of defence in 1957 shortly before he began writing his memoirs. Another of Zhukov's targets was Yeremenko – the failed saviour of the South-western Front – who was Khrushchev's right-hand man during the attack on Zhukov's military record when he was dismissed. Zhukov's desire to defend himself and to puncture the reputations of Khrushchev, Yeremenko, and others led him to compose distorted accounts of other wartime events, too.

THE YEL'NYA OFFENSIVE

While the catastrophe at Kiev was unfolding Zhukov led a successful operation at Yel'nya, near Smolensk. Zhukov's offensive was one of a complex series of Red Army operations in the Smolensk region in summer 1941 designed to block the Germans' path to Moscow. Smolensk itself fell to the Germans in mid-July but huge battles continued to rage in the surrounding area. The Red Army did not fight a defensive battle at Smolensk; its strategy was offensive and took the form of numerous counterstrokes, counter-attacks, and counter-offensives like the one at Yel'nya. The Germans were held up at Smolensk for two months but the cost was very high. The Red Army's total losses approached half a million troops dead or missing with another quarter of a million wounded.

The Reserve Front that Zhukov commanded from the end of July 1941 consisted of six armies – some fifty divisions, mostly rifle divisions but with some tank, cavalry, and motorised forces as well. It was deployed about sixty miles behind Timoshenko's Western Front on a broad front stretching from Rzhev to Viazma. Its task was to liquidate a strong German bridgehead east of the River Desna. At Khalkhin-Gol in 1939, Zhukov had prepared his offensive very carefully. In 1941 he did not have that luxury and his 24th Army was forced to launch its attack prematurely in mid-August.[48] On 21 August Zhukov reported to Stalin that the attack had so far failed to surround and destroy the enemy. He emphasised that during the ten days of the battle he had visited all the army's divisions and observed their conduct, which for the most part was very good. To continue with the battle, however, would result in casualties that would undermine the battle-worthiness of the units involved in the fighting. Zhukov asked permission for a pause of three or four days to regroup and study the situation before resuming the offensive. In the meantime the Germans would be subjected to continuous artillery and aerial bombardment. If possible, Zhukov wanted to use the 303rd Rifle Division from his reserve in the next attack.[49] The offensive was resumed on 30 August, this time with the support of the Reserve Front's 43rd Army. By 6 September Yel'nya had been recaptured and the Germans forced to withdraw. (See Map 8: The Yel'nya Offensive, August–September 1941.)

So keen were the Soviets to talk up the success of the Yel'nya offensive that they took the unprecedented step of inviting a group of western journalists to visit the battlefield. Among the participants were Alexander Werth of the London Sunday Times and the Associated Press's Moscow correspondent, Henry C. Cassidy, who wrote:

The devastation was far greater than anything I had seen after the war in the west. There, after the fall of Paris, I found the battle had passed swiftly and lightly over most places, punching only a few holes in a village here, wrecking a crossroads there. Around Yel'nya, all was consumed in a frightful, all-devastating struggle between two giants, fighting savagely to the death.[50]

MAP 8: THE YEL'NYA OFFENSIVE, AUGUST–SEPTEMBER 1941

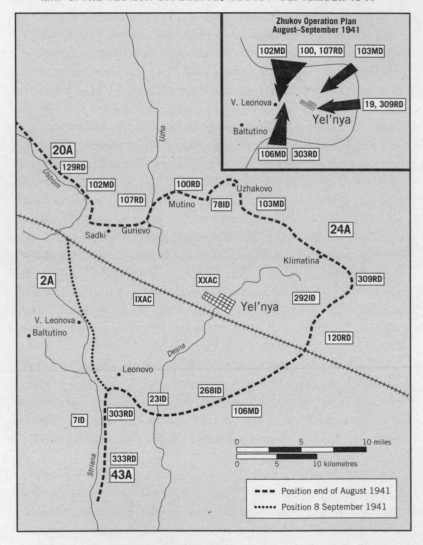

Zhukov Operation Plan
August–September 1941

102MD   100, 107RD   103MD

V. Leonova

Baltutino

19, 309RD

Yel'nya

106MD   303RD

20A
129RD
102MD
107RD

100RD
Mutino   78ID

Uzhakovo
103MD

24A

Uzha

Ustrom

Sadki   Gurievo

Klimatina

309RD

2A

IXAC

XXAC

Yel'nya

292ID

V. Leonova
Baltutino

120RD

Desna

Leonovo

23ID   268ID

106MD

7ID   303RD

Striana

333RD
43A

| 0 | 5 | 10 miles |
| 0 | 5 | 10 kilometres |

- - - Position end of August 1941
••••• Position 8 September 1941

After the operation was over Shaposhnikov wrote a critique of the Reserve Front's offensive:

> The recent 24th and 43rd Armies offensive did not provide completely positive results and led only to excessive losses both in personnel and in equipment. The main reasons for the lack of success were the absence of the required attack grouping in the armies, the attempt to attack along the entire front, and the insufficiently strong, overtly short, and disgracefully organised aviation and artillery preparation for the infantry and tank attacks. Henceforth, it is necessary to cease and not tolerate disorganized and weakly prepared artillery and aviation support of infantry and tank attacks unsupported by required reserves.[51]

Zhukov's view of the operation was very different. In his report to Stalin on 8 September he stressed the good performance of his divisions. He pointed out that enemy casualties as a result of the battle numbered between 45,000 and 47,000 while Soviet losses were about 17,000. Above all, there was the psychological impact of the victory at Yel'nya: 'As a result of this operation morale has risen in all our forces, as has the belief in victory. Now, units have the confidence to meet the attacks of the enemy, the confidence to face his fire and then quickly counter-attack.'[52] It seems Stalin agreed with Zhukov's evaluation. On 18 September he issued an order designating Zhukov's 100th, 127th, 153rd, and 161st Divisions as the first Soviet 'Guards' divisions. These were divisions that had proved themselves in battle and were to be rewarded with better pay and better supplies. Scores of divisions were so designated during the course of the war and later there were Guards armies as well.

Zhukov's conduct of the Yel'nya operation added to his reputation as a field commander and gave Stalin the confidence to make him his trusted military troubleshooter. Notwithstanding his apparent failure as chief of the General Staff, Zhukov emerged from the disaster of 22 June 1941, with both his status and his reputation enhanced. That Zhukov escaped contemporary censure for the initial failure of the Red Army seems surprising in retrospect, but it evoked no comment at the time. Contemporary observers were not particularly surprised by

German military successes – these were to be expected from a combat-hardened army that had conquered Poland, France, and most of the rest of Europe.

After Stalin's death in 1953 a critical discussion of the disaster of 22 June 1941, did develop, but most criticism focused on Stalin's personal culpability in ignoring the many warnings about an imminent German invasion and for hindering the mobilisation of the army to meet the coming attack. Zhukov, who by then had returned to Moscow from his post-war exile to the provinces to become deputy and then minister of defence, did not emphasise this particular aspect of the Khrushchevite critique of Stalin, preferring instead to concentrate his own critique on the negative effects of the Soviet dictator's pre-war purge of the Red Army. However, after he and Khrushchev fell out in 1957 the attack on Stalin was broadened to include Zhukov's role in the failure to anticipate or prepare adequately for the German 'surprise' attack.

Zhukov was not allowed to respond to that criticism until after Khrushchev's fall from power in 1964. In his memoirs, first published in 1969, Zhukov mounted a robust defence of his brief tenure as CGS, arguing that, in fact, the Red Army was well prepared for war and substantially mobilised by the time of the German attack. There had been some mistakes, admitted Zhukov, notably the miscalculation of the main direction of the German attack, which the Soviet High Command, and especially Stalin, believed would be aimed at occupying the rich lands, raw materials, and industrial resources of Ukraine rather than, as turned out to be the case, the capture of Leningrad and Moscow. Secondly, Stalin had also gravely miscalculated the timing of the German attack. Stalin, said Zhukov, believed war could be avoided and was suspicious that reports of an imminent German attack were the work of British and American agents provocateurs. Stalin also feared that premature Soviet mobilisation could accelerate the outbreak of hostilities with Hitler. 'Mobilization means war', he told Zhukov, mindful of the precedent of the July Crisis of 1914 that led to the First World War.

Stalin's caution made him reluctant to allow the General Staff to complete mobilisation and bring the Red Army to full combat readiness. The failure to mobilise fully, argued Zhukov, was a major factor in the short-term success of the German attack. But he was loath to embrace the Khrushchevite critique completely and to scapegoat Stalin for the disaster, pointing out that the High Command should have done more to convince 'the boss' of the danger of an imminent German attack.

The General Staff's focus on counter-offensive action rather than on defence was the result of the deeply ingrained offensivist ethos and doctrine of the Red Army that dated back to the civil war and had ossified into dogma when the deep battle concept was elaborated in the 1930s. As Zhukov said in a passage of his memoirs omitted from the Soviet era edition: 'We did not think that our armed forces would be such a failure at the start of the war and suffer such serious defeats in the first battles that they would be forced to retreat into the interior of the country.' In another unexpurgated passage Zhukov noted that 'at that time our military-theoretical science generally did not consider the profound problems of strategic defence, mistakenly considering it not so important'.[53]

Zhukov was not the only one of Stalin's generals to share his leader's illusions about the defensive capabilities of the Red Army. Nor was he unique in seeking, after the event and after the dictator's death, to distance himself from the disastrous consequences of that fundamental miscalculation. But Zhukov was more honest than most in accepting a share of responsibility. He was also perceptive enough to see that the origins of the error lay deep in the Red Army's history and culture.

His frankest exposition of his and the High Command's failings is not to be found in the various editions of his memoirs or even in his more private conversations with people like the Soviet writer and journalist Konstantin Simonov. In both settings he was defensive and circumspect, anxious to avoid giving ammunition to his Khrushchevite critics. A better source is the unpublished writings in his personal files in the Russian Military History Archive. As Zhukov noted in one manuscript: 'Soviet military science in the pre-war period considered only that offensive action could destroy the enemy, that defence would play a purely auxiliary role in protecting offensive groupings striving to achieve designated goals.' The result was that the Red Army neglected training for defence, especially at the operational-strategic level, and was unprepared for the defensive war it was forced to fight in 1941–1942 – a 'serious mistake', says Zhukov, that led to high casualties. The error was compounded by the failure to learn the lessons of the early years of the Second World War. The German victories in Poland, France, and other countries showed that a sudden attack by concentrated armoured forces backed by a strong air force could 'quickly overrun defences, swiftly cut off enemy lines of retreat and surround his basic groupings'. Naturally, the General Staff had studied the Germans' tactics but, Zhukov admitted, the reality did not really dawn on them until the Wehrmacht's armoured forces smashed through Soviet defences like giant battering rams. At the same time, he did not think the German invasion could have been halted at the frontier. Better defences could have reduced Soviet casualties and increased German losses, but the initial success of the surprise attack was primarily a function of the quantitative and qualitative superiority of the Wehrmacht. 'It is crystal clear', wrote Zhukov, 'that our forces could not have contained the powerful blows inflicted by the enemy during the first days of the war, that we did not have the capacity to oppose such powerful enemy blows, that the strategic initiative was in the hands of the enemy during the early days of the war.'

Neither is Zhukov very complimentary about the Soviets' top military leaders. Kiril Meretskov, his predecessor as CGS, he described as experienced and knowledgeable but over-careful and with a tendency towards passivity, while Semyon Timoshenko, the people's commissar for defence, was, Zhukov wrote, 'no more than a dilettante' when it came to grand strategy and preparing the country for war. As for himself: 'I say directly that I was not prepared for the role of Chief of the General Staff (and told Stalin so when he appointed me). In spite of all my hard work, by the beginning of the war I had still not mastered the principal question of the defence of the country and the operational-strategic preparedness of the armed forces for war with such a powerful and experienced enemy as fascist Germany.'[54]

Zhukov was also scathing of those historians and memoirists who sought to second-guess Stalin's actions and decisions with the benefit of hindsight: 'More often than not people blame Stalin for these errors and miscalculations. . . . Now that the consequences are known, nothing is easier than to return to the beginning and expound all sorts of opinions. And nothing is more difficult than to probe to the sub-stance of the problem in its entirety – the battle of various forces, the multitude of opinions and facts – at the given moment in history.'[55]

Zhukov's defence of Stalin tended to obscure a more important issue: why was a person said to be unsuitable for staff work put in charge of the General Staff on the eve of war? The answer is both simple and revealing: when the Germans attacked, the Soviets planned to respond with a strategic counter-invasion of enemy territory, and Zhukov – the victor of Khalkhin-Gol and a strong advocate of offen-sive warfare – was seen by Stalin as the man to direct such operations. While the failure of the Red Army's initial counter-offensive in late June 1941 had cast doubt on Stalin's judgment, the success at Yel'nya had restored the dictator's faith in Zhukov.

Zhukov's reward for the victory at Yel'nya was another important assignment. Throughout the battle Stalin had been urging him to come to Moscow for consultations but Zhukov demurred on grounds that he needed to stay close to his troops. By the time Zhukov met Stalin on 11 September the Soviet dictator had a pressing need for his services in a completely different zone of the battlefield. Leningrad, surrounded and besieged, was in imminent danger of falling to the Germans. Stalin needed someone with the will and the skill to stiffen and inspire the defence of the Soviet Union's second city and Zhukov fitted the job description.

STALIN'S GENERAL:
SAVING LENINGRAD
AND MOSCOW, 1941

———

STALIN'S RELATIONSHIP WITH ZHUKOV HAD THE SAME FOUNDATION AS THE Soviet dictator's relations with all his senior military: their loyalty and competence and his trust in them. Throughout his military career Zhukov had been loyal and respectful of his superiors even if not to all his subordinates and peers. His respect for Stalin's authority was reinforced by the panegyrics of the dictator's personality cult – to which Zhukov, like everyone else, subscribed, moderately in his case. But more important was the force of Stalin's personality. Stalin dominated everyone who came into close contact with him, and Zhukov was no exception.

Besides their professional relationship Stalin and Zhukov had a lot else in common. Both were from a peasant background. Both their fathers had been cobblers and prone to inflict corporal punishment on their sons. The two men's mothers had striven to ensure their sons received a good education. Both men were sentimental about their own children (in Stalin's case, more so in relation to his daughter than his two sons). The Russian Civil War had been a brutal, formative experience for Zhukov and Stalin, albeit with the former as a lowly soldier and the latter as a high-ranking political commissar. Although Stalin had some intellectual pretensions he, like Zhukov, saw himself primarily as a *praktik* – a practical man of action. Both were single-minded in pursuit of their goals and as ruthless as necessary to achieve them. Politically, Stalin and Zhukov shared not only their communist ideology but also a profound patriotic commitment to the defence of the Soviet Union as the protector of all the nationalities and ethnic groups – more than 100 of them – that constituted the multinational state that was the USSR. It was this 'Soviet' patriotism that united the Georgian Stalin and the Russian Zhukov. In the case of Hitler and the Nazis they faced not merely a foreign invader but one who sought to exterminate millions of Soviet citizens (especially the Jews) and to enslave the rest.

Zhukov's relationship with Stalin began to evolve when he became chief of the General Staff in January 1941 but was forged fully only in the crucible of war. The war showed Stalin that Zhukov could be relied upon in even the direst circumstances; that he would not panic under pressure; and that he had the talent and determination to rise to the challenge of dealing with a supreme emergency.

What Zhukov thought about Stalin is evident from a chapter in his memoirs devoted to the functioning of the Stavka (HQ) of the Supreme Command. Zhukov's primary aim in writing the chapter – added to his memoirs when he revised them in the early 1970s – was to defend the reputation of the wartime leadership of the Soviet Supreme Command, not least his own role as deputy supreme commander. But he also wanted to refute the critique of Stalin's war leadership inaugurated by Khrushchev in what became known as his Secret Speech to the 20th Party Congress in 1956. Zhukov succeeded brilliantly – his remarkable pen portrait of Stalin as supreme commander became one of the key texts in the rehabilitation of the dictator's reputation as a successful warlord.

In the course of the war Zhukov met Stalin in his Kremlin office more than 120 times, a very large number of meetings considering that he spent most of his time at the Front.[1] Many additional meetings took place at one or other of Stalin's country dachas near Moscow. When he didn't see Stalin in person Zhukov talked to him on the phone or via telegraph, sometimes daily. Not surprisingly, Zhukov came to know Stalin quite well during the war. 'I had never associated with him as closely before, and initially felt a little awkward in his presence. . . . In the early period of our association Stalin did not have much to say to me. I felt that he was sizing me up most attentively and had no fixed opinion of me. . . . But as experience accumulated I became more confident, more bold in expressing my ideas. I noticed, too, that Stalin began to give them more heed.'

Many of Zhukov's encounters with Stalin took place at night. The dictator was a late riser and he generally worked through to the early hours of the morning. His punishing work routine of fifteen-to-sixteen-hour days was as tough on his subordinates as it was on himself. The Soviet leader required briefing by the General Staff two or three times a day and he never took important operational decisions without consulting the relevant members of his Supreme Command, especially the chief of the General Staff, and from August 1942 his new deputy supreme commander, Zhukov. During briefings Stalin would pace up and down the room smoking a pipe or Russian cigarettes, stopping now and again to scrutinise the situation maps. Zhukov recalled: 'as a rule he was businesslike and calm; everybody was permitted to state his opinion. . . . He had the knack of listening to people attentively, but only if they spoke to the point. . . . Taciturn himself, he did not like talkative people. . . . I realised during the war that Stalin was not the kind of man who objected to sharp questions or to anyone arguing with him. If someone says the reverse, he is a liar.' Zhukov rated Stalin's military talent and judgment highly:

> I can say that Stalin was conversant with the basic principles of organising operations of Fronts and groups of Fronts and that he supervised them knowledgeably. Certainly, he was familiar with major strategic principles. Stalin's ability as Supreme Commander was especially marked after the Battle of Stalingrad. . . . Stalin owed this to his natural intelligence, his experience as political leader, his intuition and broad knowledge. He could find the main link in a strategic situation which he seized upon in organising actions against the enemy, and thus assured the success of offensive operations. It is beyond question that he was a splendid Supreme Commander-in-Chief.

Zhukov most liked Stalin's general informality and lack of pretension. The dictator rarely laughed out loud but he had a sense of humour and liked a good joke. On the other hand Stalin could be wilful, impetuous, secretive, and highly irritable at times: 'And when he was angry he stopped being objective, changed abruptly before one's eyes, grew paler still, and his gaze became heavy and hard. Not many were the brave men who stood up to Stalin's anger and parried his attacks.' Nonetheless, Zhukov was besotted rather than fearful and, like so many others, under Stalin's spell:

> Free of affectations and mannerisms, he won people's hearts by his simple ways. His uninhibited way of speaking, the ability to express himself clearly, his inborn analytical mind, his extensive knowledge and phenomenal memory, made even old hands and eminent people brace themselves and gather their wits when talking to him.[2]

In post-Soviet versions of his memoirs and in other material that has come to light, Zhukov was a little more critical of Stalin than in his officially published memoirs but Zhukov's positive view of Stalin as a great warlord remained.[3]

What Stalin thought about Zhukov is more difficult to know since the dictator gave little away about his private thoughts. Certainly he had a fondness for many of his generals. He admired their professionalism and was willing to learn from them, even though he had pretensions to great generalship himself. The best guess is that Stalin respected Zhukov more than most of his inner circle, many of whom were prone to fawning. Equally, Stalin was suspicious of anyone like Zhukov who displayed too much independence of mind, even when their loyalty was beyond question. Stalin's attitude to Zhukov is perhaps best summed up by his treatment of him when the two men fell out after the war: banishment for lack of deference followed by rapid rehabilitation once Zhukov had proved his loyalty again.

DEFENDING LENINGRAD

Zhukov's first assignment from Stalin after his victory at Yel'nya was to go to the defence of Leningrad. When the Germans first invaded the USSR their main goal was not to reach Moscow but to capture Leningrad. Only after Army Group North had seized Leningrad were German forces to be concentrated against Moscow. Initially, all went according to plan. Soviet defences on the Lithuanian border were easily penetrated and within three weeks the Germans had advanced 300 miles along a wide front and occupied much of the Baltic region. But the pace of the German advance slowed as the Red Army's resistance stiffened. Not until early September 1941 did the Germans reach the outskirts of Leningrad. At this point Hitler made Moscow his main target instead and decided that rather than take Leningrad by storm, the city should be besieged, its defences worn down, and its population starved into submission. The Germans were confident the city would fall sooner rather than later. On 22 September 1941, Hitler issued the following directive on Leningrad: 'the Führer has decided to erase the city of Petersburg from the face of the earth. I have no interest in the further existence of this large population point after the defeat of Soviet Russia. . . . We propose to closely blockade the city and erase it from the earth by means of artillery fire of all caliber and continuous bombardment from the air.' (*See Map 9: The German Advance to Leningrad, June–September 1941.*)

For the Soviets the threat posed to Leningrad was even more dangerous than their contemporaneous collapse in Ukraine. If Leningrad fell the way would be open for the Germans to make a flanking attack on Moscow from the north. Losing the Soviet Union's second city would also deprive the country of a pivotal centre of defence production and the negative psychological impact of the cradle of the Bolshevik Revolution falling to the Nazis would have been immense.

Stavka was not pleased with the performance of its Northwestern Front. On 10 July Zhukov – at that time still chief of the General Staff – admonished the Front command for failing 'to punish commanders who have not fulfilled your orders and who have without authorization withdrawn from defensive positions. Such a liberal attitude by you towards cowards cannot be defended . . . go immediately to forward units and deal with the cowards and criminals on the spot.'[4] That same day Stavka created a multi-Front North-western Direction to replace the North-western Front. Included in the new Direction was the Northern Front, which faced the Finns north of Leningrad, Finland having joined in the German attack in June 1941 in order to restore territorial losses sustained during the Winter War of 1939–1940.[5] Placed in command of the new Direction was Kliment Voroshilov,

MAP 9: THE GERMAN ADVANCE TO LENINGRAD, JUNE–SEPTEMBER 1941

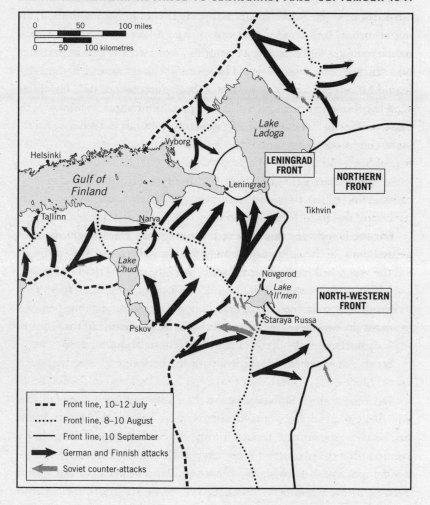

0   50   100 miles

0   50   100 kilometres

Helsinki

Gulf of Finland

Vyborg

Lake Ladoga

LENINGRAD FRONT

NORTHERN FRONT

Leningrad

Tikhvin

Tallinn

Narva

Lake Chud

Novgorod

Lake Il'men

NORTH-WESTERN FRONT

Staraya Russa

Pskov

- - - - Front line, 10–12 July

·········· Front line, 8–10 August

———— Front line, 10 September

➡ German and Finnish attacks

➡ Soviet counter-attacks

the former defence commissar. His orders from Stavka were to counter-attack in the Sol'tsy, Staraya Russa, and Dno areas near Lake
Il'men southeast of Novgorod. Voroshilov's attacks in mid-July and
again in early August held up the German advance but did not halt it
and Stavka became increasingly dissatisfied with his command, too.
On 29 August the North-western Direction was merged with the Leningrad Front, commanded by General M. M. Popov. Voroshilov was
named commander of a new Leningrad Front, with Popov as his chief
of staff. But Stalin was still not happy, and the strain of constant defeats and retreats since 22 June was beginning to tell on him. That
same day he sent a telegram to his foreign commissar, Vyacheslav Molotov, who was in Leningrad at the head of a high-powered political
commission sent to examine the city's defences:

> I fear that Leningrad will be lost by foolish madness and
> that Leningrad's divisions risk being taken prisoner. What are
> Popov and Voroshilov doing? They don't even report to us what
> measures they are thinking of taking against this danger. It is
> evident that they are busy looking for lines of retreat. Where do
> they get their enormous passivity and pure peasant fatalism
> from? What people – I can't understand anything. . . . Do you
> think that someone is deliberately opening the road to the Ger-
> mans in this decisive sector? Who is this person Popov? . . .
> I write about this because I'm very anxious about what for me
> is the incomprehensible inactivity of the Leningrad Command.[6]

On 9 September, Shlisselburg, on the banks of Lake Ladoga north-
east of Leningrad, fell to the Germans, thus cutting the last land link
to the city. Spurred to action, Stalin placed the trusted Zhukov in
command of the Leningrad Front. According to Zhukov, on 9 September he was recalled urgently to Moscow and when he arrived that
evening at the Kremlin he was ushered not to Stalin's office but into
the dictator's private apartment. After a discussion about the situation
in Leningrad Zhukov was ordered to fly to the city and take command. 'You must be aware', Stalin told him 'that in Leningrad you
will have to fly over the front line or over Lake Ladoga which is

controlled by the German air force.' Stalin then gave Zhukov a note for Voroshilov – on which was written: 'turn over command of the Front to Zhukov, and immediately fly to Moscow' – and told him that the order on his appointment would be issued when he arrived in Leningrad. 'I realized', wrote Zhukov, 'that these words reflected concern that our flight might end badly.' Zhukov also discussed the impending fall of Kiev with Stalin and suggested that Timoshenko be appointed the new commander of the South-western Front and that General Konev should take over his Western Front command. Stalin 'telephoned Shaposhnikov (Zhukov's successor as chief of the General Staff) right away and instructed him to summon Marshal Timoshenko and transmit the order to Konev'.[7] Zhukov's flight to Leningrad the next day proved almost as dangerous as Stalin feared: when his plane reached Lake Ladoga it had to dive and fly low over the water pursued by two Messerschmitts.[8]

While his flight to Leningrad may well have been as dramatic as Zhukov remembered, the rest of the story seems to be yet another colourful but inaccurate anecdote. According to the official record Zhukov met Stalin on 11 September in the dictator's office, not in his apartment. The meeting began at 5.10 P.M. and lasted four hours. Shaposhnikov was present, as was Timoshenko.[9] In the middle of the meeting – at 7.10 – a directive was sent to the Leningrad Front on the change of command, as was the norm when announcing such decisions. A few minutes later the directives on the Konev and Timoshenko appointments were also issued.[10]

Accompanying Zhukov to Leningrad were Generals I. I. Feduninskii, M. S. Khozin, and P. I. Kokorev. According to Feduninskii the plane took off for Leningrad on the morning of 13 September protected by fighters. He doesn't mention being chased by Messerschmitts but then Feduninskii's memoir was published during the Khrushchev era when Zhukov was in disgrace and his portrait of the new commander of the Leningrad Front was not very flattering. Indeed, Zhukov came across as rather vague and ill-informed, having no idea, for example, of what job he would give Feduninskii when they got to Leningrad. Even more negative was another Khrushchev era memoir, by General B. V. Bychevskii, chief of the Red Army's engineering section in Leningrad. Bychevskii depicted Zhukov as a martinet, barking out orders and throwing his weight around to little effect.[11]

It is not difficult to imagine Zhukov behaving boorishly. This was his favoured way of asserting his authority when he took over a new command. Whether he was as ineffective as the Feduninskii and Bychevskii accounts suggest is another question. When Zhukov arrived in Leningrad the situation had taken a new turn for the worse. Having closed their encirclement of the city on 9 September the Germans were now probing for weaknesses in its defences. Zhukov responded by ordering counter-attacks. His general operational order on 15 September was:

1. Smother the enemy with artillery and mortar fire and air attacks, permitting no penetration of defences.
2. Form five rifle brigades and two rifle divisions by 18 September and concentrate them in four defence lines for the immediate defence of Leningrad.
3. Strike the enemy in the flank and rear with the 8th Army.
4. Coordinate the 8th Army's operation with the 54th Army, whose objective is to liberate the Mga and Shlissel'burg regions.[12]

Two days later, on 17 September, Zhukov and his Military Council issued an order on the defence of Leningrad's vital southern sector: 'all commanders, political workers and soldiers who abandon the indicated line without a written order from the front or army military council will be shot immediately'. Stalin wholeheartedly endorsed both the spirit and letter of Zhukov's threat. On 21 September he wrote to Zhukov and the Military Council ordering them to pass on this message to local commanders:

It is said that, while advancing to Leningrad, the German scoundrels have sent forward among our forces . . . old men, old women, wives and children . . . with requests to the Bolsheviks to give up Leningrad and restore peace.

It is said that people can be found among Leningrad's

Bolsheviks who do not consider it possible to use weapons and such against these individuals. I believe that if we have such people among the Bolsheviks, we must destroy them . . . because they are afraid of the German fascists.

My answer is, do not be sentimental, but instead smash the enemy and his accomplices, the sick or the healthy, in the teeth. The war is inexorable, and it will lead to the defeat . . . of those who demonstrate weakness and permit wavering. . . .

Beat the Germans and their creatures, whoever they are, in every way and abuse the enemy; it makes no difference whether they are willing or unwilling enemies.[13]

When Zhukov took command in Leningrad he had about 450,000 troops at his disposal, deployed in the 8th, 23rd, 42nd, and 55th Armies. Facing him were an equivalent number of German troops, although the Germans had two tank divisions, whereas Zhukov had none, and the Luftwaffe had complete air supremacy. In addition, fourteen Finnish divisions were attacking Leningrad and Soviet Karelia in the north. The main battle, however, centred on the southern approaches to Leningrad, where the Germans attained positions just a few miles from the city limits. The fighting ebbed and flowed throughout September but by the end of the month the Soviets had stabilised their defences and the German attacks had petered out. (*See Map 10: The Battle for Leningrad, September 1941.*)

As the battle raged Zhukov found time to write to daughters Era and Ella:

Greetings to you from the front. As you would wish I am fighting the Germans at Leningrad. The Germans are suffering big casualties and are trying to take Leningrad but I think we will hold it and chase the Germans all the way to Berlin.

How are you getting on there? I want to see you very much but I think that only when I have beaten the Germans will I be able to come to you, or you to me. Write more often. I don't have time – there is battle all the time.

I kiss you both affectionately.[14]

MAP 10: THE BATTLE FOR LENINGRAD, SEPTEMBER 1941

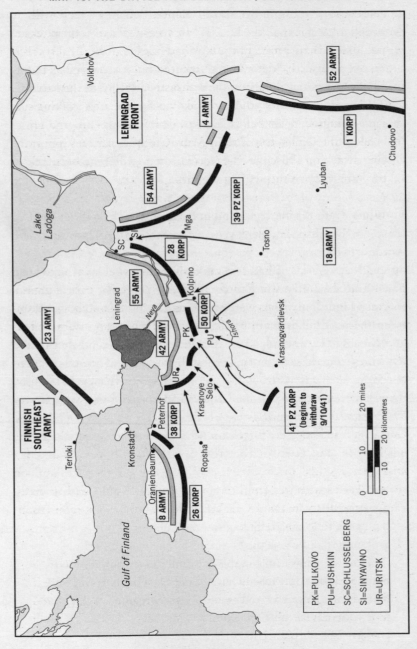

PK=PULKOVO
PU=PUSHKIN
SC=SCHLUSSELBERG
SI=SINYAVINO
UR=URITSK

Historians have differing opinions about Zhukov's performance at Leningrad. According to David Glantz, 'Zhukov's iron will . . . produced a "Miracle on the Neva." ' In a similar vein John Erickson wrote, 'in less than a month, Zhukov had mastered the gravest crisis, organised an effective defence and repaired morale, as well as restoring discipline which had crumpled disastrously before his arrival'. Evan Mawdsley was not so sure Zhukov achieved such striking success at Leningrad. Even before Zhukov's arrival in Leningrad Hitler had begun to redeploy forces from Army Group North to support the coming attack on Moscow. The Germans may well have been able to take Leningrad had they persisted with a full-force attack deploying all Army Group North's armour, argues Mawdsley, while the Russian historian Vladimir Beshanov points out that Zhukov was sent to Leningrad to lift the blockade – a task he came nowhere near to achieving.[15]

One thing was certain: Zhukov's reputation was growing. Khalkhin-Gol, Yel'nya, and now Leningrad – maybe not as great a success as the Zhukov legend came to suggest but relatively successful nevertheless. Zhukov was proving to be Stalin's lucky general; wherever he went there was success, or at least the absence of defeat, and Zhukov's achievements compared well with the disasters suffered elsewhere by the Red Army. Kiev fell in mid-September and the Germans marched on towards the Crimea and Rostov-on-Don – gateway to the Caucasus and the Soviet oilfields at Baku. In early October the Germans resumed their march on Moscow and achieved immediate results with massive encirclements of Soviet forces at Viazma and Briansk that resulted in the Red Army losses of another half million troops. Faced with yet another emergency, Stalin decided to recall Zhukov to Moscow. On 5 October Stalin phoned Zhukov in Leningrad and the following conversation took place:

STALIN: I have only one question for you: can you board a plane and come to Moscow. In view of complications on the left flank of the Reserve Front in the Ukhnov region Stavka would like your advice on the necessary measures. Maybe Khozin could take your place?

ZHUKOV: I ask for permission to fly out tomorrow morning at dawn.

STALIN: Very well. We await your arrival in Moscow tomorrow.[16]

As Zhukov left Leningrad the city's ordeal was just beginning. Leningrad was to remain encircled and besieged by German and Finnish forces for three more years. During the siege 640,000 civilians died of starvation while another 400,000 perished or disappeared during the course of forced evacuations, many into the icy waters of Lake Ladoga during the winter of 1941–1942. More than a million Soviet soldiers lost their lives fighting in the Leningrad region. The Germans tried on many occasions to breach the city's defences and to break the defenders' resistance but never again came as close to success as in September 1941. In November–December 1941 the Red Army conducted a successful counter-offensive at Tikhvin east of Leningrad, which secured Moscow against a German encirclement manoeuvre from the northwest. Thereafter, Leningrad lost its strategic importance, except for the large numbers of enemy forces it pinned down (a third of the Wehrmacht in 1941).[17]

SAVING MOSCOW

With his recall to Moscow Zhukov's moment had arrived. The impending battle for the Soviet capital would either bolster or demolish his reputation; much more importantly it would determine the fate of Operation Barbarossa – Hitler's attempt to conquer Russia in a Blitzkrieg invasion designed to avoid a costly war of attrition on the Eastern Front.

Hitler's plan had worked well so far, except that the Red Army exacted a heavier than expected toll on the Wehrmacht as it marched across Russia. In summer 1941 alone the Germans suffered twice as many casualties as they had in conquering France in 1940. But the cost to the Soviets was even greater. Although the Red Army had an available personnel pool of millions of former conscripts who had already served in its ranks for a year or two, it would take time to mobilise, retrain, and re-equip this massive reserve. The Red Army was beginning to run out of equipment as well as trained troops. The German occupation of a big chunk of European Russia denied the Soviets access to a significant portion of their industrial resources. As the Germans advanced the Soviets had performed little short of a miracle in dismantling and shipping eastward hundreds of factories together with hundreds of thousands of industrial workers. But it would take time to get the relocated factories up and running to produce desperately needed tanks, planes, and munitions. The Soviet Union's western allies – Britain, the United States, and other countries – were beginning to send aid, but this did not start arriving in significant amounts until 1942. In the meantime the Soviets faced Operation Typhoon – an attack on Moscow by seventy divisions, consisting of a million men, 1,700 tanks, 14,000 artillery pieces, and almost 1,000 planes. If Hitler could capture the Soviet capital it would be the death knell for Stalin's regime. The Soviets might have been able to survive the loss of their capital for a while but it is difficult to imagine the Red Army coming back from such a devastating defeat, particularly if Hitler's ally Japan had decided to launch an attack on the Soviet Far East rather than on the United States at Pearl Harbor in December 1941.

Zhukov was not placed in charge of Moscow's defence immediately. First, on 6 October, Stavka appointed Zhukov its representative to the Reserve Front he had commanded at Yel'nya and issued strict instructions that any decisions he took about the deployment and use of its troops were to be fully implemented. Then, on 8 October, Zhukov was named commander of the Reserve Front in place of Marshal Budenny. Finally, on 10 October Stalin unified the Western and Reserve Fronts into a single Western Front commanded by Zhukov. Konev, the existing commander of the Western Front, was made Zhukov's deputy. A few days later, however, Konev was placed in charge of a newly formed Kalinin Front, composed of armies drawn from the North-western and Western Fronts, and tasked to guard Zhukov's northern flank.[18]

The precise circumstances of Zhukov's appointment to command the new Western Front have been the subject of an arcane but instructive controversy. In Konev's contribution to a book on the battle of Moscow published in 1968 he claimed Zhukov was made head of the Western Front as a result of his recommendation. In the same book

Zhukov asserted that his appointment as commander of the new Western Front followed a telephone conversation with Stalin – one of many that he had with him after his return from Leningrad. During that conversation, wrote Zhukov, Stalin asked him if he had any objections to Konev being his deputy.[19] Another variation of the story, related by Zhukov to the journalist and writer Konstantin Simonov in 1964–1965, was that during the telephone call Stalin said he wanted to court-martial Konev because of the failures of the Western Front and only desisted when Zhukov persuaded the dictator that Konev was an honest man who did not deserve an end like Pavlov, the ill-fated commander of the original Western Front who was executed in July 1941.[20]

While Konev's version of events is supported by the documentary record,[21] Zhukov's assertion that he enjoyed Stalin's confidence is true, too. Zhukov's appointment to a central role in the defence of Moscow was inevitable because Stalin did not recall him from Leningrad simply to make him commander of the Reserve Front.

Behind this minor skirmish in the 1960s between the two retired generals lay a long history of professional rivalry and personal animosity. During the war Konev emerged as one of Zhukov's main rivals for fame and military glory – a rivalry that climaxed with their race to take Berlin in 1945. When Stalin demoted Zhukov after the war, Konev took his place as commander-in-chief of Soviet ground forces. In 1957 when Zhukov was dismissed by Khrushchev as minister of defence, Konev was the most prominent of his public critics, even going so far as to publish an article in *Pravda* that trashed Zhukov's war record. It is little wonder that Zhukov resented any suggestion he owed his appointment as commander of the Western Front to Konev. Indeed, Zhukov's memoirs are peppered with direct and indirect digs at Konev's performance as a wartime commander.

At the root of the personality clash between Konev and Zhukov were the similarities in their temperament and leadership style. Like Zhukov, Konev was an energetic and exacting commander who did not suffer fools gladly and was prone to hot-tempered outbursts. Equally, his preparation for battle was meticulous and his conduct of operations highly controlled. Unlike Zhukov, Konev's background was in artillery and he started his career in the Red Army as a political commissar during the civil war. Only in the mid-1920s did he switch to a strictly military command. He then rose through the ranks, his path paralleling that of Zhukov, but not until the battle of Moscow did the two men serve together for the first – but not the last – time.[22]

Zhukov's brief as commander of the Western Front was to halt the German advance on Moscow. His problem was that he had few forces with which to do so. The Viazma and Briansk encirclements of early October had been even more disastrous than those at Minsk and Kiev in the summer. The Briansk, Western, and Reserve Fronts lost a total of sixty-four rifle divisions, eleven tank brigades, and fifty artillery regiments,[23] leaving Zhukov with only 90,000 troops to defend the Soviet capital. Even before Zhukov's arrival Stavka had ordered a retreat to the Mozhaisk Line – a series of defensive positions about seventy-five miles west of Moscow that stretched for 150 miles from Kalinin in the north to Tula in the south. But this line did not hold for very long. By mid-October the Germans had broken through on the flanks, capturing Kalinin and threatening Tula, where there began a tremendous battle that went on for weeks. Mozhaisk was abandoned on 18 October and with the road to Moscow open, panic broke out in the Soviet capital. There were riots, looting and mass attempts to flee the city. The tense atmosphere was heightened by rumours the authorities were preparing to evacuate the city (which they were). Nerves were steadied by a radio broadcast on 17 October by A. A. Shcherbakov, the Moscow Communist Party leader, who assured citizens that Comrade Stalin remained in the capital. The situation was stabilised further by a GKO (State Defence Council) resolution published on 19 October that declared a state of siege, imposed a curfew, and announced that Zhukov was in command of the Front defending Moscow.[24] The next day Stalin rang David Ortenberg, editor of *Krasnaya Zvezda* (Red Star) – the Red Army newspaper – and ordered him to publish a picture of Zhukov. He was also told to pass the picture to *Pravda* so that they could publish it, too. When the photograph appeared in *Krasnaya Zvezda* on 21 October it was the first time the paper had printed a picture of a Front commander. The photograph was also published by *Pravda* the same day. Ortenberg claims that Zhukov later said to him the picture had only been published to ensure he got the blame if the city fell to the Germans. The more charitable explanation is that Stalin had the picture published in order to inspire people's confidence in the defence of Moscow.[25]

Zhukov responded to this grave crisis in the same way as he had in Leningrad: draconian discipline; no surrender and no retreat; counter-attack wherever and whenever possible. The first edict Zhukov issued as commander of the Western Front was a declaration on 13 October that 'cowards and panic-mongers' fleeing the battlefield, abandoning their weapons, or retreating without permission would be shot on the spot. 'Not a step back! Forward for the Motherland!' it concluded.[26] This threat was as applicable to high-ranking officers as ordinary ranks. On 3 November Zhukov announced that Colonel A. G. Gerasimov, commander of the 133rd Rifle Division, and divisional commissar G. F. Shabalov had been shot for ordering an unauthorised retreat.[27]

It is reported that Zhukov read *War and Peace* during the battle of Moscow and it may be that Tolstoy's monumental novel set during the Napoleonic Wars inspired this appeal to patriotic sentiment: 'The fields and forests where you are now standing in defence of mother Moscow are stained with the sacred blood of our predecessors who have gone down in history for their defeat of the Napoleonic hordes', Zhukov declared to his troops on 1 November. 'We are the sons of the great Soviet people. We were brought up and educated by the party of Lenin and Stalin. For a quarter of a century we have built our lives under its leadership and in this hour of danger we will not spare our forces or our lives in erecting a steel wall in defence of the Motherland and in defence of its sacred capital, Moscow. Blood for blood! Death for death! The complete destruction of the enemy! For honour and freedom, for our Motherland, for our sacred Moscow!'[28]

Exhortations notwithstanding, Zhukov was forced to retreat to new defensive positions, initially on a line running from Klin just northwest of Moscow through Istra to Serpukhov, southwest of the city. But Zhukov's policy of constant counter-attacks and withdrawal at the last possible moment had taken its toll on the enemy and by the end of October the German offensive was running out of steam. In addition, the Germans became increasingly bogged down in the autumn mud of that part of the world – what the Russians called the

Rasputitsa (the season of bad roads). The Germans decided to pause and regroup, which gave Zhukov time to bring in reinforcements. From 1 to 15 November the Western Command was replenished with 100,000 additional troops, 300 more tanks, and 2,000 extra pieces of artillery.[29]

The pause also provided a political opportunity for the Soviet leadership. On 1 November Stalin summoned Zhukov to Stavka and asked him if it was safe to go ahead with the celebration on 7 November of the anniversary of the Bolshevik seizure of power in Russia.[30] Zhukov assured him it was indeed safe, but because of the threat posed by German air raids the anniversary meeting for the party faithful was held underground, in the Mayakovsky metro station. Stalin spoke at this meeting and the next day he addressed the troops parading through Red Square on their way to the battlefield just outside Moscow. The situation was grave, Stalin told them, but the Soviet regime had faced even greater difficulties in the past:

> Remember the year 1918, when we celebrated the first anniversary of the October Revolution. Three-quarters of our country was . . . in the hands of foreign interventionists. The Ukraine, the Caucasus, Central Asia, the Urals, Siberia and the Far East were temporarily lost to us. We had no allies, we had no Red Army . . . there was a shortage of food, of armaments. . . . Fourteen states were pressing against our country. But we did not become despondent, we did not lose heart. In the fire of war we forged the Red Army and converted our country into a military camp. The spirit of the great Lenin animated us. . . . And what happened? We routed the interventionists, recovered our lost territory, and achieved victory.

In his conclusion Stalin worked the patriotic theme, invoking past Russian struggles against foreign invaders:

> A great liberation mission has fallen to your lot. Be worthy of this mission. . . . Let the manly images of our great ancestors – Alexander Nevsky [who defeated the Swedes], Dimitry Donskoy [who beat the Tartars], Kurma Minin and

Dimitry Pozharsky [who drove the Poles out of Moscow], Alexander Suvorov and Mikhail Kutuzov [the Russian hero generals of the Napoleonic Wars] – inspire you in this war. May the victorious banner of the great Lenin be your lodestar.[31]

In his memoirs Zhukov was generous in his praise of Stalin's role in saving Moscow from the Germans, noting that the dictator stayed in the city throughout the battle and played a crucial role in organising its defences: 'By his strict exactingness Stalin achieved, one can say, the near-impossible.'[32] At the same time, Zhukov was at pains to distance himself from several wrong decisions by Stalin during the battle. But reading Zhukov's orders, edicts, and records of conversations during the battle of Moscow, he comes across mainly as a general willing to execute the orders of his superiors without demur and who expected the same of those serving under him. It was, above all, Zhukov's disciplined attitude that endeared him to Stalin, not his supposed forthrightness or insubordination. One example of Zhukov's hierarchical and discipline-based command style is his response on 26 October 1941, to Rokossovsky, the commander of the 16th Army, then engaged in battle with the Germans in the Istra area, who complained about the weight of German opposition against him. Zhukov told him:

> You are wasting time for no reason. Time and again we get reports from you about the incredible forces of the enemy and the insignificant forces of your army – this is not expected of a commander. We know and the government knows what you have and what the enemy has. You must not proceed from fear, which is even more dubious, but from your missions and the real forces that you have at your disposal. The instructions of the government and its command must be implemented without any advance excuses.[33]

When the muddy roads froze in mid-November the Germans were able to resume their offensive, making some progress on the flanks, but the Red Army's defences held in the critical position directly west of Moscow. The turning point in the battle for the capital came at the end of November when Stavka released reserves to plug gaps in Zhukov's defences. Faced with fresh enemy forces and deteriorating weather conditions, the German advance on Moscow foundered only a few miles from the city centre. (*See Map 11: The Battle for Moscow, October–December 1941.*)

Zhukov and Rokossovsky clashed again during the November battles when the latter wanted to withdraw forces to the Istra River. Zhukov refused but Rokossovsky appealed over his head to Shaposhnikov, the chief of the General Staff. Shaposhnikov agreed and gave the requisite permission. When Zhukov found out he cabled Rokossovsky: 'I am the Front Commander! I countermand the order to withdraw to the Istra Reservoir and order you to defend the lines you occupy without retreating one step.'[34] 'This was like Zhukov,' complained Rokossovsky. 'In this order you could feel: I am Zhukov. And his personal ego very frequently prevailed over general interests. . . . Certain superiors . . . thought that only they could handle matters effectively and only they desired success. And shouts and intimidations had to be employed against all the rest in order to bring them over to the chief's wishes. I would also put our front commander among such individuals.'[35]

According to Rokossovsky this incident was only one of many during the battle of Moscow and it illustrated the difference between his and Zhukov's command style. Zhukov, Rokossovsky recalled, 'had everything in abundance – talent, energy, confidence in himself' and was 'a man of strong will and resolution, richly endowed with all the qualities that go into the making of a great military leader'. But, wrote Rokossovsky, 'we had different views on the extent to which a commander should assert his will and the manner in which he should do it. . . . Insistence on the highest standards is an important and essential trait for any military leader. But it is equally essential for him to combine an iron will with tactfulness, respect for his subordinates, and the ability to rely on their intelligence and initiative. In those grim days our Front Commander did not always follow this rule. He could also be unfair in a fit of temper.'

Interestingly, Rokossovsky compared the tempestuousness of his relations with Zhukov to the support and encouragement he received from Stalin. Expecting an abusive telephone call from Zhukov,

MAP 11: THE BATTLE FOR MOSCOW, OCTOBER–DECEMBER 1941

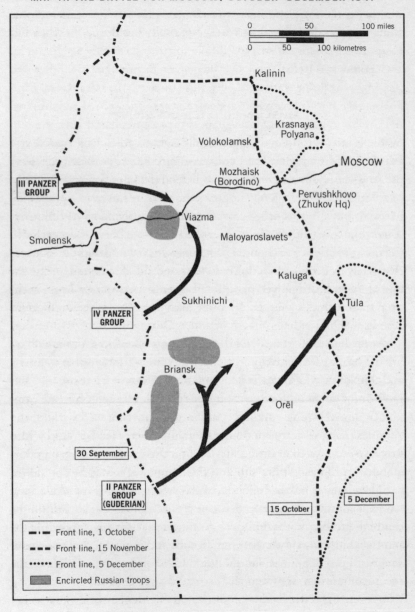

Rokossovsky picked up the phone and was pleasantly surprised to hear Stalin's 'calm, even voice' and appreciative of the 'concern displayed by the Supreme Commander. . . . The kind, fatherly intonations were encouraging and raised one's self-confidence.'[36] Much like Zhukov, Rokossovsky saw in Stalin a mirror image of himself and his own command style.

MOSCOW COUNTER-OFFENSIVE

While Zhukov fought the defensive battle of Moscow, Stavka was planning and preparing for a counter-offensive. As early as 5 October Stalin had decided to establish a strategic reserve of ten armies. Some of these were thrown into the battle to halt the German advance on Moscow but the bulk of them were reserved for the counter-offensive. According to Vasilevsky, at that time deputy chief of the General Staff, planning for the counter-offensive began in early November but was disrupted by renewed German attacks and did not resume until the end of the month.[37] Zhukov's claim to have played a central role in the preparation of the counter-offensive plan[38] seems exaggerated, given his responsibilities as Front commander. During the battle of Moscow Zhukov met Stalin in his Kremlin office only once (on 8 November).[39] On 30 November Zhukov submitted his Front's plan for a counter-attack to Stavka. This called for an attack north of Moscow by Zhukov's right flank in the direction of Klin, Solnechnogorsk, and Istra, and by his left flank south of Tula in the direction of Uzlovaya and Boroditsk. To stop the Germans switching their forces Zhukov also proposed to launch a strong attack directly in front of Moscow. On Zhukov's proposal Stalin simply wrote: 'Agreed. J. Stalin'.[40]

The aim of Zhukov's counter-offensive was to destroy the German forces attempting to envelop Moscow from the north and south. In the centre the ambition was limited to pinning down German troops. At the same time, the possibility of a more substantial advance in the centre was not ruled out if the situation developed favourably, including the prospect of a drive so deep that it would split German Army Group Centre and open the road to Smolensk on the Mozhaisk–Viazma axis.

The Moscow counter-offensive was launched by Konev's Kalinin Front on 5 December, followed by Zhukov's attack the next day, and then an advance by Timoshenko's South-western Front. The Red Army's effective combat strength was 388,000 troops supported by 5,600 guns and mortars and 550 tanks. Opposing it were the 240,000 troops, 5,350 artillery pieces, and 600 tanks of Army Group Centre.[41] Progress was slow at first, and on 9 December Zhukov issued a directive to his army commanders. The aim, he reminded them, was 'to defeat as rapidly as possible the flanking groups of the enemy, and finally, driving swiftly forwards . . . destroy all the armies which are in front of our Western Front'. Zhukov complained, however, that some units were launching attacks on the German rearguard rather than carrying out swift encirclements, methods that played into the hands of the enemy and gave them the chance to withdraw to 'new positions, to regroup, and to organize a new resistance to our forces'. The proper technique, instructed Zhukov, was to pin down the rearguard and outflank it, not to make head-on attacks on fortified positions.[42]

On 12 December Zhukov reported to Stalin that the Western Front had inflicted 30,000 fatalities on the Germans and liberated 400 towns and villages.[43] Among the liberated areas was Zhukov's home village of Strelkovka, though the Germans had burned the village, including his mother's house. But she and Zhukov's sister's family had already been evacuated. Zhukov's mother did not survive the war, however, dying of natural causes in 1944.

On 13 December the Soviet press carried the news of Zhukov's stunning success in turning the tide at Moscow, including a large photograph of him. Zhukov also featured centrally in Soviet newsreels of the battle. The western media began to take notice of Zhukov, too. In January 1942 his picture appeared on the front page of the *London Illustrated News* with the caption: 'Russia's Brilliant Commander-in-Chief Central Front: General Gregory [sic!] Zhukov'. In June 1942 Alexander Werth, *Sunday Times* correspondent in Moscow, wrote in his diary: 'The name mentioned most frequently, next to those of Stalin and Molotov, is Zhukov's. Zhukov played a leading part in organising not only the Russian counter-offensive in Moscow, but it was largely he, and perhaps entirely he, who saved Leningrad in the nick of time. Somebody today remarked that when the well-informed German military attaché was asked, shortly before the war, who was the greatest Russian general, he replied without a moment's hesitation: "Zhukov." [44]

By the end of December the Red Army had advanced 100–150 miles along a broad front. (*See Map 12: Zhukov's Moscow Counter-offensive, December 1941.*)

Zhukov's handling of the battle of Moscow was the beginning of the wartime Zhukov myth. From now on it began to be said that with Zhukov in charge success was assured. This was not true and Zhukov was to suffer many setbacks on the road to Berlin. But belief in the myth inspired confidence in him at every level of the Red Army, not least among the lower ranks to whom he became a legendary figure, a giant of Russian military history, the contemporary counterpart of Suvorov and Kutuzov, who had saved the motherland from Napoleon. Most Red Army soldiers were peasants or had a peasant heritage and Zhukov was one of their own. While he had a reputation for cruelty and crudeness he was also seen as the man who would get the job done and lead the troops to victory.

THE RZHEV-VIAZMA OPERATIONS

The success of the December counter-offensive opened up the possibility of a more ambitious offensive to encircle and destroy a significant part of Army Group Centre and Stavka began to formulate such a plan from mid-December onward. Broadly, the goal was to advance to Rzhev and Viazma and to destroy all the German forces east of the line between the two cities. The mission was entrusted to Zhukov's Western Front with the support of the Kalinin Front commanded by Konev. Initially, the hope was that the Moscow counter-offensive could be expanded to encompass this second goal but it proved impossible when the Germans – on instructions from Hitler not to retreat – dug in for defence and held the line. In response, Stavka regrouped and launched what became known as the first Rzhev-Viazma operation.

The goal of the Rzhev-Viazma operation, set out in Stavka's directive to the Kalinin and Western Fronts on 7 January 1942, was the encirclement of Army Group Centre in the Yukhnov-Viazma-Gzhatsk-Rzhev area. Some fifty divisions from Stavka's reserves were allocated

MAP 12: ZHUKOV'S MOSCOW COUNTER-OFFENSIVE, DECEMBER 1941

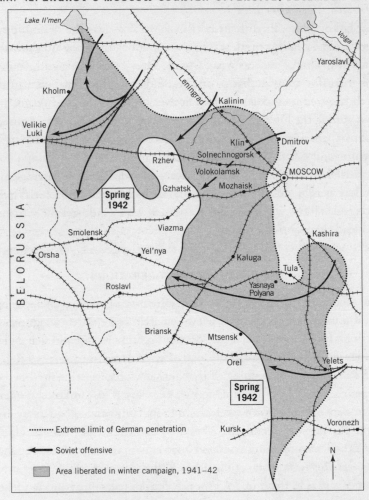

Lake Il'men

Volga

Yaroslavl

Leningrad

Kholm

Kalinin

Velikie
Luki

Klin

Dmitrov

Rzhev

Solnechnogorsk

Volokolamsk

MOSCOW

Spring
1942

Gzhatsk

Mozhaisk

Viazma

Kashira

Smolensk

Yel'nya

Kaluga

Tula

Orsha

Yasnaya
Polyana

BELORUSSIA

Roslavl

Briansk

Mtsensk

Orel

Yelets

Spring
1942

Kursk

Voronezh

N

.... Extreme limit of German penetration

◄――― Soviet offensive

Area liberated in winter campaign, 1941–42

to the operation. Between them the Western and Kalinin Fronts had fourteen armies, three Cavalry Corps, and substantial air support – a total of 688,000 troops, 10,900 guns and mortars, and 474 tanks, as against the Wehrmacht's 625,000 troops, 11,000 artillery pieces, and 354 tanks. The operation began on 8 January with an offensive by the Kalinin Front in the direction of Rzhev. Two days later the Western Front joined in the attack, driving towards Yukhnov and Viazma, while Zhukov's 1st, 16th, and 20th Armies continued their attack in the direction of Gzhatsk. At the end of January Stavka established a Western Direction (the original one having been abolished in 1941) to coordinate the Western and Kalinin Fronts. Zhukov was appointed commander of the Direction with overall responsibility for the Rzhev-Viazma operation.

Although the Rzhev-Viazma operation made little headway, it persisted for more than three months. Stalin was convinced the Wehrmacht's failure to take Moscow meant that Operation Barbarossa could be rapidly reversed and the Germans driven out of Russia. On 10 January 1942, Stalin issued the following general directive to his commanders:

> Our task is not to give the Germans a breathing space, but to drive them westwards without a halt, force them to exhaust their reserves before springtime when we shall have fresh big reserves, while the Germans will have no more reserves; this will ensure the complete defeat of the Nazi forces in 1942.[45]

In line with this view of events, the Red Army launched attacks all along the Soviet-German front, but with little or no success. By the time the Rzhev-Viazma operation was called off on 20 April the Kalinin and Western Fronts had suffered in excess of 750,000 casualties. Nor was that the end of the matter. At the end of July the two fronts launched a second offensive in the Rzhev-Viazma area that continued until the end of September, again without success, and costing nearly 200,000 more casualties. In November–December the Soviets tried once more to break through with an operation code-named Mars. While Mars's goal was limited to the destruction of the German 9th Army in the Rzhev-Sychevka area, Stavka also had in mind a much bigger encirclement of Army Group Centre. Operation Mars failed, however, at the cost of 350,000 casualties including 100,000 dead.[46] (*See Map 13: Operation Mars – the Third Rzhev-Viazma Operation, November–December 1942.*)

During the first Rzhev-Viazma operation the 33rd Army, led by General M. G. Efremov, was given the job of capturing Viazma. In support were General P. A. Belov's 1st Cavalry Corps and the 11th Cavalry Corps from the Kalinin Front. Unfortunately, the attempt to take Viazma failed and Efremov's formation found itself surrounded by the Germans. Belov's cavalry and some other units managed to escape but the bulk of Efremov's forces, including Efremov himself, were destroyed. Zhukov devoted quite a lot of space in his memoirs to this episode. His treatment included some criticism of Efremov but his overall conclusion was more self-critical: 'Viewing the events of 1942 critically I can say now that we misjudged the situation in the Viazma area. We had overrated the potential of our troops and underrated the enemy. He proved to be a harder nut to crack than we believed.'[47]

The loss of the 33rd Army has been a source of considerable controversy in Russia, with some historians arguing that Zhukov tried to take Viazma too quickly and then did not sufficiently support Efremov when the operation failed. Reading the contemporary documentation, however, it is clear that Zhukov did what he could to make the operation succeed and to save the 33rd Army. He failed for the reason stated in his memoirs: his forces were not strong enough to overcome the Germans in the given circumstances.[48]

Interestingly, during the second Rzhev-Viazma operation Zhukov received a rebuke from Stalin (and Vasilevsky) criticising the Western Front's failure to aid three of its divisions encircled by the Germans. Dated 17 August 1942, the note pointed out that when German divisions were encircled the Wehrmacht did all it could to help them. 'Stavka considers it a matter of honour that the Western Front command save the encircled divisions'.[49]

Stavka's persistence in the Rzhev-Viazma area reflected the High Command's belief that the decisive theatre of the Soviet-German war was the Moscow-Smolensk-Warsaw-Berlin axis and that the key to a Soviet victory was the destruction of Army Group Centre. The problem was that the Red Army proved incapable of delivering this

MAP 13: OPERATION MARS — THE THIRD RZHEV-VIAZMA OPERATION, NOVEMBER–DECEMBER 1942

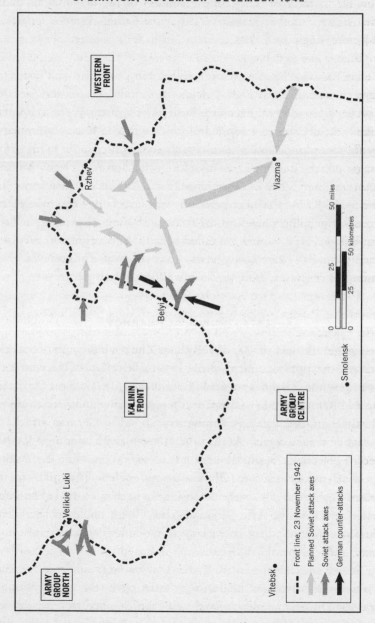

WESTERN FRONT

Rzhev

Viazma

50 miles

50 kilometres

Belyi

Smolensk

KALININ FRONT

ARMY GROUP CENTRE

Velikie Luki

Vitebsk

ARMY GROUP NORTH

- - - Front line, 23 November 1942

Planned Soviet attack axes

Soviet attack axes

German counter-attacks

objective until 1944. One reason for failure was the limited forces available to the Red Army in the context of the demands of many other fronts; another reason was that the Soviets faced a tenacious and increasingly well dug-in enemy in heavily forested regions that lent themselves to defence.

The Russians have a saying: while success has many fathers, failure is an orphan. The Rzhev-Viazma operations were Zhukov's major preoccupation in 1942. Even after he left the Western Front to become Stalin's deputy supreme commander in August 1942 he continued to devote a lot of time and attention to these operations. Yet in his memoirs he preferred to focus on his role in the Red Army's momentous victory at Stalingrad in November 1942. The little attention he did give to the Rzhev-Viazma operations was largely devoted to explaining how the failures had nothing to do with him. Zhukov argued the first Rzhev-Viazma operation failed because he was not allocated sufficient forces.[50] The record shows, however, that Zhukov was given quite a lot of troops, more than were allocated to other fronts.

CATASTROPHE AT KHARKOV

Strong doubts must also be voiced about Zhukov's account of Stavka's strategic decision-making in spring 1942. The failure of the winter offensive, wrote Zhukov, persuaded Stalin and the General Staff that the Red Army should avoid major offensive action and adopt a stance of active strategic defence, aiming to respond to German attacks as and when they occurred. At the same time, notwithstanding Shaposhnikov's objections, Stalin thought it necessary to mount a small number of offensive operations. Zhukov agreed with Shaposhnikov on the need to remain largely on the defensive but he also wanted to launch a major attack in the Rzhev-Viazma area. 'With one or perhaps two more armies at our disposal we could have combined with the Kalinin Front under General I. S. Konev and defeated the enemy not only in the Rzhev area but the entire Rzhev-Viazma German force and substantially improved the operational situation in the whole Western strategic Direction. Unfortunately, this real opportunity was missed by the Supreme Command.'[51]

The opportunity was missed, according to Zhukov, because Stalin succumbed to lobbying from Timoshenko and the Southwestern Front for a major operation in the Kharkov area. That operation was launched on 12 May and aimed to retake Kharkov – Ukraine's second city. Not only did the Soviets fail to recapture Kharkov but the three armies involved in the operation were encircled by the Germans and largely destroyed. The battle was over by 28 May and Soviet casualties numbered nearly 280,000 troops, including 170,000 killed, missing, or captured. Around 650 tanks and nearly 5,000 artillery pieces also were lost.

The party boss in Ukraine at the time was Nikita Khrushchev, who also served as the Southwestern Front's political commissar. In his Secret Speech to the 20th Party Congress in 1956 Khrushchev blamed Stalin for the Kharkov disaster, claiming that he and Timoshenko had asked Stalin's permission to call off the operation before Soviet forces were encircled by the Germans.[52] Khrushchev's self-serving version of events was duly incorporated into the official history of the Great Patriotic War published in the early 1960s when he was still leader of the Soviet Union.

Zhukov flatly denied Khrushchev's story in his memoirs and laid blame for the disaster on the leadership of the South-western Front, who had misled Stalin about their capabilities and then misinformed him about what was going on during the battle itself. Zhukov's critique of Khrushchev and Timoshenko was supported by Marshal K. S. Moskalenko, one of the army commanders involved in the operation. In his view the South-western Front underestimated the German opposition and exaggerated the capabilities of their own forces.[53] In his memoirs Vasilevsky concurred with the Zhukov-Moskalenko view of events but also confirmed Khrushchev's story of efforts made to persuade Stalin to call off the offensive. Vasilevsky argued that Stavka could have done more to help the South-western Front.[54] This latter point was also made in the memoirs of Marshal Bagramyan, chief of staff of the South-western Front, who felt the main problem was Stavka's under-resourcing of the operation.[55]

Stalin's verdict on the failure of the operation was delivered in a missive to the South-western Front on 26 June announcing that Bagramyan had been sacked as chief of staff because of his failure to provide clear and accurate information to Stavka, which 'not only lost the half-won Kharkov operation, but also succeeded in giving 18 to 20 divisions to the enemy'.[56] Stalin compared the 'catastrophe' to one of the tsarist army's biggest disasters during the First World War and pointed out that it was not only Bagramyan who had made mistakes but Khrushchev and Timoshenko. 'If we had reported to the country fully about the catastrophe . . . then I fear they would deal with you very sternly.'[57] Stalin, however, treated the guilty parties more leniently. While Bagramyan was demoted he later re-emerged as one of the most senior Soviet commanders of the war. In July 1942 Timoshenko was transferred to Leningrad to become commander of the North-western Front, but it is difficult to see this as a punishment or even a demotion. Khrushchev remained in charge of Ukraine and after the war was brought to Moscow by Stalin and groomed as one of his successors.

Stalin's treatment of the leadership of the South-western Front tacitly acknowledged that the Kharkov catastrophe was a collective responsibility of the High Command, including himself as supreme commander. In this respect the proposals and reports submitted by the South-western Front to Stavka in March–May 1942 are highly revealing.[58] These documents show that in proposing the operation the Front was confident of success and extremely ambitious, aiming not only to retake Kharkov but to reach the Dnepr – the river that bisected Ukraine and ran through the capital, Kiev. Even when it became clear during the course of the battle that the Germans were much stronger than expected and that the goals being achieved fell far short of operational expectations, the Front continued to submit optimistic reports to Moscow on its progress.

The South-western Front was not alone in formulating ambitious plans and displaying such optimism – in spring 1942 Stavka was bombarded with proposals for offensive action from front-line commanders asking for additional forces.[59] These proposals did not come out of the blue but reflected Stalin's and Stavka's optimism that the renewal of the Red Army's offensive action in the spring and summer of 1942 would lead to the expulsion of German forces from the USSR by the end of the year. Kharkov was only one of a number of ambitious offensives authorised by Stalin and Stavka in spring 1942. Arguably, it was Stavka's strategic orientation towards the offensive that lay at the root of the Kharkov disaster rather than specific operational errors by Stalin or the South-western Front. This deeper truth about Kharkov has tended to be obscured by the memoir blame game and by the widespread acceptance of Zhukov's claim that in spring 1942 Stavka decided to remain on the defensive. The credibility of Zhukov's version of events was reinforced by Vasilevsky's memoirs (published after those of Zhukov), which stated that Stavka's policy was

> simultaneously with the strategic defence to undertake local offensive operations in several sectors which, in Stalin's view, were to consolidate the successes of the winter campaign, improve the operational situation of our troops, help us maintain the strategic initiative and disrupt Nazi plans for a new offensive in the summer of 1942. It was assumed that all combined would set up favourable conditions for the Red Army to launch even greater offensive operations in summer on the entire front from the Baltic to the Black Sea.[60]

If this sounds more like a rolling programme of offensive action than strategic defence, it is because that was the concept embodied in the General Staff's planning documents of spring 1942. These envisaged the local actions mentioned by Vasilevsky, but they were to be followed by ever more ambitious offensives and by an advance to the USSR's western frontier by the end of 1942, at which point the Red Army would *then* assume the defensive.[61] This strategic perspective found public expression in Stalin's Order of the Day on 1 May 1942, which defined the current phase of the war as 'the period of the liberation of Soviet lands from Hitlerite scum' and called upon the Red Army 'to make 1942 the year of the final rout of the German-fascist troops and the liberation of the Soviet land from the Hitlerite blackguards!'[62]

Not for the first time, nor the last, was Stalin being overoptimistic. As the battle of Kharkov showed, the Germans were far from finished. Indeed, the greatest test for Stalin and his generals was yet to come. Hitler was planning another Barbarossa, this time in southern Russia. Once again, Stalin turned to Zhukov to save the day.

8.

ARCHITECT OF VICTORY?

STALINGRAD, 1942

———

IN 1942 HITLER'S STRATEGIC OPTIONS WERE MORE LIMITED THAN IN 1941. He would have preferred to launch another multipronged strategic offensive like Barbarossa but he was not strong enough to do so. The Wehrmacht had taken a severe battering at the hands of the Red Army. By March 1942 German forces had suffered 1.1 million dead, wounded, missing, or captured – some 35 per cent of their strength on the Eastern Front. Only a handful of divisions were at full strength and German mobility was severely impaired by the loss of 40,000 trucks, 40,000 motorbikes, and nearly 30,000 cars, not to mention thousands of tanks. Notwithstanding its image as a modern, up-to-date army, the Wehrmacht relied on horses and other draft animals for transport, and their losses numbered 180,000 with only 20,000 replaced.[1]

Hitler's only realistic option was an offensive on a single front and his choice fell on the Southern Direction. South of the Caucasus Mountains were the Baku oilfields – source of nearly 90 per cent of Soviet fuel. If the Germans could seize those fields the Soviet war machine would soon grind to a halt. En route to Baku the Germans could also capture the agricultural lands and mineral-rich resources of Ukraine, southern Russia, and Transcaucasia. Hitler did not necessarily expect to win the war in 1942 but he hoped to enable Germany to survive a long war of attrition on the Eastern Front. This was critically important now that the United States had formally entered the conflict following Japan's attack on the American fleet at Pearl Harbor in December 1941 and Hitler's declaration of war on the United States in support of his Japanese ally. It was clear the Americans would soon bring to bear their enormous industrial and military power in support of their Russian allies.

The goals of the German summer campaign were set out in Führer Directive No. 41, dated 5 April 1942:

> All available forces will be concentrated on the main operation in the Southern sector, with the aim of destroying the enemy before the Don, in order to secure the Caucasian oil fields and the passes through the Caucasian mountains themselves.[2]

The Soviets had intelligence the Germans would attack in the south in summer 1942 but the information was not definitive and the fact that the seventy divisions of Army Group Centre remained encamped less than 100 miles from Moscow weighed heavily in Stalin's and Stavka's calculations. A major German advance in the south was not ruled out by Stalin but it was seen as mainly aimed at contributing to a flanking attack on Moscow. Defence of Moscow was, therefore, given top priority and Stavka's reserves were placed in appropriate locations.

The idea that Hitler aimed to capture Moscow prevailed throughout 1942. Stalin, in his speech in November 1942 on the twenty-fifth anniversary of the Bolshevik Revolution – when the German advance in the south was at its height – denied the German summer campaign had been primarily about oil and insisted that the main goal was (still) to outflank Moscow from the east and then to strike at the Soviet capital from the rear.[3]

Before the start of their main campaign the Germans completed their conquest of the Crimea. Despite having conquered virtually all the Crimea in 1941 they lost control of the Kerch Peninsula in early 1942 as the result of a series of counteractions by the Red Army designed to relieve the embattled defenders of the city-fortress of Sebastopol. The German 11th Army began its campaign to recapture the

Kerch Peninsula on 8 May and within a fortnight had destroyed three Soviet armies with a total of twenty-one divisions and taken 170,000 prisoners.

The Red Army's expulsion from Kerch opened the way for a final German assault on Sebastopol, which began on 2 June with a massive aerial and artillery bombardment. During the course of a month-long siege the Luftwaffe flew more than 23,000 sorties and dropped 20,000 tons of bombs on the city. The Germans also transferred from the Leningrad Front their heaviest artillery, including guns that fired 1-ton, 1.5-ton, and even 7-ton shells. Following infantry and amphibious assaults Sebastopol fell in early July but the city's defenders had put up an awesome fight that was to be a harbinger of the titanic struggle about to begin at Stalingrad.

OPERATION BLUE

The German advance in the south – designated Operation Blau (Blue) – began on 28 June 1942. The plan was to occupy the Donets Basin (the Donbas) and all the territory west of the River Don. Soviet forces in these areas would be encircled and destroyed and a defensive line established along the Don itself. With the Red Army in the bag the Germans would then cross the Don south of Rostov and head for the Kuban, the Caucasus, and Baku. Capturing Stalingrad was not a primary goal, but the city would be brought under fire in order to disrupt the flow of oil up the Volga from Astrakhan to northern Russia. The Germans would also build a defensive land bridge from the great bend in the Don to the western banks of the Volga in the vicinity of Stalingrad to provide further cover for their advance southward.

The operation was to be executed by Army Group South, consisting of the 6th and 17th Armies and the 1st and 4th Panzer Armies, as well as the 11th Army based in the Crimea. Supporting the German armies were a large number of divisions from Hitler's Axis allies including the Hungarian 2nd, Italian 8th, and Romanian 3rd and 4th Armies. In total there were eighty-nine divisions, including nine armoured, in the nearly two-million-strong force.

Blau made rapid progress. By the end of July the Germans occupied the whole of the Donbas and much of Don country with Stalingrad and the Caucasus in sight. By the end of August the Germans were on the Volga and Stalingrad was under siege. Further south they reached the foothills of the Caucasus, occupied the Maikop oilfield, and threatened the oilfields at Grozny in Chechnya. On 21 August 1942, the German flag flew atop of Mount Elbruz, the highest peak of the Caucasus. (*See Map 14: The German Advance in the South, Summer 1942.*)

During July and August the Germans took 625,000 prisoners and captured or destroyed 7,000 tanks, 6,000 artillery pieces, and more than 400 aircraft. German casualties were high, too; some 200,000 in August alone. The Red Army's losses were significant but not on the scale of summer 1941. However, the relative ease of the German advance convinced Hitler that victory was within his grasp.

In its original conception Blau was a unitary operation whose goals would be achieved on a phased and coordinated basis. First would come control of the Don and Volga, to be followed by a major push south to the Caucasus. On 9 July, however, Army Group South was split into separate commands of Army Groups A and B. Fedor von Bock, the commander of Army Group South, took charge of Army Group B, consisting of the 6th Army, 4th Panzer Army, and the various Axis armies. His given task was to strike east from Kursk and Kharkov in the direction of Voronezh and then southeast towards the Don bend. Army Group A, headed by Field Marshal Wilhelm List, controlled the 17th Army and the 1st Panzer Army and was to capture Rostov-on-Don and then march towards Baku. On 13 July von Bock was dismissed by Hitler because of operational disagreements and replaced by Field Marshal Baron von Weichs. That same day the 4th Panzer was detached from Army Group B and directed to join Army Group A's campaign in the south.

On 23 July Hitler issued Directive No. 45. This stated 'in a campaign which has lasted little more than three weeks, the broad objectives outlined by me for the southern flank of the Eastern front have been largely achieved'. Supported by the 11th Army in the Crimea, Army Group A was now ordered to destroy the enemy south of Rostov and then 'to occupy the entire Eastern coastline of the Black Sea' and to reach Baku. Meanwhile Army Group B would 'thrust forward to Stalingrad to smash the enemy forces concentrating there, to occupy

MAP 14: THE GERMAN ADVANCE IN THE SOUTH, SUMMER 1942

the town, and to block the land communications between the Don and Volga'.[4] In other words, Hitler had decided to pursue two strategic goals simultaneously – the occupation of Baku and the capture of Stalingrad.

Hitler's decision to split his southern offensive was a fateful one. The Wehrmacht was not capable of achieving such ambitious goals and it gave the Soviets an opportunity to consolidate their defences and prepare a riposte.

Stalin's reaction to Operation Blau was coloured by his continuing belief that Moscow was the Germans' main target in 1942 – a belief confirmed by the initial weight of the German attack, aimed at Voronezh, which was closer to Moscow than to Stalingrad. Voronezh fell to the Germans on 7 July but for weeks the Red Army mounted counter-attack after counter-attack in the surrounding area. The importance that Stavka attached to these operations was signalled by its decision to establish a Voronezh Front and to appoint one of the General Staff's most talented officers, General Nikolai Vatutin, as commander.[5]

Further south the possibilities for offensive action were constrained by the weakness of Timoshenko's South-western Front following the Kharkov disaster of May 1942. When the German attack swung south in early July Timoshenko's defences crumbled and Stavka was forced to order a withdrawal towards the Don. The imminent threat to Stalingrad was undeniable and on 12 July Stavka ordered the establishment of a Stalingrad Front. This was a rebranding of Timoshenko's South-western Front with the addition of three reserve armies – the 62nd, 63rd, and 64th. Timoshenko now had thirty-eight divisions at his disposal, a force of more than half a million, including 1,000 tanks and nearly 750 aircraft. Timoshenko's tenure at the Stalingrad Front did not last long, however; on 22 July he was replaced by General V. N. Gordov. Then, in early August, it was decided to split the Stalingrad Front into two – a Stalingrad Front and a South-eastern Front. On 9 August General A. I. Yeremenko was made overall commander of the two fronts.[6]

In Russian and Soviet historiography 17 July 1942 is deemed the 'official' date of the beginning of the '200 days of fire' that constituted the battle of Stalingrad.[7] On that day forward units of the German 6th Army clashed with the 62nd and 64th Armies at the River Chir.

Within a few days the Germans pushed across the southern Don in great numbers and were advancing rapidly towards the Caucasus and Stalingrad. At the end of July the Soviets lost Rostov to the Germans, an event of symbolic as well as strategic importance. The city guarded the gateway to the Caucasus and opened the way for the Germans to occupy the Kuban, a rich agricultural zone between the Don and the mountains of Transcaucasia. The psychological impact of the loss of Rostov was considerable. Rostov had first been occupied by the Germans in November 1941 and its recapture by the Red Army a few days later had been the object of great celebrations since it was the first major city recaptured by the Soviets. Now Rostov had fallen to the enemy again.

NOT A STEP BACK!

On 28 July 1942, Stalin issued his renowned Order No. 227 – *Ni Shagu Nazad!* (Not a Step Back!). The order frankly set out the grave situation facing the USSR:

> The enemy throws at the front new forces and . . . is penetrating deep into the Soviet Union, invading new regions, devastating and destroying our towns and villages, violating, robbing and killing the Soviet people. The battle rages in the area of Voronezh, in the Don, in the south at the gateway to the Northern Caucasus. The German occupiers are breaking through towards Stalingrad, towards the Volga and want at any price to seize the Kuban and the Northern Caucasus and their oil and bread resources.

But the Red Army, said Stalin, was failing in its duty to the country:

> Units of the Southern Front, succumbing to panic, abandoned Rostov and Novocherkassk without serious opposition and without orders from Moscow, thereby covering their banners with shame. The people of our country . . . are losing faith in the Red Army . . . are cursing the Red Army for giving our

people over to the yoke of the German oppressors, while itself escaping to the east.

Underlining the extent of the losses so far, Stalin emphasised that 'to retreat further would mean the ruination of our country and ourselves. Every new scrap of territory we lose will significantly strengthen the enemy and severely weaken our defence, our motherland.' Stalin's solution was to stop the retreat and he used the same slogan Zhukov deployed during the defence of Moscow – *Ni Shagu Nazad!*

Not a step back! This must now be our chief slogan. It is necessary to defend to the last drop of blood every position, every metre of Soviet territory, to cling on to every shred of Soviet earth and to defend it to the utmost.[8]

There was nothing new in Order No. 227. Iron discipline, harsh punishment, and no retreat without authorisation had been Stalin's (and Zhukov's) main theme since the beginning of the war. But its urgent tone revealed Stalin's anxiety about mounting defeats and losses that summer.

As during the battle of Moscow, the threat of punishment was combined with an appeal to patriotism. The call to patriotic duty had been central to Soviet political mobilisation – both civilian and military – since the war began but it became even more marked in what Alexander Werth called the 'black summer of 1942', when catastrophic defeat beckoned once again.[9] The rapid German advance in the south came out of the blue for most Soviet citizens and its disillusioning effect contributed to the intense *patrie en danger* atmosphere of that summer. Soviet propaganda quickly changed tack and began emphasising the grave dangers of the situation. On 19 July an editorial in *Krasnaya Zvezda* compared the situation in the south with the battles of Moscow and Leningrad in 1941.[10]

The most important target group of the appeal to patriotic sacrifice was the Soviet officer corps. On 30 July 1942, Stalin introduced new decorations for officers only: the Orders of Kutuzov, Nevsky, and Suvorov. The pages of the Soviet press also began to be filled with articles promoting both the special role of officers in maintaining discipline and the importance of their technical expertise and professionalism. Later that year officers were issued new uniforms, complete with epaulettes and gold braid (especially imported from Britain). On 9 October 1942 – at the height of the battle for Stalingrad – a decree was issued abolishing the Institution of Commissars, ending the system under which political commissars had a veto over command decisions.[11] The power of the commissars had been restored following the German invasion in summer 1941, a move designed to strengthen the discipline and loyalty of the armed forces. A year later Stalin wanted to send a different message: that he trusted the Red Army to do its patriotic duty unencumbered by political interference from commissars.

Stalin's sense that a decisive battle was approaching at Stalingrad was evident during conversations with British prime minister Winston Churchill, who flew to Moscow in August to discuss the military and political situation. When they first met on 12 August Stalin told Churchill:

> the news was not good and that the Germans were making a tremendous effort to get to Baku and Stalingrad. He did not know how they had been able to get together so many troops and tanks and so many Hungarian, Italian and Rumanian divisions. He was sure they had drained the whole of Europe of troops. In Moscow the position was sound, but he could not guarantee in advance that the Russians would be able to withstand a German attack.

When Churchill asked if the Germans would be able to mount a fresh offensive at Voronezh or in the north, Stalin replied, 'I don't know. But in view of the length of the front, it is quite possible to take 20 divisions to create a striking force, thus creating a threat to Moscow or elsewhere.' The discussion then turned to the issue of a Second Front. The Soviets had been demanding for nearly a year that their British and American allies invade northern France in order to draw German forces away from the Eastern Front. A few weeks earlier Foreign Commissar Molotov had travelled to London and then Washington to discuss the issue with Churchill and President Roosevelt. The result of Molotov's discussions was a joint communiqué stating that 'full understanding had been reached on the urgent task of creating a Second Front in Europe in 1942'. But the British had warned that they would only open a Second Front if they could and now Churchill told Stalin that it would not be possible because there were not enough landing craft available to undertake such an operation. Churchill's news was not unexpected but Stalin reacted angrily, saying that the British and Americans 'should not be so afraid of the Germans'. He was happier with Churchill's news about Operation Torch – an Anglo-American invasion of North Africa in the autumn – but the next day he presented the British prime minister with a memorandum that claimed Soviet military plans for summer and autumn operations had been calculated on the basis of the opening of a Second Front in Europe in 1942.

On 15 August Stalin and Churchill met again and this encounter spilled over into a private dinner in Stalin's Kremlin apartment, where Stalin briefed Churchill about the military situation on the Soviet-German front. The Germans, said Stalin, were invading in two streams – one towards the Caucasus and another towards Voronezh and Stalingrad:

> The front had been broken, the enemy had achieved success, but he had not sufficient power to develop it. . . . They expected to break through to Stalingrad, but they failed to reach the Volga. [He] thought that they would not succeed in reaching it. At Voronezh they wanted to get through to Elets and Riazan, thus turning the Moscow front. Here they had also failed. . . . At Rzhev the Russians had straightened out the line somewhat and Rzhev would be taken very shortly. Then the Russians would move in a southerly direction in order to cut off Smolensk. At Voronezh the Germans had been driven across the Don. The Russians had large reserves . . . north of Stalingrad, and he hoped to undertake an offensive shortly in two directions: (a) towards Rostov, and (b) in a more southerly direction. . . . The object would be to cut off the enemy forces in the Northern Caucasia. . . . He concluded by saying that Hitler had not the strength to undertake an offensive on more than one sector of the front at any one time.[12]

As this statement shows Stalin was concerned about the situation but confident he could handle the new crisis. Stalin always displayed such confidence to foreigners and more often than not it reflected his true feelings. But that confidence must have been shaken by the failure of the Red Army's counter-attacks on the distant approaches of Stalingrad. By 23 August the Germans were at the city's gates and Stalingrad was under siege. The German attack began with massive air raids that killed at least 25,000 civilians. On 25 August the city authorities introduced martial law.

Such was the backdrop to Stalin's decision on 26 August to recall Zhukov from the Western Front and make him his deputy supreme commander (Konev replaced Zhukov as commander of the Western Front). Like Leningrad and Moscow before it, Stalingrad needed saving and Stalin wanted somebody to fight the battle the way he wanted it fought – unwaveringly, ruthlessly, and with unshakable conviction. But there was more to Zhukov's promotion than simply a desperate move to save Stalingrad. Stalin had signaled his utmost confidence in Zhukov as both his key advisor and man of action. As historian John Erickson put it, his appointment as Stalin's deputy meant 'at a stroke Zhukov was transformed from "visiting fireman" to threatened fronts into the chief engineer of the Soviet military machine'.[13]

Zhukov's promotion was also symbolic of the more equal partnership between the communist regime and the Red Army that had developed during the war, including between Stalin and his generals. Significantly, on 27 August Zhukov was also named first deputy defence commissar to Stalin's people's commissar of defence. From now on Zhukov's name as well as Stalin's would be appended to many of the most important decisions governing the Soviet war effort.

To capture Stalingrad the Germans needed to occupy the city's riverbank on the west side of the Volga, which would cut off the Red Army's access to reinforcements and supplies coming from the east side. Pitted against each other in this struggle was the German 6th Army commanded by General Friedrich Paulus and the Soviet 62nd Army commanded by General Vasily Chuikov, a general in the Zhukov mould prepared to make any sacrifice for the sake of victory.[14] The battle within the city was prolonged and intense, beginning in mid-September and lasting nearly three months. At the height of the battle the Wehrmacht occupied 90 per cent of the city but the Germans were unable to dislodge Chuikov's troops from a sixteen-mile strip along the Volga's west bank. As long as the 62nd Army held this bridgehead the Germans could not claim victory and remained vulnerable to a Soviet counter-attack that could destabilise their position not just in Stalingrad but also in the whole Don-Volga area. During the course of the battle Chuikov's forces suffered 75 per cent casualties but their will to resist did not crack. While the whole world marvelled at the famous house-to-house fighting in the city centre, equally important to the outcome of the battle was the defence of Stalingrad's flanks by the 63rd, 64th and 66th Armies, which stopped the Germans from pouring even more troops into the city. Crucial, too, was the struggle for air supremacy between the Luftwaffe and the Red Air Force and the rain of fire on German positions from Soviet artillery on the east bank of the Volga.[15] (*See Map 15: The Battle for Stalingrad, September–November 1942.*)

Stalin did not send Zhukov to Stalingrad immediately. Vasilevsky, appointed chief of the General Staff in June in succession to the sickly Shaposhnikov, was there already acting as Stavka coordinator. At the end of August, however, Zhukov flew to the headquarters of General Gordov's Stalingrad Front and remained in the area for most of September.[16] His role as Stavka's representative was to supervise and coordinate the actions of the two fronts – Gordov's Stalingrad and Yeremenko's South-eastern   involved in the defence of the city and, equally important, to report directly back to Stalin.

Zhukov's communications with Stalin during his time in Stalingrad belong to the detailed history of the complex battle for the city, but their tone is highly revealing of the relationship between the two men at this stage of the war. Stalin trusted Zhukov's reports, respected his judgment, and was prepared to defer to his advice. Typical of Stalin's phraseology was 'What are you planning?'; 'Do you think . . . ?'; 'Please report'. For example on 16 September Stalin sent a message to Zhukov asking whether he 'had considered the possibility of sending two rifle divisions into Stalingrad' in order to strengthen the defence of the city. In the same message Stalin informed Zhukov that he had

MAP 15: THE BATTLE FOR STALINGRAD, SEPTEMBER–NOVEMBER 1942

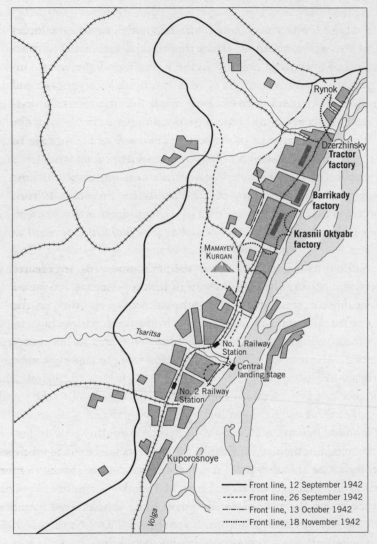

Rynok

Dzerzhinsky
**Tractor
factory**

**Barrikady
factory**

**Krasnii Oktyabr
factory**

MAMAYEV
KURGAN

Tsaritsa

No. 1 Railway
Station

Central
landing stage

No. 2 Railway
Station

Kuporosnoye

Volga

——— Front line, 12 September 1942
- - - - Front line, 26 September 1942
-·-·- Front line, 13 October 1942
········ Front line, 18 November 1942

no objections to his plans for the conduct of the battle.[17] Stalin did not usually display such deference to his generals, as evidenced by this communication to Yeremenko on 5 October:

> I think that you do not see the danger threatening the forces of the Stalingrad front. Occupying the city centre and advancing towards the Volga in northern Stalingrad the enemy intends . . . to surround the 62nd Army and take it prisoner and then to surround the 64th Army in the south and take it prisoner. The enemy can accomplish this aim if they can occupy the Volga crossings in the north, centre and south of Stalingrad. To prevent this danger it is necessary to drive the enemy back from the Volga and to occupy the streets and buildings that the enemy has taken from you. To do this it is necessary to turn every street and every building in Stalingrad into a fortress. Unfortunately, you have not managed to do this and continued to give up to the enemy block after block. This speaks of your bad work. The forces you have in the Stalingrad area are greater than those of the enemy, in spite of which the enemy continued to squeeze you out. I am not pleased with your work on the Stalingrad front and demand that you take every measure to defend Stalingrad. Stalingrad must not be yielded to the enemy and every part of Stalingrad occupied by the enemy must be liberated.[18]

OPERATION URANUS

From Stavka's point of view, while it was important to hang on to Soviet positions in Stalingrad – if only for psychological reasons – more critical was finding a solution that would repulse the Germans' whole southern campaign. The solution Stavka came up with was Operation Uranus – the Soviet counter-offensive at Stalingrad of November 1942 that encircled and then destroyed Paulus's 6th Army.

According to Zhukov the two principal authors of the plan were himself and Vasilevsky. On 12 September Zhukov flew back to Moscow to brief Stalin in person about the situation in Stalingrad. After the briefing, Zhukov and Vasilevsky moved away from Stalin and began talking quietly about the need to find 'some other solution' to the problems they faced at Stalingrad. Stalin overheard them and asked what they were talking about. Zhukov was surprised by Stalin's intervention. 'I had never imagined Stalin had such a keen ear'. The upshot was that Stalin told the two to come up with a new plan.

> Vasilevsky and I spent all the next day working at the General Staff. We concentrated on the possibility of a large-scale operation that would enable us to avoid squandering our prepared and half-prepared reserves on isolated operations. . . . After discussing all the possible options we decided to offer Stalin the following plan of action: first continue to wear down the enemy by an active defence; second prepare for a counter-offensive that would hit the enemy in the Stalingrad area hard enough to radically change the strategic situation in the south of the country in our favour.

When Zhukov and Vasilevsky returned to Stalin's office that evening, the dictator was sceptical but prepared to discuss their proposals further. In the meantime the idea of a major counter-offensive was to be kept secret. Zhukov returned to Stalingrad that night but was recalled to Moscow at the end of September for a more detailed discussion of his and Vasilevsky's draft. At this point Stalin endorsed their plan.[19]

Like so many of Zhukov's stories, this one founders on the evidentiary rock of Stalin's appointments diary, which shows no meetings with Zhukov between 31 August and 26 September. Stalin did meet Vasilevsky during this period but not on any date between 9 and 21 September. It is possible the meetings on 12 and 13 September that Zhukov describes went unrecorded in the diary or took place elsewhere or that Zhukov got the dates wrong. But the evidence suggests strongly that Zhukov imagined or invented this whole episode. The reasons why are not hard to fathom. After the war the parentage of Operation Uranus was a source of considerable controversy. When Zhukov was demoted in 1946 one charge against him was that he had falsely claimed credit for the Stalingrad counter-offensive. The same accusation was repeated by Khrushchev and his supporters when Zhukov was dismissed as minister of defence in 1957. After Zhukov's dismissal Yeremenko and Khrushchev (who had been chief political commissar at Stalingrad) claimed authorship of the counter-offensive plan and Zhukov was denied the right to comment on their claim until after Khrushchev's fall from power in 1964. There was, in fact, no foundation for the Yeremenko-Khrushchev version of events and Zhukov (and Vasilevsky) had every right to feel aggrieved. The plan may not have originated at the precise time or in the exact way Zhukov so colourfully described in his memoirs, but there is no doubt that he and Vasilevsky were the driving force behind it.

According to the Soviet General Staff's contemporaneous account of the battle for Stalingrad, planning for the counter-offensive started in the second half of September. Then, on 4 October, Zhukov had a meeting with Front commanders in which he outlined the plan.[20] From other documentary evidence we know that after this meeting the three Fronts involved in the counter-offensive – the Don, the Stalingrad, and the South-western – submitted to Zhukov and Vasilevsky their proposals for implementation. There is abundant evidence, too, that both men played an extensive role in the preparation of the counter-offensive.[21]

Another controversy concerning Operation Uranus is its relationship to the parallel offensive in the Rzhev-Viazma area – Operation Mars. In his memoirs Zhukov presented Operation Mars as a diversionary offensive designed to make sure that troops from Army Group Centre were not redeployed to the south when Uranus was launched.[22] Zhukov's characterisation of Mars as a diversionary operation has been accepted by most Russian military historians but in *Zhukov's Greatest Defeat: The Red Army's Epic Disaster in Operation Mars, 1942* American historian David Glantz claimed that Mars was an independent operation considered by Zhukov to be equally if not more important than Uranus. As Glantz pointed out, Zhukov spent more time on the preparation of Operation Mars than he did on Operation Uranus and when the two operations were launched, Zhukov took charge of the coordination of the two Fronts involved in Mars (the Kalinin and the Western) while Vasilevsky looked after Uranus. The forces deployed in each operation were more or less equal. According to Glantz's figures the equivalent of 36.5 divisions were used in the

Mars offensive and 34.5 for Uranus. Total Soviet forces deployed against Army Group Centre numbered 1,890,000 troops, 24,682 guns and mortars, 3,375 tanks and self-propelled guns, and 1,170 aircraft as against the 1,103,000 troops, 15,501 guns and mortars, 1,463 tanks and self-propelled guns, and 1,463 aircraft deployed against Army Group South.

Glantz makes a powerful case, especially when Mars is placed in the context of the series of Rzhev-Viazma operations that took place in 1942. All three operations were on a similar scale and designed to land a crippling blow on Army Group Centre. There is no reason to assume that Mars was any different. When Mars was launched on 25 November, shortly after Uranus, the two operations were accorded equal importance in the Soviet press and the headlines emphasised that a dual offensive was in progress. Such headlines did not disappear until it became apparent that Mars was failing to make the same headway as Uranus.[23]

It is clear that Mars was much more than a diversionary operation but whether it was the 'greatest defeat' dramatised by Glantz is questionable. It was more like Zhukov's latest setback in the Rzhev-Viazma area. Moreover, the first two Rzhev-Viazma operations were equally as disastrous as Mars. At the same time, the positive achievements of Operation Mars should not be underestimated. It kept the Germans busy in the central sector while Operation Uranus cut a swath through their southern campaign. Operation Mars did not succeed in expelling the Wehrmacht from the Rzhev-Viazma area but it did enough damage to prompt the Germans to withdraw of their own accord in spring 1943.

Operation Uranus, launched on 19 November 1942, was a combined three-front offensive mounted by the Stalingrad, Don, and South-western Fronts. The Stalingrad and Don Fronts had been formed on 28 September when Yeremenko's South-eastern Front was renamed the Stalingrad Front and Rokossovsky was given command of the old Stalingrad Front, renamed the Don Front. The South-western Front, adjacent to the Don Front, was set up on 31 October under Vatutin's command. The basic plan was to execute an encirclement operation, with the armies of all three fronts converging west of Stalingrad at Kalach.

MARSHAL
GEORGY
KONSTANTINOVICH
ZHUKOV.

ZHUKOV (RIGHT) AND
MARSHAL KONSTANTIN
ROKOSSOVSKY.

ZHUKOV (LEFT) ON
THE APPROACH TO
WARSAW, 1944.

ZHUKOV SIGNS THE AGREEMENT ON
THE UNCONDITIONAL SURRENDER OF
GERMANY IN BERLIN, 8 MAY 1945.

ZHUKOV AND FIELD
MARSHAL BERNARD
MONTGOMERY (ON
ZHUKOV'S LEFT) IN
BERLIN, IN MAY 1945.

ZHUKOV IN BERLIN, 5 JUNE 1945.

ZHUKOV PRESENTS THE ORDER OF VICTORY TO FIELD
MARSHAL BERNARD MONTGOMERY, 21 JUNE 1945.

ZHUKOV AT THE PARADE
OF ALLIED TROOPS IN
BERLIN, 7 SEPTEMBER
1945, IN HONOUR OF THE
VICTORY OVER JAPAN.

**THE MONUMENT
TO ZHUKOV BESIDE
THE KREMLIN,
ERECTED IN 1995.**

The counter-offensive began with an artillery barrage fired by 3,500 guns and mortars. The main attack north of Stalingrad was conducted by the 21st Army and 5th Tank Army of Vatutin's Southwestern Front. South of the city the Soviets attacked with Yeremenko's 51st and 57th armies. This dual thrust was supported by Rokossovsky's Don Front. The plan was for Vatutin's forces to advance southeast towards Kalach and for Yeremenko's forces to strike northwest towards the same objective. At the same time an outer defensive line would be established along the Chir and Krivaya Rivers. An ambitious double encirclement of both the 6th Army and the 4th Panzer Army in Stalingrad and enemy forces in the Don bend was envisaged. (*See Map 16: Operation Uranus, November 1942.*)

The counter-offensive was prepared in utmost secrecy and a number of *maskirovka* (deception and disinformation) measures were effected.[24] Front-line areas were cleared of civilians and the main assault forces were not deployed until the last moment. These measures contributed to the stunning success of Uranus in achieving complete operational surprise. By 23 November the encirclement of Paulus's forces in Stalingrad was complete. Stavka had expected to trap 100,000 or so enemy troops. In the event, they caught three times that number and Operation Uranus became the Red Army's first successfully executed grand encirclement manoeuvre. Among the enemy forces routed during the operation were the armies of Germany's Axis allies whose task was to guard Paulus's flanks. Stalingrad was the beginning of the end for Hitler's Axis alliance. The first country to defect from the Axis was Italy, which deposed Mussolini in July 1943, followed a year later by Bulgaria, Romania, Hungary, and Finland.

Hitler responded to the encirclement of Paulus's forces by attempting to keep the 6th Army supplied by air but to do so the Luftwaffe needed to fly in 300 tons of supplies a day and it did not have enough planes to do that. One reason for the shortage of planes was that the British and Americans had just invaded North Africa and transport was also needed to evacuate Field Marshal Erwin Rommel's Afrika Korps. The Germans mounted a breakthrough operation to Stalingrad but were stopped by the Soviets twenty-five to thirty miles short of the city. The operation did, however, disrupt Soviet plans for Operation Saturn. This was an ambitious follow-up to Uranus that aimed

MAP 16: OPERATION URANUS, NOVEMBER 1942

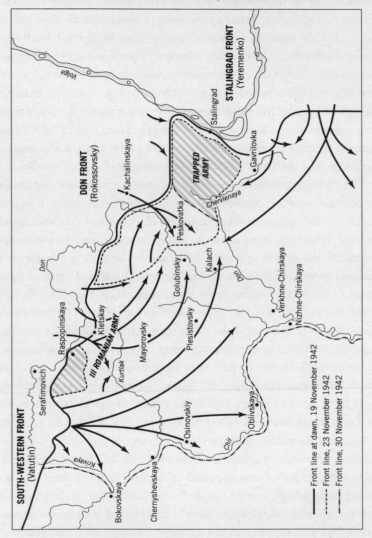

to recapture Rostov and isolate Army Group A in the Caucasus. Its counterpart in the central sector was Operation Jupiter – a grand plan to encircle Army Group Centre should Operation Mars succeed. Mars failed and Operation Jupiter was shelved. Saturn succeeded but because its execution was delayed, by the time the Soviets recaptured Rostov in February 1943 Army Group A had made good its escape. (*See Map 17: Operations Mars, Jupiter, Saturn, and Uranus.*)

When the Soviets realised the full extent of the force they had trapped in Stalingrad they prepared a major operation to tighten the encirclement ring. Seven Soviet armies commanded by Rokossovsky attacked on 10 January 1943. By the end of the month the unequal battle was won and only 90,000 Germans remained alive to surrender. Among them was Paulus, one of twenty-four German generals at Stalingrad who went into Soviet captivity.

It is worth dwelling for a moment on the audacity of Stavka's grand strategic design in autumn 1942. The aim was not only substantial encirclements in the Rzhev-Viazma and Stalingrad areas but even more gigantic encirclements of both Army Group Centre and Army Group South. As the planetary nomenclature suggested – Mars, Jupiter, Saturn, and Uranus – it was a breathtakingly cosmic strategic design. Stalin, Zhukov, and Vasilevsky intended not only to turn the tide of battle in autumn 1942 but to win the entire war. Such ambition was way beyond the capabilities of the Red Army at that time but the breadth of strategic vision was an augury of the massive offensives of 1943–1944 that were to drive the Wehrmacht out of the USSR and all the way back to Berlin.

As a result of the Stalingrad debacle the Germans and their Axis allies lost fifty divisions and suffered 1.5 million casualties. By early 1943 the Wehrmacht had been driven back to the positions they had started from when they launched Operation Blau in June 1942. The Red Army's losses were even higher, with 2.5 million casualties sustained during the course of the Stalingrad campaign. As a follow-up to Stalingrad, Stavka attempted another full-scale winter offensive. Voronezh was recaptured in January 1943 and Kharkov in February, but the Red Army was unable to hold the latter when the Germans counter-attacked. By this time Soviet operations along the front were grinding to a halt as the spring *Rasputitsa* set in.

MAP 17: OPERATIONS MARS, JUPITER, SATURN AND URANUS

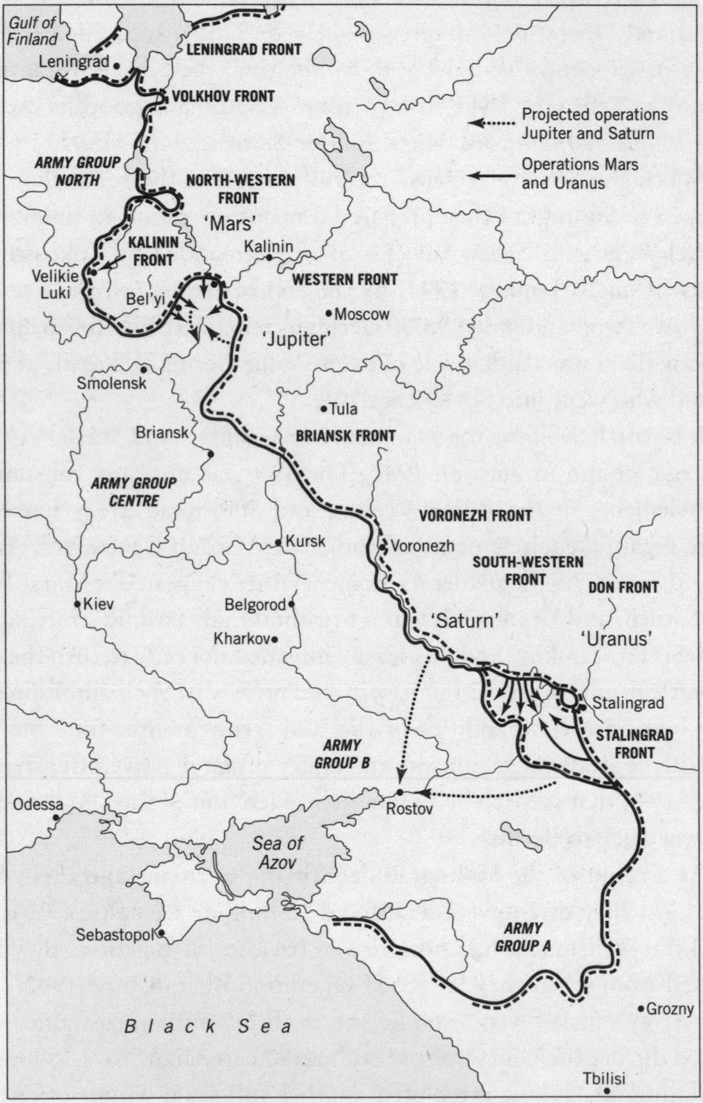

Gulf of
Finland

Leningrad

LENINGRAD FRONT

VOLKHOV FRONT

Projected operations
Jupiter and Saturn

Operations Mars
and Uranus

ARMY GROUP
NORTH

NORTH-WESTERN
FRONT

'Mars'

KALININ
FRONT

Kalinin

WESTERN FRONT

Velikie
Luki

Bel'yi

• Moscow

'Jupiter'

Smolensk

• Tula

Briansk

BRIANSK FRONT

ARMY GROUP
CENTRE

VORONEZH FRONT

Kursk

Voronezh

SOUTH-WESTERN
FRONT

DON FRONT

Kiev

Belgorod

'Saturn'

'Uranus'

Kharkov

Stalingrad

STALINGRAD
FRONT

ARMY
GROUP B

Odessa

Rostov

Sea of
Azov

Sebastopol

ARMY
GROUP A

• Grozny

B l a c k   S e a

Tbilisi

BACK TO LENINGRAD

While all this was happening Zhukov was busy elsewhere. In January 1943 he returned to Leningrad to supervise an operation by the Volkhov and Leningrad Fronts intended to break the German blockade of the city. Operation Iskra (Spark) began on 12 January and by the 18th had succeeded in re-establishing road and rail links to Leningrad. Since the land bridge to Leningrad was only a few miles wide and the constant target of German artillery, it was a case of a blockade cracked rather than broken, as David Glantz puts it.[25] But that same day Zhukov was promoted to the rank of marshal of the Soviet Union – two months before Stalin had the same rank bestowed upon himself. An editorial in *Izvestiya,* the government newspaper, entitled 'Skill of Red Army Leaders', put Zhukov's name at the head of the list of new marshals and generals and acclaimed him a 'highly talented and brave leader' who had carried out Stalin's plans for repulsing the Germans at Moscow, Leningrad, and Stalingrad. On 28 January Zhukov was decorated with the Order of Suvorov 1st Class for 'successfully carrying out the counter-offensive at Stalingrad'.[26]

Towards the end of January Zhukov returned to Moscow to begin planning Operation Polar Star. This was a grandiose plan for an offensive by the Volkhov, Leningrad, and North-western Fronts to encircle Army Group North in the Leningrad area. At the heart of the plan was an advance by Timoshenko's North-western Front to Pskov and Narva, with the Volkhov and Leningrad Fronts in a supporting role. Pivotal to the operation was a Special Group of Forces consisting of a tank army and a field army commanded by General M. S. Khozin, whose job was to close the inner ring of encirclement around Army Group North in the Lake Il'men and Staraya Russa area. (*See Map 18: Zhukov's Plan for Operation Polar Star.*)

Zhukov's name appeared below Stalin's in the operational directives to the three Fronts – orders issued as a result of an intensive series of meetings between the supreme commander and his deputy in late January and early February.[27] When the operation started Zhukov returned to the northwest to supervise its implementation. Zhukov's role in this operation was almost as important as the one he played in Mars and Uranus, yet he gave it barely a passing mention in

MAP 18: **ZHUKOV'S PLAN FOR OPERATION POLAR STAR**

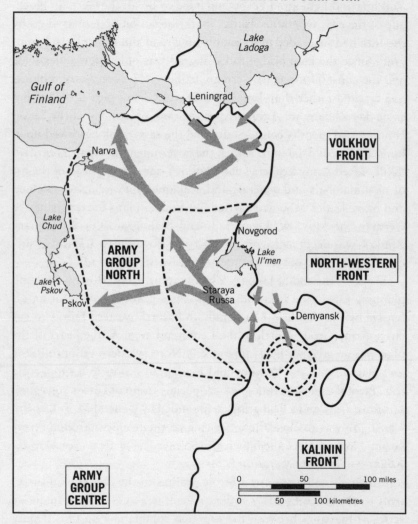

his memoirs. That may have been because like Mars, Operation Polar Star was not a success, and Zhukov did not like to dwell on his failures, which is a pity because the operation illustrated the power and authority he now wielded as Stalin's deputy.

Zhukov acted more like a multi-Front commander than a Stavka coordinator and Stalin's confidence in him was evident in the alacrity with which he agreed to Zhukov's various proposals and recommendations for the prosecution of the offensive. But perhaps more significant is the evidence of Zhukov's growing flexibility as a general, his greater willingness to change tack when faced with new conditions.

The key to the success of Polar Star was liquidating the German 16th Army in the Demyansk salient. This task was entrusted to the 1st Shock Army, instructed to encircle the Germans in the salient and then destroy it. The 1st Shock failed in its mission because by the time Operation Polar Star was launched in mid-February the Germans had already begun to withdraw from Demyansk to more defensible positions along the Lovat River. Responding to the new situation, Zhukov cabled Stalin on 28 February that Polar Star should be limited to the capture of Staraya Russa with a view to preparing the ground for a further offensive in the spring.[20] Stalin agreed and Zhukov pursued the capture of Staraya Russa for the next few weeks, but without success. The Red Army's approximate losses as a result of Polar Star were 250,000, including 50,000 dead.

In mid-March Stalin recalled Zhukov to Moscow and sent him to the Voronezh Front to investigate the situation there following the recapture of Kharkov by the Germans. It was from this vantage point that Zhukov penned a long note to Stalin on 8 April 1943, giving his estimate of the Germans' next move and how the Soviets should respond. Zhukov did not think the Germans had the reserves to renew their southern campaign or, indeed, to conduct any broad front operations. Instead, they would attack on a narrower front, where they already had forces concentrated and where an offensive would contribute to their ultimate goal of taking Moscow. Therefore, predicted Zhukov, the Germans would attack in the direction of Kursk, which lay at the centre of a salient defended by the Central, Voronezh, and Southwestern Fronts. In this attack the Germans would rely heavily on their tank divisions and might pitch as many as 2,500 tanks against the

Soviets at Kursk. To counter this threat Zhukov recommended boosting antitank defences and the transfer of as many aircraft as possible to Stavka's reserve to create the capacity to smash the enemy's tank attack. Zhukov concluded by saying that he did not think it necessary to mount a pre-emptive offensive: 'It will be better if we wear the enemy out in defensive action, destroy his tanks, and then . . . by going over to an all-out offensive we will finish off the enemy's main grouping.'[29]

It was a brilliantly prescient analysis of the next great battle of the Soviet-German war. At Moscow in 1941 the German war machine had ground to a halt in the face of dogged defence and a determined counter-offensive. At Stalingrad in 1942 the Soviets turned the tide of the war in their favour by a brilliant encirclement manoeuvre. Both these battles began with German offensives and ended with Red Army counter-offensives that dramatically turned the tables. The same was to happen at Kursk. Zhukov played a critical role in the Moscow and Stalingrad battles and was destined to star again at Kursk. One key to his success was his growing prowess as a high-level military commander. But equally important was Stalin's enduring faith in him, which survived the setbacks of Mars, Polar Star, and other failed operations. When Zhukov made the cover of *Time* magazine in December 1942 the headline could not have been more appropriate: 'Stalin's Liubimets' – Stalin's favourite.

NA ZAPAD!

FROM KURSK TO WARSAW,
1943–1944

———

FIGHTING THE WAR LEFT LITTLE TIME FOR ZHUKOV'S FAMILY LIFE. IN AUGUST 1941 his wife, Alexandra, and daughters Era and Ella were evacuated from Moscow to Kuibyshev, a city 500 miles southeast of the capital that was the destination of many government officials' families that summer. They were joined there by Zhukov's mother and by his sister, Maria, who had been forced to flee their home village of Strelkovka, occupied by the Germans in autumn 1941.

The Zhukov family did not return to Moscow until 1943. During the intervening period there was only one family reunion – a New Year's celebration at the Pervushkhovo headquarters of Zhukov's Western Front in January 1942. The family flew from Kuibyshev overnight, recalled Ella. 'In the little house where Father lived there was a fir tree and a table with loads of sweets, or so it seemed to me. Actually there weren't so many, it just seemed a lot after Kuibyshev where we never saw any sweets. But, above all, there was the holiday atmosphere. This happiness, and Father's elation, was the result of the great success [of the Moscow counter-offensive].'[1]

After their return to now secure Moscow, the family would talk to Zhukov on the telephone and see him when he visited the capital, which in 1943–1944 was not very often since he spent so much time at the Front. Zhukov's absence from home notwithstanding, 'we did not feel cut off from Father or from his big and important work', recalled Era.[2]

According to Era, her father did not write home much during the war and when he did the letters were short. But the few letters that survived do reveal a little of the man behind the commander who took decisions and gave orders that resulted in the deaths of millions of people.

On 8 January 1943, Zhukov wrote to Alexandra:

Darling Wife!

How unfortunate! I wanted to drop in on you for 30–40 minutes but, alas, you were at the theatre. Of course, you'll say that I am the guilty one for not letting you know my intentions. But it turned out that there was a delay changing from one train to another. What to do? We will divide the guilt between us.

How are you feeling? I'm fine. Healthy, except for the damned rheumatism. It's so depressing. Maybe it will be possible to treat it with salt baths and warm sunshine.

So, that's all for now.

Your Zhorzh.[3]

Complaints about his health seem to have been a theme of Zhukov's correspondence with his wife. On 5 October 1943, he wrote to her:

Greetings and affectionate kisses. Embraces and affectionate kisses to Era and Ella also. I am sending you some sunflower seeds. There is nothing to be done to them except eat them. I am sending back that warm coat, which is very lumpy . . . it would be better to have a warm sweater. Things here are not too bad. We are sitting on the Dnepr. The Germans would like to hold out on the Dnepr. But it is apparent they will not succeed. As usual I'm moving with the army . . . it is in my nature to want to be in the field, with the troops, where I am like a fish in water.

My health is not bad but my hearing is poor. It is necessary to get my ear treated again but it is difficult to organise just now. Sometimes I have a little headache and foot ache. So, that is all I would like to write to you. I wish you and the children good health.

In a similar vein, on 23 October 1943, he wrote:

> I received your letter, for which I send you two more hot
> kisses. I received the parcel with the linen. I split my sides
> laughing at how I looked in the night shirt! Things are going well
> at the front. True, some units have experienced hitches but that is
> perhaps inevitable after such an advance. I wanted to be finished
> with Kiev sooner and then return to Moscow but, unfortunately,
> there has been a delay.
>
> As usual my health gets better and then worsens. Now I have
> that foot ache again. I would like to go to Moscow for treatment.
> My hearing is the same as before – the noises have still not gone
> away. It seems that with age everything comes out.
>
> If all goes well I think I will be in Moscow in about eight
> days, if [Stalin] permits. That seems to be it. And you say I don't
> write. You see how much I scribble. Once again I kiss you and
> the children.

Perhaps with one eye on the security officials who might be reading
his mail, Zhukov could also be more formal and constrained in his
correspondence. On 10 February 1944, he wrote to Alexandra:

> Thank you for the letter, the cabbage, the berries and
> everything else. On the whole things are going well. All the
> army's plans are being fulfilled very well. It is clear that Hitler is
> heading towards complete failure and our country toward
> unconditional victory and the triumph of Russian arms. In
> general, the front is coping with its tasks. Now it is up to the
> rear. The rear has a lot of work to do to make sure the front gets
> what it needs. If the country learns well and remains morally
> strong, victory for the Russians is certain.
>
> I kiss you affectionately.

This letter was signed 'Your G. Zhukov' rather than the more
familiar diminutive 'Zhorzh'.[4]

During the war Zhukov resumed contact with Margarita, his
daughter by Maria Volokhova. When Margarita's stepfather was

killed at Stalingrad and her stepbrother went missing in action (he later died of his wounds), Maria appealed to Zhukov for help. This led to an exchange of affectionate correspondence with his daughter and when Margarita fell seriously ill from emaciation and exhaustion Zhukov sent his Douglas DC-3 to take her to a children's sanatorium run by the military and six months later flew her home again.[5]

The people who spent the most time with Zhukov during the war were the members of his personal support team – adjutants, drivers, chefs, bodyguards, and medical staff.[6] His head of security was Nikolai Bedov, who remembered the great strain that Zhukov was under, especially during the battle of Moscow when he sometimes went several nights without sleep and kept himself awake only with the aid of strong coffee. On his travels to the front line Zhukov frequently came under bombardment, recalled Bedov, and after the battle of Moscow he became a German assassination target and travelled under an assumed name. Bedov was emphatic that Zhukov was never depressed, not even during the darkest days of defeat in 1941–1942: 'the more acute and dangerous the situation, the more controlled and energetic was Zhukov'. Bedov agreed that Zhukov could be rough on subordinates but felt this was justified by wartime conditions. Asked what qualities Zhukov most admired, Bedov replied: 'Courage, decisiveness, truthfulness and, above all, exactitude in the appraisal of complex conditions.'[7]

Another of Zhukov's aides was Alexander Buchin, a driver. Buchin calculated he travelled some 170,000 kilometres with Zhukov during the war and published a memoir under that title. One of the coworkers mentioned in Buchin's memoir was Lida Zakharova, a medical aide, who joined the team during the battle of Moscow. A nicer, kinder person would be hard to find, recalled Buchin. Shy and retiring, Lida found Zhukov's rudeness and loudness hard to take and was sometimes reduced to tears by him. But she did not complain and stayed on.[8]

After his memoir was published, Buchin elaborated on Zhukov's relationship with Lida, claiming that Zhukov, attracted by her shyness, had an affair with her. They were inseparable, claimed Buchin, and given to overt displays of affection. After the war, when Zhukov was banished by Stalin, Lida followed him to the Odessa Military District and then to Sverdlovsk when he was transferred to the Urals Military District. Only when he fell in love with another young woman – Dr. Galina Semonova, who eventually became his second wife and the mother of his fourth daughter, Maria – did Zhukov's relationship with Lida end. Subsequently, Lida married and moved to Moscow, where Zhukov helped find her a flat. According to Era, her mother, Alexandra Dievna, knew about the affair but put up with it because Zhukov was discreet and because 'she knew what an interesting man Father was and how the women ran after him'.[9]

Lida Zakharova's name also came up in a deposition by a former adjutant of Zhukov's, A. S. Semochkin. This was just after the war when the Soviet security apparatus was trying to smear Zhukov. Semochkin made various allegations, including that Zhukov had shown favouritism towards Lida because of their personal relations. In January 1948 Zhukov wrote to the party Central Committee replying to these accusations. With regard to Lida, Zhukov insisted that there was no favouritism; in the work context his relations with her were honourable and honest. He did admit to having an affair with her but denied emphatically that he had carried on with her in public.[10]

During the war it was not uncommon for senior officers of the Red Army to have a 'PPZh' – a mobile field wife (*Polevaya Pokhodnaya Zhena*). Zhukov was certainly aware of the practice and did not object to it in principle. In February 1945 Zhukov complained about one of his generals spending too much time with his mistress but on practical, not moral, grounds:

> I have reports . . . that Comrade Katukov [Commander of the 1st Guards Tank Army] is completely idle, that he is not directing the army, that he is sitting around at home with some woman and that the female he is living with is impeding his work. Katukov . . . apparently never visits his units. He does not organise the operations of the corps and army, which is why the army had been unsuccessful recently. I demand . . . that the woman immediately be sent away from Katukov. If that is not done, I shall order her to be removed by the organs of *Smersh*

[the Soviet counterintelligence organization]. Katukov is to get
on with his work. If [he] does not draw the necessary conclusions, he will be replaced by another commander.[11]

In his memoirs Buchin cited one or two other examples of Zhukov's dalliances, portraying him as a bit of a ladies' man. Given his
status, looks, and powerful personality, it is not hard to imagine wom-
en's attraction to him. But, as far as we know, only four women (apart
from his mother and his daughters) were significant figures in Zhukov's personal life: Alexandra Dievna; Maria Volokhova; Lida
Zakharova; and Galina Semonova. It was apparent, too, that Zhukov
had an eye for pretty young women. The pattern of his relationships
with them suggests also that Zhukov preferred self-effacing, supportive women, who could be trusted not to interfere with his soldiering.
Indeed, the complete absence of negative testimony about Zhukov
from any of the four women, or from his four daughters, speaks volumes about their devotion to him. In his own way, Zhukov was
devoted to them, too, but his military career and service to the Soviet
state always came first.

KURSK

The hearing problem Zhukov alludes to in his letters to Alexandra
may have been the result of a close encounter with a mortar during the
battle of Kursk in July 1943.[12] After Moscow and Stalingrad, Kursk
was the third decisive battle of the Soviet-German war. In the case of
Kursk Zhukov's contribution was threefold. First, he helped to frame
the strategic concept behind the Soviet battle plan; second, he supervised the preparation of the two main Fronts involved in the Kursk
operation – the Central and the Voronezh; and third, during the battle
itself he acted as Stavka coordinator of the Briansk, Central, Steppe,
and Western Fronts.

By April 1943 the spring *Rasputitsa,* the season of bad roads caused
by rain and the thawing of the winter ice, had arrived forcing the Red
Army onto the defensive. The question Stavka faced was what to do
when summer came, when the rains stopped and the roads hardened,

and when offensive action could be resumed. As noted previously, on 8 April Zhukov wrote to Stalin proposing the adoption of a strategic defence posture with the aim of absorbing the next German attack and then launching an all-out offensive.[13] S. M. Shtemenko, the General Staff's deputy chief of operations, recalled that when Stalin received Zhukov's report he polled the Front commanders' views on what the Germans' likely next move would be. The consensus backed Zhukov's prediction of a German attack in the Kursk area.[14] Kursk was at the centre of an outward bulge in the Soviet line – a salient – at the junction of the Central and Voronezh Fronts. If the Germans pinched out the Kursk salient they could shorten their defensive line by 150 to 200 miles and free up to twenty divisions for offensive operations. Such an operation would also be a much needed, morale-boosting victory for the Germans after their failure at Stalingrad.

In mid-April 1943 at a series of meetings between Stalin, Zhukov, and Vasilevsky it was agreed the Red Army would remain on the defensive until the Germans attacked. In his memoirs Zhukov wrote, in italics: *'Thus, by mid-April the Supreme Command had already taken a preliminary decision on deliberate defence.'*[15] He was keen to emphasise this because during the Khrushchev era Zhukov had found himself written out of the history of the Kursk battle by Khrushchevites who claimed that Khrushchev – political commissar of the Voronezh Front – was the architect of Soviet strategy.

Another participant in the April discussions was the General Staff's chief of operations, General A. I. Antonov, shortly to be appointed Vasilevsky's deputy chief of the General Staff. Like Shaposhnikov and Vasilevsky, Antonov was a calm and cerebral general and much admired by Zhukov: 'Antonov was a peerlessly able general and a man of great culture and charm. It always delighted me to hear him present the strategic and tactical ideas of the General Staff. . . . Antonov had a brilliant gift for putting material into shape.'[16] That was a quality Stalin admired, too, and during Vasilevsky's frequent and prolonged absences at the front as Stavka representative, Antonov functioned as de facto chief of the General Staff – a post to which he was formally appointed in February 1945 when Vasilevsky was placed in command of the 3rd Belorussian Front. Stalin, Zhukov, Vasilevsky, and Antonov – these were the strategic brains who would guide the Red Army as it advanced *na zapad* (to the west) in 1943–1944 from Kursk to Kiev, from Viazma to Smolensk, and from Minsk to Warsaw.

After the April discussions Zhukov was sent on a mission to the north Caucasus, accompanied by Shtemenko, who had served in the area before joining the General Staff. Shtemenko remembered Zhukov's habit of playing the accordion – which he learned to play during the war – at the end of each day, usually well-known wartime tunes of a soulful character. 'The musician was lacking in skill', wrote Shtemenko, 'but he made up for it by the feeling he put into his music.' Shtemenko also recalled Zhukov's calm under fire. On one occasion Zhukov's party came under air attack but rather than waiting on the side of the road until the danger had passed Zhukov insisted on continuing the journey. In another incident Zhukov continued to observe an artillery barrage even when return enemy fire began to hit the area around his observation post.[17]

Zhukov's mission was to supervise an operation to drive the German 17th Army off the Taman Peninsula linking the Crimea to the north Caucasus coast near Novorossiisk. The Germans had been forced out of Transcaucasia as a result of the Stalingrad counter-offensive but retained a foothold on the Taman, allowing them to protect their position in the Crimea and to threaten the Soviets from the rear. Zhukov's mission was not very successful. The Germans remained entrenched on the Taman and a second major operation later in the year was required to finally dislodge them. Shtemenko returned to Moscow fearful that Stalin would castigate him and Zhukov for failure. But there were no recriminations, at least not directed against Zhukov. Indeed, the day he returned to the Soviet capital – 12 May – Stalin issued an edict stating that apart from himself only Zhukov and Vasilevsky had the right to give orders to commanders of Fronts. This edict was directed at the heads of the various branches of the armed forces – Artillery, Air Force, Cavalry, Mechanised Forces, Engineers, and so forth – and was designed to stop them from interfering in Front affairs.[18]

Zhukov's next job was to oversee the defensive and offensive preparations being made by the Central and Voronezh Fronts. The Soviet plan was simple: to construct an in-depth defence able to withstand the coming German attack and then stage a counter-offensive.[19] To this end the Soviets established several belts of defence within and behind the Kursk salient extending to a depth of 200–250 miles. Each defensive position was a maze of trenches and concrete blockhouses. Particular attention was paid to establishing antitank strongpoints since the Germans were expected to attack using a lot of armour. Between them the Central and Voronezh Fronts had available some 1.3 million troops, 19,794 artillery pieces and mortars, and 3,489 tanks and self-propelled guns. Also at their disposal was the 17th Air Army with 2,650 aircraft and the Steppe Front (commanded by Zhukov's rival, Konev) with another half million men and 1,500 tanks – a designated strategic reserve tasked to respond to enemy break-throughs and to support Soviet counter-attacks.

During preparations for Kursk the Soviets paid a lot of attention to *maskirovka* disguising their defensive buildup and their assembly of forces for counter-attack. The location of command posts was kept secret. Troops were transported and redeployed only at night. Radio communications were manipulated to deceive the enemy. Airfields, defensive fortifications, and troop assembly areas were camouflaged and mock versions created to distract enemy attention. So while German intelligence detected most of the Soviet preparations it did not grasp the full depth and strength of the Red Army's defences nor, more importantly, its capabilities to mount a counter-attack.[20]

For the first time Soviet partisans were integral to a major Red Army operation. They provided extensive intelligence on German preparations and disrupted those preparations with hundreds of small attacks and acts of sabotage, many aimed at the Wehrmacht's transportation network. When the time came to launch the Soviet counter-offensives, partisan attacks on German command and control systems lent support.

Zhukov's role in these preparations was to conduct inspections, provide progress reports to Stalin, and use his authority as Stavka representative and deputy supreme commander to deal with problems on the ground. In command of the Central Front was Rokossovsky, who recalled that 'Zhukov spent quite a long time at the Central Front in the preparatory period, and we jointly decided questions of principle pertaining to the organisation and conduct of defensive action and the counter-offensive. Thanks to him many of our requests addressed to Moscow were met.'[21] Another observer of Zhukov during the Kursk build-up was his driver, Buchin: 'Day after day, week after week, Zhukov traversed the Kursk bulge, inspecting the smallest details of the construction, consolidation and installation of [defensive] obstacles.'[22]

The Soviets had good intelligence on the Wehrmacht's intentions and attack preparations, including from their own spies in Britain who had gained access to the Ultra decrypts of high-level German codes.[23] What they did not know was exactly when the attack would begin. This uncertainty led in May and June to a series of false alerts about an impending German attack.[24] In this tense and nervous atmosphere some commanders preferred to strike pre-emptively rather than wait for the Wehrmacht to make its move. One such advocate was Vatutin, the commander of the Voronezh Front. 'We'll miss the boat, let the moment slip', he reportedly told Vasilevsky. 'The enemy is not going to move, soon it will be autumn and all our plans will be ruined. Let's get off our backsides and begin first. We've enough forces for it.'[25] Stalin and the High Command held their nerve, however, and waited.

The final alert came from Stavka on 2 July, warning Fronts to expect an attack sometime during 3 to 6 July. Operation Citadel – the German attack on the Kursk salient – began on 4–5 July. The German plan was a double envelopment, by Army Group Centre and Army Group South, of Soviet forces stationed in the Kursk salient. Hitler committed to battle eighteen infantry divisions, three motorised divisions, and seventeen panzer divisions, including large numbers of his new Tiger and Panther tanks, which outgunned anything the Soviets had in their arsenal. (*See Map 19: Operation Citadel, July 1943.*) By this time Zhukov had been appointed to coordinate the operations of the Central, Briansk, and Western Fronts (where the main action was expected to take place), while Vasilevsky was to look after the Voronezh Front. When Operation Citadel began Zhukov was with Rokossovsky at the headquarters of the Central Front. Zhukov vividly recalled the beginning of the long-prepared and intense aerial and artillery barrage the Red Army rained down on the attacking Germans:

The sounds of the heavy artillery, the explosions of the bombs and the M-31 rocket projectiles, the outburst of the Katyushas and the constant hum of the aircraft engines merged into what was like the strains of a 'symphony' from hell. The distance between our headquarters and the enemy troops was no more than 20 kilometers as the crow flies. We could hear and feel the hurricane-like fire and could not help conjuring up the terrible picture on the enemy's initial bridgehead, as he was suddenly hit by the whirlwind of . . . fire. Taken unawares the enemy officers and men probably pressed themselves to the ground or threw themselves into the first convenient hole, ditch or trench, any crack, to protect themselves somehow or other from the frightful explosions of the bombs, shells and mines.[26]

The German attacks made some progress, but for the most part Soviet defences held. The battle's climax came at Prokhorovka on 11–12 July when General P. A. Rotmistrov's 5th Guards Tank Army clashed with two panzer corps. More than a thousand tanks did battle, with hundreds of losses on both sides. The Soviets lost more tanks than the Germans, but they could afford it, and Hitler was forced to call off the attack.

Shortly after the clash at Prokhorovka Zhukov visited Rotmistrov at his command post and inspected the battlefield. According to Rotmistrov, Zhukov stopped the car several times to look at the sites of recent tank battles:

It was an awesome scene, with battered or burned out tanks, crashed guns, armoured personnel carriers and trucks, heaps of artillery rounds and pieces of tracks lying everywhere. Not a single blade of grass was left standing on darkened soil. Fields, shrubs and copses were still smouldering after devastating fires. Zhukov gazed for a long time at damaged tanks and deep craters. . . . The Marshal shook his head, awed by the scene, and he took off his cap, apparently paying tribute to our heroic tank crew.[27]

MAP 19: OPERATION CITADEL, JULY 1943

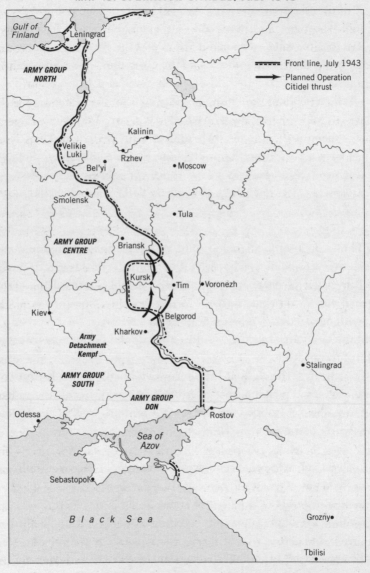

Kursk was Hitler's last throw of the dice, an attempt to regain the initiative in the Soviet-German war. After Kursk there was no possibility of the Germans surviving the grinding war of attrition the Soviets had the power and the will to inflict on them. The Red Army's road to Berlin would be long and arduous but there was no longer any doubt that it was a journey it would complete in the next two or three years.

Having absorbed the German attack at Kursk it was time for the Soviets to go over to the offensive. The Soviets planned two operations: Operation Kutuzov, an attack by the Western, Briansk, and Central Fronts on Army Group Centre in the Orel salient, and Operation Rumiantsev, an attack by the Voronezh and Steppe Fronts on Army Group South in the Belgorod-Kharkov area. (*See Map 20: The Soviet Counteroffensives at Kursk, July–August 1943.*) Kutuzov began on 12 July and by 5 August Orel had fallen to the Red Army, but not before the Germans managed to withdraw many forces from encirclement. Zhukov claimed that had additional forces been deployed the Germans could have been completely encircled in Orel but Stalin insisted that for the time being the priority was driving the Wehrmacht back, not its encirclement and destruction.

Zhukov was not directly involved in Operation Kutuzov since he had been transferred to the Voronezh and Steppe Fronts to supervise Operation Rumiantsev. Stalin had wanted to start this operation on 23 July but Zhukov persuaded him a preparatory pause was required, so Rumiantsev did not begin until 5 August.[28] Belgorod fell to the Red Army that same day, prompting Stalin to order a 120-gun salute in Moscow to mark its recapture along with the contemporaneous liberation of Orel. This was the first of 300 such celebratory salvos ordered by Stalin as the Red Army advanced towards Berlin.[29] The rest of the operation did not progress so smoothly and Kharkov was not recaptured until 23 August. In the meantime the Red Army had launched a third operation – Suvorov – to recapture Smolensk. That was achieved by September after a 150- to 200-mile advance by the Western and Kalinin Fronts.

British journalist Alexander Werth visited Kharkov not long after it was liberated. He found some grim statistics. When the Germans first took Kharkov in October 1941 the population was 700,000. By

MAP 20: **THE SOVIET COUNTER-OFFENSIVES AT KURSK, JULY–AUGUST 1943**

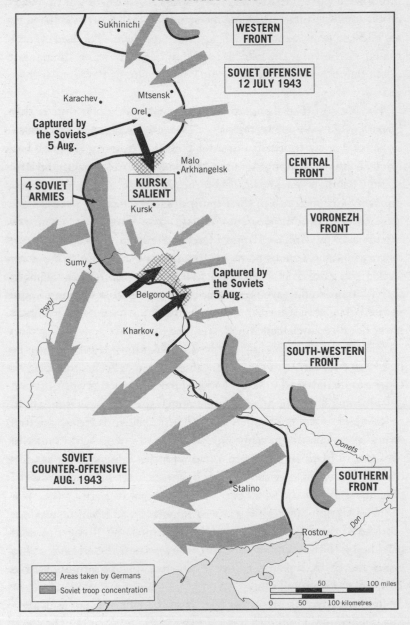

the time they had left the population had nearly halved: 120,000 people were deported to Germany as slaves; 80,000 had died of hunger, cold, and deprivation; 30,000 had been shot; and many others had fled to the countryside.[30]

BATTLE FOR UKRAINE

Operations Kutuzov, Rumiantsev, and Suvorov – named after three great Russian commanders of the eighteenth and nineteenth centuries – were part of a summer offensive intended to push the Germans back along a broad front. In the south the aim was to advance to the River Dnepr – the next natural line of defence for the retreating Army Group South. The Red Army reached and crossed the Dnepr by early autumn and the offensive then developed into a general campaign to liberate the entire Ukraine from German occupation. As Evan Mawdsley has put it, the second battle of Ukraine (the first having taken place in summer 1941) 'was extraordinary in its scope. It was the longest campaign of the war, fought over eight months . . . between August 1943 and April 1944. And it took in a vast territory, as the Wehrmacht retreated first to the Ostwall of the Dnepr River, and then far beyond it to the Carpathian Mountains and the 1938 border with Poland.'[31] No fewer than five Soviet Fronts were involved in operations: the Voronezh, the Steppe, the Southwestern, the Southern, and the Central. In October 1943 the first four of the aforementioned were renamed the 1st, 2nd, 3rd, and 4th Ukrainian Fronts, while the Central became the Belorussian Front. Zhukov was centrally involved throughout all phases of the battle for Ukraine, initially as Stavka coordinator of the 1st and 2nd Ukrainian Fronts and then as the commander of the 1st Ukrainian. (*See Map 21: The Battle for the Ukraine, 1943–1944.*)

The Ukrainian campaign was not without its problems and setbacks and there were some uncomfortable moments between Zhukov and Stalin. Now that the war had turned decisively in the Soviets' favour and the Red Army had at its disposal forces vastly superior to those of the Germans, Stalin was more demanding of success from his commanders. One general point of tension was that Zhukov favoured a campaign based on selective encirclements and then destruction of concentrated enemy groupings, as had happened at Stalingrad. Stalin

MAP 21: THE BATTLE FOR THE UKRAINE, 1943–1944

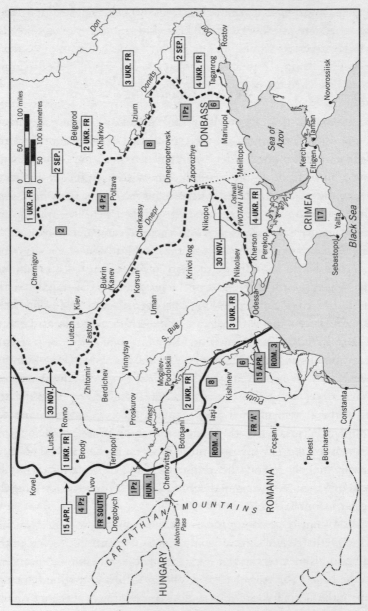

was sceptical, knowing that encirclement manoeuvres were suscepti-
ble to enemy counter-attack or breakout operations, as had happened
many times already. For political reasons also Stalin preferred a broad
front advance that would liberate as much Soviet territory as quickly
as possible. By now Zhukov knew that it was a waste of time to argue
with Stalin when the dictator had his mind made up.[32]

On 26 August 1943, the Central, Steppe, and Voronezh fronts
began a series of offensives collectively known as the Chernigov-
Poltava operation, which aimed to advance towards Kiev and the
Dnepr. By mid-September the Red Army was nearing the river along a
broad front. At this point the combined offensive entered a new stage
with an attempt to seize and hold substantial bridgeheads north and
south of Kiev on the western side of the Dnepr with the aim of surrounding and then recapturing the Ukrainian capital. Troops from all
three fronts crossed the river but the main effort was by the Voronezh
Front in the Velikii Bukrin area south of Kiev. This bridgehead was
supported by a daring drop behind German lines of two airborne brigades. On 28 September Zhukov, hitherto Stavka coordinator of the
Voronezh and Steppe Fronts, was appointed Stavka coordinator of
the Voronezh and Central Fronts. One of his first acts was to redraw
the operational boundaries between the two Fronts so the task of taking Kiev fell now to Vatutin's Voronezh Front – where Zhukov himself
was based – rather than to Rokossovsky's Central Front. This angered
Rokossovsky, who phoned Stalin to complain. The Soviet dictator
brusquely replied that it was Khrushchev and Zhukov's idea.[33]

Khrushchev was Ukraine's top communist leader and the political
commissar of the Voronezh Front and it is not difficult to see why he
would have wanted Vatutin's troops to have the honour of ejecting the
Germans from Kiev. Nor is it difficult to imagine Zhukov wanting to
share the limelight, too. Zhukov worked closely with Khrushchev
during the battle for Ukraine and they got on well. However, in the
section of his memoirs dealing with this period Zhukov did not mention the future Soviet leader at all, except for a disparaging reference
to the fact that you could always get a good meal wherever Khrushchev was to be found![34]

Zhukov was tasked by Stalin to capture Kiev by 7 October,[35] but
this proved to be a bridge too far. The paratroopers were unable to

hold their ground and it was difficult to expand the Bukrin bridgehead in the face of strong German opposition. On 24 October Zhukov reported to Stalin that the reason for the 1st Ukrainian (Voronezh) Front's lack of success so far was that the terrain favoured defence rather than attack. Enemy defences were deep and the Germans were determined, Zhukov told Stalin. Zhukov sought permission to pause the offensive and requested more ammunition and the allocation to the Front of an additional field army and a tank army. Stalin was not satisfied with Zhukov's explanation and replied with a mild rebuke: 'Stavka would like to point out that the failure of the offensive on the Bukrin bridgehead was the result of the failure to take into account local conditions, which make offensive action difficult, especially for a tank army. The reference to insufficient ammunition has no basis since the Steppe Front had no more ammunition but . . . has managed to accomplish its tasks.' Stalin did, nevertheless, agree to strengthen the 1st Ukrainian by the allocation of additional forces to enable it to capture Kiev quickly.[36]

The new timetable was to recapture the Ukrainian capital by 7 November – the anniversary of the Bolshevik Revolution. In accordance with Stavka's instructions, the focus of the offensive shifted from Bukrin to another bridgehead on the west bank of the Dnepr at Lutezh, north of Kiev. The attack began on 3 November with the greatest artillery barrage so far seen on the Soviet-German front – 2,000 guns and mortars with fifty Katyusha rocket launchers, 480 guns to the mile – one third of the entire artillery strength of the 1st Ukrainian.[37] Within three days Kiev fell to the Red Army and Zhukov and Vatutin were able to telegram Stalin: 'Immensely happy to report that the task set by you to liberate our beautiful city of Kiev, the capital of the Ukraine, has been accomplished by the troops of the 1st Ukrainian Front. The city of Kiev has been completely cleared of the Nazi invaders.'[38]

Like Kharkov, Kiev had been devastated: 6,000 buildings and 1,000 factories plundered or destroyed; 200,000 civilians killed and another 100,000 deported.[39] Just outside Kiev, at Babi Yar, was the site of one of the most infamous massacres of the Second World War, where 30,000 Jews were shot by the SS in retaliation for the Germans killed by the delayed-action time bombs the Red Army left behind in the city centre when it evacuated the Ukrainian capital in September 1941.

After the recapture of Kiev the Soviet offensive in Ukraine continued and by the end of 1943 the Red Army had consolidated its positions west of the Dnepr, pushing the Germans back fifty to eighty miles.

In December Zhukov was recalled to Moscow to take part in a high-powered Supreme Command conference. Stalin had just returned from the Tehran summit with Churchill and Roosevelt at which they had promised Stalin that western Allied forces would, at long last, invade northern France in summer 1944. It was also agreed to coordinate the strategic operations of the USSR and its Western allies and Stalin pledged to support the Allied invasion of France by launching a major offensive on the Soviet-German front around the same time.

The Supreme Command conference in Moscow, attended by Stalin, Zhukov, Vasilevsky, and Antonov, by General Staff officers and by members of the Soviet political leadership, was convened to assess the strategic situation and agree on a plan of action for the next set of large-scale operations. At the conference the General Staff presented statistics on the results of the war so far. By the end of 1943 half of all Soviet territory occupied by the Germans had been liberated. Since Stalingrad the Germans had lost 56 divisions and suffered devastating damage to 162 others. While the Wehrmacht no longer had the capacity to wage large-scale offensive warfare, it could sustain an active defence: Germany and its allies still had an army five million strong with 54,500 guns and mortars, 5,400 tanks and assault guns, and more than 3,000 planes. Despite cumulative losses that far exceeded those of the German, the Soviet armed forces had 30 per cent more manpower, 70 per cent more artillery, and 230 per cent more aircraft. (It also had the advantage of greatly increased supplies from the United States, Canada, Britain, Australia, and other allies.)

While in Moscow Zhukov dined with Stalin in the dictator's private Kremlin apartment. On one such occasion Zhukov again raised the issue of encirclement operations, as opposed to broad front advances, and Stalin indicated that he was more favourably disposed towards them now that the Red Army was stronger and more experienced. While the conference decided to mount a winter offensive along a broad front, from Leningrad in the north to the Crimea in the south, the focus was to be the operations of the 1st, 2nd, 3rd and 4th Ukrainian Fronts and the aim of liberating the entire Ukraine west of the Dnepr.[40]

In mid-December Zhukov returned to the 1st Ukrainian Front and at the end of the month Vatutin's troops launched the Zhitomir-Berdichev operation, designed to push the Germans further from Kiev. A month later Konev's 2nd Ukrainian Front launched a joint operation with the 1st Ukrainian to eliminate a German salient in the Korsun-Shevchenkovskii area. Zhukov supervised both operations, later claiming that it was his idea to encircle the Germans in the Korsun-Shevchenkovskii salient with a two-Front pincer movement.[41] The encirclement operation was successful but tightening the ring proved more difficult as the Germans refused to surrender. Stalin was not happy about the delay and blamed Zhukov, sending him a stinging rebuke on 12 February:

> Notwithstanding my personal instructions you did not have a well-thought out plan for the destruction of the German Korsun grouping by the 1st and 2nd Ukrainian Fronts. . . . I made you responsible for coordinating the actions of the 1st and 2nd Ukrainian Fronts but from your report today it seems that in spite of the sharpness of the position you are not well-informed about the situation.[42]

A few hours later Stalin sent Zhukov another message telling him that Konev had been given responsibility for liquidating the Korsun-Shevchenkovskii grouping and that his new task was to protect Konev's operation from a German attempt at a breakthrough from outside the ring.[43]

It took Konev about a week to tighten the Korsun-Shevchenkovskii ring and destroy the German force trapped in the encirclement. Stalin ordered an artillery salute in Moscow in honour of the 2nd Ukrainian Front. 'Not a word was said about the troops of the 1st Ukrainian Front,' complained Zhukov later. 'I feel that was a mistake on the part of the Supreme Commander. There is no denying that success in surrounding and destroying an enemy grouping depends on the action of both the inner and outer Fronts; in this instance, equal success was achieved by the brilliant action of both Fronts – Vatutin's and Konev's.'[44]

Vatutin was a dedicated and well-liked officer. Zhukov was fond of him and in his memoirs went out of his way to defend Vatutin's reputation. He was shocked to learn on 29 February 1944, that Vatutin had been ambushed and shot by anti-Soviet Ukrainian nationalists. The next day Zhukov was appointed commander of the 1st Ukrainian Front in his place. Vatutin was hospitalised in Kiev, and Stalin flew in the chief surgeon of the Red Army to treat him, but two weeks later he died of his wounds.

The 1st Ukrainian Front was Zhukov's first direct operational command since the battle of Moscow. His mission was to continue the offensive in western Ukraine and reach the River Dnestr, thereby cutting off the retreat of Army Group South into Romania. On 26 March *Krasnaya Zvezda* carried an editorial extolling Zhukov's latest exploits: 'During the past days the 1st Ukrainian Front under the command of Marshal Zhukov has achieved a new series of outstanding victories over the enemy. . . . The art of Soviet commanders and the determination of Soviet troops has once again foiled the plans of the Germans. . . . These victories are a victory for both our valour and our skill. . . . In London the radio is broadcasting that events in the Ukraine are a catastrophe for Nazi Germany.'[45] The fighting in the Dnestr area continued for several more weeks but Zhukov's attention was increasingly focused on planning for the Red Army's next grand strategic operation: Bagration.

OPERATION BAGRATION

Operation Bagration was devised to surround and destroy Army Group Centre – the Wehrmacht's last major intact force on the Eastern Front – and to expel the Germans from Belorussia. As with all the spectacularly successful Red Army operations of the Great Patriotic War the authorship of the plan is a matter of some dispute. According to General Shtemenko, the chief of operations, the plan was drafted by the General Staff in April–May 1944 aided by the relevant Front commanders. Particularly important, in Shtemenko's view, was the contribution made by Rokossovsky, commander of the 1st Belorussian Front (formerly the Central Front).[46] According to Zhukov, however, the basic idea of an envelopment of Army Group Centre in Belorussia was proposed by him during a meeting in Stalin's office on 22 April.[47] However, according to Stalin's appointments diary Zhukov did not meet Stalin at all during March or April 1944. If such a meeting took place, it must have been somewhere else in the Kremlin. What is known is that on 15 May Stalin issued an order stating that in view of the possibility that Zhukov could be called upon to 'lead the actions of several fronts' he was relieving him of his 'temporary' command of the 1st Ukrainian.[48] His replacement as commander of 1st Ukrainian was Konev. It is also known that on 25, 26 and 27 May, Zhukov, Vasilevsky, Antonov, Shtemenko, and other senior officers had three lengthy meetings with Stalin.[49] It must have been then that the final decisions regarding Operation Bagration were taken. A few days later – on 31 May – directives were issued to the relevant Fronts instructing them to draw up detailed operational plans for Bagration's implementation. These directives were signed by Zhukov as well as Stalin, reaffirming his high status among the dictator's generals and marshals and indicating, perhaps, that his role in devising the operational concept behind Bagration was as important as he later claimed.[50]

Bagration – named after a Georgian hero of the Napoleonic Wars – involved a combined attack by four Fronts: the 1st, 2nd, and 3rd Belorussian and the 1st Ukrainian. The 1st Belorussian was to advance in the direction of Baronovichi, Brest, and Warsaw; the 2nd Belorussian towards Minsk; and the 3rd Belorussian to Vilnius, capital of Lithuania. In support were the Leningrad and Baltic Fronts and Konev's 1st Ukrainian. Operations were to begin with the Leningrad Front's advance into Finland in early June, followed by a surprise attack in Belorussia later that month and then an advance by the 1st Ukrainian in the direction of Lvov to prevent the transfer of enemy forces from the southern sector. (*See Map 22: The Plan for Operation Bagration, June 1944.*) Between them the four main Fronts had 2.4 million troops, 5,200 tanks, 36,000 artillery pieces, and

MAP 22: THE PLAN FOR OPERATION BAGRATION, JUNE 1944

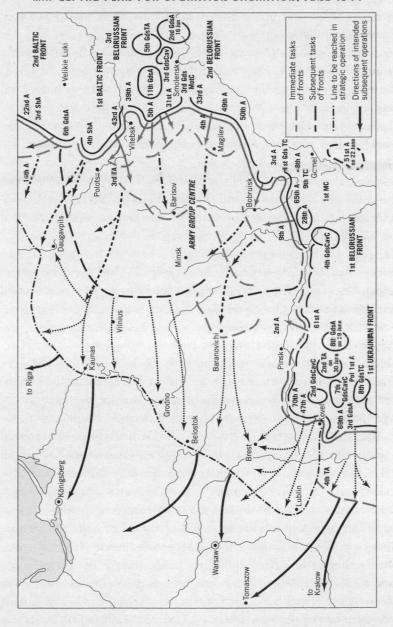

Immediate tasks of fronts
Subsequent tasks of fronts
Line to be reached in strategic operation
Directions of intended subsequent operations

2nd BALTIC FRONT
Velikie Luki
3rd BELORUSSIAN FRONT
5th GdsTA
2nd GdsA 16 Jun
2nd BELORUSSIAN FRONT
1st BALTIC FRONT
22nd A
3rd ShA
6th GdsA
4th ShA
43rd A
39th A
5th A (11th GdsA) 31st A 3rd GdsCav
Smolensk
3rd Gds MotC
33rd A
49th A
50th A
1st A
3rd TA
Polotsk
Vitebsk
Barisov
Magliev
4th A
3rd Gds TC
8th A
9th TC
1st MC
51st A on 22 June
Gomel
Daugavpils
Minsk
ARMY GROUP CENTRE
Bobruisk
65th A
28th A
9th A
4th GdsCavC
1st BELORUSSIAN FRONT
Vilnius
Baranovichi
2nd A
61st A
8th GdsA on 29 June
1st UKRAINIAN FRONT
Pinsk
2nd TA on 30 June
Kaunas
to Riga
Grodno
Belostok
70th A
47th A
2nd GdsCavC
7th GdsCavC
8th GdsTC
69th A
Pol 1st A
3rd GdsA
Königsberg
Brest
4th TA
Lublin
Warsaw
Tomaszow
to Kraków

5,300 military aircraft, giving the Soviets a two-to-one superiority over the Germans in personnel, six times as many tanks, and four times as many planes and artillery.

Soviet plans for Operation Bagration were closely coordinated with the launch of the long-awaited Second Front in France. The Soviets were informed of the approximate date of D-Day in early April and on 18 April Stalin cabled Roosevelt and Churchill that 'as agreed in Tehran, the Red Army will launch a new offensive at the same time so as to give maximum support to the Anglo-American operation'. When the D-Day landings began on 6 June 1944, Stalin cabled Churchill and Roosevelt his warmest congratulations and informed them that, in keeping with the agreement reached at Tehran, the Soviet summer offensive would soon be launched on 'one of the vital sectors of the front'.[51]

Zhukov's role in Operation Bagration was Stavka coordinator of the 1st and 2nd Belorussian Fronts. Vasilevsky had the same role in relation to the 1st Baltic Front and the 3rd Belorussian Front. Serving alongside Zhukov was Shtemenko, who was given special responsibility for the 2nd Belorussian Front.

Zhukov spent most of his time with the 1st Belorussian, and having served in Belorussia for six years before the war he knew its area of operations quite well. As before Kursk, Zhukov spent a lot of time on inspection tours. In his memoirs he detailed the thoroughness of the preparations for Bagration. There was intensive training of troops in fire tactics and attack techniques, with particular attention paid to the coordination of infantry, tanks, artillery, and aviation. Advanced HQs and command and observation posts were established and procedures worked out to move them forward as the attack developed. Reconnaissance units reviewed their intelligence and tweaked the tactical and operational maps provided to front-line units. As always, there was a huge logistical effort to secure and put in place the necessary supplies of food, fuel, and ammunition. In mid-June details of the operation were reviewed and a series of war games conducted at army level. In attendance were corps and divisional commanders and other senior officers. 'We were able', commented Zhukov, 'to better acquaint ourselves with the officers who were to lead the troops to rout a major enemy grouping. . . . Theirs was a great responsibility since the defeat of Army Group Centre spelled the complete expulsion of the enemy from Belorussia and Eastern Poland.'[52]

It is likely that, given his knowledge of the area and the opportunity presented by the lull between operations, Zhukov went hunting, his favourite pastime. He was a dedicated hunter and often took his officers and commissars on hunting trips during the war. When asked why he insisted his officers go hunting with him, even when they were not hunters, he explained that it was to show confidence that the rear areas under his control were safe and secure.[53]

One of the units Zhukov visited during the preparations for Bagration was General P. I. Batov's 65th Army, which was part of the 1st Belorussian Front. In his memoirs, published in 1962, Batov painted an unflattering portrait of Zhukov as a blundering bully. He recalled a failed attempt by Zhukov to climb an observation post up a tree. Halfway up Zhukov lost his footing and fell. Zhukov was 'beside himself with rage', wrote Batov, and he ordered the corps commander to be relieved and the divisional commander to be sent to a penal company.[54] However, Batov's memoirs were published during the Khrushchev era at the height of the campaign to discredit Zhukov and his conclusions about Zhukov's personality and behaviour are largely a construct derived from the critical attacks on Zhukov made during that time.

Zhukov could indeed be abrasive, a not untypical trait of the Red Army's higher commanders. Not everyone appreciated his overly assertive leadership style and he must have upset a lot of senior officers who were stressed enough by the war. There was also jealousy about Zhukov's exalted status, especially his personal relationship with Stalin. Many of Stalin's generals – for example, Konev – were equally egotistical and after the war would take the opportunity to settle their personal scores with Zhukov. Animosity towards Zhukov was not universal, however. For every Batov and Konev there was a Bagramyan or Vasilevsky willing to spring to Zhukov's defence. Even Konev balanced his personal animosity towards Zhukov with an appreciation of his military talents and the same was true of Zhukov's attitude towards Konev.

Operation Bagration began with a wave of partisan attacks on the Germans. Belorussia was the main centre of Soviet partisan operations

and by summer 1944 there were as many as 140,000 partisans organised in some 200 detachments operating behind the Wehrmacht's
lines. On 19–20 June the partisans launched attacks on German communications, staff headquarters, and airfields. The partisans also
acted as forward observers for massive bombing attacks on the Germans on 21–22 June. The main ground attack began on 23 June and
was a stunning success. Attacking across a 500-mile front the Red
Army smashed through Army Group Centre's defences and rapidly
converged on Minsk. The Belorussian capital was recaptured by the
Soviets on 3 July. Zhukov visited the city shortly afterwards:

> The capital of Belorussia was barely recognizable. I had
> commanded a regiment there for seven years and knew well
> every street, and all the main buildings, bridges, parks, stadi-
> ums and theatres. Now everything was in ruins; where whole
> apartment buildings had stood, there was nothing but heaps of
> rubble. The people of Minsk were a pitiful sight, exhausted and
> haggard, many of them in tears.[55]

In a poignant reversal of the Red Army's catastrophe at Minsk in
June 1941, 100,000 Germans were encircled and trapped east of the
city. At Stalingrad the symbol of Soviet success had been the iconic
newsreel footage of the surrender of the 6th Army's commander, Field
Marshal Friedrich Paulus. In the case of Operation Bagration the
memorable sight was of 57,000 German POWs being led by their generals through the streets of Moscow in July 1944.

Minsk was followed by the recapture of Vilnius on 13 July. In mid-
July Konev's 1st Ukrainian Front began the Lvov-Sandomierz operation. He was joined by Zhukov, who was appointed Stavka coordinator
of the operation. Lvov fell to the Red Army on 27 July. Two days later
Zhukov was made a Hero of the Soviet Union for a second time in
honour of his role in liberating Belorussia and Ukraine. That same
day Stalin issued an edict stating that henceforth Zhukov was not only
in charge of coordinating the 1st Ukrainian and 1st and 2nd Belorussian Fronts but of their operational decisions, too. An identical edict
was issued concerning Vasilevsky and the 3rd Belorussian and 1st and
2nd Baltic Fronts.[56] It is not clear what motivated Stalin's decision or

what difference it made in practice, but the edict endorsed the status and authority of Zhukov and Vasilevsky as Stalin's trusted chief troubleshooters.

Between 22 June and 4 July, Army Group Centre lost twenty-five divisions and well over 300,000 troops; another 100,000 troops were lost in the weeks that followed. By the end of July it had ceased to exist as an effective fighting force. The destruction of Army Group Centre did not come cheap. The four main Fronts involved in Operation Bagration suffered 750,000 casualties during the course of the campaign to liberate Belorussia. But there was no gainsaying the magnitude of the Soviet victory. By the end of the operation Belorussia and western Ukraine were back in Soviet hands; Finland was about to capitulate; the Red Army had penetrated deep into the Baltic states and in the south was heading for Belgrade, Bucharest, and Budapest. John Erickson went so far as to argue that 'when the Soviet armies shattered Army Group Centre, they achieved their greatest single military success on the Eastern Front. For the German army in the east it was a catastrophe of unbelievable proportions, greater than that of Stalingrad.'[57]

THE WARSAW UPRISING

The main aim of Operation Bagration was to liberate Belorussia, but the collapse of Army Group Centre and the rapid advance of the Red Army propelled Soviet forces forward to the borders of East Prussia and into central and southern Poland. By the end of July the Red Army was closing on the Polish capital, Warsaw, from a number of directions. The extent of the Red Army's penetration westward raised the question of the future direction of the offensive now that Belorussia had been liberated. On 19 July Zhukov proposed to Stalin a series of operations to occupy East Prussia, or at least cut it off from the main body of Germany.[58] His proposals were considered at meetings between Stalin, Zhukov, Vasilevsky, Antonov and Shtemenko at the end of July.[59] It was ultimately decided East Prussia was too tough a nut to crack, although operations to establish the basis for a future assault would continue. But the main Soviet effort would focus on the capture of Warsaw. On 27 July, 1st Belorussian was ordered to attack the

Warsaw suburb of Praga, on the eastern side of the Vistula, and to establish bridgeheads on the river's western banks to the north and south of the Polish capital. These tasks were to be accomplished by 5–8 August.[60] Pride of place in the coming capture of Warsaw was allocated to the Soviet-organised 1st Polish Army. Recruited from among Polish citizens deported to the USSR following the Soviet invasion of Eastern Poland in September 1939, the 1st Polish had begun forming up in July 1943. Its leadership was pro-communist and many of its officers Russian. By July 1944 it was about 20,000 strong and formed part of Rokossovsky's 1st Belorussian Front. Rokossovsky was himself part Polish, bilingual, and spoke Russian with a Polish accent. After the Second World War he was to become minister of defence in communist-controlled Poland.

Soviet plans soon ran into trouble as the Red Army came up against strong German defences in the Warsaw area. The Wehrmacht was down but not out, and the Germans quickly rebuilt Army Group Centre by transferring divisions from other sectors of the Eastern Front and from Western Europe. Warsaw barred the way to Berlin and was a crucial strategic outpost for the Germans to defend. Working in favour of the Germans' stabilising their defensive position was the fact that the Soviet offensive was progressively losing momentum. Soviet troops were tiring, the Red Army's supply chains were now stretched hundreds of miles, and the Red Air Force's relocation to forward airfields had disrupted its operations, allowing the Luftwaffe to regain some initiative in the air. The Soviets were able to establish some small bridgeheads on the western bank of the Vistula but couldn't hang on to them and were forced to retreat from Praga after their 2nd Tank Army received a severe mauling at the hands of six German divisions, of which five were armoured. The 1st Polish Army also incurred high casualties in its unsuccessful attempts to establish a bridgehead on the western bank of the Vistula.

On 8 August Zhukov and Rokossovsky submitted to Stavka a new plan for the capture of Warsaw that involved securing a strong bridgehead across the Vistula north of Warsaw in the Pultusk-Serock area and strengthening existing bridgeheads south of Warsaw. Once this was achieved the 1st Polish Army would then advance north along the western bank of the Vistula and capture Warsaw. Zhukov and

Rokossovsky estimated that the operation could begin on 25 August.[61] In the event there was further delay and on 29 August Stavka issued a series of directives to the Fronts ordering them to go over to the defensive. However, the right wing of the 1st Belorussian was exempted from this directive and ordered to continue its efforts to establish a bridgehead in the Pultusk-Serock area.[62]

In mid-September Rokossovsky renewed the attack on Praga and revived his efforts to establish a bridgehead for the 1st Polish Army west of the Vistula. While the first goal was achieved, his persistent efforts to secure a position for the 1st Polish Army across the river failed. By early October the Soviet attack on Warsaw had petered out and its bridgeheads west of the Vistula were precarious at best. On 12 November the right wing of the 1st Belorussian Front was ordered to go over to the defensive[63] and the Red Army did not resume offensive operations in the Warsaw area until January 1945.

The course of military events shows that the Soviets did indeed want to capture Warsaw and expected to do so quickly. When their first efforts failed, they tried again. Only when Operation Bagration had run its course did Stavka shelve the aim of capturing Warsaw in the short term.[64] (*See Map 23: The Soviet Advance on Warsaw, Summer 1944.*) However, an alternative scenario has been posited, one in which the Red Army deliberately halted its offensive at the Vistula in order to allow the Germans time to crush a popular uprising in Warsaw. The uprising had begun on 1 August and was staged by the Polish Home Army (the AK) – the partisan arm of Poland's government-in-exile in London. Like the Soviets, the Polish nationalist partisans expected Warsaw to fall to the Red Army quickly and easily. Their aim was to liberate Warsaw from the Germans and seize control of the city before the Red Army could arrive.

Stalin was undoubtedly hostile to the uprising, which was anti-communist and anti-Soviet in its inspiration, and directed as much against him as against Hitler. But there is no evidence he saw the AK as much of a threat. He had every confidence that when the Red Army captured Warsaw he would be able to deal with the anticommunist Poles. This confidence was shared by his Front commanders. 'Do you think that we would not have taken Warsaw if we had been able to do it?' Rokossovsky rhetorically asked journalist Alexander Werth in an

MAP 23: THE SOVIET ADVANCE ON WARSAW, SUMMER 1944

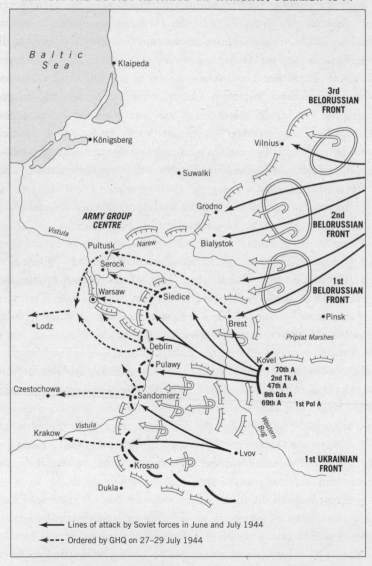

Baltic Sea

• Klaipeda

3rd BELORUSSIAN FRONT

• Königsberg

Vilnius •

• Suwalki

Grodno •

2nd BELORUSSIAN FRONT

ARMY GROUP CENTRE

Vistula

Pultusk •

Narew

Bialystok •

Serock

1st BELORUSSIAN FRONT

Warsaw

• Siedlce

• Pinsk

• Lodz

Brest

Pripiat Marshes

Deblin

Pulawy

Kovel

• 70th A
2nd Tk A
47th A
8th Gds A
69th A   **1st Pol A**

Czestochowa •

Sandomierz

Vistula

Krakow

Western Bug

• Lvov

1st UKRAINIAN FRONT

• Krosno

Dukla •

⟵— Lines of attack by Soviet forces in June and July 1944

⟵--- Ordered by GHQ on 27–29 July 1944

off-the-record interview at the end of August 1944. 'The whole idea that we are in any sense afraid of the AK is too idiotically absurd.'[65]

Stalin's refusal to aid the insurgents also aroused suspicion that he was happy to see the Germans crush them. At first he had been inclined to give some help, even though he thought the uprising ill-judged militarily and doomed to failure. But his attitude changed when the western press began to publish reports that the AK's action had been coordinated with the Red Army, which having encouraged an uprising was now refusing aid to the insurgents. When the British and Americans approached Stalin with a request for Soviet landing and refuelling facilities for their planes dropping supplies to the insurgents, he refused. On 16 August he wrote to Churchill explaining why:

> Now, after probing more deeply into the Warsaw affair, I have come to the conclusion that the Warsaw action is a reckless and fearful gamble, taking a heavy toll of the population. This would not have been the case had Soviet headquarters been informed beforehand about the Warsaw action and had the Poles maintained contact with them. Things being what they are, Soviet headquarters have decided that they must dissociate themselves from the Warsaw adventure.

On 20 August Churchill and Roosevelt jointly appealed to Stalin to drop supplies to Warsaw, if only to propitiate world opinion. Stalin replied on 22 August:

> Sooner or later the truth about the handful of power-seeking criminals who launched the Warsaw adventure will out. . . . From the military point of view the situation . . . is highly unfavourable both to the Red Army and to the Poles. Nevertheless, the Soviet troops . . . are doing all they can to repulse the Hitlerite sallies and go over to a new large-scale offensive near Warsaw. I can assure you that the Red Army will spare no effort to crush the Germans at Warsaw and liberate it for the Poles. That will be the best, really effective, help to the anti-Nazi Poles.[66]

But by September, with their attack on Warsaw delayed, the Soviets began to worry more about the public relations aspects of the affair. On 9 September the People's Commissariat for Foreign Affairs sent a memorandum to the British embassy in Moscow proposing to establish an independent commission to investigate who was responsible for launching the Warsaw uprising and why it had not been coordinated with the Soviet High Command. The memo also announced that the Soviets would now cooperate with British and American supply drops. In mid-September the Soviets also began to step up their own airdrops to Warsaw – a move that coincided with renewed Red Army efforts to take the city. Indeed, Soviet airdrops of supplies to the insurgents were broadly equivalent to those of the British and included 156 mortars, 505 antitank guns, 2,667 submachine guns and rifles, three million cartridges, 42,000 hand grenades, 500 kilos of medicine, and 113 tons of food.[67]

By the time the uprising failed in early October the AK had incurred about 20,000 fatalities and many thousands more wounded, while the civilian population, caught in the crossfire, suffered somewhere between 150,000 and 200,000 dead. To cap the whole horrific affair the Germans demolished the Warsaw city centre and deported the surviving population to concentration camps. After the war the issue of who was to blame for the catastrophe was the subject of prolonged and often virulent controversy. Was it the AK for launching a premature uprising? Was it Stalin for holding back the Red Army? Was it the British and Americans for failing to do all they could for the insurgents or for encouraging a lost cause?[68]

Because of the controversy both Rokossovsky and Shtemenko devoted entire chapters of their memoirs to demonstrating that the Red Army had done all it could to capture Warsaw and to aid the insurgents. In his memoirs Zhukov said much the same thing, but devoted little space to the details of events.[69] In truth, Zhukov regarded the capture of Warsaw as a sideshow compared to the more strategically important goal of an invasion of Germany. He was disappointed by Stalin's rejection of his proposal for a large-scale offensive into East Prussia, which he saw as a missed opportunity to take advantage of the Germans' disarray and weakness following the stupendous success of Bagration – an error of judgment he thought would cost the Red Army dearly when it invaded Germany in 1945.[70]

Another reason for his retrospective lack of interest in the Warsaw uprising was that at the end of August he was given a new mission. Stalin had decided to declare war on Bulgaria. The country was not at war with the USSR but it had aided Nazi Germany in various ways. The 3rd Ukrainian Front was tasked with the invasion of Bulgaria and Zhukov was sent to supervise the operation. In command of the 3rd Ukrainian was Marshal Tolbukhin, a former classmate of Zhukov's from the Frunze Military Academy. On 4 September Zhukov and Tolbukhin submitted to Stavka an invasion plan that was approved by Stalin the next day. The plan called for an attack by three armies (twenty-seven infantry divisions) and two mechanised corps. On 5 September the USSR declared war on Bulgaria. A couple of days later the 3rd Ukrainian invaded. It was not much of a war. The Red Army was welcomed as a liberator by most of the population, including by the Bulgarian army, and on 9 September the pro-German government was overthrown by a communist-led coup in Sofia. The new Bulgarian government promptly declared war on Germany.[71]

By the middle of September Zhukov was back in Poland coordinating the 1st and 2nd Belorussian Fronts but not until the end of October was he formally relieved of his responsibility for the 3rd Ukrainian Front.[72] According to Stalin's appointments diary the dictator did not meet Zhukov at all during September and October 1944. However, they did meet on 2 November and this was the first of a series of meetings[73] leading to a portentous decision: on 12 November Zhukov was appointed commander of the 1st Belorussian Front.[74] By this time planning had begun for the Red Army's next strategic operation – the invasion of Germany. The 1st Belorussian's role in the invasion would be to advance in the centre from Warsaw to Berlin. To Zhukov's north would be the 2nd Belorussian Front, commanded by Rokossovsky, while to the south there was Konev's 1st Ukrainian Front. Rokossovsky was not happy with his transfer from the 1st to the 2nd Belorussian Front even though Stalin assured him that his was not a secondary task. 'If you and Konev don't advance,' Stalin told him, 'neither will Zhukov.'[75]

Zhukov was convinced that Rokossovsky blamed him for his removal from the command of the 1st Belorussian and wrote in his memoirs: 'It seems to me that after this conversation [between Rokossovsky and Stalin] Konstantin Konstantinovich and I did not have the warm friendly relations we had had over many years. It seems that he thought . . . I had asked to head the 1st Belorussian Front. If that is so, he was profoundly mistaken.'[76]

There is no reason to doubt Zhukov's word on this matter. The decision was Stalin's and he had decided that the honour and glory of leading the Soviet storm on Germany belonged to his deputy supreme commander.

RED STORM:
THE CONQUEST OF GERMANY,
1945

AFTER THE BATTLE OF MOSCOW, ZHUKOV IS BEST KNOWN FOR HIS ROLE IN the capture of Berlin in April 1945. It was Zhukov's troops who fought their way into the city centre where, on 30 April, they famously planted the Soviet flag on top of the ruined German parliamentary building, the Reichstag. By this time Hitler was dead, having committed suicide in his bunker that afternoon. Two days later the German defenders of Berlin surrendered and on 9 May Zhukov had the honour of accepting Germany's unconditional surrender on Stalin's behalf. Victory came at a high price. During the assault on Berlin the Red Army suffered 300,000 casualties, including nearly 80,000 dead.

Stalin and Stavka began to plan the invasion of Germany in autumn 1944 with an eye to capturing Berlin by the end of February 1945 after an operation of no more than forty-five days. A pause would then follow before the resumption of large-scale offensive operations in the summer designed to finish off the Nazi regime. In other words, the Soviets expected the war to follow the same pattern as in the previous three years: winter offensive, spring pause, summer campaigning. It should be noted that the Soviets did not equate the fall of Berlin with the end of the war. They fully expected the Germans to fight on for a few more months, including in Hitler's much vaunted Bavarian stronghold – the birthplace of the Nazi movement and where it was widely expected to make its last stand. The struggle for Berlin only became the last great battle of the Soviet-German war because of various military and political contingencies, not least Stalin's determination that the Red Army capture the German capital before the British and Americans. Zhukov – Stalin's deputy, the saviour of Leningrad and Moscow, the victor of Stalingrad and Kursk, and the liberator of Poland, Belorussia, and the Ukraine – was always destined to play a significant role in the conquest of Germany and the capture of Berlin. But no one anticipated the dramatic finale of the Soviet-German war that would cement Zhukov's reputation as one of the greatest generals in history.

In early November 1944 Zhukov participated in several long discussions with Stalin, Vasilevsky, Antonov, and Shtemenko about winter operations.[1] The main idea to emerge was that in early 1945 the Red Army would stage a multi-Front strategic operation to take it from the Vistula to the Oder – the two great rivers that bisected eastern Poland and eastern Germany, respectively – and then on to Berlin. The two main Fronts involved in what became known as the Vistula-Oder operation would be Zhukov's 1st Belorussian and Konev's 1st Ukrainian. Between them Zhukov and Konev had 163 divisions with a total of 2.2 million troops, 32,000 guns and mortars, 6,460 tanks and self-propelled guns, and 4,800 aircraft. Relative to the Germans, Konev and Zhukov had 5.5 times more manpower, 7.8 times more artillery, 5.7 times more armour, and 17.6 times more aircraft.[2] In addition, they had the flanking support of the 2nd and 3rd Belorussian Fronts in the north and the 2nd, 3rd, and 4th Ukrainian Fronts in the south.

Zhukov's mandate was to capture Warsaw, advance to Poznan, and then take Berlin. Konev was to head for Breslau and the important industrial area of Silesia, which Stalin was keen to capture for economic as well as strategic reasons.[3] The task of Rokossovsky's 2nd Belorussian Front was to strike out across northern Poland towards Danzig. In charge of the 3rd Belorussian was I. D. Chernyakhovsky – the only Jewish general to command a Front during the Great Patriotic War – who was to destroy the strong German forces in East Prussia, capture Königsberg, and link up with Rokossovsky's forces in a joint advance along the Baltic coastal lands. However, in February 1945 Chernyakhovsky was killed in action and his place was taken by

Vasilevsky, hitherto Stavka coordinator of the 1st and 2nd Baltic Fronts. That Vasilevsky did not have a central role in the invasion of Germany from the outset was not a sign of Stalin's disfavour but of his plan for Vasilevsky to command an attack on the Japanese in Manchuria later that year. Although the Soviet Union remained neutral in the Pacific War Stalin was pledged to enter the war against Japan soon after the defeat of Germany. In return the Soviets would regain the territory and military bases in China they had lost as a result of the Russo-Japanese War of 1904–1905.

Although the Vistula-Oder operation was a complex, multi-Front offensive, Stalin decided to coordinate the operation himself rather than to rely on Stavka coordinators on the ground, roles that Zhukov and Vasilevsky would normally have played. Zhukov speculated that Stalin decided this because he wanted to be in direct command of the Red Army when it marched into Berlin, just as Tsar Alexander I had been when the Russian army occupied Paris in 1814. Indeed, when the American ambassador, Averell Harriman, later congratulated Stalin on the capture of Berlin, the dictator told him 'Alexander got to Paris'. In any event, by this stage of the war Stalin was supremely self-confident as a military leader and had at his disposal the very able assistance of General Antonov – soon to succeed Vasilevsky as chief of the General Staff – and the equally able General Shtemenko, his chief of operations.

Shtemenko was the General Staff's deputy chief of operations for most of the war. A striking-looking man who in later life sported a dramatic handlebar moustache, he would publish an influential insider account, *The Soviet General Staff at War,* in the late 1960s and early 1970s.[4] After the war Shtemenko served as deputy and chief of the General Staff but was banished to the provinces when he fell out with Khrushchev. When Zhukov became minister of defence in 1955 he brought Shtemenko back into the fold, making him deputy chief of the General Staff. But when Zhukov was removed as defence minister in 1957 Shtemenko found himself once again serving in a regional military command. After Khrushchev's fall from power in 1964 the Zhukov-Shtemenko alliance was renewed in the battle for the historical memory of the Great Patriotic War that raged in the 1960s, even though the two men's memories did not always coincide.[5]

THE VISTULA-ODER OPERATION

The Vistula-Oder operation was to launch on 8–10 January but was delayed by bad weather. Stalin then set 20 January as the start time but brought it forward in response to Churchill's request for help in relieving pressure on the Western Front following the success of the Germans' Ardennes offensive of December 1944 (known as the Battle of the Bulge). Konev began his attack on 12 January, followed the next day by Zhukov, Rokossovsky and Chernyakhovsky.

Zhukov's first objective was to take Warsaw, which he did by using existing bridgeheads on the west bank of the Vistula to launch a flanking attack on the city from the south. The pro-communist 1st Polish Army was tasked to enter Warsaw first and it did so on 17 January 1945. Zhukov recalled:

> Listening to people from Warsaw tell about Nazi atrocities during the occupation, and especially before the retreat, one found it hard to understand the psychology and moral character of the enemy. Polish officers and men took the destruction of the city especially hard. I saw battle-scarred Polish soldiers shed tears, and pledge then and there to take revenge on the fiendish foe. As for Soviet soldiers, we were all embittered and determined to aptly punish the enemy for the atrocities committed.[6]

Zhukov's next advance was from Warsaw to Poznan, 120 miles to the west, not far from Poland's pre-war border with Germany. The mission was to reach Poznan by early February but Soviet forces achieved this goal within a week, albeit by circumventing rather than assaulting the heavily defended city. One reason for the astounding speed of the Soviet advance was that Zhukov did not introduce his tank armies into the battle until day two or three of the offensive, when enemy defences had already been breached, thereby preserving their capability for in-depth exploitation of the breakthrough.[7] Speed was the characteristic feature of the Vistula-Oder operation. During the first twenty days of the operation Soviet troops advanced at the rate of fifteen to twenty miles a day, with some tank units going twice as fast.[8] (*See Map 24: The Vistula-Oder Operation, January–February 1945.*)

MAP 24: THE VISTULA-ODER OPERATION, JANUARY–FEBRUARY 1945

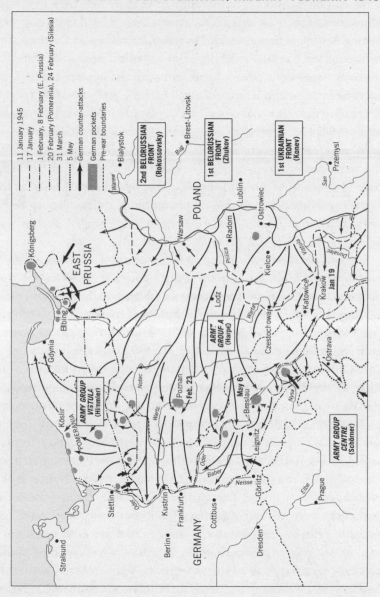

11 January 1945
17 January
1 February, 8 February (E. Prussia)
20 February (Pomerania), 24 February (Silesia)
31 March
5 May
German counter-attacks
German pockets
Pre-war boundaries

2nd BELORUSSIAN FRONT (Rokossovsky)

1st BELORUSSIAN FRONT (Zhukov)

1st UKRAINIAN FRONT (Konev)

ARMY GROUP A (Harpe)

ARMY GROUP VISTULA (Himmler)

ARMY GROUP CENTRE (Schörner)

Königsberg

Elbing

Gdynia

Köslin

POMERANIA

Stralsund

Stettin

Berlin

Kustrin

Frankfurt

Cottbus

GERMANY

Dresden

Görlitz

Prague

Bialystok

Brest-Litovsk

Warew

Warsaw

POLAND

Lublin

Ostrowiec

Radom

EAST PRUSSIA

Lodz

Kielce

Katowice

Krakow

Jan 19

Przemysl

Poznan
Feb. 23

Czestochowa

Ostrava

Breslau
May 6

Leignitz

Neisse

Elbe

Bug

Pilica

Warta

Notec

Oder

Baber

Nysa

Vistula

San

Dunajec

Warte

On 26 January Zhukov proposed to Stalin an advance to the Oder by the end of the month, to be followed in early February by Soviet troops forcing their way across the river along a broad front and then skirting Berlin north and south.[9] In effect, it was a plan for the encirclement of the German capital. Stalin approved and on 27 January Zhukov informed his troops, 'if we can seize the western bank of the Oder the operation to seize Berlin will be fully guaranteed'.[10] The 1st Belorussian did reach and cross the Oder by early February, establishing a bridgehead west of the river in the Kustrin area. German resistance was strong, however, and Zhukov was forced to regroup with a view to preparing, as he put it, a 'sweeping assault to capture Berlin on 15 or 16 February'.[11] On 10 February Zhukov submitted his plan for the capture of Berlin to Stalin, an operation now scheduled to begin on 19–20 February.[12] But on the evening of 18 February Zhukov was ordered by Stavka to halt his attack on Berlin.[13]

Stavka's decision was made in response to the situation on Zhukov's northern flank. While in the south Konev's progress had been as spectacular as Zhukov's, Rokossovsky's advance to the northern Oder had lagged behind. The 3rd Belorussian Front had run into trouble in East Prussia and the right flank of Rokossovsky's 2nd Belorussian Front was ordered to lend assistance. The knock-on effect of the redeployment slowed Rokossovsky's left flank and opened a gap with Zhukov's rapidly advancing armies in the central sector. This exposed Zhukov's drive to Berlin to a counter-attack by strong Wehrmacht forces stationed in Pomerania (the north German province adjacent to East Prussia). To counter this threat Stavka ordered Zhukov to turn his right flank north, away from Berlin, and attack Pomeranian positions. Another complication was that Konev's rapid advance in the south was slowing down. The 1st Ukrainian reached and crossed the southern Oder by the end of January and Konev formulated grandiose plans for a further advance all the way to the River Elbe, including a strike at Berlin from the south in late February. The first phase of this mission – an advance from the Oder to the River Neisse – was completed by mid-February but after forty days of continuous fighting and an advance of some 300–400 miles Konev's troops were in no condition to continue the offensive.[14]

This series of events became the subject of a sharply contested controversy in the 1960s when Marshal Vasily Chuikov published an article claiming that Zhukov could have successfully stormed Berlin in February 1945, thereby bringing the war to an early conclusion. Chuikov was commander of the 62nd Army during the siege of Stalingrad. After the battle the 62nd was renamed the 8th Guards Army and Chuikov was still in command when it took part in Zhukov's drive on Berlin.[15]

Chuikov argued that Zhukov had enough forces to storm Berlin in February 1945 and that the threat represented by the Pomeranian grouping was exaggerated. Zhukov wanted to continue the advance to Berlin, said Chuikov, but he was overruled by Stalin, who insisted the 1st Belorussian Front turn north into Pomerania. In the article Chuikov claimed to have overheard a telephone conversation between Stalin and Zhukov on 4 February during which the Soviet dictator ordered a halt to the attack on Berlin. Concluded Chuikov:

> To this very day, I do not understand why Marshal Zhukov, as First Deputy Supreme Commander and as someone who knew the situation perfectly, did not attempt to convince Stalin of the necessity of waging the offensive against Berlin instead of Pomerania. All the more so since Zhukov was not alone in his view; he was well aware of the mood of the officers and the troops. Why then did he agree with Stalin without a murmur?[16]

Chuikov was not the first person to suggest that Berlin could have been taken by the Red Army in February 1945. On 19 February 1945, *Time* magazine published a report under the headline: 'In Zhukov's Good Time'. Reported the magazine:

> Last week, Marshal Zhukov had to call upon all his will power. Temptation was great. Berlin, the great prize for which he had fought and planned since the battles of Moscow and Stalingrad, was almost within range of his big guns. . . . With one more massive lunge Zhukov might have carried the battle to Berlin. . . . But Zhukov paused to strengthen his grip. Perhaps there was no great danger, but there was still some danger in attempting a quick blow against Berlin. Zhukov knew well

what the Germans knew too well: that a sprawling city becomes a fortress, that an attacking force risks being pinched into its ruins by flank attacks. That was what Zhukov had done to the Germans at Stalingrad.

Time was close to reading Zhukov's mind, as evidenced by his remarks to a Red Army conference in Berlin in April 1946. Convened to discuss the lessons of the Vistula-Oder operation, the conference heard suggestions that the operation could have culminated with the capture of Berlin in February 1945. Zhukov responded:

> Of course, at this time Berlin did not have strong defences. On the west bank of the Oder the enemy had only individual companies, battalions, tank units and no real defence along the Oder. This was well known. It would have been possible to send tank armies . . . directly to Berlin and they might have got to Berlin. The question, of course, is whether or not they would have been able to take it, and that is difficult to say. But it was necessary to resist temptation – not an easy business. A commander must not lose his head, even in the face of success. You think that comrade Chuikov did not want to dash to Berlin or that Zhukov did not want to take Berlin? It was possible to go to Berlin; it was possible to throw mobile forces at Berlin. But . . . it would not have been possible to turn back since the enemy could easily have closed the path of retreat. The enemy attacking from the north could easily have broken through our infantry, reached the Oder crossings and placed our forces in a difficult position. I emphasise again that it is necessary to keep a grip, to resist temptation and avoid adventures. When taking decisions a commander must never lose his common sense.[17]

Zhukov's response to Chuikov's later critique was considerably less relaxed, not surprisingly given the personal barbs directed at him by his former subordinate. Zhukov emphasised the reality of the threat posed by the Pomeranian grouping and denied Chuikov's claim that enough forces were available to isolate that threat *and* march on Berlin. Zhukov also denied that the 4 February telephone conversation with Stalin took place, noting he was elsewhere on the given date. Zhukov also took on Chuikov's argument that in war it was necessary to take risks. 'Historical experience shows', retorted Zhukov, 'that risks have to be taken, but not excessive ones.'[18]

The dispute between Zhukov and Chuikov centred on the evaluation of the threat posed by the German armies in Pomerania. The severity of this threat can be gauged by the fact that the right wing of Rokossovsky's 2nd Belorussian and the left wing of Zhukov's 1st Belorussian did battle with the Germans in Pomerania for nearly two months. During the course of those operations the Red Army destroyed more than twenty enemy divisions but at the cost of 50,000 dead and 170,000 wounded and the loss of 3,000 tanks, aircraft, and artillery pieces.[19]

When the issue was discussed at a Moscow military history conference in January 1966, Zhukov's view received overwhelming support from the participants, who included many high-ranking veterans of the Great Patriotic War. Chuikov (but not Zhukov) attended and defended his position but among Zhukov's supporters were Konev and Rokossovsky – neither of whom were his friends – and both of whom contested the idea that German defences would have crumbled if the Vistula-Oder operation had been continued.[20] His later defence of Stavka's strategic decisions notwithstanding, Zhukov seems to have been less enthusiastic about the Pomeranian operation at the time. When Stavka ordered Zhukov to transfer his 1st Guards Tank Army to the 2nd Belorussian for the duration of the Pomeranian operation, he told Rokossovsky: 'I warn you that the Army must be returned in the same state as you received it.'[21]

During the lull in the Red Army's advance to Berlin that set in at the end of February 1945 Zhukov had a chance encounter with someone who was to become one of the most famous foot soldiers of the Second World War. Sergeant Joseph R. Beyrle is thought to be the only American soldier who served in both the U.S. Army and the Soviet army during the Second World War. Beyrle was a paratrooper captured by the Germans in France just after D-Day. In January 1945 he escaped from prison camp in eastern Germany and headed for the Soviet lines where he met up with a Red Army tank unit. Beyrle was experienced in the use of explosives and he persuaded the tank unit's commanders to allow him to fight alongside them. A month later he was wounded in action and found himself in a Soviet military hospital in what was then called Landsberg (it is now part of Poland). One day there was a commotion in the hospital ward when Zhukov came to visit. Zhukov was intrigued to learn of the wounded American soldier and through an interpreter conducted a conversation with Beyrle, who told him he had no papers, which meant it was difficult for him to get home. The next day Beyrle was supplied with a document authorised by Zhukov that enabled him to travel to Moscow and then to the United States.

Sergeant Beyrle's story gained worldwide attention in 1994 on the fiftieth anniversary of D-Day when at a ceremony in the White House President Bill Clinton and President Boris Yeltsin of Russia both presented him with medals. Beyrle died in 2004 – four years before his son John was appointed United States ambassador to Russia. In an interview in Moscow in April 2011 Ambassador Beyrle stated that as far as he was concerned 'Zhukov had helped save his father's life'.[22]

ZHUKOV VERSUS KONEV: THE RACE TO BERLIN

Zhukov's eye remained on Berlin and at the end of March he submitted to the General Staff a plan with two variants for renewing the attack on the German capital: first, an expansion of the existing bridgehead west of the Oder in the Kustrin area; second, the establishment of a new bridgehead north of Kustrin and south of Schwedt, while also strengthening a small bridgehead at Frankfurt-on-Oder.[23] Zhukov traveled to Moscow to discuss his plans with the General Staff but his proposals were about to be overtaken by events.

On 31 March Stalin received a message from General Eisenhower, the western commander-in-chief, detailing Anglo-American strategic plans. Eisenhower told Stalin his immediate objective was to destroy German forces defending the Ruhr. He would then head for Erfurt, Dresden, and Leipzig and link up with Soviet forces in this area. It was possible, too, that western forces would conduct a secondary advance towards Regensburg-Linz, with the aim of foiling German plans to establish a last redoubt in the south. Eisenhower concluded by asking Stalin for information about Soviet plans.[24]

Eisenhower's message was delivered to Stalin in his office that evening by Averell Harriman, the American ambassador. After Harriman left, Stalin was joined by Zhukov, Antonov and Shtemenko, who stayed for an hour or so.[25] Presumably, Stalin discussed the contents of Eisenhower's message. Stalin replied to Eisenhower the next day to say that western and Soviet strategic plans coincided. He agreed that Soviet and western forces should link up in the Erfurt-Leipzig-Dresden area and said his High Command thought their main thrust of attack would be in that direction. The German capital, Stalin stated, 'has lost its former strategic significance so the Soviet Supreme Command is thinking of setting aside only secondary forces for Berlin'. The main Soviet attack, Stalin informed Eisenhower, would begin in the second half of May.[26]

Stalin's reply later became a matter of controversy when it was suggested that he had deliberately misled Eisenhower about Soviet intentions in relation to Berlin. It is possible, however, that Stalin meant what he said at the time but later changed his mind. The clue to what might have prompted such a change is provided by Konev's memoirs. On 2 April Konev joined Zhukov, Antonov, and Shtemenko for a two-hour meeting in Stalin's office. According to Konev, Shtemenko read out a telegram, evidently from a Soviet intelligence source, stating that the British and Americans were preparing an operation to take Berlin before the Red Army. Stalin then turned to Konev and Zhukov and asked them: 'Well, then, who is going to take Berlin, we or the Allies?' 'It is we who will be taking Berlin', replied Konev, 'and we shall take it before the Allies.'[27]

On the following day, Antonov, Konev, Shtemenko, and Zhukov returned to Stalin's office for a shorter meeting.[28] That same day Stalin signed directives to Zhukov and Konev ordering that Berlin be captured as soon as possible. Zhukov's 1st Belorussian Front was to launch an offensive to capture Berlin and to reach the Elbe River (the agreed Soviet-western military demarcation line in Germany) within twelve to fifteen days of the launch of the operation. Konev's 1st Ukrainian Front was to rout the Germans south of Berlin and advance to Dresden within ten to twelve days and then consider an attack on Leipzig. The demarcation line between the 1st Belorussian and the 1st Ukrainian was fixed at Lübben about forty miles southeast of Berlin, effective from 15 April – an indication that the dual offensive was to commence on 16 April.

The plan meant Zhukov would strike directly towards the German capital and envelop the city from the north, while Konev's forces were to surround the city from the south. A supporting role would be played by Rokossovsky's 2nd Belorussian Front opening an offensive towards Berlin on 20 April to protect Zhukov's right flank from a northern counter-attack by the Germans.[29] (*See Map 25: The Berlin Operation, April 1945.*) The rapid preparation signalled Stalin's determination to seize Berlin before his western allies. Weather permitting, he could be confident of success, albeit at the cost of the lives of many Soviet soldiers who might otherwise have survived the war.

In his memoirs Shtemenko suggested Stalin manipulated the demarcation line between the 1st Belorussian and the 1st Ukrainian Fronts to create a race to Berlin between Zhukov and Konev. According to Shtemenko the original demarcation line was much further south and was changed by Stalin when Konev protested that he should be given a chance to deploy his forces closer to Berlin. Later, Stalin supposedly told Shtemenko and the General Staff: 'Whoever reaches Berlin first, let him take it'.[30] Shtemenko's story is probably a little overdramatic but it is not difficult to imagine Stalin manipulating the rivalry between Zhukov and Konev to ensure Berlin was taken as quickly as possible.

According to Konev the change in the boundary between the 1st Belorussian and the 1st Ukrainian Fronts was Stalin's idea, not his. 'Was this demarcation line at Lübben', wondered Konev, 'an implicit call for competition between the Fronts? I cannot deny the possibility. At any rate, it is not to be excluded.'[31] Zhukov, however, emphatically denied Shtemenko's story and insisted that 1st Belorussian alone was tasked to take Berlin, with Konev's 1st Ukrainian playing an auxiliary role only if needed.[32]

Berlin was a formidable target, notwithstanding the battering the city had taken during the previous five years. Between 1940 and 1945 the British RAF dropped more than 60,000 tons of bombs on Berlin, killing 200,000 people and destroying up to 75 per cent of buildings in the centre of the city. A great number of the city's inhabitants were homeless. Before the war the population of Berlin was nearly 4.5 million.

MAP 25: THE BERLIN OPERATION, APRIL 1945

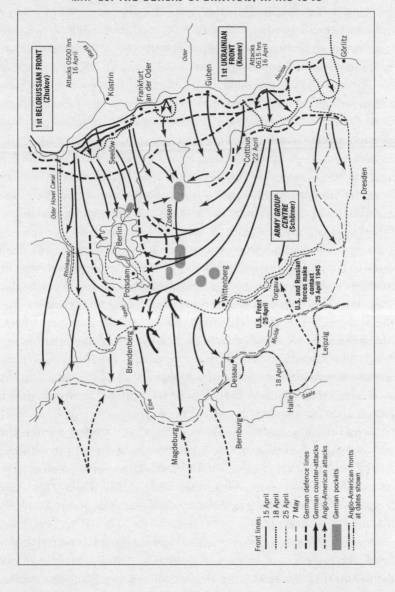

Attacks 0500 hrs
16 April

**1st BELORUSSIAN FRONT
(Zhukov)**

Warta

Oder

Küstrin

Frankfurt
an der Oder

Guben

**1st UKRAINIAN
FRONT
(Konev)**

Attacks
0615 hrs
16 April

Neisse

Görlitz

Seelöw

Oder Havel Canal

Cottbus
'22 April

Dresden

Rhinkanal

Berlin

Zossen

**ARMY GROUP
CENTRE
(Schörner)**

Potsdam

Havel

Wittenberg

Torgau

U.S. and Russian
forces make
contact
25 April 1945

Brandenberg

U.S. Front
25 April

Mulde

Leipzig

Elbe

Dessau

18 April

Halle

Saale

Magdeburg

Bernburg

Front lines:

— 15 April
··· 18 April
-··- 25 April
--- 7 May
··········· German defence lines
➤ German counter-attacks
➤ Anglo-American attacks
▮ German pockets
-··-··- Anglo-American fronts
at dates shown

By early 1945 the population was little more than three million, including 120,000 children and some two million women. The city was bursting with refugees from the east, with the remnants of foreign volunteers in SS divisions that had fought on the Eastern Front, and with hundreds of thousands of slave labourers conscripted by the Germans to work in their war factories.

The city's defences extended to a depth of thirty miles and were organised in three defensive zones, which bristled with machine gun nests, bunkers, and strongpoints, concealed trench systems, antitank ditches, artillery, and tanks and antitank guns. Forward zones were riddled with minefields and many areas were flooded to slow the Soviet advance. Huge flak towers containing Berlin's antiaircraft defences were adapted to take part in the coming land battle. A million German troops supported by 1,500 tanks and assault guns and nearly 10,000 mortars and artillery pieces defended the city and its approaches. The German plan was to conduct a fighting retreat from zone to zone and, if possible, prevent a Soviet breakthrough into or around Berlin. By 1945 the Germans had been on the defensive for more than two years and had become adept at fighting retreats.

In truth, the German defenders were a motley bunch of under-strength and under-supplied units containing a good number of young boys and old men conscripted for the final fight with the Soviets. Nevertheless, the Germans inflicted a high number of casualties on the Red Army, proportionally more than it had suffered in any campaign since the disastrous early months of the war.[33]

Why did the Germans fight on when it was evident to even the most fanatical Nazi that the only outcome could be catastrophic defeat? The short answer is that they feared Soviet retaliation more than defeat. As the Red Army advanced through eastern Germany Nazi propagandists regaled the population with stories of Soviet atrocities against German civilians as well as soldiers. Though exaggerated, some of the stories were true and were confirmed by German refugees from the east. The Germans also hoped that if they fought on, something might turn up – the western allies would reach Berlin first, Stalin would fall out with Churchill and Roosevelt, or Hitler's much vaunted secret super-weapons would materialise and turn the tide of the war.

In the limited time available Zhukov prepared as thoroughly as he could for the challenge of taking the biggest and most heavily defended urban target the Red Army had ever confronted. He assembled a force of 77 rifle divisions supported by 3,155 tanks and self-propelled guns, 14,628 artillery pieces and mortars, and 1,531 rocket launchers. Forty ferry crossings and twenty-five bridges were constructed across the Oder. Zhukov's engineers built models of the city centre and preparations were made for street fighting on the scale of Stalingrad. On the eve of the main attack a reconnaissance in force was conducted to draw enemy fire and to probe for weaknesses in the Germans' defences.

The main operational problem Zhukov faced was how to break out of the Kustrin bridgehead. This would entail seizing the Seelow Heights – a 100- to 200-foot sandy ridge with steep slopes. Heavily defended by the Germans, the Heights dominated the surrounding countryside, which was marshy and in places waterlogged because of the spring thaw. Zhukov decided on a frontal assault by his field armies, followed by an exploitation of the breakthrough by two tank armies that would then encircle Berlin north and south. To catch the enemy by surprise Zhukov decided on a night attack preceded by a short but intensive artillery barrage. The attack began at 3.00 A.M. on 16 April 1945, with more than a million shells fired at enemy positions. At 3.30 A.M., Zhukov switched on 140 searchlights that illuminated the battlefield with light equivalent to 100,000 million candles. 'It was a striking picture', Zhukov recalled, 'and I remember having seen nothing like it during my whole life.' Dramatic though it was, some of Zhukov's generals were not so sure about the effectiveness of this tactic, pointing out later that the searchlights blinded Soviet troops as well as the Germans. Also controversial in retrospect was Zhukov's decision to commit his tank armies to battle just a few hours after the opening attack. He did this to support the faltering assault of his field armies on the Seelow Heights. But the Kustrin bridgehead was a small and congested area and the tanks clogged the roads and further hampered the advance of the infantry. It took Zhukov nearly three days to take the Heights.

Captain Anatoly Mereshko of the 8th Guards Army recalled Zhukov's frustration at this turn of events: 'Zhukov was angry and used clipped, hard-toned phrases, each one accompanied by a threat. I was to find the XXIX Infantry Corps commander, and tell him to organize the storming of the Seelow Heights by 3:00 P.M. or he would be demoted and lose his Hero of the Soviet Union award. Further threats were made against the commanders of the 47th and 82nd Guards Divisions. The order was duly delivered but its recipients all made the same point. Our reconnaissance had belatedly discovered that the main German position was on the reverse side of the Seelow Heights, and this had not been suppressed by our artillery barrage.'[34]

While Zhukov was bogged down in the Kustrin bridgehead, Konev stormed ahead. According to Konev, during the evening of 17 April he had a conversation with Stalin that led to a Stavka directive ordering his tank armies to break into Berlin from the south.[35] This spurred even greater efforts from Zhukov to break through the Seelow Heights. On 18 April he ordered his commanders to personally inspect forward units and determine what was holding up the advance. Officers who showed themselves 'incapable of carrying out assignments' or 'displayed lack of resolution' faced immediate dismissal.[36] This was vintage Zhukov.

Zhukov's troops eventually broke through and by 20 April his artillery was in position to open fire directly on Berlin. But the race with Konev to be the first to break into the city was still on. That evening both issued instructions to their tank commanders ordering them to penetrate the outskirts of Berlin by the following day. Zhukov's order specified that as soon as the mission was accomplished the news would be transmitted not only to Stalin but also to the press. As John Erickson has commented: 'This order left nothing to the imagination. Zhukov intended to be the first into Berlin and not only Stalin but the world's press would know it.'[37] In the event the suburbs of Berlin were penetrated simultaneously by troops from both 1st Belorussian and 1st Ukrainian.

The ruined Reichstag building was a massive, imposing structure in the centre of Berlin. It was a mere shell, having been burned out in February 1933 shortly after Hitler came to power. The fire was supposedly started by a Dutch communist, Marinus van der Lubbe, and it was used by the Nazis as a pretext to impose a repressive regime on the country – the first step in establishing Hitler's dictatorship. Among those tried for the alleged crime alongside Lubbe was a Bulgarian communist, Georgy Dimitrov, who later became the leader of the Communist International and a close confidant of Stalin's. Following an international protest campaign only Lubbe was convicted while Dimitrov was deported to the Soviet Union. From the Soviet point of view the Reichstag, as the British military historian Chris Bellamy put it, 'had all the attributes needed for an iconic victory symbol'.[38]

On 23 April Stalin issued an order specifying the demarcation line between Konev's and Zhukov's two Fronts in the coming battle for inner Berlin. It bisected Berlin just south of the city centre about 150 yards from the Reichstag building, which lay in Zhukov's designated zone. The race between Konev and Zhukov to claim the capture of Berlin was effectively over. Konev would share in the glory of capturing Hitler's capital but the palm of victory would go to Zhukov when his troops stormed the Reichstag.[39]

In the following week Konev's and Zhukov's troops fought their way towards the city centre, street by street, building by building, much as the Germans had done in Stalingrad in 1942. One of the most common Soviet techniques was to fire their artillery directly at buildings, destroying them and their defenders. The demolition of Berlin begun by the RAF was completed by the Red Army. The battle culminated in the capture of the Reichstag building on 30 April. That evening two soldiers from Zhukov's 3rd Shock Army raised the Soviet flag on top of the building. Later, the Soviet photographer Yevgeni Chaldei re-enacted the scene with two other soldiers, aiming to create as iconic a picture of the Red Army's conquest of Berlin as the hoisting of the Stars and Stripes by U.S. troops over Iwo Jima two months earlier. But whereas the Americans suffered 25,000 casualties at Iwo Jima, Soviet losses during the Berlin operation numbered hundreds of thousands. It was a high price to pay but there is little doubt that the determination of Stalin, Zhukov, and Konev to take Berlin was shared by the rest of the Red Army.

The consolation for Konev was that it was his troops who met the American forces for the first time on 25 April, the linkup taking place on the Elbe at Torgau, about seventy miles southwest of Berlin. The joyous event was reenacted for the newsreel cameras and celebrated by a massive artillery salute in Moscow.

On 1 May Stalin announced the capture of Berlin to the world: 'The troops of the First Belorussian Front, supported by the troops of the First Ukrainian Front . . . have gained full control of Berlin, the capital of Germany – the centre of German imperialism and the hot-bed of German aggression.' The next day the remaining German defenders of Berlin surrendered. By the end of the battle Soviet casualties during the Berlin operation exceeded 350,000 while the Germans lost half a million with another half a million taken prisoner by the Soviets. Among the casualties were the 125,000 German civilians who died, including 4,000 who committed suicide in April 1945 alone.

One of Zhukov's immediate concerns in taking control of Berlin was to verify Hitler's suicide. Like Stalin, Zhukov was sceptical that the Nazi dictator had killed himself and feared he might have escaped with his deputy, Martin Bormann. Zhukov went to the Imperial Chancellery to search for the burned bodies of Hitler and Joseph Goebbels, the Nazi propaganda chief, who had also committed suicide. He found nothing but was told that in Hitler's bunker were the bodies of Goebbels's six children, poisoned by their parents. 'I must admit', recalled Zhukov, 'I had not the heart to go down and look at the children.'[40] Only after an extensive investigation by a Soviet forensics team did Zhukov and Stalin reluctantly accept that Hitler had indeed killed himself.[41]

At the Reichstag Zhukov added his signature to the thousands of graffiti inscriptions made by Red Army soldiers on the columns at the entrance to the building. Zhukov's visit to the Reichstag and the Chancellery was filmed and the newsreel footage added to his renown as the top Soviet general. A few days later an even more famous moment was captured on film. On 7 May the German armed forces signed a capitulation agreement at Reims in France. But since only a relatively junior Soviet officer was present, Stalin insisted that this agreement was provisional and that Zhukov should sign a proper act of capitulation in Berlin. The ceremony took place in a villa in Karlshorst in eastern Berlin on 8 May. The Americans were represented by General Carl Spaatz, commander of the U.S. Strategic Air Forces, the British by Air Marshal Arthur Tedder, and the French by the commander-in-chief of their army, General Jean de Lattre de Tassigny. Signing on behalf of Germany was Field Marshal Wilhelm

Keitel. The actual signing of the document took place just after midnight on 9 May – hence the annual celebration of Victory Day in Russia on this date. After the signing ceremony Zhukov congratulated everyone present. Then, he recalled, 'incredible commotion broke out in the hall. Everyone was congratulating one another and shaking hands. Many had tears of joy in their eyes. I was surrounded by my comrades in arms.' Afterwards there was a reception that went on all night and ended in singing and dancing: 'The Soviet generals were unrivalled as far as dancing went. Even I could not restrain myself and, remembering my youth, did the Russkaya dance.'[42]

On 19 May Zhukov returned to Moscow where he learned that Stalin had decided to appoint him commander of the Soviet occupation forces in Germany and to make him the Soviet representative to the Allied Control Council (ACC). During the war it had been decided to divide post-war Germany into American, British, French, and Soviet occupation zones. Berlin was also divided into occupation zones, even though it lay deep in eastern Germany, which was controlled by the Soviets. (*See Map 26: Allied Occupation Zones in Germany.*) The ACC would be based in Berlin and coordinate the Allied occupation, oversee the implementation of common policies, and prepare the way for the eventual reunification of Germany after the country had been thoroughly demilitarised, de-nazified and democratised.

While in Moscow Zhukov attended a series of meetings in Stalin's Kremlin office along with Antonov, Shtemenko, and other senior officers. Further meetings were held at the end of June. The topic of discussion was the forthcoming Soviet invasion of Manchuria.

When Japan attacked the United States at Pearl Harbor in December 1941 the Soviet Union remained neutral but Stalin promised to enter the war in the Far East as soon as possible. At the Yalta conference in February 1945, Stalin told President Roosevelt the Red Army would attack Japanese forces in Manchuria three months after Germany's surrender. In the event, that meant August 1945.

The designated commander of the Soviet invasion was Vasilevsky. The operation began on 8 August. And within a few days Japan's Kwantung Army was defeated, suffering massive casualties, including 80,000 dead. The Red Army's attack coincided with the American atom bombing of Hiroshima and Nagasaki, and it was the dual shock

MAP 26: ALLIED OCCUPATION ZONES IN GERMANY

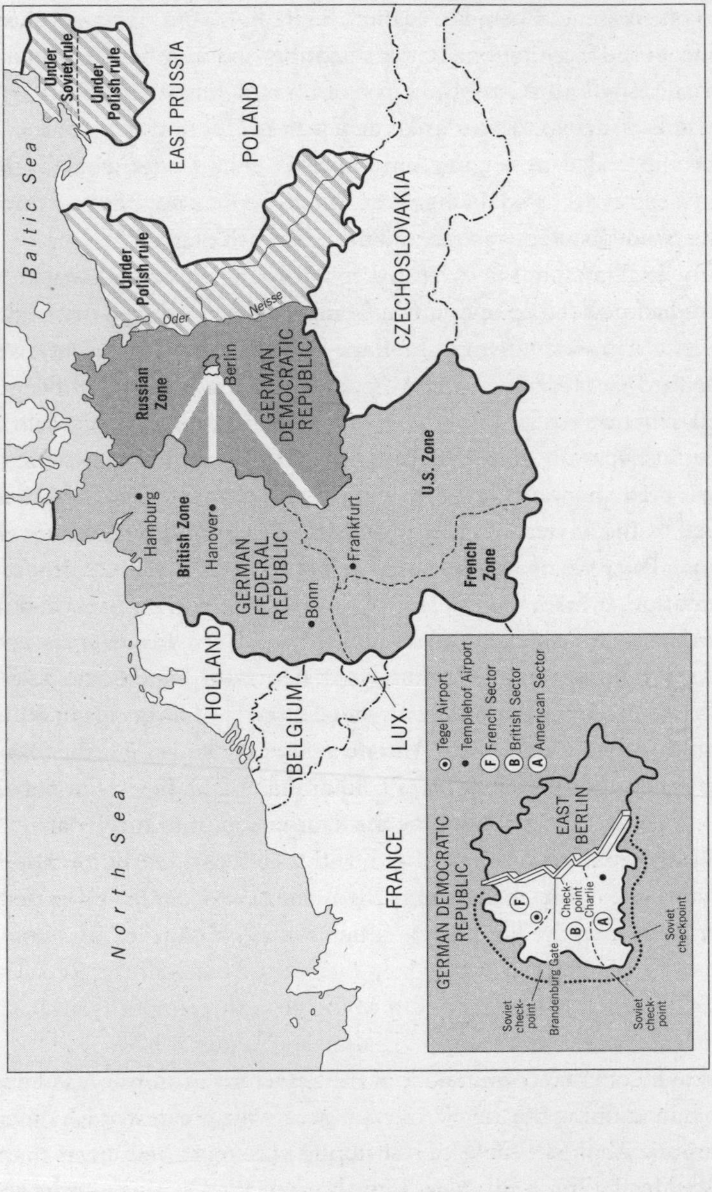

of these two sets of events that precipitated the Japanese surrender on 14 August.

Zhukov was not involved in the Manchurian operation but he must have taken some satisfaction from the Red Army's stunning success and from the fact that one of the starting positions of the Soviet invasion was Khalkhin-Gol – the scene of his triumph in August 1939.[43]

Zhukov was appointed to his new post in Germany on 30 May. On 9 June he held a press conference in the German capital at which he replied to verbal as well as written questions from Soviet and foreign correspondents. He was particularly expansive about the battle for Berlin, emphasising the careful preparation of the Soviet assault and the audacity of the opening night bombardment designed to catch the Germans unawares. Asked about the comparison between the battles of Berlin and Moscow, Zhukov pointed out that at Moscow the Soviets had launched a major counter-offensive as well as successfully defended the city. Asked about Khalkhin-Gol and the comparison between German and Japanese soldiers, Zhukov tactfully replied that the Germans were no longer enemies but that he thought they were technically superior to the Japanese he had fought in 1939. It was an impressive performance by Zhukov, notable for the absence of the usual panegyric to Stalin.[44]

Among those in attendance was Alexander Werth, the *Sunday Times* correspondent in Moscow during the war. 'With Zhukov, one felt in the presence of a very great man', remembered Werth. 'But his manner was simple, and full of bonhomie.' Werth also noted that while Zhukov paid tribute to Stalin's military leadership he also 'had a very high opinion of himself and, with a curious mixture of modesty and almost boyish boastfulness, he tended to take credit for practically *all* the decisive victories the Red Army had won'.[45]

VICTORY PARADES

Zhukov's conceit was understandable given the immense role he had played in winning the Soviet-German war – the greatest clash of arms in history. Zhukov's sense of self-importance must have been further boosted by Stalin's decision to allow him to take the salute at the great Victory Parade in Red Square.

In the middle of June Zhukov returned to Moscow to receive his third award of Hero of the Soviet Union. Around 18 or 19 June Stalin summoned him to his dacha and asked him if he remembered how to ride a horse.[46] When Zhukov answered in the affirmative Stalin informed him that he would take the salute while Rokossovsky would command the parade. Zhukov demurred, suggesting that the supreme commander should take the salute himself but Stalin said he was too old to review parades.[47] The next day Zhukov went to the Central Airfield in Moscow where training for the parade was taking place. There he met Stalin's son Vasily, an air force officer, who told him his father had wanted to take the salute himself but had fallen off the horse during a practice – the same horse that Zhukov was to ride. This story appeared in the post-Soviet edition of Zhukov's memoirs and it has to be said that Vasily – who had drink and discipline problems and did not get on well with his father – was not the most reliable witness. Moreover, there is no evidence that Stalin had ever learned to ride.[48]

The horse Zhukov rode at the parade was a magnificent white Arabian called Tspeki recommended by Marshal Budenny, Zhukov's old cavalry boss from the 1930s. The parade took place on 24 June. As the Kremlin clock struck 10.00 A.M. Zhukov and his escort rode into Red Square. Awaiting them were columns of combined regiments representing all the Fronts and branches of the Soviet armed forces. At the head of each column were many of the generals and marshals with whom Zhukov had served during the war, including Vasilevsky, Konev, Meretskov, Tolbukhin, Bagramyan and Yeremenko. The Victory Parade was a supreme moment of triumph for Zhukov but the glory was shared by the rest of the members of the Soviet High Command, not least Stalin their commander-in-chief. The Soviet dictator watched the proceedings from the rostrum above Lenin's mausoleum and received the laurels of the 200 captured Nazi banners piled against the Kremlin wall by the parading troops.

After the parade a reception was held in the Kremlin for 2,500 generals and officers. Stalin's toast at the reception may have surprised the assembled elite of the Soviet armed forces. When he raised his glass it was not to his generals but to the millions of 'little people', the cogs in the great state machine, upon whom he and his marshals had depended to win the war. Four days later Stalin was proclaimed Generalissimo – the superlative general. The message to Zhukov and the High Command could not be clearer: they could bask in the glory of victory, but Stalin was still the boss.

Because the Moscow Victory Parade was such a success the Soviets decided to hold a similar event in Berlin. The parade took place on 7 September and once again Zhukov took the salute. Zhukov did not impress the senior American general present, George Patton, not unknown to be irascible himself. 'He was in full-dress uniform much like comic opera and covered with medals', he wrote to his wife. 'He is short, rather fat, and has a prehensile chin like an ape but good, blue eyes.' It was a pity Patton, a former cavalryman, did not see Zhukov ride at the Victory Parade in Moscow. He might have been more impressed.[49]

Another assignment for Zhukov was hosting the Potsdam summit of Stalin, Churchill, and Harry Truman, the new president of the United States, succeeding Roosevelt, who had died in office in April 1945. In summer 1945 hopes were still high that the wartime Grand Alliance of Britain, the Soviet Union, and the United States would continue to collaborate and construct a peaceful and prosperous post-war order. The conference venue was the Cecilienhof Palace, one of the few large buildings left intact in the Greater Berlin area. Stalin arrived in Berlin by train on 16 July 1945. Unlike Churchill and Truman he evinced no interest in touring the ruins of the city and ordered Zhukov to receive him without ceremony. But Stalin was in a good mood, Zhukov recalled, as well he might be on the eve of a summit in the former capital of Hitler's Germany with the leaders of the two other great victor states of the Second World War.

Zhukov was not a delegate to the conference. Stalin's main military advisor at Potsdam was Antonov, the new chief of the General Staff, and the military discussions concerned the coming Soviet attack on Japanese forces in Manchuria, an operation in which Zhukov was not involved. But Zhukov did attend several sessions of the conference. After one session Truman told Stalin that America had successfully tested the atomic bomb and intended to drop it on Japan. Stalin did not react to the news but he talked about it afterward with Zhukov and Molotov and gave orders to speed up the development of the

Soviet atomic bomb. Another incident recorded in Zhukov's memoirs happened during a reception at which he spent a long time talking to Churchill about various battles. When the toasts began Churchill unexpectedly toasted Zhukov. In his replying toast Zhukov mistakenly addressed Churchill as 'comrade' but quickly recovered by proposing a toast to all his allied 'comrades-in-arms'. The next day, however, Stalin ribbed Zhukov about his new 'comrade'.[50]

The main political discussion at Potsdam concerned the future of Germany. It was agreed the country would be demilitarised, denazified, and democratised and forced to pay reparations for war damages (mostly to the Soviet Union). When the time was right the Allied occupation zones would be unified and a central German government established to preside over a peaceful and democratic state. That, at least, was the theory. In practice the Soviet and western zones of occupation became the basis for the political and economic division of Germany when the Grand Alliance fractured in 1947–1948 and the Cold War began.

ZHUKOV AND EISENHOWER

As head of the Soviet military administration in Germany, Zhukov presided over what soon became a vast machinery of occupation. Although on paper he exercised complete civil and military control in the Soviet zone, his powers were more limited than those of his counterparts in the western zones. The Foreign Ministry and Communist Party ran political affairs in the Soviet zone, while teams of Soviet reparations officials roamed at will, stripping it of industrial resources and shipping them back to the USSR. Soviet security police controlled the massive operation to repatriate to the USSR the millions of Soviet POWs and slave labourers liberated from German concentration camps. Even in the military sphere Zhukov's control was indirect, exercised through five provincial military governors.[51]

As Soviet representative on the Allied Control Council Zhukov had a highly visible role in the occupation regime. Zhukov's first meeting with the western representatives on the ACC came on 5 June 1945, when they visited him in Berlin to co-sign a declaration on the assumption by the occupying powers of supreme authority in Germany.[52] The western representatives wanted the ACC to start functioning immediately but Zhukov insisted British and American troops first withdraw from the Soviet zone of occupation. This problem arose because during the course of military operations the agreed Allied demarcation lines in Germany had been contravened. The Soviets, intent on exercising power in their zone without fear of interference by western troops, wanted the British and Americans out. Zhukov's delaying tactic did not please General Eisenhower, the American representative on the ACC, who was keen to get on with business. When the American went to leave the banquet arranged by the Soviets for their guests, Zhukov exclaimed jovially, 'I shall arrest you and make you stay!' But Eisenhower stayed only for the first toasts.[53] Apart from this incident Zhukov and Eisenhower got on well and formed a good working relationship. Indeed, during their first meeting Eisenhower bestowed on Zhukov the award of Chief Commander of the Legion of Merit. When Zhukov visited Eisenhower's HQ in Frankfurt a few days later, he reciprocated by decorating his host with the Soviet Order of Victory.

In August 1945 Eisenhower (and his son John) visited Moscow accompanied by Zhukov, giving the two men an opportunity for prolonged conversation. There was much talk about the battle for Berlin, during which Eisenhower disavowed any previous intention to seize the German capital before the Soviets and blamed Churchill for any impressions to the contrary.[54] During this trip to Moscow Eisenhower observed 'Zhukov was patently a great favourite with Stalin. . . . The two spoke to each other in terms of intimacy and cordiality.'[55]

One of the events the two men attended was a physical culture parade in Red Square on 12 August. Eisenhower reviewed the parade from the rostrum above Lenin's mausoleum, Stalin standing on his left and Zhukov on his right. Stalin was impressed by Eisenhower, calling him a 'very great man' who was not 'coarse' like most military men. Reporting this statement to Eisenhower, John Deane, the head of the American military mission in Moscow, told him 'you evidently sold a bill of goods while you were here'.[56]

Stalin's invitation to Eisenhower to come to Moscow had been prompted by a prior invitation from Truman that Zhukov visit the United States. Forwarding the invitation on 2 August, U.S. ambassador Harriman emphasised the president's high regard for Zhukov and the warm feelings of the American people towards both him and the Red Army.[57] When the Soviets replied to this invitation on 17 September they suggested that Zhukov visit the United States at the beginning of October.[58] But this did not happen and in April 1946 the Americans had to renew their invitation. By this time Zhukov had been recalled from Berlin to Moscow to take up a new post as commander-in-chief of Soviet ground forces and had to decline the reissued invitation due to work.[59] But the real reason for Zhukov's failure to visit the United States may have been the significant deterioration of Soviet-western relations that occurred in early 1946. In March, for example, Churchill delivered his (to the Russians) notorious 'Iron Curtain' speech in Fulton, Missouri, which complained of the Soviet and communist take-over of a number of Central and East European countries and the exclusion of western influence from the region. The Soviets were able to erect such an Iron Curtain because of the Red Army's occupation of Bulgaria, Hungary, and Romania – states that had fought on the side of Germany during World War II – while in Czechoslovakia, Yugoslavia, and, to a lesser extent, Poland, the communists were very strong. From the Soviet point of view their control of Eastern Europe was necessary protection against a revival of Germany and the possibility of another war. Stalin reacted to Churchill's speech angrily, denouncing the former British prime minister (he had lost power in July 1945) as a warmonger and an inveterate anticommunist, pointing out that he had been one of the main organisers of the western anti-Bolshevik crusade during the Russian Civil War.

Zhukov served in occupied Germany for only a few months in 1945–1946, at a time when relative harmony prevailed in Soviet-western postwar relations. In his memoirs Eisenhower was complimentary about Zhukov. He disagreed with Zhukov's communist ideology but was respectful of his political conviction: 'there was no doubt in my mind that Marshal Zhukov was sincere. . . . His own adherence to the Communist doctrine seemed to come from inner conviction and not from any outward compulsion.' In relation to

Zhukov's abilities as a military commander, Eisenhower wrote that he 'had longer experience as a responsible leader in great battles than any other man of our time . . . it was clear that he was an accomplished soldier'.[60]

Zhukov's memoirs published twenty years later, after two decades of Cold War, depicted Eisenhower as a decent person but also as a representative of capitalist and imperialist interests who had failed to do what he could to avert the postwar breakup of the Grand Alliance. In the post-Soviet edition of Zhukov's memoirs, however, there appeared a much more balanced appraisal of Eisenhower. 'I liked his simplicity, informality and sense of humour', wrote Zhukov of his first impression of Eisenhower. 'It seemed to me that he understood the great sacrifices of the Soviet people.'[61]

Eisenhower was recalled to the United States at the end of 1945 and Zhukov's last meeting with him in Berlin took place on November 7. Zhukov readily agreed when Eisenhower asked if he could report to Washington that the work of the Allied Control Council had been carried on in a friendly spirit, without serious disagreements, and in terms of a common language.[62]

THE RED ARMY AND RAPE

After the Potsdam Conference, Zhukov briefed key officials in the Soviet Military Administration in Germany in a speech setting out policy priorities: the extraction of Soviet reparations from Germany; the elimination of fascist ideology from every sphere of German life and support for the anti-Nazi parties in Germany; and winning the respect of the German people as the basis for future Soviet-German relations. To achieve this latter goal it was necessary to abandon the old enmities, something that certain elements among the Soviet occupation forces did not understand, said Zhukov, since they continued to engage in illegal acts and in robbery and violence directed against the local population. During the war such things had gone on unnoticed because people were hiding from the fighting but now 'when the war was over, when the people were beginning to forget about the war, it was intolerable to go to the Germans and pick their pockets'.

Unfortunately, because of the existence of 'criminal elements' among the Soviet occupation forces, this was still happening and was undermining efforts to build friendship with the German people:

> In the early days [of the occupation], when the Germans saw that we weren't going to shoot them and gave them bread, they took this to heart. [Nazi] propaganda said that we would destroy, slaughter, rob and shoot the Germans. Our conduct belied this. The Germans saw this and were grateful. Now the Germans are more demanding. Every illegal act, every cruelty, every occurrence of lawlessness, has a bad effect on mutual relations. I do not consider this to be a complicated matter and I personally demand of every official of the Soviet Military Administration, of every soldier, of every member of our staff, that it must cease. If it is necessary to take extreme measures, if we have to shoot people, we will do it; we will not refrain from shooting the criminal elements.[63]

The problem to which Zhukov alluded was not one he liked to discuss in public. When the Red Army invaded Germany a reign of terror descended on the civilian population. Though exaggerated by Nazi propaganda, there was widespread looting, shooting, and, above all, rape. Zhukov's assertions to the contrary notwithstanding, these acts were not confined to a tiny criminal minority and the lawlessness continued during the Soviet occupation of Germany.

To what extent were Zhukov and the High Command responsible for this lack of control over Soviet troops? Certainly, Soviet soldiers were left in no doubt that no quarter was to be given when they invaded Germany. On the road to Berlin the Red Army was fed a steady diet of anti-German hate propaganda. On the eve of the Vistula-Oder operation, for example, Zhukov issued an order to the 1st Belorussian Front: 'Woe to the land of the murderers. We will get our terrible revenge for everything.' On the other hand, Red Army soldiers needed little or no encouragement to wreak their own vengeance. They were witnesses to the murderous occupation policies of the Germans that had resulted in the death of millions of Soviet citizens. The troops' hostility to the Germans was reinforced by the string of Nazi extermination camps they liberated as they swept through Poland: Auschwitz, Belzec, Chelmno, Sobibor, Treblinka. Among the surviving inmates were not just Jews – the main victims of the Nazi Holocaust – but Soviet POWs. During the war the Germans captured six million Soviet soldiers, half of whom died in captivity from starvation, disease, neglect, and brutality. In such circumstances retaliatory atrocities were all but inevitable. But the scale of the violence and disorder was obscenely disproportionate, not least the mass rape of German women. Estimates of the number of German women raped by Soviet soldiers ranges from the tens of thousands to the low millions, with the true figure probably somewhere in between. A large number of these rapes took place in the Greater Berlin area after the city's capture by the Red Army.[64] Another city that suffered greatly was Vienna, where there were perhaps 70,000–100,000 rapes. In the case of the Austrians there was no official incitement to hatred since their country was considered a victim of the Nazi takeover in 1938. However, many Austrians had fought with the Germans on the Russian front, especially in Ukraine, and it was Konev's 1st Ukrainian Front – which included many Ukrainians in its ranks – that 'liberated' Vienna.

The Red Army was not the only Allied army to commit atrocities against German civilians either during the war or during the occupation. American, British, Canadian, and French soldiers were also guilty, although the scale of their rape and pillage was much less than that of the Soviets. When stories about Red Army atrocities began to appear in the western press Soviet propagandists responded by pointing to the 'indiscipline' of the western Allied armies.[65]

There is no evidence that Zhukov sanctioned or condoned criminality by Red Army troops. Indeed, he took steps to combat it, not only in words but also in action. On 30 June 1945, he issued an order noting complaints about robbery and rape by 'individuals wearing Red Army uniforms' and directed his soldiers to remain on army premises unless they were engaged in official business. To stop Soviet soldiers from liaising with German women he ordered that anyone seen entering or leaving a private house would be arrested. Zhukov also threatened to punish officers incapable of maintaining discipline over their men. On the other hand, the Soviets' public insistence that the Red Army was a model of discipline and that there was no problem apart from the activities of a tiny criminal minority was part of the problem and helps to explain the persistence of rape during the occupation. There was also a hint of frivolity and indulgence in Zhukov's attitude towards the rape problem. 'Soldiers, make sure that in looking at the hemlines of German girls', Zhukov reportedly said, 'you don't look past the reasons the homeland sent you here.'[66] Stalin was even more explicit in the leeway he was prepared to allow his troops when it came to women. 'Imagine', he told a delegation of Yugoslav communists in April 1945, 'a man who has fought from Stalingrad to Belgrade – over thousands of kilometres of his own devastated land, across the dead bodies of his comrades and dearest ones. How can such a man react normally? And what is so awful in his having fun with a woman, after such horrors.'[67] Stalin's comments about 'fun' could only contribute to a blinkered view of sexual violence against women.

Zhukov himself was not without sin when it came to pillage. While in Germany he amassed a hoard of trophies, including 70 pieces of gold jewellery, 740 items of silverware, 50 rugs, 60 pictures, 3,700 metres of silk and 320 furs. Zhukov later claimed that he bought these items or they were gifts but their acquisition sat ill with his supposed socialist principles and with his self-righteous insistence, both at the time and in his memoirs, that the Red Army was a model of good discipline in both the invasion and occupation of Germany.

In February 1946 elections were held to the Supreme Soviet, the USSR's parliament. Zhukov was a candidate in one of a number of special constituencies created to facilitate the participation of voters serving in the armed forces in Germany and elsewhere. As was usual in the Soviet system, only Communist Party–backed candidates were allowed to stand for office and Zhukov's election was a foregone conclusion. But there seems to have been genuine enthusiasm for his candidacy in the immediate afterglow of victory, as there was for Stalin and other Soviet leaders, and *Pravda* published a laudatory account of an election meeting that Zhukov addressed.[68]

Shortly after the election Zhukov was recalled to Moscow to become commander-in-chief of Soviet ground forces. His appointment on 22 March was one of a number of high-level military appointments. Vasilevsky returned as chief of the General Staff and Nikolai

Bulganin, who had served as Zhukov's political commissar during the war, was made Stalin's deputy in the Ministry of the Armed Forces (the new name of the People's Commissariat of Defence).[69] Within three months of his return to Moscow, however, Zhukov had been sacked and banished to the command of a provincial military district. This turn of events was extraordinary enough, but it proved merely the opening act in the drama of Zhukov's post-war political career.

11.

EXILED TO THE PROVINCES:

DISGRACE AND REHABILITATION,
1946–1954

———

WHEN ZHUKOV RETURNED TO MOSCOW FROM BERLIN IN APRIL 1946 HE HAD no idea his fortunes were about to take a marked turn for the worse. As he reviewed the May Day Parade in Red Square the hero of the Great Patriotic War seemed set for a prolonged and glorious tenure as Stalin's right-hand military man. Just a month later Zhukov was arraigned before the Higher Military Council and accused of egoism and disrespect for his peers.

Chaired by Stalin himself, the meeting, held on 1 June, was attended by top party leaders Lavrenty Beria, Nikolai Bulganin, Georgy Malenkov and Vyacheslav Molotov as well as an array of generals and marshals, including Semyon Budenny, Filipp Golikov, Leonid Govorov, Ivan Konev, Konstantin Rokossovsky, Pavel Rybalko, Sergey Shtemenko, Vasily Sokolovsky, Alexander Vasilevsky and Nikolai Voronov. Konev and Sokolovsky later claimed to have come to Zhukov's defence at the meeting and Zhukov himself recalled that the majority of the military leaders supported him.[1] It is difficult to imagine, however, that their opposition to Stalin was any more than perfunctory. We do not have the stenographic record of this session of the Higher Military Council but the likely scenario is that after a reading of the indictment there would have been a few speeches in support of the charges followed by a mea culpa from Zhukov. Those present may have had some kind words about Zhukov's loyalty and record of service, but that is all. Any stronger protest would likely have resulted in them sharing Zhukov's fate. What we know for certain is that the meeting resolved to remove Zhukov as commander-in-chief of the ground forces and transfer him to the command of a military district, a resolution implemented by the Council of Ministers on 3 June. The next day Zhukov handed over command to his deputy, Konev.[2]

DENOUNCED BY NOVIKOV

The events leading to Zhukov's fall from grace began in March 1946 with the removal of Marshal A. A. Novikov as head of the Soviet Air Force. Novikov was a victim of the so-called Aviators Affair – a purge of the Soviet aircraft industry following accusations that during the war the fighter planes produced had been of poor quality. Zhukov was a member of the commission charged with investigating the affair, although he does not appear to have taken an active part in its proceedings.

Novikov was arrested in April and interrogated by Soviet security officers. On 30 April the head of the Ministry of State Security (in Russian: Ministerstva Gosudarstvennyi Bezopastnosti – MGB), Viktor Abakumov, sent Stalin a statement from Novikov denouncing Zhukov as 'an exceptionally power-loving and self-obsessed person, who loves glory, demands respect, expects submissiveness and cannot bear dissent'. Novikov then recounted how Zhukov was only interested in the importance of his own role during the war and discounted the contribution of others. Most damagingly Novikov detailed what he claimed was Zhukov's disrespectful attitude towards Stalin as the supreme commander.[3]

When Novikov was released from prison and rehabilitated after Stalin's death he claimed his attack on Zhukov was prompted by interrogation pressure and torture. This is very likely true, but it may be that Novikov was encouraged to point the finger at Zhukov because he saw Zhukov's membership of the investigation commission as instrumental in his downfall. In any event, Stalin chose to accept Novikov's claims at face value and on 9 June he issued a decree to the higher ranks of the military repeating the accusations and announcing Zhukov's posting to the Odessa Military District in the Crimea. Zhukov was deemed guilty of 'unworthy and harmful conduct' in his relations with the Supreme Command. As a man of overweening personal ambition, said the decree, Zhukov had falsely claimed credit for all the big operational successes during the Great Patriotic War and had gathered around himself a group to whom he had expressed criticisms and disagreements with the government. One of the successes that Zhukov took credit for was the Berlin operation. But, said the decree, Berlin would not have been taken in such a short time had it not been for the support of Konev's and Rokossovsky's armies. Zhukov, the decree noted, had recognised that his 'serious mistakes' made it impossible for him to continue as commander-in-chief of the ground forces.[4]

Why did Stalin decide to use Novikov's accusations to remove Zhukov from a post to which he had so recently appointed him? One possibility is that Stalin had his own sources of information on Zhukov that confirmed some of Novikov's claims. At this time it was common for Soviet military and political leaders to be kept under close security surveillance, including bugging of their apartments and dachas.[5] While it is hard to believe that Zhukov would have disparaged Stalin even in private, it is not difficult to imagine him making exaggerated claims of credit for wartime victories. Demoting Zhukov might seem an extreme response relative to the sin of boastfulness – a common trait of generals, after all – but Stalin was in a brittle mood after the war. An aging man of nearly seventy by then, the war had taken its physical and emotional toll on the dictator. He was tetchy and disposed to upbraid or censure the members of his inner circle for even minor perceived transgressions. Zhukov was only one of many to suffer such a fate in the 1940s. In 1949, for example, Stalin removed Molotov from the post of foreign minister because he refused to vote for the expulsion of his own wife (who was Jewish and accused of association with Zionist supporters of Israel) from the Communist Party.[6] Stalin was also determined to bring the Soviet military to heel and to prevent the overlauding of its war record. Stalin's demotion of Zhukov showed the Red Army he was still the boss and warned other generals that he would not tolerate any sign of disloyalty.[7]

When asked in the 1960s about his demotion Zhukov blamed jealousy but not so much on the part of Stalin as those around the dictator, especially Beria.[8] Another theory of Zhukov's was that Bulganin had turned Stalin against him. Bulganin was Stalin's political deputy within the Defence Ministry and, indeed, was to succeed Stalin as armed forces minister in 1947. In the post-Soviet edition of Zhukov's memoirs a passage describes how he clashed with Bulganin shortly after his return to Moscow in 1946 about the chain of command and relations between the military and Stalin. Bulganin wanted the chain of command to run through him to Stalin whereas Zhukov wanted direct access to the Soviet leader. Unfortunately for Zhukov, when the dispute was reported to Stalin the dictator sided with Bulganin. In another unpublished writing Zhukov described how he clashed with Bulganin over command of demobilised troops who had been placed on the reserve list.[9]

Zhukov left for Odessa in mid-June intent on behaving normally. 'I firmly resolved to remain myself', he told Konstantin Simonov. 'I understood that they were waiting for me to give up and expecting that I would not last a day as a district commander. I could not permit this to happen. Of course, fame is fame. At the same time it is a double-edged sword and sometimes cuts against you. After this blow I did everything to remain as I had been. In this I saw my inner salvation.'[10] One outer sign of normality was that Zhukov took his family on their first postwar holiday in August – to the popular Soviet resort of Sochi on the opposite side of the Black Sea from Odessa. Marshal Rokossovsky was among his fellow holidaymakers.[11] But Zhukov's troubles were far from over. On 23 August Bulganin reported to Stalin that a train with seven wagons containing eighty-five cartons of German-made furniture had been stopped by customs on the Soviet-Polish border. The furniture was bound for Zhukov in Odessa. The train was allowed to continue its journey but customs officials in Odessa were instructed that the cargo was not to be given any privileged treatment.[12]

In February 1947 Zhukov was excluded from candidate (i.e., non-voting) membership of the party Central Committee on grounds that he had an antiparty attitude. On 21 February Zhukov wrote to Stalin:

> My exclusion as a candidate member of the party central committee hurt me deeply. I am not a careerist and I had no problem with my transfer from Commander of the ground

forces. For nine months I have worked diligently as the commander of a military district even though my transfer was based on a statement that was slanderous. I would like to give you my word that all the mistakes I have committed will be rectified. For nine months I have not received a single reproof that the district is not in good order. I think that I am working well now but it seems that the slander begun against me continues. I ask you, comrade Stalin, to hear me out and I will convince you that you are being deceived by the malicious people slandering me.

On 27 February Zhukov wrote to Stalin again, admitting that during the war he had made mistakes, including claiming too much credit for successes and failing to acknowledge fully the role of the supreme commander. But he remained adamant that Novikov's accusation that he was hostile towards the government was slanderous: 'Comrade Stalin, you know that without regard for my own life, without hesitation in the most dangerous situations, I always tried as much as I could to fulfill your instructions.'

By Soviet standards Zhukov's pleas were quite dignified. It was not uncommon for people who found themselves in Zhukov's position to go to much greater lengths to ingratiate themselves with Stalin, usually by praising the Great Leader's genius. Both letters were passed to Stalin by Bulganin but the dictator did not reply and never met Zhukov again.[13] Instead the campaign against Zhukov continued. In June 1947 he was censured for awarding a military medal to the singer Lidiya Andreevna Ruslanova when she visited Berlin in August 1945. (After one of her performances Zhukov accompanied her on the accordion. He did not play badly 'for a marshal', the singer later recalled.) Also censured was one of Zhukov's long-serving political officers, General K. F. Telegin, who had signed the award decree. While Zhukov's punishment was a reprimand, Telegin was dismissed from the army and reduced from full membership of the party to candidate membership. In 1948 Telegin, Ruslanova, and her husband, General V. V. Krukov, were arrested and imprisoned because of their connections with Zhukov.[14] 'In 1947 I feared arrest every day', recalled Zhukov, 'and I had a bag ready with my underwear in it.'[15]

The next development was even more ominous: an investigation into the war booty that Zhukov had extracted while in command of the Soviet zone of occupation in Germany. In January 1948 Stalin authorised covert searches of Zhukov's Moscow flat and country dacha. On 10 January Abakumov, head of state security, reported to Stalin on the extensive haul of gold, jewellery, silverware, silk, expensive books, furs, and foreign furniture that his officers had found. Looking around the dacha, Abakumov wrote to Stalin, it was difficult to tell if it was located in Moscow or in Germany.[16]

Among the haul was a collection of twenty handmade hunting weapons, including shotguns made by the elite British company Holland & Holland.

The pressure on Zhukov increased with the arrest of a number of officers who had served with him in Germany, among them Colonel A. S. Semochkin, who had served as Zhukov's adjutant from 1940 to 1946. Semochkin's statement was sent to Zhukov for comment. On 12 January 1948, Zhukov replied to A. A. Zhdanov, Stalin's ideology chief, who had been appointed chair of a commission investigating Zhukov's 'trophy items'. His defence was that he had either bought the items with his own money or they had been given to him as gifts. He denied Semochkin's allegation that he received extra money from official funds to pay for his purchases. He also pointed out that many of the furnishings in his dacha had been supplied by the Ministry of State Security! However, he did express regret for purchasing so many items for himself and his family and said that some of the goods should be given to the state. Zhukov concluded with a plea to remain a member of the party so that he could continue the correction of his mistakes and strive to be a good communist.[17]

The Zhdanov commission was not impressed by Zhukov's plea or by his explanations, characterising them as insincere and evasive. On 20 January the Politburo – the executive body of the Central Committee – decreed that Zhukov would be allowed to remain in the party but that all the misappropriated items must be handed over to the state. It was also resolved to demote him to the command of a less important military district. Hence Zhukov's transfer on 4 February 1948, to the command of the Urals Military District based in Sverdlovsk.[18]

Zhukov blamed Abakumov and Beria for this further punishment and not Stalin. Indeed, he thought the Soviet dictator had protected him from arrest.[19] After Stalin's death Abakumov was tried and executed for abuse of power and became a convenient scapegoat for many of the purges of the late Stalin era, including that of Zhukov. But Abakumov could only have moved against someone of Zhukov's standing with Stalin's blessing and probably only at his prompting. It was the Soviet dictator who was responsible for the purge of Zhukov and it was Stalin who determined the level of punishment. The punishment itself – removal of material perks and banishment to the provinces – was relatively mild. Probably the worst indignity was being written out of the history of the Great Patriotic War. Paintings of the Victory Parade omitted him from the picture. A 1948 documentary film about the battle of Moscow barely mentioned Zhukov. When General Rybalko died in August 1948 Zhukov's name was omitted from the death announcement in *Pravda* that listed all other Soviet marshals.[20] In a 1949 poster tableau depicting Stalin and his top generals plotting and planning the great counter-offensive at Stalingrad, Zhukov was nowhere to be seen.

Many of those caught up in the 'Zhukov affair' suffered far worse fates. Ruslanova, Telegin, Semochkin and others were imprisoned. The worst case concerned General Gordov (who had commanded the Stalingrad Front in 1942) and General Rybalchenko, his chief of staff in the Volga Military District. They were recorded by the MGB exchanging disloyal remarks about Stalin's treatment of Zhukov. Both were arrested and shot.[21]

All the victims of the Zhukov affair were rehabilitated after Stalin's death, posthumously in the case of Gordov and Rybalchenko. Zhukov himself was active in securing a pardon for Krukov.[22] Zhukov's own rehabilitation began while Stalin was still alive, a process aided perhaps by the appointment of Vasilevsky as armed forces minister in 1949 in place of Bulganin. The personal ties between the two men were cemented by the marriage of Zhukov's daughter Era to Vasilevsky's son Yuri in 1948. In October 1949 *Pravda* carried a funeral notice of the death of Marshal F. I. Tolbukhin and Zhukov was listed among the signatories.[23] In 1950 Zhukov, along with a number of other senior officers, was re-elected to the Supreme Soviet of the USSR, in his case as a deputy for Sverdlovsk. In 1951 he was a member of a government delegation to Warsaw where he met Rokossovsky, now Poland's defence minister. During the trip Zhukov delivered a speech on Polish-Soviet relations that was published in *Pravda*. In 1952 the second edition of the official *Great Soviet Encyclopedia* carried a short but favourable entry on Zhukov, stressing his importance in the realisation of Stalin's military plans during the war.[24]

In October 1952 Zhukov was a delegate to the 19th Party Congress – the first such congress since the end of the war – and he was restored to candidate membership of the Central Committee. The writer and journalist Konstantin Simonov met Zhukov at the congress and found him in good spirits, albeit a little surprised at his re-election to the Central Committee. Zhukov also seemed pleased that Simonov's novel about Khalkhin-Gol had been published. The novel did not name Zhukov directly but it provided a flattering portrait of the fictional commander in charge of the operation.[25]

Simonov was also elected to the Central Committee at the 1952 congress. He had first met Zhukov at Khalkhin-Gol in 1939 and was destined to write a series of biographical sketches that cemented Zhukov's reputation as a heroic but human figure of Soviet history. A playwright, novelist, poet, and war correspondent, Simonov was almost as famous as Zhukov. In February 1942 *Pravda* published his poem 'Wait for Me', a tragic lament that captured the feelings of a whole generation of Soviet people and is still immensely popular in Russia today:

> *Wait for me, and I'll return, only wait very hard.*
> *Wait, when you are filled with sorrow as you watch*
>   *the yellow rain;*
> *Wait, when the winds sweep the snowdrifts,*
> *Wait in the sweltering heat.*
> *Wait when others have stopped waiting . . .*
> *Wait, for I'll return, defying every death.*
> *And let those who did not wait say I was lucky;*
> *They will never understand that in the midst of death,*
> *You, with your waiting, saved me . . .*

Another sign of Stalin's softening attitude towards Zhukov in the early 1950s was the dictator's directive that Emmanuil Kazakevich's novel about the Vistula-Oder operation should mention Zhukov by name rather than refer to an anonymous 'Front Commander'. 'Zhukov has his shortcomings and we have criticised him for them', Stalin reportedly said. 'But Zhukov did a good job at Berlin, at any event, not a bad job.'[26] Amazingly, Zhukov himself believed that had Stalin lived longer he would have rehabilitated him fully and even appointed him minister of defence.[27]

The late 1940s and early 1950s was a complicated period in Zhukov's personal as well as his political life. When Zhukov was sent to Odessa in 1946 his wife, Alexandra, went with him (their two daughters stayed in Moscow and visited during the holidays), but so did his wartime lover, Lida Zakharova, although he kept the two women apart. Lida followed Zhukov to Sverdlovsk, too, but she returned to Moscow when Zhukov met another woman he fell in love with.[28]

In summer 1950 Zhukov was hospitalised in Sverdlovsk because of heart trouble (he had already had one heart attack). The attending physician was Dr. Galina Semonova. Zhukov was soon drawn to the young woman. 'What especially attracted me to her', recalled Zhukov, 'were her big, beautiful warm eyes, her shapely figure and her shy modesty. The more I saw her the more I liked her. . . . In 1951–1952 Galina and I became closer and closer. Even then I could not think of life without her.'[29] At the beginning of 1953 Galina went to Moscow for a medical course. She was soon joined there by Zhukov, who had been recalled to the Soviet capital following Stalin's death in March. The dramatic political events in which he soon became involved did nothing to dampen his ardour for Galina. A flavour of their relationship is captured in a letter he wrote to her in August 1953, while she was on holiday at a sanatorium and he was preparing to take part in a military exercise simulating a nuclear attack:

How are you finding the sea, the southern sun and the mountains? I would like to be there in their place, to be near you my darling Galina. After you left Moscow I missed you very much. Every day I recall to memory those last days, your nervousness, and our conversations. . . .

Have you started your course of treatment? Are you sticking to the regime that we agreed many times? Don't forget, darling, that you must be good and rest. It is necessary to sleep well and long, to try to eat and to keep going for longer, but no later than 22.00. Don't forget, darling, that you have given me your word that you will gain at least 5 kilos.

Tomorrow I will be in Prague by 11.00. It seems that I will be detained there for several hours and then I will go to Karlsbad. I don't know what it will be like there but I am going in a depressed mood. . . .

I wish you darling all the best. I would very much like to embrace you hard, but you are not here. I send you my kisses with this letter. Your G.[30]

This was typical of the letters Zhukov wrote to Galina in the 1950s when he was away from Moscow. It is clear that Zhukov had switched his romantic allegiance to Galina, although he did not move in with her until the late 1950s.[31] Indeed, Alexandra only found out about the affair in 1957 after the birth of Galina and Zhukov's daughter, Maria.

After the war Zhukov also resumed contact with his illegitimate daughter, Margarita, who visited him in both Odessa and Sverdlovsk. In 1948 Margarita entered Moscow State University to study law. Era was also at the university and in the same faculty (she later became a specialist in international law). In the early 1950s the paths of the two half-sisters crossed by accident. Unfortunately, when Alexandra found out she insisted that Era cease contact with Margarita and that Zhukov, as a sign of good faith, should renew the registration of their marriage, the original certificate having been lost in the 1920s.[32]

These events were the first in a series of complications in Zhukov's personal life that continued until the mid-1960s when he finally divorced Alexandra.

THE DEATH OF STALIN AND THE ARREST OF BERIA

When Zhukov wrote his memoirs he ended his narrative with his return to Moscow from Berlin in April 1946. There is, however, an unpublished coda in which he related some of his experiences after

Stalin's death that takes the story up to his 1957 dismissal by Khrushchev.[33] According to this memoir on 4 March 1953, Zhukov received an urgent message in Sverdlovsk to telephone Bulganin, who told him to fly to Moscow the next day. When he arrived Bulganin whisked him off to a high-level meeting of party leaders, where he learned that Stalin was gravely ill; indeed the dictator died later that day. At this meeting a number of personnel changes were agreed, including Bulganin's appointment as war minister, with Zhukov and Vasilevsky (the incumbent minister) to serve as his deputies. Other appointments included Georgy Malenkov, who was named chairman of the council of ministers (i.e., prime minister), and Vyacheslav Molotov, who was reappointed foreign minister, a post he had previously held from 1939 to 1949. The meeting was chaired by Khrushchev, thus signalling his pre-eminence as the most important party leader apart from the dying Stalin. Zhukov was surprised by his new appointment since it was well known he did not have a great deal of respect for Bulganin. Later, Zhukov heard that Bulganin had objected to his appointment but was overruled by the rest of the party leadership. Before starting his new job Zhukov had a frank conversation with Bulganin and told him: 'You have caused me much unpleasantness, exposing me to attack by Stalin . . . but if you sincerely want to work together on a friendly basis let's forget about past troubles.'[34]

Zhukov was prominent in the military guard of honour at the dictator's state funeral on 9 March, although it was Vasilevsky who spoke on behalf of the armed forces at the mass meeting in Red Square.[35] 'Notwithstanding that Stalin treated me badly after the Great Patriotic War,' recalled Zhukov, 'I was genuinely regretful. . . . After Stalin's funeral the Soviet people sincerely mourned his death and entrusted all their hopes to the party.'[36]

Zhukov's appointment as deputy minister was confirmed by the Supreme Soviet on 15 March. At this same meeting the name of the Ministry of War was changed to the Ministry of Defence and it was merged with the Ministry of the Navy. A further sign of Zhukov's rapid rehabilitation was *Pravda*'s publication in May 1953 of an article by him marking the eighth anniversary of the Soviet victory over Nazi Germany. The article was notable for two themes: the continued celebration of Stalin's war leadership and the Great Leader's military genius and the Soviet Union's commitment to peaceful coexistence with all states, including the United States.

Zhukov's first big chance to shine in the post-Stalin era came with his role in the arrest of security chief Lavrenty Beria. On the morning of 26 June 1953, Bulganin telephoned Zhukov and asked him to come to the Kremlin, where he met Malenkov, Khrushchev, Molotov and other party leaders. Malenkov told the gathering that Beria was plotting against the party leadership and had to be arrested. When Khrushchev interjected to ask if there were any doubts, Zhukov replied: 'what doubts could there be? The mission will be fulfilled.' When Khrushchev pointed out that Beria was a strong man who might be armed, Zhukov responded, 'I am not a specialist in arrest and I have never done this before but I will not hesitate.' Zhukov and several other senior military men who had been called to the Kremlin were then told to wait until they heard a prearranged signal from Malenkov to enter the room where the party leaders were meeting with Beria. When that signal came two hours later Zhukov went in, marched briskly up to Beria, told him that he was under arrest and grabbed both his arms. Zhukov and his team then hustled Beria out of the room and sent him on his way to prison.[37]

Beria was found guilty of terrorism and counter-revolutionary activities, sentenced to death, and shot. Sometime later, when he was asked what was the most important thing he had done in his life, Zhukov replied: 'the arrest of Beria'.[38]

The use of senior army officers to deal with Beria was a significant symbol of the new post-Stalin-era relationship forged between the communist regime and the Soviet military. After Stalin's death the status of the armed forces was raised, even glorified, particularly in relation to the victory in the Great Patriotic War. The military was allowed more autonomy in its professional sphere and a greater say in political decision-making, albeit in a context in which the party leadership remained firmly in control. Under Stalin the internal security forces had been the main coercive prop of the regime. Now more reliance was placed on the army as the state's guarantor of last resort. The choice of Zhukov to lead the arrest of Beria was no accident. He was a popular war hero and, with him on their side, party leaders could be sure not only of support from the armed forces but from a good part of the general population, too. In time Zhukov would come to personify both the more equitable power balance between the party and the army as well as the new political activism of the military – a phenomenon not seen in the Soviet Union since the 1920s and 1930s when Zhukov's heroes Frunze and Tukhachevsky were in charge of the armed forces.

Despite his role in the Beria affair, Zhukov did not move to centre stage in Soviet politics until he was appointed defence minister in 1955. In the meantime Bulganin made sure he was sidelined politically. What responsibilities Zhukov did have as deputy defence minister kept him out of the limelight and away from Moscow.

NUCLEAR TESTS

One of Zhukov's jobs was to oversee the development of the Soviet armed forces' nuclear-war-fighting capabilities.[39] The USSR had tested its first nuclear bomb in August 1949. In the 1950s there was a further series of tests, including the explosion in August 1953 of the first Soviet H-bomb. During this same period the Soviets found themselves threatened by the growing American arsenal of more than 1,000 atom bombs, including tactical and battlefield nuclear weapons sited in Europe. Since the Soviet nuclear arsenal at that time numbered only fifty bombs this meant the USSR had to rely for its defence on conventional as well as nuclear forces.

In autumn 1953 the Soviets conducted a field exercise in the Carpathian Military District in western Ukraine in which troops were subjected to a simulated battlefield nuclear attack. In charge of the district was Konev, who had been posted there in 1951 following stints as commander-in-chief of Soviet ground forces (1946–1950) and chief inspector of the Soviet army (1950–1951). Zhukov assisted in the preparation and conduct of the exercise. It was also decided to conduct a live exercise as well – to detonate a nuclear bomb with troops in the vicinity and to observe the effects on their performance. Preparations for this test, which took place at Totskoe in the southern Urals in September 1954, began in April with Zhukov in charge.

Ahead of the planned detonation the local population was evacuated and/or given instructions about protection from radioactive fallout. Troops were trained, equipped with protective clothing, and placed in specially constructed fortifications. Zhukov visited the test zone frequently. On one occasion he watched a tank attack passing through a supposedly contaminated zone. They moved so slowly that Zhukov stopped them, gathered the tank commanders together, and asked if any of them had taken part in the advance on Berlin. On being told that some had, he asked them to conduct a proper tank attack, which they then did. Zhukov was also concerned about troops being frightened by all the precautions being taken. 'You have frightened people too much with your safety measures,' he reportedly told the exercise commanders. 'Now you'll have to "unfrighten" them.'

The live bomb exercise began on 14 September when a medium-size atomic bomb was exploded 1,000 feet above the ground. Troops were entrenched as close as three or four miles from ground zero while Zhukov, Bulganin, and members of the High Command watched from about ten miles away. The shock wave blew off their hats, including Zhukov's.

Overall, the exercise was judged a great success and its lessons were distilled into a new set of Field Regulations, adopted in 1955, which assumed use of battlefield nuclear weapons as well as the strategic bombing of cities. On Zhukov's urging the transfer of nuclear weaponry from the industrial ministry responsible for building the bombs to the military and the Ministry of Defence took place around the same time.[40]

As deputy defence minister, Zhukov occupied an important but secondary place in the military and political hierarchy. There is no evidence he exercised any real influence over the government's defence policy and he did not feature prominently as a national public figure. Zhukov might well have languished in that middling position in the Soviet hierarchy until retirement were it not for the vagaries of Soviet internal politics. In January 1955 they took a twist that propelled him into the country's top leadership, indeed made him the kingmaker in the sharply contested post-Stalin succession struggle.

MINISTER OF DEFENCE:
TRIUMPH AND TRAVESTY, 1955–1957

———

IN JANUARY 1955 THE SOVIET PRIME MINISTER, GEORGY MALENKOV, WAS RE-
moved from office. Malenkov's place was taken by Nikolai Bulganin,
thus creating a vacancy at the Defence Ministry. The obvious candidate for the job was Zhukov. He had the status, the charisma, and the
requisite energy and determination. When the matter came up at the
Presidium (the new name for the Politburo), Zhukov modestly deferred to Vasilevsky, who had previously served as war minister. But
Vasilevsky insisted that Zhukov had more experience and was the outstanding figure among the armed forces.[1]

Behind both Malenkov's fall and Zhukov's elevation was the rise
of the new party leader, Nikita Khrushchev. While there were some
policy differences between Malenkov and Khrushchev the conflict
that led to Malenkov's dismissal was mainly personal. Since succeeding Stalin as party leader in March 1953 Khrushchev had become
more and more domineering. Malenkov was not the only Soviet leader
with whom Khrushchev fell out. Next was Foreign Minister Vyacheslav Molotov, sacked by Khrushchev in 1956, followed by Zhukov himself in October 1957.

Khrushchev was forceful, flamboyant, and volatile. He deferred to
no one (except Stalin when he was alive) and he didn't like sharing the
limelight.

Like many in the Soviet leadership Khrushchev was born into a
peasant family. He joined the Bolshevik Party in 1918 when he was

twenty-four and served as a political commissar in the Red Army during the Russian Civil War. In the 1920s and 1930s he worked his way up the party hierarchy, becoming head of the Moscow party organisation in 1934. In 1937 Stalin appointed him secretary of the Ukrainian Communist Party. One of Khrushchev's more unsavoury career episodes was his role in the infamous Katyn Massacre of March–April 1940. This was the name given to the execution by the Soviet authorities of some 20,000 Polish POWs deemed to be incorrigible enemies of the communist system. It was Khrushchev, together with Stalin's later disgraced security chief, Lavrenty Beria, who had proposed the further security measure of deporting the POWs' families to Kazakhstan for ten years – an operation completed by mid-April 1940.[2]

When Ukraine was invaded and occupied by the Germans in 1941 Khrushchev reverted to the role of political commissar, serving at Stalingrad in 1942–1943 and then in Ukraine. After the war Stalin brought Khrushchev back to Moscow and once again appointed him head of the capital's Communist Party, placing him in a prime position to succeed as party leader when the dictator died in March 1953. The post-Stalin leadership was supposedly collective – and for a couple of years it was. But Khrushchev's control of the party – the key institution of the Soviet state – made him first among equals with control over key appointments and policies.

One of the ways Khrushchev asserted his leadership was by promoting the de-Stalinisation of the Soviet system – a break with many of the policies and practices of the Stalin era. The most significant was ending the practice of mass repression and releasing millions of political prisoners from the Gulag – the Soviet system of labour camps. At the same time there was a thaw in Soviet cultural policy. Writers, musicians, and other artists were allowed more freedom of artistic expression and the country was open to increasing contact with the outside world. There was also a more relaxed atmosphere within the Communist Party, although discussion that challenged the leadership was still not allowed. In other words, Khrushchev presided over a much more benign form of authoritarianism than had prevailed in Stalin's time. There was repression but dissent within certain limits was permitted and outright opposition to the system was more likely to get you imprisoned than shot.[3]

Khrushchev first encountered Zhukov in 1940 when the latter commanded the Kiev Special Military District. Their paths crossed again at Stalingrad and when the two men worked closely together during the Ukrainian campaign of 1943–1944. In his memoirs, published in 1971, Khrushchev expressed a high opinion of Zhukov:

> He was a talented organiser and a strong leader. He was to prove his mettle in the war. I still have great respect for him as a commander, despite our subsequent parting of the ways. He didn't correctly understand his role as Minister of Defense, we were compelled to take action against him. . . . But even then I valued him highly as a soldier. . . . Nor did I disguise my admiration for Zhukov after the war when he fell out of favour with Stalin.[4]

Khrushchev must have seen in Zhukov what Stalin saw: a powerful but reliable and loyal personality. Khrushchev was right about Zhukov's loyalty to him, but he was no Stalin and Zhukov expected a certain autonomy to go along with his promotion. Nor could Zhukov resist the temptation to bask in the glory of his war record, something that rankled with the insecure Khrushchev even more than it did with Stalin. Zhukov was not outwardly hostile to Khrushchev when he served with him during the war or as his defence minister but his later attitude to Khrushchev was one of barely concealed contempt. Indeed, he came to consider Khrushchev's betrayal of him in 1957 as having been greater than Stalin's in 1946.[5] Unlike Khrushchev, Stalin didn't deny Zhukov his military career, nor did he orchestrate a distortion of Zhukov's war record or make ridiculous claims about his own role in particular battles. And for Zhukov military honour and pride were of utmost importance.

MINISTER OF DEFENCE

Zhukov was formally appointed minister of defence on 7 February 1955, and that day he gave a lengthy interview to a group of American journalists.[6] Asked whether he thought the battle of Moscow was more important than Stalingrad, Zhukov replied that the tide of war turned as a result of a series of operations: Moscow, Stalingrad, and Kursk. While he had directed preparations for the Stalingrad operation, it was Vasilevsky who had carried it through. Asked about Hitler's mistakes during the war, Zhukov said that at the strategic level the German dictator had underestimated the capacity of the Soviet Union, while at the tactical level Hitler had underrated the importance of the coordination of the different branches of the armed forces and underestimated the value of artillery as opposed to aircraft: 'The air force is a delicate arm. It is greatly dependent on weather and a number of other factors.' When the conversation switched to the question of atomic weapons Zhukov emphatically denied they made the world a safer place because of their deterrent effect:

> The very existence of nuclear weapons harbours the possibility of their employment, and certain madmen might go to the length of using them in spite of everything. It is our duty to do our utmost to have these weapons banned. . . . It should be remembered that atomic weapons are double-edged. Atomic war is just as dangerous to the attacker as to the attacked.

Zhukov also noted that 'war cannot be won by atomic bombs alone'. Much of the interview concerned American-Soviet relations and Zhukov expounded the Soviet line that the USSR posed no threat to the United States and wanted only peaceful relations. Zhukov complained about American military bases ringing the Soviet Union and called for an end to the arms race. He concluded by recalling the good relations he had with President Eisenhower when they served together on the Allied Control Council in Germany, urging a renewal of friendly relations. Notwithstanding his completely conventional responses, it was an impressive political debut, one that exuded confidence and a good command of his brief.

When Zhukov took office as defence minister he faced a myriad of issues but first and foremost was an ongoing programme of troop reductions.[7] At the end of the Second World War the Red Army was eleven million strong but dropped to three million in the war's aftermath. However, the outbreak of the Cold War in 1947–1948 resulted in an increase to 5.4 million by the early 1950s. After Stalin's death in

1953 that number was cut by 600,000 and in August 1955 Khrushchev announced a further reduction of a similar order. In May 1956 another demobilisation of 1.2 million was announced.

During Zhukov's term as defence minister from February 1955 to October 1957 the armed forces were reduced by some two million people. The cuts were made for a mixture of strategic and economic reasons. Zhukov seems to have acknowledged that in the nuclear age fewer conventional forces were necessary due to the deterrent of the atomic bomb, especially since in the mid-1950s the USSR had begun to develop the rocket technology that could guarantee delivery of bombs to distant targets. (In 1957 the Soviets launched Sputnik – the world's first orbital satellite.) 'Unlike so many thick-headed types you find wearing uniforms,' recalled Khrushchev, 'Zhukov understood the necessity of reducing our military expenditures.'[8]

Related to these troop reductions were Soviet proposals for arms control and nuclear disarmament. On 10 May 1955, the USSR called on the United Nations to establish an international control agency to supervise significant reductions in armaments and armed forces and to initiate a process leading to the prohibition of nuclear weapons.[9] Full implementation of the proposals would have resulted in a Soviet army of 1.5 million troops – a surprisingly small number for a country the size of the USSR. Zhukov was an ardent supporter of the proposals and proved more flexible than Khrushchev in responding to western objections to the Soviet disarmament programme. The Americans, for example, demanded that their spy planes be allowed to overfly Soviet territory to verify Soviet compliance with disarmament agreements. Zhukov was prepared to concede this demand if the United States agreed to Soviet aerial inspection of the United States. Some have suggested that Zhukov's motive was purely instrumental – that he expected to get more military intelligence on the Americans than they would get in return. But that underestimates the importance Zhukov attached to achieving nuclear disarmament and the lengths to which he was prepared to go to secure that goal. When Zhukov warned of the devastation that would result from nuclear war it was the heartfelt plea from someone who had seen such large-scale destruction firsthand.

At the same time, running somewhat in contradiction to Soviet efforts to control the spiralling arms race, was Moscow's decision to establish the Warsaw Pact. This was the Soviet response to the rearmament of West Germany and its admission into NATO in May 1955. This eventuality had been in prospect for several years and the Soviets had waged an extensive campaign for a pan-European collective security treaty to protect all European states and preclude the need for German rearmament, an action designed to counter a supposed Soviet threat to Western Europe. While the Soviets had political and ideological ambitions in Europe – in the long run they wanted to see the spread of communism to the whole continent – they had no military designs. Indeed, they saw themselves as the ones under threat from NATO and the United States.

When the campaign for European collective security failed the Soviets decided to set up the Warsaw Pact, initially not so much a military counterpart to NATO but more as an exemplar of a non-aggressive collective security organisation open to all states.[10] It was Zhukov and Foreign Minister Molotov who drafted the terms of the 'Treaty of Friendship, Co-operation and Mutual Assistance' signed by the Soviets and their communist allies in Eastern Europe in Warsaw in May 1955. Zhukov's involvement in drafting the pact stemmed from the Presidium's decision to establish a joint military command of the signatory states – much like what existed under the umbrella of NATO. In April 1955 Zhukov and Molotov presented to the Soviet leadership a proposal for a military organisation of the Warsaw Pact consisting of eighty-five divisions, thirty-two contributed by the USSR.[11] But it was to be some time before the Warsaw Pact developed into a full-fledged military alliance like NATO.

Despite the deepening Cold War divide in Europe, the first great power summit since the Potsdam Conference of 1945 was held in Geneva in July 1955. In attendance were the leaders of France, Great Britain, the Soviet Union, and the United States. The Soviet delegation was led by Bulganin in his capacity as prime minister. He was accompanied by Khrushchev, Molotov, and Zhukov. Khrushchev later claimed that Zhukov was specifically included on the delegation because of his prior relationship with President Eisenhower, but as the subject of the summit concerned European security it was likely he would have attended anyway.

Geneva was Khrushchev's first trip outside the communist bloc and he was eager to make an impact on the world stage. But standing in his way was the media attention lavished on the prospect of Zhukov's encounter with Eisenhower. In May 1955 Zhukov made the front cover of *Time* magazine. The accompanying story was almost fawning. According to *Time*, 'Zhukov is the nearest thing the Soviet Union has to a popular hero; the victorious Red Army is its only esteemed public institution. . . . In the confused power situation following Stalin's death, Zhukov and the Red Army give the regime a reassuring semblance of stability.' Readers of the piece were also led to believe that Zhukov had single-handedly masterminded the Soviet victory over Germany. Among the legends repeated in the article was that he had once demonstrated the importance of spit and polish by personally cleaning the boots of one of his soldiers. Another was that Zhukov's family in his home village of Strelkovka had been saved in the nick of time from being burned alive in their house by the Germans. In relation to Zhukov and Eisenhower the magazine speculated: 'Could the friendship of two old soldiers provide the basis for a genuine easing of tensions between the U.S. and Russia?'[12]

A few weeks before the Geneva summit the American ambassador in Moscow, Charles Bohlen, met Zhukov at a British embassy reception. Zhukov, Bohlen reported to Washington, emphasised the need to improve Soviet-American relations and expressed hope for bilateral conversations between the United States and the USSR as well as those at the four-power summit. Bohlen was struck by how deeply Zhukov emphasised disarmament:

He said that the arms race was senseless and dangerous and given the development of atomic weapons any new war would be unbelievably destructive. He said he had made a special study of the effect of atomic weapons and in his May 8 article on the anniversary of the end of the war published in *Pravda* he originally had several paragraphs giving graphic description in understandable local terms of their power of destruction. However, 'the Editors' had felt it unwise to publish these paragraphs since they might 'frighten' people.

Later Bohlen and Zhukov were joined by Bulganin and Anastas Mikoyan, the deputy prime minister. Bulganin said good-naturedly that Zhukov was considered an 'Americanphile'. When Bohlen replied that the relationship between Zhukov and Eisenhower was well known and showed that friendship between military men was more solid than that between diplomats and politicians, 'both Mikoyan and Zhukov looked at Bulganin and laughed'.[13] In his memoirs Bohlen said of Zhukov that he 'looked like a soldier – stocky, sturdy as a Russian oak, a slightly ruddy complexion and clear blue eyes. Although he had a pleasant smile, he was very reserved, particularly with foreigners. . . . He conveyed a tolerance, even a respect, for the United States, and there was no doubt in my mind that his affection for Eisenhower was genuine.'[14]

ZHUKOV AND EISENHOWER

At Geneva Zhukov had two official conversations with Eisenhower, recorded separately by Bohlen, who acted as Eisenhower's interpreter, and by Oleg Troyanovsky, the Foreign Ministry official who translated for Zhukov.[15] Zhukov, recalled Troyanovsky, behaved with great dignity and diplomacy at the summit, taking an active part in the proceedings while accepting the pre-eminence of Bulganin and Khrushchev. Zhukov did not come across at all like the severe commander he was reputed to be: 'He could adapt, it seems, to a different situation.'[16]

Zhukov's first conversation with Eisenhower took place during lunch in the president's villa on 20 July. Recalling the good relations between the United States and the Soviet Union during the war and the joint work he and Eisenhower had done on the Allied Control Council, Zhukov noted that towards the end of the war Hitler had tried, unsuccessfully, to disrupt the alliance between the two countries. Unfortunately, after the war 'dark forces' had succeeded in undermining the alliance by portraying the Soviet Union as an aggressive state that was planning attacks on other countries. Zhukov gave Eisenhower his word as a soldier that this was not so and claimed the only reason he had come to Geneva was to meet the president and to help improve Soviet-American relations. When Eisenhower responded that the development of the Cold War was the result of aggressive Soviet actions, Zhukov refused to be drawn into the argument, stating that mistakes had been made by both sides and that it was better to look to the future rather than to dwell on the past.

In political terms Zhukov's main theme was the need for disarmament and the establishment of a collective security system in Europe to facilitate the dissolution of the Cold War blocs. When Eisenhower raised the issue of a system of inspection to make sure arms controls and disarmament agreements were being kept, Zhukov did not object. The two men also discussed the Chinese question with Zhukov urging Eisenhower to recognise Communist China and admit it to the United Nations. In relation to Germany, Zhukov repeated the Soviet line that the two Germanys could be reunited in the context of a pan-European system of collective security that would provide protection for all states in Europe.

Ideological and political differences aside, the tone of the conversation between the two men was relaxed and conciliatory. The friendly talk continued at Zhukov's next meeting with Eisenhower on 23 July though much of the conversation was devoted to a procedural dispute at the summit over which issue was to be discussed and resolved first: German reunification or European collective security. While the Americans wanted to settle the German question first, the Soviets said reunification should follow the establishment of a European collective security system to reassure them that a united Germany would not threaten the USSR. When Eisenhower appealed to him to use his good offices to resolve this dispute, Zhukov responded that efforts to reach a compromise should continue until the end of the summit. The conversation concluded with Zhukov expressing the hope that he would be able to visit the president's grandchildren in the United States and Eisenhower his in Moscow.

Despite his and Zhukov's warm relations Eisenhower would later recall:

In our wartime association he had been an independent, self-confident man who, while obviously embracing communist doctrine, was always ready to meet cheerfully with me on any operational problem and to cooperate in finding a reasonable solution. . . . Now in Geneva, years later, he was a subdued and worried man. . . . He spoke as if he was repeating a lesson which had been drilled into him until he was letter perfect. He was devoid of animation, and he never smiled or joked, as he used to do. My old friend was carrying out the orders of his superiors. I obtained nothing from this private chat other than a feeling of sadness.[17]

According to Andrei Gromyko, at that time deputy foreign minister, Zhukov was as disappointed as Eisenhower and said the president 'withdrew into himself and merely mouthed a few platitudes. I could see that Zhukov was upset and, on our way back home he made the comment that the Soviet Union must "keep its powder dry." '[18]

Neither post hoc recollection is borne out by the contemporary record of the two men's conversations at Geneva. What had happened was that both men had become politicians and were disappointed the other was not the old soldier they had known in Berlin a decade earlier. As Zhukov commented to Troyanovsky when they were leaving the president's villa: 'President Eisenhower is not the same person as General Eisenhower.'[19]

Years later, Troyanovsky ran into Zhukov at a cinema in Moscow screening *The Bridge on the River Kwai* – David Lean's classic POW epic starring Alec Guinness as the British officer who collaborates with the Japanese in building the bridge as a means of keeping up his men's morale. When Troyanovsky asked what he thought of the film, Zhukov replied that it was 'too pacifist for me. I prefer something with shooting like *The Guns of Navarone*. I'm a military man, a different business from yours.'[20] In fact, in 1955 Zhukov had performed very well in his new political and diplomatic role. He had also mellowed personally and acquired some humility as a result of his post-war disgrace – qualities that would serve him well when he was forced into exile a second time.

The only practical result from the Geneva summit was an agreement to hold a further meeting of the foreign ministers of the four states. The first item on the agenda would be the German question *and* European security – thus circumventing the procedural dispute that had dogged the summit. When the foreign ministers met in October 1955 the meeting started well, everyone agreeing on the need to establish a common system of security in Europe. But the western price for a deal on pan-European security was German reunification on terms that would mean a loss of communist control over East Germany. Molotov wanted to pursue negotiations along these lines but was overruled by Khrushchev, who took a more hawkish line. As a result the foreign ministers meeting collapsed without agreement.

The skirmish between Khrushchev and Molotov over the resolution of the German question was part of a running battle between the two men that had begun earlier in the year over relations with communist Yugoslavia. Khrushchev wanted to end the ideological split that had developed between Stalin and the Yugoslav leader, Marshal Tito, in 1948. As Stalin's right-hand man Molotov had been at the forefront of the campaign to expel Tito from the communist bloc and was reluctant to rescind or repudiate his sharp ideological critique of the Yugoslav leader. Zhukov was drawn into the dispute when he published an article in *Pravda* on the tenth anniversary of the victory in the Great Patriotic War that praised Tito's leadership of the partisan movement in Yugoslavia during the war and expressed the hope that relations between Belgrade and Moscow would improve. At the Presidium meeting on 19 May 1955, Molotov expressed his disagreement with the article, saying, 'the Red Army was founded by Trotsky but we don't glorify him'. He also characterised Zhukov's piece as 'anti-Leninist' but later withdrew this remark as being made in the heat of the moment.[21] Molotov lost the battle and relations with Tito's communists were restored. At a meeting of the Central Committee in July Molotov was sharply criticised for his stance on Yugoslavia. Zhukov attended the meeting but did not speak, thereby avoiding direct involvement in the battle between the two titans of the post-Stalin Soviet leadership.[22]

THE 20TH PARTY CONGRESS

By the end of 1955 the focus of the struggle between Khrushchev and Molotov had switched to preparations for the forthcoming 20th Party Congress. Khrushchev was planning to deliver a wide-ranging critique of Stalin at the congress and Molotov objected on grounds that the achievements as well as the failings of the Soviet dictator should be recognised. He pointed out, too, that not long ago everyone had been praising Stalin to the skies, including Khrushchev. Molotov's position gained some traction with other Presidium members, notably the disgruntled Malenkov, and Lazar Kaganovich, another former member of Stalin's inner circle. But Khrushchev commanded a majority on the Presidium and his Secret Speech, as it came to be called, went ahead as planned.

Khrushchev's famous speech denouncing Stalin and the cult of his personality was delivered on 25 February 1956 to a closed and private session attended only by congress delegates. Khrushchev electrified them with his account of Stalin's reign of terror that peaked in the late 1930s with mass repressions of party and state officials. Among the victims were members of the Soviet officer corps and Khrushchev reported that since 1954 more than 7,500 military victims of the purges had been rehabilitated, many of them posthumously. Khrushchev also attacked Stalin's war leadership. The country had not been prepared adequately for war and Stalin had refused to heed warnings of the imminent German attack. Khrushchev claimed that when war broke out Stalin suffered a nervous breakdown and only came back to work at the behest of the rest of the Soviet leadership. After his recovery Stalin continued to interfere in military affairs in an amateurish way and only the country's talented military leaders had saved the Soviet Union from an even greater disaster than the catastrophic losses the Red Army suffered during the early years of the war. Khrushchev also went out of his way to present himself as Zhukov's loyal friend who had defended him when he came under attack by Stalin. After the war, Khrushchev said, Stalin had sought to magnify his own role in winning victory and minimise that of his generals, including Zhukov. 'Not Stalin', concluded Khrushchev, 'but the party as a whole, the Soviet Government, our heroic army, its talented leaders and brave soldiers, the whole Soviet nation – these are the ones who assured the victory in the Great Patriotic War. (*Tempestuous and prolonged applause*).'[23] Khrushchev's Secret Speech was not officially published but it was read out at party meetings throughout the Soviet Union, causing much confusion and divided opinions.

A week before Khrushchev's dramatic intervention Zhukov had delivered a more sedate report on military matters to a public session of the congress. This was an important moment for Zhukov personally as it was the first time he had addressed a party congress and it was also an opportunity to make a wide-ranging statement on Soviet defence policy in the new, nuclear age. A future war, Zhukov told the delegates, would be very different from past wars. It would be characterised by extensive use of planes and rockets to deliver weapons of mass destruction, not only atomic bombs but chemical and bacteriological weapons as well. This new form of warfare required that resources be transferred to the air force and to air defences. At the same time, conventional land, air, and sea forces continued to be essential since only they could prosecute a war to a successful conclusion. Zhukov did not ignore the human factor: 'Military equipment, even the most effective, cannot by itself decide a battle or an operation or achieve victory. The outcome of armed struggle in future wars will be determined by people who have complete control over their military equipment, who believe in the rightness of the war, who are deeply devoted to their government and are always ready to defend their people.'[24] Zhukov concluded his speech the way he had begun it, pledging the armed forces' eternal loyalty to the Soviet motherland.

At the congress Zhukov was elected an alternate (i.e., nonvoting) member of the Presidium, propelling him to the highest level of Soviet political decision-making. Zhukov immediately aligned himself with Khrushchev and the critique of Stalin. Shortly after the congress he drafted a speech on the impact of the cult of personality on military affairs. The speech was intended for a plenum of the Central Committee held in June 1956 but for some reason Zhukov did not get to deliver it, possibly because the party leadership had decided to moderate its denunciations of Stalin.

As might be expected, Zhukov's draft report to the Central Committee followed the main lines of Khrushchev's Secret Speech: Stalin was criticised for the pre-war purge of the Red Army, for his role in the debacle of 22 June 1941, and for operational mistakes during the early years of the war. But Zhukov also introduced some new criticisms, including the unjust execution of General Pavlov and the members of the Western Front command in July 1941, linking this episode to a more general defence of the Red Army's honour against Stalin's accusation that it had been too prone to retreat during the war. Zhukov pointed to the Red Army's astronomical number of casualties during the early years of the war and argued that it had 'honorably and valiantly fulfilled its military duty, defending the socialist motherland'. Zhukov also raised the question of the treatment of surviving Soviet POWs after the war, most of whom had been captured through no fault of their own. Not only had many of them suffered post-war repression, they were still being treated badly by party and state bodies: 'it is necessary to remove the moral disapproval of the former POWs, to repudiate their illegal punishment, and to eliminate reservations about them'.[25]

Pressure to alleviate the suffering of former POWs had been building for some time. In September 1955 the government had granted amnesty to former POWs convicted of voluntarily entering captivity. In April 1956 a commission headed by Zhukov was established to examine the status of former POWs, including the issue of whether they should be readmitted to the party. Zhukov's commission reported in June, proposing a range of measures to end discrimination against the former POWs. payments for time spent in captivity; pensions for them and their families; and a propaganda campaign to extol the POWs' heroic contribution to the wartime struggle. In September 1956 the government issued a directive ordering the full implementation of the year-old amnesty decree.[26]

The issue of Pavlov and the Western Front command was trickier for Zhukov to resolve. There was no problem with repudiating their execution and rehabilitating their reputations as patriots and communists. Many such rehabilitations took place in the years following Stalin's death. Those involved in the Aviators Affair that had led to Zhukov's demotion in 1946 were rehabilitated as early as June 1953. In July 1954 the heads of the Red Air Force who had been executed in October 1941 were rehabilitated. Tukhachevsky and the group of generals and marshals shot for supposedly conspiring against Stalin in 1937 were rehabilitated in January 1957. The problem with Pavlov's case was that there was no denying the disaster that had befallen the Western Front in June 1941. The solution to this tricky problem was to hold a General Staff inquiry into the command failures of the leadership of the Western Front. Completed in November 1956, the General Staff review concluded that because Pavlov lacked experience of high command he had been unable to cope with the demands of wartime decision-making but he had not been guilty of cowardice or of deliberately allowing his troops to succumb to German encirclement without a fight.[27] This verdict suited Zhukov because while Pavlov was partly exonerated the spotlight remained on his mistakes rather than those of the General Staff who had ordered the overambitious counter-offensive that led to the destruction of the Western Front. Pavlov and his colleagues were formally rehabilitated by the party in July 1957.

HUNGARY 1956

With his promotion to the Presidium Zhukov became an active participant in high-level political as well as military decision-making, most notably in the Hungarian crisis of 1956. This crisis was preceded by and, indeed, prompted by a crisis in Poland. When news of Khrushchev's Secret Speech leaked it encouraged hopes in Poland that there could be a fundamental reform of the authoritarian communist system imposed after the Second World War. Popular dissent increased, as did agitation by reform-minded communists seeking a change in the Polish party leadership. Matters came to a head during the Poznan riots of June 1956 when hundreds of demonstrators were shot by Polish security forces. Polish communists responded to the crisis by restoring the leadership of Wladyslaw Gomulka, who had been the party's leader in the 1940s until he was purged as a communist considered too nationalist. Among the reforms Gomulka proposed was sacking Rokossovsky as minister of defence – a proposal that caused particular alarm in Moscow since he was seen as the guarantor of Poland's continued alignment with the Soviet Union. As the protests and street demonstrations escalated, Khrushchev flew into Warsaw unannounced on 19 October accompanied by Molotov, Mikoyan, Kaganovich, Konev, and Zhukov. Their aim was to browbeat Gomulka into retaining Rokossovsky as defence minister and to insist that political reform in Poland proceed at a more moderate pace. In the background lurked the threat of military action to impose the Soviets' will.

Gomulka refused to capitulate but he managed to convince the Soviet delegation that neither communist rule nor Poland's alliance with the USSR within the Warsaw Pact was under threat.[28] But the Soviets could not save Rokossovsky, who was dismissed as defence minister and returned to Moscow in November 1956.

Meanwhile an even bigger political crisis had developed in Hungary, also inspired by Khrushchev's denunciation of Stalin. On 23 October Hungarian security police opened fire on anticommunist crowds attempting to storm Budapest's main radio station. An armed revolt broke out across the city and the communist government asked for Soviet military assistance to suppress the rebellion. That evening Zhukov reported to the Presidium that 100,000 people had demonstrated in Budapest and that the radio station was ablaze. The consensus of the meeting was that troops should be used to restore order. Zhukov agreed: 'It is different from Poland. It is necessary to introduce troops . . . declare martial law and introduce a curfew.'[29]

Soviet troops had been stationed in Hungary since the end of the war. They remained even after the signature of a peace treaty with Hungary in 1947, the ostensible rationale being the need to protect supply routes for Soviet troops based in eastern Austria, which, like Germany, was divided into zones of military occupation after the war. In May 1955 the Soviet-western occupation of Austria was ended by the Austrian State Treaty. By this time the Warsaw Pact had been signed, providing a pretext for Soviet troops in Hungary and those formerly based in Austria to be reorganised into a Special Corps. According to Colonel E. I. Malashenko, commander of the Soviet troops based in Budapest, the Special Corps was Zhukov's idea, inspired by his experience commanding a similar formation at Khalkhin-Gol in 1939.[30]

When the Hungarian crisis erupted the Soviets had five divisions stationed in or proximate to Hungary and on 24 October they mobilised some 30,000 troops and 1,000 tanks to seize strategic locations in Budapest and seal the Austrian-Hungarian border. Contingency plans for such an operation had been drawn up in July 1956 and the Soviets achieved their tactical goals with relative ease.[31] However, the military intervention further inflamed those in armed revolt and the question arose of Soviet troops being withdrawn as part of a political compromise similar to that achieved in Poland. When the Presidium discussed the matter on 26 October Zhukov opposed troop withdrawal, characterising it as 'capitulation'. He urged instead the use of more troops and maintenance of a 'firm position'.[32]

In Budapest the situation stabilised when a new government headed by the reform communist Imre Nagy came to power. Nagy seemed to be a Hungarian Gomulka and appeared to offer the possibility of a political compromise that would satisfy both the insurgents and the Soviets. At the Presidium meeting on 28 October Zhukov spoke in favour of a limited troop withdrawal and of the need to support the Nagy government.[33] That same day a cease-fire was arranged and Soviet troops began to withdraw to barracks outside Budapest. Replying to questions from journalists the next day Zhukov said that 'in Hungary, the situation has improved. A government had been formed in which we have confidence.'[34] The conciliatory mood was continued at the Presidium meeting on 30 October when it was agreed to issue a statement about the development of more equitable relations between the Soviet Union and all the socialist countries, not only Hungary. Zhukov said the statement should express 'sympathy for the people' and 'call for an end to the bloodshed'.[35] But by the next day, 31 October, the mood in Moscow had hardened once again and Zhukov was ordered to draft a plan for further military intervention.

The Soviet change of heart was prompted by two separate and distinct developments. First, signs that Nagy was preparing to withdraw Hungary from the Warsaw Pact and declare the country a neutral state (which on 1 November he did). Second, the Anglo-French-Israeli attack on Egypt on 29 October aimed at regaining control of the Suez Canal. Egypt was a Soviet ally and as Khrushchev told the Presidium on 31 October: 'If we leave Hungary it will encourage the American, British and French imperialists. They will see weakness on our part and go on the offensive. . . . To Egypt they will then add Hungary.'[36] At the next meeting of the Presidium, on 1 November, there was a discussion of whether the second military intervention should go ahead. Zhukov was adamant that decisive action was necessary: 'Remove all the rotten elements. Disarm the counter-revolution. Everything must be brought to order.'[37]

The Soviet military intervention of 4 November 1956, was as

bloody as it was decisive. Code-named Whirlwind, it was directed by Konev, with units in Hungary supplemented by forces from the neighbouring Carpathian Military District, from Romania, and from the Odessa Military District. A total of seventeen divisions took part in combined tank, infantry, and air actions designed to quash the rebellion in Budapest and other urban areas. The fighting was particularly fierce in Budapest, where the insurgents fought back with barricades, small arms, and Molotov cocktails. The Soviets suffered more than 2,000 casualties, including nearly 700 dead. Civilian and insurgent casualties numbered 25,000 (including 5,000 dead). Another 200,000 Hungarians fled into Austria, notwithstanding Soviet efforts to keep the border closed.

Zhukov provided the Presidium with regular progress reports on the action in Budapest.[38] Within a few days order had been restored and a new Soviet-supported government headed by Janos Kadar was installed. After the uprising thousands of Hungarians were arrested and hundreds later executed, Imre Nagy most prominently. Zhukov gave no indication he had any doubts about the brutal suppression of the popular uprising in Hungary. For Zhukov and all the Soviet leaders, it was not only in Hungary that communist power and the socialist system was at stake. They all feared a domino effect of popular uprisings against communist rule that would destabilise the whole eastern bloc – threatening the buffer zone between Germany and the USSR, which the Soviets were determined to maintain at all costs.

Zhukov's status in the leadership was enhanced considerably by his decisive role in the Hungarian crisis. On his sixtieth birthday in December 1956 he was awarded his fourth Order of Lenin, his picture published on the front page of Soviet newspapers together with birthday greetings from both the party Central Committee and the Council of Ministers.[39]

In January and February 1957 Zhukov went on a highly publicised tour of India and Burma – a follow-up to a similar tour by Khrushchev and Bulganin in November–December 1955 – aimed at consolidating Soviet relations with the two recently independent states. The tour was a great success and Zhukov was warmly received. In India Zhukov was photographed riding an elephant and one wonders if he thought of Hannibal and his famous victory over the Romans at

Cannae – the battle most often compared to Khalkhin-Gol. When Zhukov returned home the Soviets released a colour documentary film entitled *The Friendship Visit of Marshal of the Soviet Union G. K. Zhukov to India and Burma*.[40] While in India Zhukov gave a speech at a military staff college on 5 February 1957, in which he addressed the question of nuclear war:

> Will nuclear and thermonuclear weapons be used in the event of war between coalitions of the great powers? Yes, undoubtedly, since the introduction of these weapons into the armed forces has gone too far and have already made their influence felt on organisation, tactics and operational-strategic doctrine. . . . We think that as long as atomic and thermonuclear weapons remain in countries' arsenals they will have no little significance for ground, sea and air forces. In the postwar construction of our armed forces we proceeded from the fact that victory in a future war can only be achieved by the unified force of all types of arms and armed forces and their coordinated use in war.[41]

In March 1957 Zhukov went to East Berlin to sign a defence agreement with the East German government. While there he delivered a speech to senior troop commanders of Soviet forces in East Germany. The mission of Soviet forces in Germany was in the event of a NATO attack to hold up the advance of western forces and to buy time for second-echelon Warsaw Pact forces to move forward. But Zhukov made it clear he did not necessarily intend to wait for NATO to attack. As soon as it became apparent that NATO intended to launch an attack the Soviets would implement a pre-emptive strike aimed at reaching the English Channel within two days. In other words, the Soviets intended to pursue the kind of pre-emptive strategy that they had considered but failed to implement in summer 1941 when they waited for the Germans to attack. A leaked version of the speech concocted by the Soviets for disinformation purposes reported Zhukov as saying that Soviet strategy was counter-offensive rather than pre-emptive and that nuclear rather than conventional weapons would be employed from the outbreak of war.[42] The aim of this dissimulation was both to mislead NATO about Soviet intentions and to deter a western attack with the threat of an immediate nuclear escalation.

The idea of launching a pre-emptive attack came up again at a military conference in Moscow in May 1957 attended by more than 200 of the most senior officers of the Soviet army, navy, and air force. In his speech Zhukov concentrated on the initial period of the war and reviewed the lessons of the armed forces' lack of preparedness in June 1941. He emphasised the importance of studying the enemy's plans and intentions:

> The basic concept of our enemies is the maximum use of all forces and means during the initial period of the war on the basis of a sudden attack on command and control systems. It is therefore necessary to raise to a high and constant level of preparedness the air defences of the country, particularly in the spheres of radar and anti-rocket defence. Under all circumstances our armed forces must be prepared to deliver attacks by land, air and sea that would liquidate the enemy's attempt to deliver a disorganizing blow. Some say – for example Bagramyan – that our strategy must be built around a system of anticipatory surprise preventative blows that aim to destroy the attack preparations of the enemy. About this we cannot talk openly.

Was this statement a signal to the audience that they should not discuss the pre-emptive strategy that was being devised? Or was it a warning that such talk would only encourage the enemy to strike pre-emptively? It is difficult to say and Zhukov may well have been of two minds.[43] When he reported on the conference to the party leadership Zhukov highlighted the discussion of the initial period of the war but did not mention pre-emption. The conference had been a success, he said, but it had revealed that military theory had still not caught up with contemporary developments in military technology.[44]

ZHUKOV SAVES KHRUSHCHEV

During the Polish and Hungarian crises Khrushchev's dominance of the Presidium slipped as the other members began to assert their independence. The main beneficiary of the return to a more collective leadership style was Molotov. He had been dismissed as foreign minister by Khrushchev in June 1956 but remained on the Presidium and in November 1956 was given the job of minister of state control with responsibility for ensuring that government decrees were enforced. He used this new position to challenge Khrushchev's authority on a range of domestic and foreign issues. Molotov was supported by Kaganovich and Malenkov and these three formed the core of a growing opposition to Khrushchev on the Presidium. Throughout these disputes Zhukov remained a staunch supporter of Khrushchev's. As he later recalled: 'Personally, I thought that Khrushchev's line was more correct than that of Kaganovich and Molotov, who stuck to the old dogmas and did not want to change in accordance with the spirit of the times.'[45]

Khrushchev's power struggle with Molotov came to a head following a speech given by the Soviet leader in Leningrad in May 1957 in which he pledged that the USSR would overtake the United States in the production of meat, butter, and milk within a few short years. This entirely unrealistic target was announced by Khrushchev without consultation and asserted a style of decision-making that threatened to usurp the power and prerogatives of the Presidium. In short, the post-Stalin collective leadership was being subverted by the emergence of a new boss. This development was unwelcome to a majority of Presidium members, including Bulganin and Dmitry Shepilov, Molotov's short-lived successor as foreign minister (he had been replaced by Gromyko in February 1957). With a majority of full (voting) members of the Presidium on their side the Molotov group attempted a coup against Khrushchev.

On 18 June the conspirators lured Khrushchev to a meeting, supposedly of the Council of Ministers but which metamorphosed into an impromptu gathering of the Presidium. Khrushchev was not without his supporters and he managed to fend off the demand that he resign immediately as party leader. Zhukov and Mikoyan were his strongest backers. Indeed, before the meeting Zhukov had rebuffed an attempt by Malenkov to recruit him to the conspiracy. According to Zhukov, Khrushchev was confused and demoralised at the Presidium meeting and it was only his support that saved the day. 'Georgy, you have saved the position,' Zhukov recalled Khrushchev telling him, 'only you could do it. I will never forget that.'[46] With Zhukov's help Khrushchev arranged military transport for Central Committee members to fly to Moscow to demand the convening of a full Central Committee plenum. By day three of the Presidium meeting the Molotov group – dubbed the 'antiparty group' by their opponents – were forced to agree to a Central Committee meeting to decide on Khrushchev's leadership.[47]

The 200 or so members of the Central Committee had been elected at the 20th Party Congress and were overwhelmingly pro-Khrushchev. At the plenum from 22 to 29 June the members of the so-called antiparty group found themselves in a tiny minority and Zhukov was at the forefront of the attack on Molotov and his co-conspirators. The first speech at the plenum was made by Khrushchev's ideology chief, Mikhail Suslov, but the second came from Zhukov, who launched a ferocious attack on the antiparty group focused on their culpability for the crimes of the Stalin era. Zhukov revealed to the plenum that between 27 February 1937, and 12 November 1938, Stalin, Molotov and Kaganovich had personally sanctioned 38,679 political executions. On one day alone – 12 November 1938 – Stalin and Molotov signed death warrants for a list of 3,167 people. 'I don't know whether they even read the list,' commented Zhukov. After giving more details of killings, Zhukov concluded: 'I think it is necessary to discuss this question at the Plenum and to demand from Malenkov, Kaganovich and Molotov an explanation for their abuse of power.' Zhukov's intervention notwithstanding, the crimes of the Stalin era did not become a major theme of discussion, not least because it raised too many uncomfortable questions about Khrushchev's role in those events.

Zhukov did not speak again at the plenum but he did make numerous interjections, often working in tandem with Khrushchev to heckle the members of the antiparty group when they spoke. 'Speak about the responsibility for the criminality, for the shootings,' he demanded of Kaganovich. 'This is the most important question.' He seems to have taken particular pleasure at the discomfort of Bulganin, who had supported the antiparty group at the Presidium but now tried to explain away his actions. At one point during Bulganin's speech Zhukov began to interrogate him and told him not 'to twist things around if you want to be an honest man'. Reading the transcript of the plenum Zhukov comes across as someone who was enjoying himself.[48]

The result of the plenum was a foregone conclusion. Molotov, Malenkov, and Kaganovich were stripped of their government posts and expelled from the Presidium and the Central Committee. Molotov was subsequently exiled to the ambassadorship of the People's Republic of Mongolia while Malenkov was sent to direct a power station in Kazakhstan and Kaganovich became manager of a potash factory in the Urals. Bulganin escaped with a censure but he was soon ousted as prime minister by Khrushchev, who took the post himself. The plenum was undoubtedly a great triumph for Khrushchev but Zhukov was the real star of the show. His reward was promotion to full membership of the Presidium.

While the struggle against the antiparty group was in progress another drama was being played out in Zhukov's personal life. At the age of sixty Zhukov had become a father once again. On 19 June Galina gave birth to their daughter, Maria. Zhukov was delighted and wrote to Galina wanting to know all about the new baby, promising to visit as soon as he could but explaining that he was involved in a 'terrible battle' and had not had much sleep for four days. However, Maria was sick – jaundiced and passive, Galina wrote to Zhukov – and both she and the doctors feared for her life. Zhukov was distraught and wrote to Galina on 26 June: 'I haven't slept all night since receiving your letter about the health of our daughter. How could this happen? I am very afraid for her. . . . I ask you to be strong and not to give in to fate. . . . Weakness never brings victory in the struggle.'[49] Happily, baby Maria recovered and survived.

After the plenum the campaign against the antiparty group was broadened. A truncated version of the Central Committee resolution on the antiparty group was published in the press. Party meetings were convened to condemn Molotov, Malenkov and Kaganovich. On 2 July Zhukov addressed the party group based in the Ministry of Defence. In attendance were Antonov, Bagramyan, Vasilevsky, Konev, Meretskov, Rokossovsky and other marshals and generals. Zhukov repeated what he had said at the plenum, focusing in particular on the role of the antiparty group in the mass repressions of the Stalin era. This time he highlighted Bulganin's 'unseemly' role in the affair.

According to Zhukov, part of the plot was to hand control of the KGB over to Bulganin. At the Presidium meeting Bulganin had gone along with this conspiracy but when he saw the way the wind was blowing at the plenum he turned against the antiparty group.[50]

Another opportunity to denounce the plotters came in mid-July when Zhukov went to Leningrad to take part in Navy Day celebrations. On the 15th he gave a widely publicised speech in which he criticised the antiparty group for opposing Khrushchev's commitment to overtake the United States in per capita production of meat, milk, and butter (a remark greeted by stormy applause) and for resisting decentralisation of economic and political decision-making. But the bulk of Zhukov's critique was directed at the antiparty group's opposition to the campaign against Stalin's cult of personality.[51] Zhukov was accompanied on this trip by 'Mrs. Zhukov' – a sign that despite his relationship with Galina the marriage to Alexandra was not yet over.

THE KHRUSHCHEVITE ATTACK

In October 1957 Zhukov toured Yugoslavia and Albania, aiming to replicate the publicity and success of his earlier tour to India and Burma. Zhukov was accompanied by a large group of senior officers and, rather than flying to Belgrade, they travelled to Yugoslavia in style on board the modern Soviet cruiser *Kuibyshev,* which sailed from Sebastopol on 5 October. This was Zhukov's first sea voyage and he appears to have enjoyed it, even though relations with the navy were not of the best at this time. Apart from perennial interservice rivalries, there had recently been a clash between Khrushchev and the naval chief, Admiral N. G. Kuznetsov, over plans to build a large surface fleet. Zhukov had backed Khrushchev's preference for a submarine-based fleet and Kuznetsov was dismissed following the accidental blowing up of a battleship at Sebastopol in October 1955 that had killed hundreds of sailors.

While sailing through the Bosporus the *Kuibyshev* came across ships from the U.S. Sixth Fleet (an aircraft carrier, a cruiser, two frigates, and several destroyers). As was customary the crews of the U.S. ships lined up on deck and messaged their greetings to the Soviet minister of defence. Zhukov was not amused, complaining: 'Why is it necessary for them to be here? Why aren't their ships in their own waters?' On a happier note, the voyage allowed Zhukov the opportunity to play his accordion and he joined in the ship's concert party.[52]

The *Kuibyshev* arrived in the Yugoslav port of Zadar on October 8 and there began the usual round of visits, meetings, ceremonies, and speeches. Zhukov's most important encounter was with Tito, whom he met at the Yugoslav's hometown in Croatia where they went hunting for mountain goats. 'For me it was a very successful hunt,' recalled Zhukov. 'I killed four goats. Tito killed only one and it was clear to me that he was not very happy with his results.'[53] On 16 October Zhukov submitted to Moscow a report on his conversations with Tito that emphasised Yugoslavia's desire to improve relations with the Soviet Union and to act together on a common anti-imperialist platform. On 17 October Zhukov left Belgrade for the Albanian capital of Tirana, where he undertook a similar round of visits and met Albania's communist chief Enver Hoxha.[54]

But Zhukov was not happy with the limited press coverage his trip received back home. On 12 October he wrote to Khrushchev to complain that *Pravda* only carried short reports of his visit and did not publish the full texts of his and the Yugoslavs' speeches. This was creating a bad impression on the Yugoslav leadership. If the Central Committee thinks it inadvisable to publish my speeches, telegraphed Zhukov, then perhaps it should announce my departure from Yugoslavia. The Presidium replied on 14 October that there were two Soviet delegations abroad just now – a visit by parliamentarians to China and the 'military' delegation to Yugoslavia. If first billing was given to Zhukov's visit, that might not go down too well with either world public opinion or the Chinese. Zhukov was not satisfied with this explanation and on 16 October he wrote to Khrushchev again, giving him a little political lecture: 'We are a great country, the material and spiritual base of the world communist and workers' movement, we must not – in the interests of China – give offence to small countries.'[55]

It may be that this testy exchange was the last straw for Khrushchev, particularly as it came in the wake of yet another policy disagreement with Zhukov. Earlier in the year Zhukov had advocated

compromise with the United States on the question of aerial reconnaissance as a means of ensuring agreements were being kept. The
Americans favoured Open Skies – first proposed by Eisenhower at the
Geneva summit – which meant that the USSR would be required to
open its airspace to American spy planes in return for access to U.S.
airspace. The Soviets initially agreed to a limited version of Open
Skies, but in August 1957, when the question of a more extensive
agreement on Open Skies arose, while Zhukov was in favour, Khrushchev was opposed. 'I do not entirely agree with comrade Zhukov's
point of view,' he told the Presidium. 'The potential of the enemy is
higher. Whoever has the higher potential the more interested they are
in intelligence. They do not know about everything we have. I agree
with comrade Zhukov that the enemy will not accept it. But what if it
is accepted? That will be bad.'[56] The upshot of this discussion was that
the Soviet Union stuck with its existing position of limited Open Skies.
However, after Zhukov was ousted from office Khrushchev rescinded
even the limited Open Skies proposal and withdrew the Soviet Union
from U.N. disarmament negotiations.

The drama of Zhukov's second fall from grace began while he was
still in Albania. On 17 October A. S. Zheltov, head of the armed forces
political administration, denounced him at a Presidium meeting. Political work in the armed forces was belittled, Zheltov told the meeting. Zhukov had said that he would make sure the military councils
(i.e., the political organs of the armed forces) were subordinate to
military commanders. According to Zheltov, Zhukov described political workers as 'red beards' who would kill all commanders if they
were given knives. Zheltov complained he was not allowed to make
trips to troops without permission and that Zhukov treated him with
hostility. 'Why? Because I was supposedly against his appointment as
minister. Because I object to his glorification.' Zheltov's denunciation
must have been a setup since he would not have dared to criticise
Zhukov in such terms without Khrushchev's blessing. Present at the
Presidium meeting were Konev and Marshal Rodion Malinovsky,
commander-in-chief of ground forces. They defended the state of
political work in the army (although not Zhukov personally) but
their objections to Zheltov's comments were swept aside as the meeting decided to establish a commission to examine the question of

strengthening party work in the armed forces. This commission reported to the Presidium two days later and a resolution was adopted which specified that military councils were responsible for all important decisions of the armed forces. It was also decided to convene meetings of party activists in the armed forces in Moscow and Leningrad.

Khrushchev addressed two such meetings in Moscow on 22 and 23 October. His direct criticisms of Zhukov were muted but it was clear that Zhukov's days were numbered. One of Khrushchev's complaints concerned a documentary film about the battle of Stalingrad that depicted Zhukov and Vasilevsky as the main architects of the counter-offensive of November 1942, whereas the credit should go to himself and Yeremenko. Two days later the minister of culture wrote to the Central Committee detailing Zhukov's interference in the film's editing, concluding that its content 'propagated the cult of the personality of comrade Zhukov'.[57]

At the meeting on 23 October Khrushchev made a rather ominous comment. He pointed out to his audience that he had dismissed General Shtemenko as head of Soviet military intelligence because he and Zhukov had established a special school to train military saboteurs without the permission of the party leadership. Khrushchev reminded those present that Shtemenko had previously been dismissed as deputy chief of the General Staff because of his connections with Beria. He was then posted to serve as chief of staff of the Siberian Military District. However, when Zhukov became defence minister he recalled Shtemenko to Moscow and put him in charge of military intelligence.[58] Khrushchev's point was that Zhukov had shown bad judgment both in appointing Shtemenko and in authorising the establishment of the saboteurs school without the party's permission.

News of what was happening may or may not have filtered through to Zhukov in Albania. When he returned to Moscow on 26 October he had influenza and was not in good form when he attended the Presidium meeting later that day. Nevertheless, he mounted a spirited defence of his position, denying he wanted to separate the armed forces from the party and demanding a commission to investigate the charges. He accepted that there were problems with a cult of personality around him but he denied any personal interest in glory. In his contribution to the discussion Khrushchev raised Zhukov's willingness to accept the Americans' Open Skies proposal and it was Khrushchev who proposed that Zhukov be removed as minister of defence in a resolution that was adopted unanimously, as was the decision to appoint Malinovsky in his place.[59]

After the Presidium meeting Zhukov telephoned Khrushchev to ask him what was going on. When Khrushchev replied that all would be revealed at the forthcoming meeting of the Central Committee, Zhukov replied: 'I consider that our previously friendly relations give me the right to ask you personally why you have become unfriendly in relation to me.' To which Khrushchev responded: 'Don't get so excited, we will still have work for you.'[60]

On 28 and 29 October 1957, the Central Committee met to ratify the dismissal and condemnation of Zhukov. Once again Suslov was Khrushchev's chief hatchet man but he was supported by a galaxy of generals and marshals anxious to settle personal scores with Zhukov as well as to demonstrate their loyalty to the party leadership. The charges against Zhukov were that he was attempting to split the army from the party and he claimed too much credit for the victory in the Great Patriotic War. Suslov also introduced a new element into the critique: that Zhukov had a tendency to accumulate power. Suslov's charges were supported by Zheltov and then Zhukov was given a chance to reply. Naturally, he proclaimed his loyalty to the party and denied any intention to undermine its authority within the armed forces. On the contrary, it had been his policy to utilise military commanders – most of whom were experienced communists as well as officers – to strengthen the role of the party within the armed forces. While he was speaking Zhukov suffered the same sort of heckling from Khrushchev that he himself had inflicted on the members of Molotov's antiparty group at the June plenum of the Central Committee.

Zhukov's fellow officers piled on with a litany of charges. In his contribution to the discussion Sokolovsky, chief of the General Staff, claimed that Zhukov had without consultation altered a General Staff document stating that the Soviet Union would never start a war to a statement that it might attack first. Marshal Timoshenko reiterated Suslov's point about Zhukov's power seeking and noted his tendency to claim infallibility. Konev, like Sokolovsky, claimed to have

defended Zhukov against Stalin's attack in 1946 but he now criticised
Zhukov's cult of personality. Yeremenko, who had served alongside
Khrushchev at Stalingrad, harped on the falsity of Zhukov's claims in
relation to the organisation of the counter-offensive there. Chuikov,
another Stalingrad general, complained that Stalin's cult had been replaced by Zhukov's. Rokossovsky highlighted Zhukov's vulgarity and
his insulting behaviour towards fellow officers, giving as an example
his dispute with Zhukov during the battle of Moscow. It wasn't that
Zhukov 'was just rude during the war,' said Rokossovsky. 'His way
of commanding was literally obscene; we heard nothing but continuous cursing and swearing mixed with threats to shoot people.' Malinovsky also stressed Zhukov's vulgarity, saying he had never heard
him deliver a speech that did not contain some vulgarity. Absent from
the plenum was Vasilevsky, who was ill. It is difficult to say whether
he would have joined in the condemnation of Zhukov. Certainly, he
would have been expected to and relations between the two men remained distant until Zhukov was rehabilitated for a second time in
the 1960s.

Towards the end of the plenum Zhukov spoke again, thanking the
Central Committee members for their criticism and admitting he had
made mistakes. But on one point he stood firm. It had been pointed
out that this was not the first time he had been hauled before the Central Committee to account for his mistakes and in 1946 he had refused
to recognise the errors of his ways. Zhukov's riposte was that while he
accepted the criticism levelled at him now he did not and would not
accept that he had been wrong in 1946.

The last word at the plenum was Khrushchev's. In a typically ram-
bling speech he broadened the attack on Zhukov to include aspects of
his war record, especially in relation to the fall of Kiev in 1941, the
Kharkov debacle of 1942, and the battle of Stalingrad. Khrushchev
also accused Zhukov of not understanding modern military technology. At the end of the meeting a resolution was passed confirming the
Presidium's decision to sack Zhukov as defence minister and to expel
him from the Central Committee as well as the Presidium.[61] He would
remain a member of the party but within weeks he had been stripped
of all power.

After the plenum the campaign against Zhukov was carried into the armed forces, the party, and the wider public domain. At a meeting of party members in Moscow on 31 October Marshal Moskalenko denounced Zhukov's 'vanity, egoism, limitless arrogance and narcissism', while Malinovsky blasted his 'stubbornness, despotism, ambition, and search for self-glorification'. Perhaps the unkindest cut came from his old friend Bagramyan, who reportedly said that Zhukov was 'simply a sick man. Self-aggrandizement is in his blood'.[62]

That Zhukov had been replaced by Malinovsky as defence minister was announced to the world even before the plenum in a brief statement on the back page of *Pravda* on 27 October.[63] On 3 November the Soviet press published the Central Committee resolution 'On Improving Party Political Work in the Soviet Army and Navy', revealing that Zhukov had been sacked because he had pursued a policy of curtailing the work of the party in the armed forces. The resolution criticised the cult of Zhukov's personality and its distorting effect on the 'true history' of the Great Patriotic War. The resolution referred also to Zhukov's 'adventurism' in foreign policy – presumably an oblique reference to his dispute with Khrushchev over disarmament negotiations with the United States. That same day *Pravda* carried a long article by Konev attacking Zhukov's war record. Konev pointed out that when the Germans attacked in June 1941 Zhukov was chief of the General Staff and should share responsibility for the ensuing debacle. Konev also criticised Zhukov for claiming unwarranted credit for operations such as the Stalingrad counter-offensive and the assault on Berlin. According to Konev the successes of the Great Patriotic War were more the result of the efforts of Front commanders (like himself) than Stalin, Stavka, and Zhukov. And, Konev pointed out, while Zhukov was fond of attacking the Stalin cult Zhukov's purpose was not to critique the cult but to build up his own cult following.[64] A few months later Zhukov came across Konev in the street. Zhukov did not want to talk to him but Konev offered him a lift in his car, saying that he had not forgotten their old friendship. Zhukov refused, reminding Konev of his performance at the plenum when he was far from being a friend.[65]

While there had developed a personality cult around Zhukov since his appointment as minister of defence it was not a development he encouraged. Regarding party-army relations Zhukov's ousting has often been interpreted as evidence of institutional conflict between the two groups and of his own personal desire to assert the independence of the armed forces. The truth of the matter is both more simple and more complex. At the time and in retrospect Zhukov flatly denied seeking to undermine party control of the armed forces. 'For me personally, the word of the party was always the law,' he said later,[66] and he went out of his way to praise the role of political commissars and to emphasise the leadership role of the party. Zhukov, it should never be forgotten, was a lifelong communist himself. But he did have a particular view of how the party's control and influence within the armed forces should be exercised. Zhukov had been a strong supporter of *edinonachalie* – one-man command – since the Frunze reforms of the 1920s. Like Frunze, Zhukov believed commanders should be able to control military decision-making without interference from political commissars whose role was propaganda within the armed forces. The guarantee of party control was that the commanders would or should be dedicated communists themselves. Zhukov also urged that commissars be good soldiers as well as good communists.

During Zhukov's tenure at the Ministry of Defence there were numerous initiatives and instructions designed to strengthen both *edinonachalie* and the effectiveness of political work in the armed forces. For example, an instruction on the organisation of the party in the armed forces issued in April 1957 had one line forbidding party meetings from criticising the orders of commanders but the remainder of the text was devoted to strengthening the position of communists in the military, including in relation to the political behaviour of professional officers.[67] Many of the policies on party work in the armed forces implemented by Zhukov predated his term as minister of defence. When Zhukov issued a decree in May 1956 on improving military discipline through strengthening one-man command he was ordering the implementation of a policy that had been adopted in 1951 – during the Stalin era.[68] The accusation that Zhukov was seeking to undermine the party's role within the armed forces was a politically powerful pretext for removing him from office but the charge had no substance.

Zhukov believed that Khrushchev's decision to cut him adrift was mainly personal and was prompted by Zhukov's independence of mind and his refusal to pander to the growing cult of Khrushchev's personality. Khrushchev also feared that Zhukov, like Eisenhower, aspired to higher political office. 'I never wanted state power – I am a military man and the army was my business,' said Zhukov.[69]

Zhukov later claimed he saw Khrushchev's attack coming, but there is no contemporaneous evidence to support this assertion. All the signs are that in 1957 Zhukov was afflicted by the same combination of political naïveté and personal hubris he displayed when Stalin purged him in 1946.

As soon as Zhukov's fall from grace became known in the West speculation was rife as to the causes and consequences of his disgrace. One of the most accurate of the near-contemporary analyses was a CIA briefing paper dating from June 1959, which concluded: 'The causes of the Zhukov ouster appear to have been his devotion to his duty as he saw it, his lack of political tact, and his insistence on genuinely assuming the theoretical prerogatives of a full member of the party presidium and USSR minister.'[70]

The most prescient comment was that of the Indian ambassador in Moscow, K.P.S. Menon, who recorded in his diary on 5 November 1957:

> No star shone in the Russian firmament after Stalin's death with greater lustre than Zhukov's. The attempts that are now being made to blot it out can only be called pitiful. The Party may succeed in keeping Zhukov's figure out of the public eye, but it will not succeed in keeping his memory out of the hearts of men. . . . Ultimately truth will triumph, and Clio will place Zhukov by the side of such favourites as Alexander Suvorov, Mikhail Kutuzov and Alexander Nevsky. . . . And the grateful Russian land will always hold his memory in esteem and affection.[71]

FINAL BATTLE:
THE STRUGGLE FOR HISTORY,
1958–1974

———

ZHUKOV RECOVERED FROM THE ORDEAL OF THE OCTOBER PLENUM BY GOING home and sleeping. 'I was determined not to be a victim,' he told Konstantin Simonov, 'not to break down, not to fall apart, not to lose my will to live. . . . Returning home, I took a sleeping pill. I slept for several hours. I got up. I ate. I took a sleeping pill. Again I fell asleep. I got up again, took a sleeping pill and fell asleep. This went on for 15 days. . . . In my dreams I relived everything that had been tormenting me. . . . I disputed. I proved my point. I grieved – all in my sleep. Then, after 15 days, I went fishing.'[1]

Zhukov's distress was compounded by the continuing complications of his private life. Following his dismissal as defence minister his wife found out about his affair with Galina. Alexandra had known about Galina from her time in Sverdlovsk but did not know she had moved to Moscow. Nor did Alexandra know about Galina's daughter, Maria; indeed, she only found out about Maria four years later when Zhukov needed the permission of his legal wife to officially adopt Maria as his daughter. Zhukov responded to his personal crisis by swapping his flat on Granovsky Street for two smaller apartments – one for Alexandra and one for daughter Ella – while he himself went to live at his dacha with Galina and Maria. Neither Ella nor Era knew about their parents' de facto separation until the couple divorced in 1965. When they did find out they took their mother's side and did not speak to Zhukov for more than a year.[2] Then, in 1966, Zhukov married Galina.

IN RETIREMENT

When Khrushchev dismissed Zhukov as defence minister he promised to find him other work but the promise came to nothing and in February 1958 the Presidium retired Zhukov from the armed forces, albeit on comfortable terms by Soviet standards. He was awarded a good pension, generous medical aid and security support, and a small car for personal use. He was also allowed to keep his flat and dacha and to wear military uniform if he so desired.[3]

Less welcome was the surveillance of the KGB. From their reports we know that in retirement and in the privacy of his own home Zhukov was prone to criticise the Khrushchev regime. And not just at home; in September 1959 the KGB reported to Khrushchev that at the funeral of General V. V. Krukov (the husband of the singer Lidiya Ruslanova) Zhukov, in conversation with other mourners, had criticised party policy on military pensions and said that the growing authority of political officers was weakening the armed forces.

In May 1963 the KGB reported that Zhukov described as a 'toady' Marshal Malinovsky, his successor as defence minister. He criticised the amount of money spent on the Soviet space programme, and the gifts lavished on visiting foreign VIPs, something that would not have happened in Stalin's time. Zhukov was scathing about the multivolume official Khrushchevite *History of the Great Patriotic War* that began publication in 1960,[4] which claimed that western Allied aid to the Soviet Union during the war had not been important. According to Zhukov, however, American supplies enabled the USSR to build up its reserves of equipment and to switch production to essential items such as tanks. The KGB official concluded his report by noting that Zhukov and family were due to go on holiday soon, presenting an opportunity to find out what he was writing in his memoirs.

This particular KGB report touched a nerve. In June 1963 the Presidium resolved to send a delegation headed by Leonid Brezhnev to warn Zhukov that if he did not desist from such criticism he would be

expelled from the party and arrested. But when Brezhnev visited Zhukov later that month the marshal was unrepentant. He was unable to
accept the resolution passed by the October 1957 plenum, he told
Brezhnev, because he had not been given an opportunity to comment
on it. He was particularly incensed by the resolution's charge of adventurism: 'When and where was I an adventurist? In relation to what
was I an adventurist? I have been in the party for 43 years, I have
fought in four wars, I have sacrificed my health for the motherland
and yet somehow and somewhere I have committed adventurist acts?
Where are the facts? Such facts there are not.' Zhukov denied he had
criticised the party in conversation with others and demanded an opportunity to confront his accusers. On the other hand, Zhukov
pledged his eternal loyalty to the party and reassured Brezhnev that he
had nothing to fear from what he was writing in his memoirs.[5]

WRITTEN OUT OF HISTORY

Zhukov had begun writing his memoirs in the late 1950s in the context of a continuing campaign to discredit both his historical reputation and his personal integrity. The first salvo of criticism had been
fired by Konev in his post-plenum *Pravda* article of November 1957
that attacked various aspects of Zhukov's war record. In 1958 an authoritative article by General E. A. Boltin, a leading Soviet military
historian, criticised Zhukov for his failure when chief of the General
Staff in 1941 to make adequate preparations for war. His failings as
chief of the General Staff also featured in the second volume of the
official history of the Great Patriotic War, with Timoshenko, the people's commissar for defence in 1941, accused alongside Zhukov. More
damaging still was Malinovsky's accusation at the 21st Party Congress in 1959 that Zhukov had 'Bonapartist' tendencies – namely, as-
piring to supreme power – a charge repeated by Khrushchev at the
22nd Party Congress in 1961.[6] These very public attacks on his reputation paved the way for military memoirists to criticise Zhukov's performance during the war. Typically, they characterised him as ignorant
of sophisticated military matters and bullying in his dealings with fellow officers.[7] In February 1964 Zhukov wrote to Khrushchev to complain that memoirists and historians were depicting him not just as a

Bonapartist, but as an adventurist, a revisionist, and someone who was hostile to party criticism of the armed forces.[8]

For Zhukov the deafening silence of many historical publications regarding his role in the war was as galling as the frontal attacks. A 1958 study of the blockade of Leningrad omitted any mention of his crucial role in defending the city in September 1941. A 1960 study of the East Pomeranian operation did not even name Zhukov as the commander of the 1st Belorussian Front – one of the main fronts involved in liquidating a major German threat to the impending Soviet assault on Berlin. The first volume of the *History of the Great Patriotic War* acknowledged that Zhukov was in command at Khalkhin-Gol but gave him no credit for the Red Army's defeat of the Japanese. In 1962 Marshal V. D. Sokolovsky, former chief of the General Staff and Zhukov's deputy when he was defence minister, published the definitive Soviet textbook *Military Strategy*. Sokolovsky had served alongside Zhukov in many different capacities during and after the war but his former boss did not figure at all in the section dealing with the development of Soviet strategic thinking during the Second World War. Zhukov was no great strategic thinker but his practice of generalship during the Great Patriotic War did contribute greatly to the refinement of Soviet operational art. Nor did Sokolovsky mention Zhukov's pronouncements on military strategy when he was defence minister in 1955–1957 – a key period in the Soviet transition from conventional to nuclear concepts of warfare. In 1964 Sokolovsky edited a book on the battle of Moscow that barely mentioned Zhukov, despite the fact that he had served as Zhukov's chief of staff during that battle and well knew the central role Zhukov had played at this turning point of the war. In 1965 Rokossovsky was the editor-in-chief of a definitive text on the battle of Stalingrad that limited its recognition of Zhukov's role in events to the statement that he had served as Stalin's Stavka representative during the battle.[9] By this time, Zhukov must have felt a bit like the Duke of Wellington, who in old age remarked that when reading some historians' accounts of Waterloo he began to wonder whether he himself had been present at the battle![10]

Against this backdrop it is not surprising that in his memoirs Zhukov went to inordinate lengths to defend his war record while displaying a marked reluctance to discuss his failures and shortcomings, not least to avoid providing critics with yet more ammunition with which to attack him.

When Zhukov began writing his memoirs it was an act of faith since there was no possibility they would be published while Khrushchev remained in power. When Ella asked why he bothered, he told her that he was writing 'for the table' and 'for history'.[11] In October 1964, however, the Presidium, disillusioned by the failure of Khrushchev's domestic and foreign policies and fed up with his domineering leadership style, removed him from power. Like Zhukov, Khrushchev retired to his country dacha to write his own memoirs. Published in the West in the 1970s, they caused a sensation and the revelations they contained dominated western views of Soviet history for many years. In the second volume, published in 1974, Khrushchev devoted a whole chapter to Zhukov's dismissal in 1957. He reiterated that, in his opinion, Zhukov had Bonapartist tendencies and that was why it had been necessary to dismiss him as defence minister. At the same time Khrushchev was careful to show Zhukov some respect: 'I respected Zhukov for his intellect and for his common sense. We spent a lot of time talking business and also duck hunting together. . . . Zhukov was exceptionally perceptive and flexible for a military man.'[12]

REHABILITATION OF AN UNPERSON

Zhukov's rehabilitation after Khrushchev's fall was not immediate but it was not long delayed. In March 1965 Zhukov wrote to the party leadership arguing for his rehabilitation on grounds that he had been a victim of Khrushchev's dictatorial tendencies.[13] There does not appear to have been a reply to this letter but a month later TASS, the official Soviet news agency, broadcast some remarks about Zhukov by his old adversary, Konev. Zhukov had his shortcomings, said Konev, but he was a great military commander who should rightly take part in the imminent celebrations of the twentieth anniversary of victory in the Great Patriotic War. On 8 May Brezhnev, the new Soviet leader, delivered a keynote speech in the Kremlin on that anniversary. Zhukov was invited to attend and when he entered the meeting hall he was given a standing ovation. There was more applause when Brezhnev mentioned Zhukov's (and Stalin's) name in his speech. The next day

Zhukov was among the marshals standing once again on the rostrum above Lenin's mausoleum reviewing the Victory Parade. At the post-parade reception in the Kremlin the crowd applauded Zhukov as he took his place at his table. Later, Zhukov went to the Moscow Writers' Club where he gave an unscripted speech that impressed Konstantin Simonov for its restraint and modesty.[14] It was clear that years of Khrushchevite attacks had done little to dent Zhukov's popularity. He was – and would remain – the great general who had saved the Soviet Union from catastrophic defeat by Hitler and then led the country to a great victory.

In November 1966 Zhukov attended a conference celebrating the twenty-fifth anniversary of the battle of Moscow along with other 'Marshals of Victory', including Konev, Rokossovsky and Chuikov. When the marshals gathered on the platform the audience burst into applause that lasted several minutes. As the clapping died a delegate shouted 'glory to Marshal Zhukov!' and the applause started all over again – a display of adulation that did not please the party representative chairing the gathering.[15] That same month, on the eve of his seventieth birthday, Zhukov was awarded his fifth Order of Lenin – one of nearly seventy medals and decorations he received during his lifetime that included awards from Britain, France, the United States, Poland, Mongolia, Italy, Bulgaria, Czechoslovakia, Yugoslavia, Egypt and China.[16]

In June 1965 the main Soviet military history journal, *Voenno-Istoricheskii Zhurnal,* published Zhukov's reply to Chuikov's criticism of his failure to capture Berlin in February 1945. This was the signal that it was once again permissible to publish Zhukov's writings and from then until the end of his life he was in constant demand to write, give interviews, and make personal appearances.[17] In his public appearances Zhukov mainly spoke or wrote about the war but he also took an interest in contemporary events. For example, in one piece he warned that the Vietnam War must not be allowed to develop into a new world war, criticised China's role in world affairs and its attacks on the USSR (this was the time of the Sino-Soviet split), and warned of a possible rapprochement between Beijing and Washington.[18]

Among Zhukov's more notable publications were articles in weighty tomes on the battles of Moscow and Stalingrad published in

1968 and on Kursk in 1970.[19] Zhukov was also interviewed for documentary films about the two battles. The script for the Stalingrad film was subjected to extensive correction by Zhukov, who advised the producers against the use of slang because it could damage the education of young people.[20] Simonov observed Zhukov's interviews for the documentary on the battle of Moscow and was impressed by his iron concentration and recall of detail, even though he was in pain from a fall the day before.[21] Zhukov's performance in both documentaries was somewhat stilted but confident and commanding. In August 1969 he was interviewed by Georgian television and told his viewers that their compatriot Stalin was 'a great organiser of the struggle against Germany and its allies' who had demonstrated outstanding ability in the conduct of strategic operations and the will to fight the war through to final victory.[22]

Zhukov did not, however, spend all his time engaged in public activities or writing his memoirs. He looked after his daughter Maria, while Galina, now his second wife, who was a doctor and a specialist in infectious diseases, worked in a Moscow hospital. He also repaired relations with Era and Ella. He often went to the theatre with Galina, including the Bolshoi, but preferred opera to ballet. He spent time in his garden and gathered mushrooms in the local woods. His dacha had a cinema room and the family watched many films together. He read a lot, not only military history and theory, but the classics of Russian literature. And, as ever, he went hunting and fishing.[23]

MEMOIRS

In July 1965 Zhukov was approached by Anna Mirkina, an editor at APN – the publishing arm of the Novosti press agency – about writing his memoirs. According to Mirkina, the approach was prompted by a proposal from a French publisher to produce a series of Soviet military and political memoirs. Zhukov had already been in some contact with Novosti. In early 1965 the agency had commissioned him to write an article on Germany's surrender. In March 1965 APN copied the article to the party leadership and requested permission to publish. The article was never published but the material it contained was later incorporated into the memoirs.[24]

Zhukov invited Mirkina to meet him at his dacha in Kuntsevo on the west side of Moscow. Zhukov's dacha (given to him by Stalin in 1942) was no small country cottage but a rather grand two-story house. Mirkina recalled the walls of the entrance hall as being decorated with photographs of Zhukov and his staff taken during the battle of Moscow. The hall led into a large and formally furnished dining room, in the middle of which stood a big oval table covered with a white cloth. Suspended over the table was a beautiful crystal chandelier. Along one wall there was a heavy oak sideboard and in one corner a chiming clock. Beside the clock was a small table on which stood a bust of Zhukov and a model of a T-34 tank. The dining room opened onto a terrace with a small round table and two easy chairs.

Zhukov, dressed informally in his at-home clothes, led Mirkina through to his study, a fair-sized but comfortable and well-lit room. It contained a large writing table covered with worn green leather that Zhukov sat at with his back to the window, taking advantage of the light. The room was full of the books Zhukov used in writing his memoirs and a picture of his mother hung on the wall.[25]

Once Mirkina had satisfied Zhukov that APN was a legitimate publisher who would support him in telling the truth about the war he was happy to allow them to publish the memoirs. The contract was signed in August 1965 and it galvanised Zhukov to finish writing. By autumn 1966 he had delivered to the publisher a 1,430-page typed manuscript.[26] Zhukov did not type it himself, nor did he like to dictate. He wrote longhand because, he told Mirkina, it enabled him to organise his thoughts. His pages were then typed up by Galina's mother, Klavdiya Evgeniya.[27]

By the mid-1960s Zhukov had been granted access to the Ministry of Defence archive at Podolsk on the outskirts of Moscow where he studied some 1,500 documents.[28] The inclusion of many citations from archive documents lent his memoirs a unique air of authenticity and authority and made them a key source for historians in the era before the collapse of the USSR and the opening of Soviet archives to scholarly research.

Zhukov did not write his memoirs in isolation but in consultation, conversation, and correspondence with former colleagues in the High Command and other wartime comrades. Among them were

Vasilevsky, Bagramyan, and Rokossovsky. He also talked with the editors of *Voenno-Istoricheskii Zhurnal* and with the representatives of various publishing houses, journals and newspapers seeking his contributions and advice. Not all of these interactions were positive. In April 1965, for example, he wrote to Rokossovsky to correct mistakes he alleged the marshal had made in an interview about the war with *Literaturnaya Gazeta*. Zhukov was particularly concerned about Rokossovsky's failure to challenge myths about the war spawned during the Khrushchev era, not least the exaggeration of the importance of Khrushchev's role in events.[29]

Zhukov's closest confidant during this period was General A. N. Antipenko, who had been his supplies officer when he commanded the 1st Belorussian Front in 1945 and had also served with him in Germany after the war. Antipenko recalled that shortly after the October 1957 plenum he came across Zhukov at a health centre. When they embraced Zhukov asked him why he was not afraid. When Antipenko asked him what there was to be afraid of Zhukov replied that on the way to the centre he had met two other generals of his acquaintance who had crossed the street to avoid him. Why would he want to do that, responded Antipenko, when he had served with Zhukov during the war? Thereafter the two men spent a lot of time together – hunting, fishing, going to the theatre, and discussing Zhukov's memoirs.[30] After Khrushchev's fall Antipenko became the leading advocate of Zhukov's rehabilitation, pointing out to Brezhnev and other party leaders that such a move would be very popular both at home and abroad. After publication of Zhukov's memoirs in 1969, Antipenko wrote a letter to the main party journal, *Kommunist*, urging a reversal of the verdict of the October 1957 plenum.[31] This letter was not published and there is no evidence that such a radical step was even contemplated during the Brezhnev era. The problem with repudiating the 1957 plenum was that it would have called into question Brezhnev's judgment as well as that of all the other members of the Central Committee who had supported Khrushchev's assault on Zhukov, including Mikhail Suslov, who had led the attack and remained the party's top ideologist under Brezhnev. It could also have raised questions about the treatment of Molotov, Malenkov, and Kaganovich – the antiparty group expelled from the party leadership by the June 1957 plenum – who were lobbying for their political rehabilitation, too.

Zhukov's close relationship with Antipenko during his retirement was an anomaly. During his adult life Zhukov had many followers, admirers, comrades in arms, drinking and hunting buddies, and professional associates, but few intimate male friends. Apart from Antipenko, only Bagramyan could be said to have sustained a deep and long-lasting friendship with Zhukov. At certain times in his life Zhukov was close to Vasilevsky, too, but not during his disgrace under Khrushchev, after which the relationship between the two men never recovered fully. The partial estrangement was no doubt reinforced by Era's divorce from Vasilevsky's son Yuri.

Having finished the writing of his memoirs Zhukov now faced the problem of negotiating their contents with Soviet censors. All Soviet publications had to undergo some process of official vetting and editing and it proved to be a long drawn-out process for Zhukov. In December 1967 an impatient Zhukov appealed personally to Brezhnev to expedite matters, and he did so again in February 1968. But it was not until April 1968 that a group headed by Marshal Grechko, minister of defence, reported on the memoirs. The group's appraisal was generally positive but critical of Zhukov's tendency to inflate his own role and not pay sufficient attention to the collective contribution of the party, especially its leadership. The report focused in particular on Zhukov's treatment of the immediate pre-war period, arguing that he undervalued the significance of the party's preparations for war. One specific point was that Zhukov was deemed to attribute too much importance to the negative impact of the 1930s purges of the Red Army. Grechko's conclusion was that the memoirs should be published but only after further editing and correction.[32]

The memoirs were then handed over to a specialist editorial group headed by historian G. A. Deborin. The Deborin group worked on the required changes in consultation with Zhukov, and with V. G. Komolov, a journalist employed by APN to mediate relations between the author and the editors. According to Komolov the editing was a fraught process and Zhukov bridled at many of the proposed changes.[33] Nevertheless, the work proceeded quickly and by summer

1968 an approved text for publication had been agreed upon by the Central Committee.[34] The hundreds of photographs published in the book also had to be approved by the censor.

Without access to the unexpurgated text of Zhukov's original manuscript it is difficult to gauge the full extent of the changes wrought by the process of censorship, but certainly hundreds of pages and entire passages were excised or significantly altered. There were also many additions. One notorious example was the inclusion of a passage in which Zhukov stated that he would have liked to have been able to consult political commissar Colonel Leonid Brezhnev while on a trip to the north Caucasus in April 1943 but unfortunately the future Soviet leader was not available. 'The wise will understand', daughter Maria recalled Zhukov saying – meaning that marshals did not seek the counsel of colonels. According to Maria, it was her mother who convinced Zhukov that 'no one would believe he had written these lines and that if he did not make a compromise, the book would not come out at all'.[35]

The officially sanctioned memoirs were finally published in April 1969. Although the plan was to print half a million copies paper shortages meant that only 100,000 could be printed followed by a further print run of 200,000 in a format that required fewer pages.[36] These soon sold out and eventually millions more copies of the memoirs would be printed and sold, not only in the Soviet Union, but throughout the world and in numerous translations. The Soviet public was wildly enthusiastic and Zhukov received thousands of letters from readers offering congratulations, corrections, and suggestions for future editions.[37] The official reception was more muted, at least initially; in April 1969 the party Central Committee issued a directive that no reviews, commentaries, or excerpts from Zhukov's memoirs were to be published.[38] In July, however, *Kommunist* published a long and very positive review by Vasilevsky, who wisely played down Zhukov's personal exploits, emphasising instead his patriotism and his loyalty to the Communist Party and the Soviet state. The article was entitled 'Sovetskomu Soldatu Posvyashchaetsya' (Dedicated to the Soviet Soldier) – the same dedication that adorned Zhukov's memoirs. Another highly positive review appeared in *Voenno-Istoricheskii Zhurnal* in November.[39]

TRIUMPH AND TRAGEDY

Although publication of his memoirs was a triumph for Zhukov it came at an increasingly difficult time in his personal life. In December 1967 Galina had an operation that revealed she had cancer and the prognosis was that she had five years to live. That same month Alexandra died of a stroke. Zhukov was ill and unable to attend the funeral but he locked himself in his room for a whole day.[40]

As if these were not troubles enough, in January 1968 Zhukov himself suffered a severe stroke while resting at a sanatorium at Arkhangel'skoe outside Moscow that left him paralysed on his left side. He was incapacitated for a month. After his recovery his speech remained slurred and he could walk only with assistance. In December 1968 Zhukov wrote to Brezhnev asking if he could swap his fifteen-year-old Zil for a more comfortable Chaika. He had to visit the clinic for treatment quite often, he explained to Brezhnev, and the Chaika was a better-constructed car that would give him a 'softer ride'.[41] What action Brezhnev took in relation to Zhukov's request is not known.

Galina's illness and Zhukov's incapacity forced the couple to spend long periods apart while Galina was being treated at different clinics. 'Day and night, I think only about you', he wrote to her in July 1973. In November 1973 Galina's condition took a turn for the worse and she died on 13 November at the age of forty-seven. Zhukov was unable to get to see her in the hospital before her death. Galina was buried in the Novodevichy cemetery, a famous Moscow resting place for many of the most prominent figures of the Soviet era, including Khrushchev, who had died in 1971. Zhukov attended the funeral walking with the aid of a cane and the assistance of Bagramyan. 'Such a blow I will not survive,' he told Maria.[42]

But he did survive and indeed completed revisions for the second edition of his memoirs, incorporating corrections and adding new chapters based on reviews and reader feedback: the siege of Leningrad, the Yel'nya battle, and the workings of Stavka and the Soviet High Command. To help Zhukov with the Stavka chapter the publishers drafted in the historian Evgeny Tsvetaev, who had worked with General Shtemenko on his memoirs. Preparation of the second edition began in 1973 but progress was slow because of Zhukov's poor health and the doctor's orders that he should work only an hour a day. Tsvetaev wanted Zhukov to provide a detailed account of the workings of Stavka but Zhukov insisted he was writing a memoir, not a scientific tract. The result was a compromise – a chapter that combined elements of memoir with a general description of the operation of Stavka. Even so, it was a chapter that was destined to become a key text for historians seeking to understand how the Soviet High Command operated during the war.[43]

Despite his and Galina's poor health Zhukov continued to respond to requests for interviews and articles. In February 1972, for example, TASS asked for an article that would be published in the country's youth papers on 23 February – Soviet Army Day. 'Defence of the motherland and service in the Soviet army', Zhukov told his young readers, 'is a sacred obligation, an honourable and noble duty, a matter of honour and pride.' In December 1972 Zhukov contributed the preface to a book by a group of war veterans: 'Years pass. Many war veterans are no longer with us. Old age is catching up with others. But veterans never give up. They retain their youthful spirit, they remain indefatigable.'[44]

It was an apt epitaph for Zhukov himself, whose struggle with bad health and old age was nearing its end. After Galina's death Zhukov's own health deteriorated and he did not live to see the publication of the second edition of his memoirs. He died in the Kremlin hospital on 18 June 1974. His revised memoirs were published just a few weeks later.

Zhukov's funeral was the biggest state occasion in the Soviet Union since the death of Stalin. Among those in attendance were his four daughters – Era, Ella, Margarita, and Maria – the one and only occasion they were seen together.

The death notice was published in *Pravda* on 20 June. Heading the long list of signatures by senior Soviet political and military leaders was party general secretary Brezhnev. The announcement stated:

> The Soviet people and their armed forces have suffered a
> grave loss. From us has been taken a distinguished military

figure and a renowned hero of the Great Patriotic War. . . . The communist party sent him to the most difficult sectors of the struggle with the German-Fascist invaders. As commander of the Leningrad and Western Fronts he was one of the organisers of the defence of Leningrad and Moscow . . . he coordinated the actions of the Stalingrad and Don Fronts and played a prominent role in the destruction of the Hitlerite forces at Kursk and in the liberation of the Ukraine and Belorussia. In the final stage of the war G. K. Zhukov commanded the 1st Belorussian Front which together with other Fronts finished off the enemy in his own lair. In all the posts entrusted to him by the party G. K. Zhukov displayed unbending willpower, courage and organisational talent. . . . The memory of Georgi Konstantinovich Zhukov – a true son of the Leninist party, a brave soldier and a talented commander – will always be preserved in the hearts of the Soviet people.[45]

A second eulogy, written by Vasilevsky, was published in *Pravda* the next day. He paid particular tribute to Zhukov's operational art – his ability to plan, prepare and execute large-scale military operations. 'Possessing great military talent Georgi Konstantinovich excelled in the ability to understand complex strategic situations and make the correct analysis of developing events. . . . In preparing plans for operations he always took a creative, original approach.'[46]

As Zhukov lay in state in the Central House of the Soviet army in Moscow thousands of citizens queued to pay their respects. When his ashes were interred in the Kremlin wall on 21 June the chief pallbearer was Brezhnev and at the memorial service that followed the main speaker was Minister of Defence Grechko.[47]

More ambivalent feelings about Zhukov were apparent in 'On the Death of Zhukov' (1974) – a poem by the exiled Soviet writer Joseph Brodsky:

> How much soldiers' blood he did spill in foreign fields!
> Was he sorry?
> Did he remember them as he lay dying in civilian sheets?

Silence.
What will he tell them when he meets them in hell?
   'I waged war.'[48]

RISE OF THE ZHUKOV CULT

As is so often the case, Zhukov achieved an even greater reputation in death than he had latterly enjoyed in life. His funeral marked the beginning of a Zhukov cult that lauded his status as the greatest Soviet general of the Second World War. Although the cult was kept somewhat under control by Brezhnev, Zhukov was celebrated in official historiography, in numerous documentary films about the war, and even in a specially produced book about his exploits produced for children and young adults.[49] His birth village was renamed Zhukov in his honour and in 1980 a newly discovered planetoid was named after him, too.

In the late 1980s two collections of reminiscences about Zhukov were published.[50] Among the contributors were Era and Ella, who both depicted a devoted husband and a loving father, a family man who did his best to overcome the difficulties his military career imposed on his personal life. The two sisters also published letters written by their father to them and to their mother, showing that in private Zhukov could be attentive, caring, and gentle, notwithstanding his professional persona as a tough commander.

Equally fervent in support of her father was Maria, who inherited his private papers when Zhukov died. A number of files were taken away by party officials and deposited in state archives but among the remaining papers were the original manuscripts of his memoirs. Most of the material excluded by the party censors was only of scholarly interest but included, for example, an extensive discussion by Zhukov of the pre-war purge of the Soviet armed forces, including an account of how he almost became one of Stalin's victims himself. The original draft of the memoirs also showed Zhukov was more critical of Stalin than he appeared to be in the officially approved version published in 1969 and revised in 1974. The tenth edition of Zhukov's memoirs, published in 1990 with Maria's support, incorporated a large amount of the excluded material and the eleventh edition published two years later included even more.[51] This new version of the memoirs put some distance between Zhukov and Stalin.

Another important event shaping Zhukov's image in the 1980s was the posthumous publication in 1987 of Konstantin Simonov's 'Notes Towards a Biography of G. K. Zhukov'. The famous Soviet writer had died in 1979 and the notes were based on meetings and conversations he had with Zhukov from the late 1930s through the mid-1960s. Simonov's treatment of Zhukov focused on the person rather than the general, in particular on how he had coped emotionally with the travails of his post-war career. The book's overall effect humanised Zhukov and redrew the Khrushchevite picture of him as an egotistical brute. Simonov showed Zhukov as emotionally vulnerable as well as tough-minded, self-reflective as well as self-confident, strong-willed but flexible to change if experience warranted.[52]

Another influential publication of the late 1980s – the era of Mikhail Gorbachev, glasnost, and more openness in the USSR about the Soviet past – was a series of articles on Zhukov by Lieutenant General N. G. Pavlenko entitled 'Reflections on the Fate of a Commander'. Pavlenko, a former editor of *Voenno-Istoricheskii Zhurnal,* had been instrumental in getting Zhukov published again in 1965. Like Simonov, Pavlenko highlighted the injustice of the party's post-war treatment of Zhukov, not only during his periods of exile under Stalin and Khrushchev but also in the failure to rehabilitate him fully during the Brezhnev era. One example of ill treatment cited by Pavlenko was Zhukov's exclusion from the 24th Party Congress in 1971, even though he had been elected to attend as a delegate, because of the fear that his popularity at the congress would outshine Brezhnev's.[53]

When the Soviet Union collapsed in 1991, post-Soviet Russia needed new heroes to replace the icons of the discredited communist regime. Zhukov fitted the bill perfectly. In the late 1980s he had been successfully reinvented as an independent figure whose patriotism and professionalism were seen as more significant than his loyalty to Stalin and the Soviet system. He was the hero of the Great Patriotic War, a war that the vast majority of Russians still considered sacred. He was also an authentically, ethnically *Russian* hero. As his daughter Era put it, Zhukov 'was completely Russian by nature. He loved everything Russian: land and people, music and arts, customs and food.'[54]

Zhukov's specifically Russian identity was important to the post-Soviet regime, which replaced socialism with nationalism as the legitimising foundation of the state.

An early sign that Zhukov was destined for celebrity status in the new Russia was the striking of a commemorative rouble adorned with his image. In May 1994 Boris Yeltsin, then Russian president, issued two further decrees in relation to Zhukov. The first directed that a memorial to Zhukov be built in time for the fiftieth anniversary of victory in the Great Patriotic War in May 1995. The second created two new military decorations – a Zhukov Medal and an Order of Zhukov. The memorial – a large statue by the sculptor V. M. Klykov and architect U. Grigoriev depicting Zhukov riding his horse at the 1945 Victory Parade – was finished in time for the anniversary and duly erected at the main entrance to Red Square where it remains as a major attraction for Russian and foreign tourists. On the 100th anniversary of his birth in 1996 the boundaries of Zhukov village were extended and the area upgraded to town status and a museum in his honour opened. In 1999 the Yeltsin government published the report of a presidential commission exonerating Zhukov of all charges levelled against him by Khrushchev in 1957. It also resolved to publish the records of the Central Committee plenum of October 1957 at which Zhukov had confronted and replied to his Khrushchevite accusers.[55]

These government initiatives were only one component of a rash of recognition of Zhukov's status as Russia's national hero: special exhibitions, commemorative plaques, celebratory conferences, adulatory press articles, respectful TV documentaries, poems and songs dedicated to him, and the publication of yet more glowing memoirs by those who had known him. In 1992 the first of many Russian biographies of Zhukov was published[56] and throughout the 1990s and into the twenty-first century barely a year went by without the publication of at least several books about him and his exploits. Most of this literature was dedicated to promoting Zhukov as the 'Marshal of Victory'. Equally, dissident voices promoting a critique of Zhukov's mistakes and shortcomings continued to be heard. For those critics Zhukov was not a hero but a villain, a loyal and ruthless servant of Stalin and the Soviet state who stood for a cause – communism – and a past that Russia needed to excoriate rather than celebrate.[57]

There have also been numerous fictional representations of Zhukov, including a short story by Aleksandr Solzhenitsyn, published in 1995, shortly after he returned to Russia from exile in the United States. In it, Solzhenitsyn imagined Zhukov writing his memoirs and grappling with the problem of how to depict his relationship with Stalin. In Solzhenitsyn's treatment, Zhukov had been dominated personally by Stalin, but during the war his confidence grew and their more equal relations prompted the Soviet dictator to exile him in 1946. But Zhukov did not blame Stalin for his misfortune, and his faith in the Soviet dictator was shaken but not destroyed by Khrushchev's revelations at the 20th Party Congress in February 1956.

Solzhenitsyn's story, based on Zhukov's various memoirs, contains a lot of truth in its portrayal of a dedicated communist who loved soldiering and whose brutal command style was driven more by his judgments of military necessity than by personal choice. More doubtful is Solzhenitsyn's speculation that in 1956 Zhukov wondered whether he should move against the party. There is no evidence for such a supposition, and Solzhenitsyn's own astute account of Zhukov's communist conscience makes it difficult to believe that his faith in the party ever wavered.[58]

Towards the end of his life Zhukov completed one of those celebrity questionnaires now so common in newspapers and magazines the world over. His answers were preserved by his daughter Maria:

Q. What is the most important thing in a person's life?
Z: *A sense of duty fulfilled.*
Q. What quality in people do you value above all?
Z: *Integrity.*
Q. On the part of men?
Z: *Courage and audacity.*
Q. On the part of women?
Z: *Faithfulness and tenderness.*
Q. Your favourite colour?
Z: *Sky-blue.*
Q. Favourite writers?
Z: *Lev Tolstoy, Mikhail Shokolov, Alexander Tvardovsky.*
Q. Most talented Russian commanders?

Z: Suvorov and Kutuzov. It is impossible to separate them.

Q. Favourite composer?

Z: Tchaikovsky.

Q. What won't you forgive?

Z: Betrayal!

Q. Are you envious of any of your friends?

*Z: Yes! I've always envied [Marshal] Budenny. He is a virtu-*oso on the accordion.[59]

14.

Marshal of Victory

———

ZHUKOV COMPLETED WORK ON THE SECOND EDITION OF HIS MEMOIRS SHORTLY before he died in June 1974. Writing a new conclusion was his last authorial task. The first edition had finished with a conventional paean to the Communist Party, the glorious socialist system, the wonderful Soviet people, and the great victory over Nazism. Although these pieties were repeated in this second edition Zhukov, ailing and nearing the end of his life, was in a more reflective mood: 'My life like that of any other person was marked by joys, sorrows, and losses. For me the most important thing in my life was my service to my country, to my own people. And I can say with a clear conscience that I did everything I possibly could to do my duty.'

Keen to pass on the torch of patriotic service to the younger generation, Zhukov urged them to appreciate the colossal sacrifices of those who had fought in the war, to be kind to surviving veterans, and, above all, to learn the lessons of history: 'It is young people who will have to further our cause. It is very important that they should learn from our mistakes and our successes.'

Zhukov ended by recalling his boyhood, noting the decisive impact the Russian Revolution had in transforming his prospects as a young man, offering him 'the opportunity to live a completely different way of life, a vivid interesting life full of exciting experiences and important deeds'.[1]

Zhukov died satisfied with his life's work, content that he had given good service to his party and to his homeland. The Soviet people were mostly satisfied, too. To them Zhukov was a patriotic hero who had served his motherland well through turbulent periods of deep crisis when only total, unwavering commitment to a cause would ensure the Soviet Union's survival. This view of Zhukov-as-hero remains alive for present-day Russians, though few now share his unshakable commitment to communism.

It is not hard to understand why Zhukov continues to be held in such high esteem. In the galaxy of talented Soviet generals who fought and won the Great Patriotic War of 1941–1945 no one's light continues to shine more brightly than Zhukov's. Only Zhukov was involved in each and every one of the critical turning points and battles that saved Russia and the Soviet Union from Hitler. Zhukov is and forever will be the 'Marshal of Victory' in a war that cost the Soviet Union 25 million dead, destroyed a third of its national wealth, and devastated tens of thousands of its villages, towns, and cities. In some ways it was a Pyrrhic victory but the alternative of enslavement as part of Hitler's racist empire was even worse.

During the war Zhukov experienced many setbacks and the troops under his command suffered horrendous numbers of casualties on the way to victory. But winning in war tends to trump all criticism of the conduct of particular battles or operations and obviates all what-might-have-been discussions concerning different courses of action or different command decisions. In Russia Zhukov's reputation as a great general will endure for generations for the simple reason that whatever his mistakes or defeats he also won the greatest – and most decisive – victories.

This popular view of Zhukov is shared by Russia's military professionals. In his 2004 study of the top Soviet generals of the Great Patriotic War, General M. A. Gareev, president of the Russian Academy of Military Science and himself a veteran of the battle of Moscow, assessed Zhukov's qualities as a commander: inexhaustible reserves of creative energy; deep understanding and flexibility in the face of battle; meticulous planning and preparation of each and every operation; and the bravery and determination to pursue his goals. In the military history of Russia, concluded Gareev, only Alexander Suvorov, the eighteenth-century tsarist general and strategist who never lost a battle, could be considered Zhukov's equal as a great commander.[2]

Yet while Zhukov was a great commander he was not the unrivalled military genius of legend. He made no lasting contribution to strategic theory or to military doctrine. Nor did he bequeath any profound insights into the conduct of modern warfare. He certainly had his brilliantly incisive moments on the battlefield – at Khalkhin-Gol, during the battles of Moscow and Stalingrad, and on the road to Berlin in 1944–1945 – but his talent was for deployment, not for creative innovation or imaginative flair in battle. Similarly while Zhukov's tough and often coarse leadership style had its utility in the crises of all-out war, its transfer value is questionable. Threatening people with dire disciplinary action is not necessarily the most effective way to elicit their best efforts. Many other Soviet generals adopted very different but equally successful leadership styles, the most obvious example being Rokossovsky, who believed in using encouragement and coaxing as well as implementing discipline.

What distinguished Zhukov was his exceptional will to win. Throughout his life he displayed an intense determination to succeed, allied to a powerful energy for getting things done. For those around him Zhukov's wilfulness generated confidence in the possibility of success even in the most adverse of circumstances. This was never more evident than during the critical summer months of 1941 and again in 1942 at Stalingrad when the German and Axis forces threatened to sweep away all before them. At no time did Zhukov waver or allow himself to be perturbed by the prospect of defeat and his decision-making remained crisp and unequivocal.

Zhukov's legendary poise when confronted with seemingly insurmountable odds was less a matter of personal courage – although he was not lacking in bravery – and more a matter of supreme self-discipline. The self-control and obedience Zhukov expected of officers and troops was akin to that which he imposed upon himself. As an operational commander Zhukov fought hard within the Stavka central command for the decisions he favoured and for the forces and resources he needed to implement his orders. But once decisions had been made and directives issued – even if he had not achieved all he wanted – Zhukov executed his orders and he expected everyone else to behave in the same way.

These character-traits of Zhukov's – willpower, discipline, decisiveness, and self-assurance under fire – were complemented by important intellectual qualities: clarity of vision and purpose combined with a willingness to learn from experience. All great generals must have the capacity to penetrate the complexities of their strategic situation and see through battlefield confusion to identify what are the critical positions, decisions, and objectives so as to take appropriate, effective action. Equally important is that persistent pursuit of their military goals be balanced by the flexibility to change course when necessary.

In the early war years Zhukov did not always display this necessary adaptability. One example was his failure as chief of the General Staff to abandon offensive operations in summer 1941 and to instead adopt a strategic defence posture that might have better contained the German Blitzkrieg invasion. Another example was his continual pursuit in 1942 of the Rzhev-Viazma series of operations designed to dislodge Army Group Centre from its positions in front of Moscow but that culminated in the failure of Operation Mars. But as the war progressed Zhukov learned that it was sometimes necessary to retreat, when it was more effective to disengage, and when long-term success could be achieved by a pause or by ending an operation.

The scale of his strategic vision was another facet of Zhukov's generalship. Time and again during the war he embarked on operations with hugely ambitious goals. When the Germans invaded in June 1941 his ambition was to mount a strategic counter-invasion of enemy territory in order to turn the tables almost immediately, just as he had done during the map-based war games of January 1941. The aim of the Moscow counter-offensive in December that year was not only to drive the German forces away from the Soviet capital but to initiate a Barbarossa-in-reverse and drive them out of Russia altogether. The Soviet entrapment of the German 6th Army at Stalingrad in November 1942 was envisaged as a prelude to more gigantic encirclements of both Army Group South and Army Group Centre. Operation Polar Star in January 1943 aimed to encircle Army Group North as well as end the blockade of Leningrad. These grandiose ambitions were not realised but the successes that were achieved formed the building blocks of Operation Bagration and the Vistula-Oder operation in 1944–1945 that liberated Belorussia and Poland and took Zhukov to within striking distance of Berlin.

Zhukov's ambitious operations were not simply his own dreamed-up conceits. They were the shared vision of Stalin and Stavka and also reflected the Soviet tradition of grand projects of transformation. Zhukov's military comprehension had been formed in this tradition and although it could allow for creativity it was also highly authoritarian and hierarchical with an emphasis on discipline and conformity. Zhukov's reliance more on energy and vigour than on imagination to achieve his goals was consonant with the prevailing ethos of the whole Soviet system. So a particular component of Zhukov's great success was that he was a *Soviet* general and it is unlikely he would have been so effective a general in any other army.

As a Soviet general, Zhukov commanded a particular kind of army: an army of peasant conscripts of limited education and of little more than basic military training. Many of these peasants-in-uniform, together with their parents and grandparents, had experienced the traumatic consequences of forced collectivisation. While some were sincere and committed supporters of the communist cause, at least as many were hostile, ignorant, or indifferent. It is difficult to envisage how such an army could have been held together in the terrifying conditions of the ferocious fighting that obtained during the Soviet-German war except by a regime of harsh discipline and exemplary punishment. And harsh and merciless it undoubtedly was. The Soviets executed an astonishing 158,000 of their own troops during the war. Tens of thousands of others were punished by being dispatched to serve in so-called penal battalions where they had an opportunity to redeem themselves for their crimes and misdemeanours – if they were lucky enough to survive the 50 per cent fatality rate in such cannon fodder units. There is no hint that Zhukov ever regretted – or even had second thoughts about – any of the harsh measures he authorised.

It should be remembered that Zhukov was one of a number of highly talented Soviet generals who served under a very effective supreme commander – Stalin. If Zhukov was the greatest general of the Second World War – in the sense that he made a decisive contribution to all the war's significant turning points – it was not through his efforts alone. He was a member of a Soviet High Command that collectively performed brilliantly. Arguably, it was Stalin's management of his generals that mattered as much as their individual talents, skills, and exploits. By using his leadership and authority to create a coherent group of powerful and often clashing personalities, Stalin elicited the best from their individual and collective talents, and inspired and demanded a loyalty that held them together through disaster and triumph. Zhukov was Stalin's greatest individual asset from among this group. Time and again Zhukov delivered military victories to the Soviet dictator, unhesitatingly if not always unquestioningly. He never challenged the dictator's supremacy or showed ambition beyond achieving victory. He was indeed Stalin's general.[3]

How does this Soviet legend compare with other great commanders of the Second World War? And what should be compared? A simple tally of victories says nothing about how hard fought the individual battles may have been. A personality profile does not reveal military prowess. Generating popularity or provoking hostility among peers cannot measure talent and skill. Comparisons are made even more difficult when it comes to Zhukov because, as Eisenhower noted, the Soviet general 'had longer experience as a responsible leader in great battles than any other man of our time'.

Perhaps the most apposite comparisons would be with other top Soviet commanders, particularly Konev, Rokossovsky, and Vasilevsky. But none of those generals had as many diverse roles as did Zhukov, who was variously chief of the General Staff, Front commander, Stavka coordinator, and deputy supreme commander. Vasilevsky had various duties but mainly functioned as a Stavka representative and it was not until towards the end of the war that he commanded a Front. Zhukov, Konev, and Rokossovsky all experienced failure as well as success and it is difficult to adjudicate their relative merits as Front commanders. After the war Konev and Rokossovsky often complained of the interference in their Fronts' operations by the General Staff and by Stavka representatives such as Zhukov and Vasilevsky, claiming that as the on-the-spot commander they knew what was best. But neither Konev nor Rokossovsky ever had to meet the challenge of centrally coordinating and directing operations being conducted across multiple Fronts, so it remains unknown how well they would have performed and whether such experience would have changed their command style or altered their success rate.

The temperaments and leadership styles of Zhukov and Konev were quite similar. As multi-army Front commanders they both drove their troops forward with a relentless determination to achieve their prescribed goals at whatever cost was necessary. Both were aggressive, offensive-minded commanders but knew when to call off an attack and regroup. Rokossovsky had a more subtle and intellectual approach, at least in relation to his immediate colleagues and subordinates. As Rokossovsky noted in his memoirs Stalin, too, was adept at using a softly-softly approach when necessary, although the Soviet dictator was also capable of throwing tantrums, issuing threats, and delivering insults – behaviours typical of Zhukov's and Konev's leadership style.

Compared with non-Soviet generals Zhukov appears to combine many of their traits, both good and bad.[4] Zhukov's favourite American general was Eisenhower, who like himself was able to manage effectively a large and complex organisation responsible for millions of soldiers. Both men achieved this by surrounding themselves with loyal and talented lieutenants who got on with the job. Zhukov, however, lacked Eisenhower's diplomatic skills. After the war both men became successful politicians but Zhukov turned out to be the more politically naive of the two.

General Patton is famous for slapping two sick soldiers he thought were malingerers. There are reports that Zhukov, too, occasionally hit his subordinates, a practice picked up from his time in the tsarist army, where it was common. More happily, Patton and Zhukov shared a devotion to constant training and drilling as the basis for strong discipline on the battlefield. Both men were also fervent believers in offensive action and conveyed to their troops the need to close with the enemy in order to destroy them. Like Zhukov, Patton attained legendary status during the war and was held in high esteem and affection by the general public as well as by his troops. Both commanders liked nothing better than to be in action with their troops and as close to the front line as possible.

Another general who commanded respect and affection and

generated confidence in the ranks was the British Field Marshal Bernard Montgomery. Zhukov shared with Montgomery a dedication to meticulous planning and preparation of operations. Both men devoured resources to assemble the overwhelming force required to guarantee victory. Less happily, both men provoked jealousy and hostility among their peers as well as love and respect from other senior commanders.

Zhukov was dismissive of the German generals, partly because of their pro-Nazi politics but mainly because those who survived annoyed him with their memoir claims that they had lost the war because of Hitler's strategic errors, the severity of the Russian weather, and the Red Army's sheer weight of numbers, which enabled the Soviets to absorb far more casualties than the Wehrmacht. What none of them would admit, according to Zhukov, was that superior Soviet generalship was the primary reason they had lost the war.

The only German general who approached Zhukov's mass popularity during the war was Field Marshal Erwin Rommel. But Rommel was a battlefield tactician not a strategist or an organiser of large-scale operations. During the North African campaign – which he ultimately lost – Rommel commanded only a few divisions. Set-piece battles may not have been Zhukov's strongest skill but his prosecution of the fighting at Khalkhin-Gol and during the Yel'nya offensive in August 1941 is certainly comparable to Rommel's achievements in North Africa. Rommel was also fortunate not to have served on the Russian front – the destroyer of many German generals' lives and reputations.

Two German generals who did live to tell the tale of fighting on the Eastern Front were General Heinz Guderian and Field Marshal Erich von Manstein, whose names occur often in Zhukov's memoirs. Indeed, he cites their books as evidence for the veracity of his own account of various battles. But in his writings Zhukov made no effort to assess the merits of either as generals, except for a passing reference to von Manstein as 'enterprising'.

During Operation Barbarossa, Guderian's forces and Zhukov's fought head-to-head in the battle for Moscow. Guderian blamed the weather for his defeat in front of the Soviet capital but, as Zhukov was fond of pointing out, the cold did not discriminate between German and Soviet soldiers. When the 6th Army was surrounded at Stalingrad, von Manstein commanded the force charged with breaking the Soviet encirclement. This operation failed but Manstein later played an important role in securing the withdrawal of German forces south of Rostov-on-Don taking part in Hitler's failed drive to capture the Soviet oilfields at Baku. Like Zhukov, Manstein proved himself as adept at defensive battles as offensive ones.

Perhaps the most intriguing comparison is between Zhukov and General Douglas MacArthur. Like Zhukov, MacArthur was surprised by the weight of enemy attack at the beginning of the Pacific War and as a result suffered a series of disastrous and costly defeats in battles with the Japanese in the Philippines in 1941–1942. But MacArthur staged a comeback with a series of brilliant amphibious operations to recapture those islands, together with Borneo and New Guinea. Had the Japanese not surrendered in August 1945 following the dropping of atomic bombs on Hiroshima and Nagasaki and the Soviet invasion of Manchuria, MacArthur would have spearheaded the invasion of Japan and faced a military test of a scale that Zhukov encountered many times during the war. With Zhukov, MacArthur shared the trait of trusting his own intuition and judgment above others' and of being reluctant to admit his mistakes. But Zhukov did not go as far as MacArthur did in his memoirs where he concluded he had made no major mistakes in his military career.

The conclusion to be drawn from this survey of comparable generals is that while Zhukov did not excel as 'the best ever' in any one field of military endeavour, he was the best all-around general of the Second World War. He combined prowess and courage in battle with ambitious strategic vision, determination, and organisational ability. He inspired the affection and confidence of his troops – as well as their fear – if not the ungrudging respect of all his peers. He was stoic in defeat and exuberant in victory. He had seemingly inexhaustible reserves of energy and the will to succeed however challenging the circumstances.

These were qualities Zhukov needed to deploy again after the war when he came under personal and political attack from Stalin and then from Khrushchev. On both occasions he held his nerve and resolved to make a comeback after his fall from grace. Zhukov's resilience in the post-war period is almost as impressive as his war record.

As he had done during the war, Zhukov emerged triumphant from defeat and adversity.

A Soviet system that no longer exists provided the political and cultural context in which the dramatic triumphs and adversities of Zhukov's life and career took place. As a committed communist, he supported this system; it was a system he served, a system to which he was loyal, whatever its faults. Ironically, it is only because the Soviet regime collapsed in 1991 that it has been possible to undertake research to strip away the myths and political distortions and reveal an accurate measure of Zhukov as a general and as a man.

The Zhukov legend has continued to grow in post-Soviet times. But new sources of evidence make it possible to disentangle the seductive myth from the often ordinary reality and to truly capture the complexity and contradictions of a man who rose from peasant poverty to become a great general and a hero not only to the Russian people but to all those who value his incomparable contribution to the victory over Nazi Germany.

NOTES

―――

ABBREVIATIONS

The following abbreviations and short titles are used in the Notes:

RGVA: Rossiiskii Gosudarstvennyi Voennyi Arkhiv
(Russian State Military Archive)

Zhukov, *Reminiscences:* G. K. Zhukov. *Reminiscences and Reflections*,
2 vols. Moscow: Progress Publishers, 1985

Zhukov, *Vospominaniya:* G. K. Zhukov. *Vospominaniya i Razmyshleniya*,
11th ed., 3 vols. Moscow: APN, 1992

CHAPTER 1: SIC TRANSIT GLORIA

1 My account of the Victory Parade is based mainly on the Soviet newsreel
   film of the event: *Parad Pobedy 1945*. The typescript of Zhukov's speech
   was on display at an exhibition in Moscow in April 2010 celebrating the
   sixty-fifth anniversary of the victory in the Great Patriotic War. The information about Zhukov's rehearsal of the speech comes from his daughter Era, interviewed by the author in Moscow in April 2010.

2 Author interview with Era Zhukova, Moscow, April 2010.

3 K. Simonov, *Glazami Cheloveka Moego Pokoleniya* (Moscow: APN,
   1989), p. 330.

4 A. Mirkina, *Vtoraya Pobeda Marshala Zhukova* (Moscow: Vniigmi-
   Mtsd, 2000), p. 24.

5 *Georgy Zhukov: Stenogramma Oktyabr'skogo (1957g.) Plenuma TsK
   KPSS i Drugie Dokumenty* (Moscow: Democratiya, 2001), part one,
   docs. 9–10.

6 'F. I. Tolbukhin', *Pravda*, 19 October 1949.

7 *Bol'shaya Sovetskaya Entsiklopediya*, 2nd ed. (Moscow: Ogiz, 1952),
   pp. 222–23.

8 *Marshal Zhukov: Polkovodets i Chelovek*, vol. 2 (Moscow: APN, 1988),
   p. 70.

9 'U Groba Velikogo Vozhdya', *Krasnaya Zvezda*, 9 March 1953.

10 *Time,* 9 May 1955.

11 *Istoriya Velikoi Otechestvennoi Voiny Sovetskogo Souza,* 6 vols. (Moscow: Voenizdat, 1960–1965).

12 C. Ryan, *The Last Battle* (London: NEL, 1968), p. 169.

13 E. Salisbury (ed.), *Marshal Zhukov's Greatest Battles* (London: Sphere, 1971; originally published by Harper & Row in 1969), p. 4.

14 Erickson's review may be found in an archive file of Zhukov's containing foreign press cuttings about himself in the Russian State Military Archive – Rossiiskii Gosudarstvennyi Voennyi Arkhiv (hereafter RGVA), F. 41107, Op. 1, D. 85.

15 G. K. Zhukov, *Vospominaniya i Razmyshleniya* (Moscow: APN, 1969). An English translation was published as *The Memoirs of Marshal Zhukov* (London: Jonathan Cape, 1971).

16 G. K. Zhukov, *Vospominaniya i Razmyshleniya,* 2 vols. (Moscow: APN, 1974). This edition was published in English as G. Zhukov, *Reminiscences and Reflections,* 2 vols. (Moscow: Progress Publishers, 1985).

17 'V Poslednii Put': Pokhorony Marshala Sovetskogo Souza G. K. Zhukova', *Pravda*, 22 June 1974.

18 V. Suvorov, *Ten' Pobedy* (Donetsk: Harvest, 2003), pp. 17, 26.

19 G. K. Zhukov, *Vospominaniya i Razmyshleniya,* 3 vols., 10th and 11th eds. (Moscow: APN, 1990–1992). Both these editions italicise the material previously excluded. According to Otto Preston Chaney's count the tenth edition added 125 pages to previous editions and the eleventh a further thirty-five pages: O. P. Chaney, *Zhukov,* rev. ed. (Norman: University of Oklahoma Press, 1996), p. 527.

20 The files of Zhukov's Lichnyi Fond (personal file series) may be found in RGVA. There are c. 190 files consisting of manuscripts and materials relating to his memoirs, speeches, articles, correspondence, and personal memorabilia (F. 41107, Ops. 1–2). The archive also houses a series of Zhukov files on the battle of Khalkhin-Gol (F. 32113, Op. 1).

CHAPTER 2: FABLED YOUTH

1 Unless otherwise stated, the biographical information contained in this chapter is derived from the first three chapters of Zhukov's memoirs: G. Zhukov, *Reminiscences and Reflections,* vol. 1 (Moscow: Progress Publishers, 1985) (hereafter: Zhukov, *Reminiscences*). This 1985 English translation of the revised Russian edition of Zhukov's memoirs published in 1974 is the one that will be referred to throughout the book. Note that Zhukov celebrated his birthday on 2 December and this was the date recorded in many Soviet reference works. This was because when Zhukov was born the Julian calendar was still used in Russia, which at that time was twelve days behind the Gregorian calendar used by other countries. In the twentieth century the gap between the two calendars widened to thirteen days. In 1918 the Bolsheviks adopted the Gregorian calendar, which meant everyone had to change their birthdays. Many, like Zhukov, added thirteen days rather than the twelve they should have.

2   V. Daines, *Zhukov* (Moscow: Molodaya Gvardiya, 2005), p. 9.

3   M. Zhukova, *Marshal Zhukov – Moi Otets* (Moscow: Izdanie Sretensk-ogo Monastyriya, 2005), p. 25. Another source gives Zhukov's mother's age as twenty-nine when she married Konstantin.

4   Zhukov, *Reminiscences,* vol. 1, p. 19.

5   M. Zhukova, *Marshal Zhukov,* p. 34.

6   A. N. Buchin, *170 000 Kilometrov s G. Zhukovym* (Moscow: Molodaya Gvardiya, 1994), pp. 29–30.

7   See his daughter Era's memoir 'Otets' in *Marshal Zhukov: Polkovodets i Chelovek,* vol. 1 (Moscow: APN, 1998), p. 30.

8   Zhukov, *Reminiscences,* vol. 1, p. 24.

9   Cited by A. Axell, *Marshal Zhukov: The Man Who Beat Hitler* (London: Pearson, 2003), p. 2.

10   E. Zhukova, 'Interesy Ottsa', in *Marshal Zhukov: Polkovodets i Che-lovek,* vol. 1, pp. 47–48. An analysis of Zhukov's surviving books and his annotations of them may be found in V. S. Astrakhanskii, 'Biblioteka G. K. Zhukova', *Arkhivno-Informatsionnyi Bulleten',* no. 13, 1996.

11   *Marshal Zhukov: Moskva v Zhini i Sud'be Polkovodtsa* (Moscow: Glav-arkhiva Moskvy, 2005), pp. 21–22.

12   G. K. Zhukov, *Vospominaniya i Razmyshleniya,* 11th ed., vol. 1 (Mos-cow: APN, 1992), p. 64 (hereafter: Zhukov, *Vospominaniya*). This, the eleventh Russian edition of Zhukov's memoirs, will be referred to through-out the book. It is the fullest published version of Zhukov's memoirs. This exchange was omitted from the version published in the Soviet era. Bol-shevik (i.e., communist) policy was to oppose the war and seek the over-throw of the tsarist government, whereas Zhukov's statement indicated that his politics at the time were patriotic rather than socialist. Later in life Zhukov always maintained that he had fought in four wars on behalf of his country: the First World War, the Russian Civil War, the war with Japan in Mongolia in 1939, and the Second World War.

13   Zhukov, *Reminiscences,* vol. 1, p. 43.

14   Ibid., p. 49.

15   RGVA, F. 41107, Op. 1, D. 86, L. 5.

16   Zhukov, *Reminiscences,* p. 52.

17   M. von Hagen, *Soldiers in the Proletarian Dictatorship: The Red Army and the Soviet Socialist State, 1917–1930* (Ithaca, N.Y.: Cornell University Press, 1990), p. 39.

18   Daines, *Zhukov,* p. 28.

19   V. Krasnov, *Zhukov: Marshal Velikoi Imperii* (Moscow: Olma-Press, 2005), pp. 18–19. In his memoirs he confused this chronology by the inac-curate claim that candidate membership of the party did not exist when he joined on 1 March 1919.

20   B. V. Sokolov, *Georgy Zhukov: Triumf i Padeniya* (Moscow: Ast, 2003), p. 44.

21   These documents may be found in Krasnov, *Zhukov,* pp. 24–31.

22   Zhukov, *Reminiscences,* vol. 1, pp. 85–87.

23   E. Zhukova, 'Otets', in *Marshal Zhukov: Polkovodets i Chelovek,* p. 30.

CHAPTER 3: A SOLDIER'S LIFE

1   Zhukov, *Reminiscences,* vol. 1, p. 75.
2   On the Red Army during the interwar period: J. Erickson, *The Soviet High Command: A Military-Political History, 1918–1941,* 3rd ed. (London: Frank Cass, 2001); M. von Hagen, *Soldiers in the Proletarian Dictatorship: The Red Army and the Soviet Socialist State, 1917–1930* (Ithaca, N.Y.: Cornell University Press, 1990); R. R. Reese, *Stalin's Reluctant Soldiers: A Social History of the Red Army, 1925–1941* (Lawrence: University Press of Kansas, 1996); R. R. Reese, *Red Commanders: A Social History of the Soviet Army Officer Corps, 1918–1991* (Lawrence: University Press of Kansas, 2005); S. W. Stoecker, *Forging Stalin's Army: Marshal Tukhachevsky and the Politics of Military Innovation* (Boulder, Colo.: Westview, 1998); W. J. Spahr, *Stalin's Lieutenants: A Study of Command Under Stress* (Novato, Calif.: Presidio, 1997); L. Samuelson, *Plans for Stalin's War Machine: Tukhachevskii and Military-Economic Planning, 1925–1941* (London: Palgrave, 2000); and D. R. Stone, *Hammer and Rifle: The Militarization of the Soviet Union, 1926–1933* (Lawrence: University Press of Kansas, 2000).
3   J. Stalin, *Leninism* (London: Allen & Unwin, 1942), p. 366.
4   In my interview with her in Moscow in April 2010, Zhukov's daughter Era said that in the Zhukov household Stalin was neither worshipped nor denigrated.
5   Zhukov, *Reminiscences,* vol. 1 p. 97.
6   Ibid., p. 98.
7   V. A., Afanas'ev, *Stanovlenie Polkovodcheskogo Iskusstva G. K. Zhukova* (Moscow: Svyatigor, 2006), p. 22.
8   A number of these documents are reproduced in V. Krasnov, *Zhukov: Marshal Velikoi Imperii* (Moscow: Olma-Press, 2005), p. 44ff.
9   A. L. Kronik, 'Molodost' Marshala', in I. G. Aleksandrov (ed.), *Marshal Zhukov: Polkovodets i Chelovek* (Moscow: APN, 1988), p. 66.
10   Zhukov, *Reminiscences,* vol. 1, p. 107.
11   K. Rokossovsky, *A Soldier's Duty* (Moscow: Progress Publishers, 1970), p. 84. On Rokossovsky: R. Woff, 'Rokossovsky', in H. Shukman (ed.), *Stalin's Generals* (London: Phoenix, 2001).
12   I. K. Bagramyan, *Tak Shli My k Pobede* (Moscow: Voenizdat, 1988), p. 7. On Bagramyan: G. Jukes, 'Bagramyan', in Shukman (ed.), *Stalin's Generals.*
13   Zhukov, *Reminiscences,* vol. 1, p. 108.
14   Ibid., pp. 109–13.
15   I. Mastykina, *Zheny i Deti Georgiya Zhukova* (Moscow: Komsomol'skya Pravda, 1996). This booklet contains Mastykina's interviews with Zhukov's daughters and others that were originally published in the newspaper *Komsomol'skya Pravda,* 7 June 1996, 23 August 1996, 30 August 1996 and 4 October 1996.
16   Afanas'ev, *Stanovlenie Polkovodcheskogo Iskusstva G. K. Zhukova,* p. 33.
17   On the development of Soviet military doctrine before the Second World

War: M. R. Habeck, *Storm of Steel: The Development of Armour Doctrine in Germany and the Soviet Union, 1919–1939* (Ithaca, N.Y.: Cornell University Press, 2003); S. Naveh, *In Pursuit of Military Excellence: The Evolution of Operational Theory* (London: Frank Cass, 1997); H. Fast Scott and W. F. Scott (eds.), *The Soviet Art of War* (Boulder, Colo.: Westview, 1982); and S. J. Main, 'The Red Army and the Future War in Europe, 1925–1940', in S. Pons and A. Romano (eds.), *Russia in the Age of Wars, 1941–1945* (Milan: Feltrinelli, 2000).

18   On Tukhachevsky: S. Naveh, 'Tukhachevsky', in Shukman (ed.), *Stalin's Generals*.

19   Zhukov, *Reminiscences*, vol. 1, pp. 137–39.

20   Erickson, *The Soviet High Command*, p. 800.

21   Afanas'ev, *Stanovlenie Polkovodcheskogo Iskusstva G. K. Zhukova*, p. 22.

22   *Marshal Zhukov: Moskva v Zhizni i Sud'be Polkovodtsa* (Moscow: Glavarkhiva Moskvy, 2005), pp. 48–49.

23   In the 1980s it was reported that Rokossovsky had said in a private conversation with two Soviet journalists that Zhukov had not so much been promoted as removed from the position of brigade commander following complaints from his subordinates that he was too strict and too rude (N. G. Pavlenko, 'Razmyshleniya o Sud'be Polkovodtsa', *Voenno-Istoricheskii Zhurnal*, no. 10, 1988, p. 17). The conversation with Rokossovsky reportedly took place in summer 1966 at a time when Zhukov had yet to be fully rehabilitated following his isolation during the Khrushchev era. Relations between the two men were still at a low ebb because of Zhukov's belief that Rokossovsky had collaborated with the Khrushchevites in their minimising his role during the Great Patriotic War.

24   A. M. Vasilevsky, *A Lifelong Cause* (Moscow: Progress Publishers, 1981), pp. 485–86. On Vasilevsky: Jukes, 'Vasilevsky', in Shukman (ed.), *Stalin's Generals*.

25   Krasnov, *Zhukov*, pp. 74–76.

26   Zhukov, *Reminiscences*, vol. 1, p. 119.

27   Ibid., pp. 136–39.

28   Ibid., p. 141, 162.

29   L. F. Minuk, 'Komandir Divizii' in *Marshal Zhukov: Polkovodets i Chelovek*, vol. 1 (Moscow: APN, 1998), pp. 100–15.

30   The two daughters' memoirs may be found in ibid. See also the following interview with them: 'Papa Chetverok ne Lyubil. Dnevnik Smotrel Pridirchivo', *Izvestiya*, 1 December, 2006. (I am grateful to Professor Stephen White for a copy of this article.)

31   Zhukov, *Reminiscences*, pp. 171–74.

32   M. Fainsod, *How Russia Is Ruled* (Cambridge, Mass.: Harvard University Press, 1963), p. 479.

33   On Stalin's prewar purge of the Red Army, see R. R. Reese, 'The Impact of the Great Purge on the Red Army', *The Soviet and Post-Soviet Review*, vol. 19, nos. 1–3, 1992, and R. R. Reese, 'The Red Army and the Great Purges', in J. A. Getty and R. T. Manning (eds.), *Stalinist Terror: New Perspectives* (Cambridge, U.K.: Cambridge University Press, 1993); O. F.

Suvenirov, *Tragediya RKKA, 1937–1938* (Moscow: Terra, 1998); P. P. Wieczorkiewicz, *Lancuch Smierci: Czystka w Armii Czerwonej, 1937–1939* (Warsaw: RYTM, 2001); and A. A. Pechenkii, *Voennaya Elita SSSR v 1935–1939gg: Repressii i Obnovlenie* (Moscow, 2003).

34 The literature on the Great Terror is vast. A good documentary collection is: J. Arch Getty and O. V. Naumov (eds.), *The Road to Terror: Stalin and the Self-Destruction of the Bolsheviks, 1932–1939* (New Haven, Conn.: Yale University Press, 1999).

35 Zhukov, *Reminiscences,* vol. 1, p. 171.

36 Zhukov *Vospominaniya,* vol. 1, chap. 6 passim.

37 Cited by O. P. Chaney, *Zhukov,* rev. ed. (Norman: University of Oklahoma Press, 1996), pp. 54–55.

38 In the early 1990s evidence was published that Zhukov himself had made at least one accusation against a purge victim. However, it transpired the 'G. Zhukov' named in the supposedly incriminating evidence was another Zhukov. See W. J. Spahr, *Zhukov: The Rise and Fall of a Great Captain* (Novato, Calif.: Presidio, 1993), pp. 234–35.

CHAPTER 4: KHALKHIN-GOL, 1939

1 The text of most of Voroshilov's order is reproduced in V. Krasnov, *Zhukov: Marshal Velikoi Imperii* (Moscow: Olma-Press, 2005), p. 98. The original order, together with a number of other documents cited by Krasnov, was on display at an exhibition on Khalkhin-Gol in RGVA in Moscow in April 2010.

2 The letter is reproduced in E. Zhukova, 'Interesy Ottsa', in *Marshal Zhukov: Polkovodets i Chelovek,* vol. 1 (Moscow: APN, 1998), pp. 52–53. In his memoirs Zhukov wrote that he saw Voroshilov on 2 June and arrived in Mongolia on 5 June. He also implies that he was sent to Khalkhin-Gol with a view to taking over command rather than just conducting an inspection. The documentary record shows otherwise. See Zhukov, *Reminiscences,* vol. 1, pp. 177–78.

3 See E. O. Clubb, 'Armed Conflict in the Chinese Borderlands, 1917–1950', in R. L. Garthoff (ed.), *Sino-Soviet Military Relations* (New York: Praeger, 1966); J. Colvin, *Nomonhan* (London: Quartet, 1999); and G. Lenson, *The Damned Inheritance: The Soviet Union and the Manchurian Crisis, 1924–1935* (Tallahassee, Fla.: Diplomatic Press, 1974).

4 J. Haslam, *The Soviet Union and the Threat from the East, 1933–1941* (London: Macmillan Press, 1992), pp. 93–94.

5 Krasnov, *Zhukov,* pp. 100–101.

6 Ibid., pp. 101–2.

7 V. Daines, *Zhukov* (Moscow: Molodaya Gvardia, 2005), p. 95.

8 Krasnov, *Zhukov,* pp. 112–14. This section of Krasnov's book contains the text of a number of orders issued by Zhukov during this period. The originals (seen by me) may be found in RGVA, F. 32113, Op. 1, Dd. 3, 5.

9 Krasnov, *Zhukov,* pp. 118–20, cites the text of Zhukov's conversation with Shaposhnikov and Voroshilov with Kulik as well as Voroshilov's instruction to Kulik not to interfere.

10 Daines, *Zhukov,* pp. 114–16.
11 V. A. Afanas'ev, *Stanovlenie Polkovodcheskogo Iskusstva G. K. Zhukova* (Moscow: Svyatigor, 2006), p. 83; J. Erickson, *The Soviet High Command: A Military-Political History,* 1918–1941, 3rd ed. (London: Frank Cass, 2001), p. 533.
12 Zhukov, *Reminiscences,* vol. 1, pp. 185–86.
13 Ibid., pp. 186–88.
14 The text of the order may be found in Afanas'ev, *Stanovlenie Polkovodcheskogo Iskusstva G. K. Zhukova,* pp. 233–34.
15 Zhukov, *Reminiscences,* vol. 1, p. 192.
16 Krasnov, *Zhukov,* p. 137.
17 Cited by B. V. Sokolov, *Georgy Zhukov* (Moscow: Ast, 2003), p. 143.
18 K. Simonov, *Glazami Cheloveka Moego Pokoleniya* (Moscow: APN, 1989), pp. 319–20.
19 Further evidence of strained relations between Shtern and Zhukov can be found in Major General Petro G. Grigorenko's memoirs. Grigorenko, a Soviet dissident in the 1960s and 1970s, spent several years in psychiatric confinement, imprisoned by the authorities on the grounds that if he opposed the communist system he must be mad. Grigorenko died in 1987 – a decade after his enforced emigration to the United States. In June 1939 Grigorenko had been among recent graduates of the Red Army's General Staff Academy who were posted to the Far East, where he served in Shtern's Front Group. Grigorenko paints a very unflattering portrait of Zhukov as a military commander, claiming that during the June battles Zhukov responded to successive Japanese attacks by transferring elements from one sector to another, thus creating a front line consisting of a confusion of temporary detachments. This elementary error Grigorenko attributed to the fact that Zhukov had not attended the General Staff Academy and lacked a military education. He reports, too, that the problem was only sorted out after Shtern's intervention. It has to be said that this story is most unlikely to be true. Zhukov had not been educated at the General Staff Academy but he had attended plenty of other command courses and was an experienced senior officer who would not have made such a gross error. In truth, Grigorenko's memoirs are extremely biased against Zhukov. Shtern, by contrast, comes across as an almost saintly figure and is given credit for the victory at Khalkhin-Gol. The difference in Grigorenko's attitude towards Shtern and Zhukov may be partly related to the subsequent fate of the two men. While Zhukov became the Soviet Union's most famous soldier, Shtern fell victim to a Stalinist purge in October 1941 and was executed. See P. G. Grigorenko, *Memoirs* (New York: Norton, 1982), pp. 105–29.
20 The letter is reproduced in E. Zhukova, 'Interesy Ottsa', pp. 53–54.
21 Daines, *Zhukov,* pp. 126–27.
22 A. D. Coox, *Nomonhan: Japan Against Russia, 1939* (Stanford, Calif.: Stanford University Press, 1990), p. 572. The battle of Cannae took place in 216 B.C. during the Second Punic War between Rome and Carthage.
23 W. J. Spahr, *Stalin's Lieutenants: A Study of Command Under Stress* (Novato, Calif.: Presidio, 1997), p. 213.

24 O. P. Chaney, *Zhukov,* rev. ed. (Norman: University of Oklahoma Press, 1996), pp. 68, 72, 74.

25 Simonov, *Glazami Cheloveka Moego Pokoleniya,* pp. 309–10. Another journalist present was D. I. Ortenberg, who was editor of *Krasnaya Zvezda* during the Great Patriotic War. His memoir of Zhukov at Khalkhin-Gol, which conveys a similar impression to Simonov's, may be found in his 'Nezabyvaemoe', in S. S. Smirnov et al. (eds), *Marshal Zhukov: Kakim My Ego Pomnim* (Moscow: Politizdat, 1988).

26 K. Simonov, *Tovarishchi po Oruzhiu* (Moscow: Gosudarstvennoe Izdatel'stvo Khudozhestvennoi Literatury, 1961). The novel was first published in 1952.

27 'O Kampanii 1939g v Raione r.Khalkhin-Gol', RGVA, F. 32113, Op. 1, D. 2. The report was co-signed by political commissar M. S. Nikishev.

CHAPTER 5: IN KIEV

1 For Stalin's speech, see O. A. Rzheshevsky and O. Vekhvilyainen (eds), *Zimnyaya Voina, 1939–1940* (Moscow: Nauka, 1999), pp. 272–82. An English translation may be found in A. O. Chubaryan and H. Shukman (eds.), *Stalin and the Soviet-Finnish War, 1939–1940* (London: Frank Cass, 2002).

2 *'Zimnyaya Voina': Rabota nad Oshibkami, Aprel'-Mai 1940g.* (Moscow: Letnii Sad, 2004), doc. 82; and *Glavnyi Voennyi Sovet RKKA, 1938–1941: Dokumenty i Materialy* (Moscow: Rosspen, 2004), p. 5. A good summary of the Timoshenko reforms may be found in W. J. Spahr, *Stalin's Lieutenants: A Study of Command Under Duress* (Novato, Calif.: Presidio, 1997), chap. 10. Zhukov became a member of the Main Military Council on 24 July 1940.

3 J. Colvin, *Nomonhan* (London: Quartet, 1999), p. 13.

4 See V. Anfilov, 'Timoshenko', in H. Shukman (ed.), *Stalin's Generals* (London: Phoenix, 2001). Timoshenko published no memoirs.

5 *Na Priyome u Stalina* (Moscow: Novyi Khronograf, 2008), p. 300. The next day Zhukov met Stalin again for a much longer meeting, but in the company of a number of other senior officers (p. 301). In his memoirs Zhukov mistakenly dated the meeting with Stalin and his posting to Kiev to early May 1940.

6 Zhukov, *Vospominaniya,* vol. 1, p. 287.

7 'O Prisvoenii Voinskikh Zvanii Vyeshemu Nachal'stvuushemu Sostavu Krasnoiarmii', *Pravda,* 5 June 1940.

8 Many details may be found in R. S. Irinarkhov, *Kievskii Osobyi* (Minsk: Harvest, 2006), and M. Mel'tukhov, *Upushchennyi Shans Stalina* (Moscow: Veche, 2000).

9 Zhukov, *Reminiscences,* vol. 1, pp. 227–28.

10 R. R. Reese, *Stalin's Reluctant Soldiers: A Social History of the Red Army, 1925–1941* (Lawrence: University Press of Kansas, 1996), pp. 175–85. Reese's treatment is based on the Kiev District's records in RGVA.

11 The Soviet invasion was mostly peaceful and incident-free but in his memoirs Zhukov described an episode in which he ordered two airborne

brigades supported by two tank brigades to seize control of bridges over the Prut River. His aim was to prevent the Romanians from violating an agreement that prohibited the removal of equipment and supplies from the occupied territories. The next day Stalin telephoned Zhukov and told him the Romanian ambassador had complained that Soviet tanks had landed on the Prut River. Stalin wanted to know how that was possible and laughed when Zhukov explained that only the airborne troops had flown to the bridges; the tanks had made their way there separately by road. The humour seems to have been lost on the Soviet censors, who had the whole passage expunged from Zhukov's memoirs. After the Second World War communist-controlled Romania became a Soviet ally but the loss of Bessarabia and North Bukovina remained a sore point for many Romanians. The offending passage did not reappear in Zhukov's memoirs until the tenth edition published in 1990. Zhukov, *Vospominaniya,* vol. 1, pp. 289–91.

12 The text of this directive is reproduced in V. Krasnov, *Zhukov: Marshal Velikoi Imperii* (Moscow: Olma-Press, 2005), pp. 150–54. See also: Reese, *Stalin's Reluctant Soldiers,* p. 184.

13 K. Rokossovsky, *A Soldier's Duty* (Moscow: Progress Publishers, 1970), p. 5.

14 O. P Chaney, *Zhukov,* rev. ed. (Norman: University of Oklahoma Press, 1996), pp. 81–82. An extract from Kalashnikov's memoir may be found in *Marshal Zhukov: Moskva v Zhizni i Sud'be Polkovodtsa* (Moscow: Glavarkhiv, 2005), pp. 97–99.

15 *Khrushchev Remembers* (London: Sphere, 1971), p. 144.

16 See O. Rzheshevsky 'Shaposhnikov', in H. Shukman (ed.), *Stalin's Generals.*

17 *God,* vol. 2 (Moscow: Demokratiya, 1998), pp. 557–71.

18 Ibid., vol. 1, doc. 95.

19 Ibid., doc. 117.

20 Ibid., doc. 134.

21 G. Gorodetsky, *Grand Delusion: Stalin and the German Invasion of Russia* (New Haven, Conn.: Yale University Press, 1999), pp. 121–24.

22 M. V. Zakharov, *General'nyi Shtab v Predvoennye Gody* (Moscow: Ast, 1989), pp. 220–24.

23 *God,* vol. 1, doc. 224.

24 Zhukov, *Reminiscences,* vol. 1, p. 121.

25 I. Kh. Bagramyan, *Tak Shli My k Pobede* (Moscow: Voenizdat, 1977), pp. 7–9.

26 V. A. Afanas'ev, *Stanovlenie Polkovodcheskogo Iskusstva G. K. Zhukova* (Moscow: Svyatigor, 2006), pp. 110–13.

27 The record of the conference proceedings may be found in 'Nakanune Voiny: Materialy Soveshchaniya Vyschego Rukovodyashchego Sostava RKKA 23–31 Dekabrya 1940g', *Russkii Arkhiv: Velikaya Otechestvennaya Voina, 1941–1945,* vol. 12 (1) (Moscow: Terra, 1993).

28 G. Zhukov, 'Kharakter Sovremnnoi Nastupatel'noi Operatsii', in ibid., pp. 129–51.

29 Ibid., pp. 152–72.

30 D. G. Pavlov, 'Ispol'zovanie Mekhanizirovannykh Soedinenii v Sovre-
    mennoi Nasupatel'noi Operatsi i Vvod Mekhanizirovannogo Korpusa v
    Proryv', in ibid., pp. 252–300. On Pavlov's role in the development of So-
    viet tank doctrine, see M. R. Habeck, *Storm of Steel: The Development
    of Armour Doctrine in Germany and the Soviet Union, 1919–1939*
    (Ithaca, N.Y.: Cornell University Press, 2003), passim.

31 'Zakluchitel'naya Rech' Narodnogo Komissara Oborony Souza SSR
    Geroya i Marshala Sovetskogo Souza S.K. Timoshenko na Voennom
    Soveshchanii 31 Dekabrya 1940g', *Russkii Arkhiv: Velikaya Otechestven
    naya Voina, 1941–1945*, vol. 12 (1) (Moscow: Terra, 1993), pp. 338–72.

32 *Na Priyome u Stalina*, p. 322.

33 The fullest version of this episode may be found in the unexpurgated edi-
    tion of Zhukov's memoirs: Zhukov, *Vospominaniya*, vol. 1, pp. 291–92. It
    seems that Stalin's corrections were taken into account by Timoshenko
    prior to the publication of his speech as a booklet for internal circulation
    with the armed forces. See *1941 God*, vol. 1, p. 498, no. 2. A copy of Ti-
    moshenko's speech as published in 1941 may be found in the Volkogonov
    Papers in the Library of Congress Manuscript Division.

34 On the war games, see Zakharov, *General'nyi Shtab v Predvoennye Gody*,
    pp. 239–50; Gorodetsky, *Grand Delusion*, pp. 127–29; P. N. Bobylev, 'K
    Kakoi Voine Gotovilsya General'nyishtab RKKA v 1941 godu', *Otechest-
    vennaya Istoriya*, no. 5, 1995; and B. Fugate and L. Dvoretsky, *Thunder
    on the Dnepr: Zhukov-Stalin and the Defeat of Hitler's Blitzkrieg* (No-
    vato, Calif.: Presidio, 1997), chap. 1. Fugate and Dvoretsky's treatment of
    the war games is commensurate with their hypothesis that the Soviet plan
    for coping with a German attack involved the deliberate sacrifice of Pav-
    lov's Western District with the aim of drawing the Wehrmacht deep into
    Russia before the launch of a counter-offensive, which finally came at
    Moscow in December 1941. In this connection they posit a third war
    game in February 1941, from which Pavlov was excluded, in which this
    scenario was played out. It is an intriguing, speculative idea but there is no
    direct evidence to support it; it gives Stalin, Zhukov, and Timoshenko far
    too much credit for prescience.

35 Cited by Chaney, *Zhukov*, p. 89.

36 E. Mawdsley, 'Crossing the Rubicon: Soviet Plans for Offensive War in
    1940–1941', *International History Review*, December 2003, pp. 826–27.

37 K. Meretskov, *Serving the People* (Moscow: Progress Publishers, 1971),
    pp. 122–27; *Na Priyome u Stalina*, p. 322.

CHAPTER 6: ARCHITECT OF DISASTER?

1 Zhukov, *Reminiscences*, vol. 1, pp. 379–80.

2 *Russkii Arkhiv: Velikaya Otechestvennaya Voina, 1941–1945*, vol. 13 (1),
   Prikazy Narodnogo Komissara Oborony SSSR, 1937–41, Iunya 1941g
   (Moscow: Terra, 1994), doc. 108.

3 On Soviet-German relations in 1939–1941, see G. Roberts, *Stalin's Wars:
   From World War to Cold War, 1939–1953* (London: Yale University Press,
   2006), chap. 2.

4   The available Soviet military intelligence reports are collected in: *Voennaya Razvedka Informiruet: Dokumenty Razvedypravleniya Krasnoi Armii, 1939–1941* (Moscow: Demokratiya, 2008).

5   Ibid., docs. 7.13, 7.22, 7.33, 7.38, 7.47, 7.57, 7.65, 7.82.

6   E. Mawdsley, *Thunder in the East: The Nazi-Soviet War, 1941–1945* (London: Hodder Arnold, 2005), pp. 33–34.

7   *God*, vol. 1, docs. 273–74, vol. 2, doc. 549. D. M. Glantz, *Stumbling Colossus: The Red Army on the Eve of World War* (Lawrence: University Press of Kansas, 1998), pp. 100–101; E. Mawdsley, 'Crossing the Rubicon: Soviet Plans for Offensive War in 1940–1941', *International History Review*, December 2003; M. Mel'tukhov, *Upushchennyi Shans Stalina* (Moscow: Veche, 2000), pp. 347–48.

8   *God*, vol. 1, doc. 315. Note: the text of the March plan as published is incomplete.

9   Ibid., vol. 2, doc. 473.

10 A. Werth, *Russia at War, 1941–1945* (London: Pan, 1965), p. 132.

11 See: J. Forster and E. Mawdsley, 'Hitler and Stalin in Perspective: Secret Speeches on the Eve of Barbarossa', *War in History*, vol. 11, no. 1, 2006.

12 Mawdsley, 'Crossing the Rubicon', p. 838.

13 *God*, vol. 2, docs. 481–83; L. Rotundo, 'Stalin and the Outbreak of War in 1941', *Journal of Contemporary History*, vol. 24, 1989, p. 283.

14 Mawdsley, 'Crossing the Rubicon'.

15 *Na Priyome u Stalina* (Moscow: Novyi Khronograf, 2008), pp. 334–35.

16 *Voennaya Razvedka*, docs. 7.90, 7.91, 7.95, 7.97, 7.98, 7.104.

17 G. Gorodetsky, *Grand Delusion: Stalin and the German Invasion of Russia* (New Haven, Conn.: Yale University Press, 1999), pp. 287–93.

18 *Voennaya Razvedka*, doc. 7.107.

19 Zhukov, *Reminiscences*, vol. 1, p. 276.

20 In relation to Stalin and 22 June 1941, see: Gorodetsky, *Grand Delusion*, and Roberts, *Stalin's Wars*.

21 Zhukov, *Reminiscences*, vol. 1, p. 277.

22 On the timing of Zhukov and Timoshenko's meetings with Stalin on 21/22 June, see *Na Priyome u Stalina*, pp. 337–38.

23 A translation of the text of the three directives may be found in D. M. Glantz, *Barbarossa: Hitler's Invasion of Russia, 1941* (Stroud, U.K.: Tempus, 2001), pp. 242–43.

24 Zhukov, *Reminiscences*, vol. 1, pp. 284–85.

25 I. K. Bagramyan, *Tak Shli My k Pobede* (Moscow: Voenizdat, 1988), p. 65.

26 *Na Priyome u Stalina*, p. 339. In his memoirs Zhukov recalled that he arrived in Moscow late in the evening of 26 June and went directly to Stalin's office (Zhukov, *Reminiscences*, vol. 1, p. 305). According to Stalin's appointments diary he was there between four and five and again between nine and ten.

27 Zhukov, *Reminiscences*, vol. 1, p. 309. Stalin's appointments diary confirms that he was absent from his own office that day.

28 A. Mikoyan, *Tak Bylo* (Moscow: Vargrius, 1999), p. 390.

29 *The Memoirs of Marshal Zhukov* (London: Jonathan Cape, 1971), p. 268.

30 *Russkii Arkhiv: Velikaya Otechestvennaya Voina, 1941–1945,* vol. 16 (1), Stavka VGK: Dokumenty i Materialy 1941 god (Moscow: Terra, 1996), doc. 41.

31 *God,* vol. 2, doc. 635.

32 *Organy Gosudarstvennoi Bezopasnosti SSSR v Velikoi Otechestvennoi Voine,* vol. 2, book 1 (Moscow: Rus', 2000), docs. 379, 436, 437, 438.

33 G. Jukes, 'Meretskov', in H. Shukman (ed.), *Stalin's Generals* (London: Phoenix, 1997).

34 See *Organy Gosudarstvennoi Bezopasnosti,* docs. 293, 306, 384, 413, 424, 490, 550.

35 A number of these directives may be found in vol. 16 (1), Stavka VGK: Dokumenty i Materialy 1941 god.

36 Ibid., docs. 115, 117. A number of other conversations are reproduced by Zhukov in his memoirs.

37 Stavka VGK: Dokumenty i Materialy 1941 god, doc. 101.

38 Zhukov, *Reminiscences,* vol. 1, pp. 379–80.

39 RGVA, F. 41107, Op. 1, D. 54, L. 57.

40 *Na Priyome u Stalina,* pp. 343–45.

41 *Russkii Arkhiv,* vol. 13 (2), Prikazy Narodnogo Komissara Oborony SSSR, 22 Iunya 1941g–1942g, doc. 36.

42 Stavka VGK: Dokumenty i Materialy 1941 god, 168.

43 Ibid., doc. 10, p. 361.

44 Stavka VGK: Dokumenty i Materialy 1941 god, doc. 255.

45 Cited by A. M. Vasilevsky, *A Lifelong Cause* (Moscow: Progress Publishers, 1981), p. 110.

46 Stavka VGK: Dokumenty i Materialy 1941 god, doc. 280.

47 Ibid., doc. 130.

48 Zhukov, *Reminiscences,* vol. 1, p. 383.

49 Stavka VGK: Dokumenty i Materialy 1941 god, doc. 15, pp. 365–66.

50 H. C. Cassidy, *Moscow Dateline* (Boston: Houghton Mifflin, 1943), p. 123. For Werth's account of the visit, see A. Werth, *Russia at War, 1941–1945* (London: Pan, 1965), pp. 188–95.

51 Cited by Glantz, *Barbarossa,* pp. 90–91.

52 Cited by V. Krasnov, *Zhukov: Marshal Velikoi Imperii* (Moscow: Olma-Press, 2000), pp. 210–12.

53 Zhukov, *Vospominaniya,* vol. 1, pp. 304–5.

54 RGVA, F. 41107, Op. 1, D. 17, Ll. 1–50. This fifty-page typescript, entitled 'Nachal'nyi Period Velikoi Otechestvennoi Voiny' (The Initial Period of the Great Patriotic War), is a variant chapter of his memoirs. The citations are from pp. 38–41 of the document. This file contains a number of such documents, including several handwritten fragments.

55 Ibid., p. 265.

CHAPTER 7: STALIN'S GENERAL

1 *Na Priyome u Stalina* (Moscow: Novyi Khronograf, 2008), pp. 614–15.

2 The summary of Zhukov's view of Stalin is drawn from Zhukov, *Reminiscences,* vol. 1, chap. 11. When the Soviet regime came to an end, this

chapter was more than a little embarrassing for his publishers, who wanted to present Zhukov as an anti-Stalinist, so they began adding an editorial note pointing out that Zhukov's treatment of Stalin was in accordance with the 'spirit of the times' (Zhukov, *Vospominaniya*, vol. 2, p. 73).

3 See, for example, 'Korotko o Staline', *Pravda*, 20 January 1989.

4 *Russkii Arkhiv: Velikaya Otechestvennaya Voina, 1941–1945*, vol. 16 (1), Stavka VGK: Dokumenty i Materialy 1941 god (Moscow: Terra, 1996), doc. 82.

5 Ibid., doc. 83.

6 Cited by N. Lomagin, *Neizvestnaya Blokada*, vol. 1 (Moscow: Olma-Press, 2002), p. 63.

7 Zhukov, *Reminiscences*, vol. 1, pp. 398–401. In another version of the story in the archives Zhukov gives the date of his meeting with Stalin as 7 September and says that Stalin asked him where he wanted to go next. He suggested Leningrad or the southwest. When Stalin decided to send him to Leningrad, Zhukov suggested Timoshenko for the Southwestern Front command. RGVA, F. 41107, Op. 1, D. 54, L. 58.

8 Zhukov, *Reminiscences,* vol. 1, pp. 417–18.

9 *Na Priyome u Stalina*, p. 349.

10 Stavka VGK: Dokumenty i Materialy 1941, docs. 252, 253.

11 Extracts from the Feduninskii and Bychevskii memoirs may be found in S. Bialer, *Stalin and His Generals: Soviet Military Memoirs of World War II* (London: Souvenir Press, 1970).

12 Cited in D. M. Glantz, *The Battle for Leningrad, 1941–1944* (Lawrence: University Press of Kansas, 2002), p. 76.

13 Ibid., pp. 81–82.

14 Cited by Ella Zhukova, 'Interesy Ottsa', in I. G. Aleksandrov (ed.), *Marshal Zhukov: Polkovodets i Chelovek* (Moscow: APN, 1988), pp. 54–55.

15 Glantz, *The Battle for Leningrad*, p. 83; J. Erickson, 'Zhukov', in M. Carver (ed.), *The War Lords: Military Commanders of the Twentieth Century* (Barnsley, U.K.: Pen & Sword, 2005), p. 250; E. Mawdsley, *Thunder in the East: The Nazi-Soviet War, 1941–1945* (London: Hodder Arnold, 2005), pp. 84–85; V. Beshanov, *Leningradskaya Oborona* (Minsk: Kharvest, 2006), pp. 124–25.

16 Stavka VGK: Dokumenty i Materialy 1941, doc. 339.

17 On the siege of Leningrad, see Harrison E. Salisbury's unsurpassed *The 900 Days* (New York: Harper & Row, 1969).

18 *G. K. Zhukov v Bitve pod Moskvoi: Sbornik Dokumentov* (Moscow: Mosgorarkhiv, 1994), docs. 3, 5, 7, 17.

19 I. S. Konev, 'Osen'u 1941 goda', and G. K. Zhukov, 'Vospominaniya Komanduushchego Frontom', in *Bitva za Moskvu*, 3rd ed. (Moscow: Moskovskii Rabochii, 1975), pp. 55–56, 68–69. The first edition of this book was published in 1968. Before Konev's article was published the editors sent a copy to Zhukov for comment. Zhukov responded vehemently, writing to the editors that Konev's draft contained so many falsehoods, including in relation to his own appointment as commander of the Western Front, that if it was published as it stood he would withdraw his

contribution to the book (RGVA, F. 41107, Op. 1, D. 77, L.8). In the event, Konev's piece was published more or less unchanged, together with Zhukov's own article.

20 K. Simonov, *Glazami Cheloveka Moego Pokoleniya* (Moscow: APN, 1989), p. 364.

21 See V. Krasnov, *Zhukov: Marshal Velikoi Imperii* (Moscow: Olma-Press, 2000), pp. 237–41. Vasilevsky's version of events falls midway between Konev's and Zhukov's: 'On 9 October during a routine conversation with the Supreme Commander the decision was taken to combine the Western and Reserve Fronts into the Western Front. All of us, including Konev . . . agreed with Stalin's suggestion to appoint Zhukov commander of the combined front'. A. M. Vasilevsky, *A Lifelong Cause* (Moscow: Progress Publishers, 1981), p. 115.

22 On Konev, see: O. Rzheshevsky, 'Konev', in H. Shukman (ed.), *Stalin's Generals* (London: Phoenix, 2001) and J. Erickson, 'Konev', in Carver (ed.), *The War Lords*. Konev's memoirs were published in English as *Year of Victory* (Moscow: Progress Publishers, 1969). The fuller version of the memoirs in Russian is: I. S. Konev, *Zapiski Komanduushchego Frontom* (Moscow: Voenizdat, 1981).

23 Mawdsley, *Thunder in the East,* p. 95.

24 *G. K. Zhukov v Bitve pod Moskvoi,* doc. 23. On the panic in Moscow, see R. Braithwaite, *Moscow 1941* (New York: Knopf, 2006), chap. 12; A. Nagorski, *The Greatest Battle* (London: Aurum, 2007), chap. 7; and A. Werth, *Russia at War, 1941–1945* (London: Pan Books, 1965), pp. 224–33.

25 W. J. Spahr, *Zhukov: The Rise and Fall of a Great Captain* (Novato, Calif.: Presidio, 1993), p. 72. One version of Ortenberg's memoir may be found in S. S. Smirnov et al. (eds.), *Marshal Zhukov: Kakim My Ego Pomnim* (Moscow: Politizdat, 1988).

26 *G. K. Zhukov v Bitve pod Moskvoi,* doc. 12.

27 Stavka VGK: Dokumenty i Materialy 1941, doc. 66.

28 Ibid., doc. 32.

29 Zhukov, *Reminiscences,* vol. 2, p. 31.

30 Ibid.

31 J. Stalin, *On the Great Patriotic War of the Soviet Union* (London: Hutchinson, 1943–44), pp. 21–23.

32 Zhukov, *Reminiscences,* vol. 2, p. 66.

33 *G. K. Zhukov v Bitve pod Moskvoi,* doc. 37.

34 K. Rokossovsky, *A Soldier's Duty* (Moscow: Progress Publishers, 1970), p. 78.

35 Cited by O. P. Chaney, *Zhukov,* rev. ed. (Norman: University of Oklahoma Press, 1996), p. 179. This statement was omitted from the published edition of Rokossovsky's memoirs.

36 Ibid., pp. 85–86. In his memoirs Vasilevsky made a similar comment about Stalin during the battle of Moscow: 'Stalin could be very irascible and abrasive; but even more striking was [his] concern for his subordinates at such a grave time'. Vasilevsky, *A Lifelong Cause,* p. 118.

37 Vasilevsky, *A Lifelong Cause,* p. 121.

38 Zhukov, *Reminiscences,* vol. 2, pp. 44–46.

39 *Na Priyome u Stalina*, p. 355.

40 G. K. *Zhukov v Bitve pod Moskvoi*, doc. 62.

41 D. Glantz, *Barbarossa: Hitler's Invasion of Russia, 1941* (Stroud, U.K.: Tempus, 2001), p. 188.

42 Cited by E. Mawdsley, *December 1942: Twelve Days That Began a World War* (London: Yale University Press, 2011), pp. 219–20.

43 *Bitva za Moskvu: Moskovskaya Operatsiya Zapadnogo Fronta, 16 Noyabrya 1941g.–31 Yanvarya 1942g* (Moscow: Tranzitkniga, 2006), p. 240. This is the Soviet General Staff's own study of the Moscow counter-offensive. It was one of a number of such studies written and circulated in secret during the war with the aim of distilling and disseminating the experience of major operations. These studies are invaluable for the clarity of their description of the course of battles from the Soviet point of view and for references to important archive documents that cannot be found anywhere else.

44 A. Werth, *The Year of Stalingrad* (London: Hamish Hamilton, 1946), p. 99.

45 Cited by Vasilevsky in *A Lifelong Cause*, p. 152.

46 My summary of the Rzhev-Viazma operations of 1942 is based on S. Gerasimova, *Rzhev 42: Pozitsionnaya Boinya* (Moscow: Yauza-Eksmo, 2007). The book contains a number of maps and an appendix with the relevant Stavka orders. Gerasimova's casualty figures have been challenged by General M. A. Gareev: 'O Nashikh Poteryakh podo Rzhevom i Vyaz'moi', *Voenno-Istoricheskii Zhurnal* no. 3, 2002.

47 Zhukov, *Reminiscences,* vol. 2, p. 62. In an unpublished interview with the editors of *Voenno Istoricheskii Zhurnal* in the 1960s Zhukov was more critical of Efremov's conduct than he was in his memoirs but he accepted his own responsibility for the failure and pointed out that this was far from being the only operation during which mistakes were made (*Kommunist* no. 14, 1988, p. 96).

48 See V. Mel'nikov, *Ikh Poslal na Smert' Zhukov? Gibel' Armii Generala Efremova* (Moscow: Eksmo, 2009). Also: Krasnov, *Zhukov*, pp. 304–31; Spahr, *Zhukov*, pp. 84–87; and Chaney, *Zhukov*, pp. 197–200.

49 A copy of this document may be found in the Volkogonov Papers, Library of Congress, Manuscript Division.

50 Zhukov, *Reminiscences,* vol. 2, pp. 52–55.

51 Ibid., p. 86.

52 *Khrushchev Remembers* (London: Sphere, 1971), pp. 536–37.

53 K. S. Moskalenko, *Na Ugo-Zapadnom Napravlenii*, 2nd. ed., vol. 1 (Moscow: Nauka, 1975), pp. 168–213.

54 Vasilevsky, *A Lifelong Cause*, pp. 163–64.

55 I. K. Bagramyan, *Tak Shli My k Pobede* (Moscow: Voenizdat, 1998), pp. 305–53.

56 These documents may be found in D. M. Glantz, *Kharkov 1942: Anatomy of a Military Disaster Through Soviet Eyes* (Shepperton, U.K.: Ian Allan, 1998). Glantz's invaluable book also contains a detailed narrative of the battle and an extensive account of the Soviet discussion of the disaster.

57   Ibid., pp. 224–25.

58   Ibid.

59   See M. N. Ramanichev, 'Nevidannoe Ispytanie', in G. N. Sevast'yanov (ed.), *Voina i Obshchestvo, 1941–1945*, vol. 1 (Moscow: Nauka, 2004), p. 88.

60   Vasilevsky, *A Lifelong Cause*, p. 157.

61   See P. P. Chevela, 'Novye Ispytania', in V. A. Zolotarev and G. N. Sevast'v yanov (eds.), *Velikaya Otechestvennaya Voina, 1941–1945*, vol. 1 (Moscow: Nauka, 1998–99), pp. 325–27. Also Ramanichev, 'Nevidannoe Ispytaniye'.

62   Stalin, *On the Great Patriotic War of the Soviet Union*, pp. 32, 34.

CHAPTER 8: ARCHITECT OF VICTORY?

1   B. Wegner, 'The War Against the Soviet Union, 1942–1943', in H. Boog et al. (eds.), *Germany and the Second World War*, vol. 6 (Oxford, U.K.: Clarendon Press, 2001).

2   H. R. Trevor-Roper, *Hitler's War Directives, 1939–1945* (London: Sidgwick & Jackson, 1964), p. 117.

3   J. Stalin, *On the Great Patriotic War of the Soviet Union* (London: Hutchinson, 1943–44), p. 38.

4   Trevor-Roper, *Hitler's War Directives*, pp. 129–30.

5   Extensive extracts from the Soviet General Staff's daily briefing reports may be found in *Stalingradskaya Bitva*, 2 vols. (Moscow: Olma-Press, 2002). The volumes also contain reprints of many articles from the Soviet press as well as Stavka directives, Front and army reports, and many other documents.

6   *Stalingrad, 1942–1943: Stalingradskaya Bitva v Dokumentakh* (Moscow: Biblioteka, 1995), docs. 109–10, 120.

7   *Khronika Ognenykh Dnei, 17 Iulya 1942, 2 Fevralya 1943*, Volgograd, 2002. The date derives from the Soviet General Staff's study of the Stalingrad battle prepared in 1943. See L. Rotundo (ed.), *Battle for Stalingrad: The 1943 Soviet General Staff Study* (London: Pergamon-Brassey's, 1989), pp. 12–13.

8   A full English translation of Order No. 227 is appended to G. Roberts, *Victory at Stalingrad: The Battle That Changed History* (London: Pearson/Longman, 2002).

9   A. Werth, *Russia at War, 1941–1945* (London: Pan, 1965), part 4.

10   'Na Uge', *Krasnaya Zvezda*, 19 July 1942.

11   'Ob Ustanovlenii Polnogo Edinonachaliya i Uprazdnenii Instituta Voennykh Komissarov v Krasnoi Armii', *Krasnaya Zvezda*, 10 October 1942.

12   On the Stalin-Churchill conversations of August 1942, see G. Roberts, *Stalin's Wars: From World War to Cold War, 1939–1953* (London: Yale University Press, 2006), pp. 134–43.

13   J. Erickson, 'Zhukov', in M. Carver (ed.), *The War Lords: Military Commanders of the Twentieth Century* (Barnsley, U.K.: Pen & Sword, 2005), pp. 251–52.

14 On Chuikov: R. Woff, 'Chuikov', in H. Shukman (ed.), *Stalin's Generals* (London: Phoenix, 2001).

15 On the battle for Stalingrad see Roberts, *Victory at Stalingrad*; A. Beevor, *Stalingrad* (London: Penguin, 1999); W. Craig, *Enemy at the Gates* (London: Hodder & Stoughton, 1973); M. Jones, *Stalingrad: How the Red Army Triumphed* (Barnsley, U.K.: Pen & Sword, 2007); D. M. Glantz & J. M. House, *Armageddon at Stalingrad* (Lawrence: University Press of Kansas, 2009); and J.S.A. Hayward, *Stopped at Stalingrad: The Luftwaffe and Hitler's Defeat in the East, 1942–1943* (Lawrence: University Press of Kansas, 1998).

16 In his memoirs Zhukov wrote that he went to Stalingrad on 27 August. However, Stalin's appointments diary and other documentation indicates that he was in Moscow until 31 August.

17 *G. K. Zhukov v Stalingradskom Bitve: Sbornik Dokumentov* (Moscow: Biblioteka, 1996) pp. 66–67.

18 *Stalingrad, 1942–1943,* doc. 220.

19 Zhukov, *Reminiscences,* vol. 2, pp. 93–99.

20 Rotundo (ed.), *Battle for Stalingrad,* p. 415.

21 See *Stalingrad, 1942–1943,* docs. 221, 225, 227, 228, 229, 231, 258.

22 Zhukov, *Reminiscences,* vol. 2, p. 129.

23 Various articles, editorials, and statements published in *Izvestiya, Pravda,* and *Krasnaya Zvezda* from 29 November 1942, onwards.

24 D. M. Glantz, *Soviet Military Deception in the Second World War* (London: Frank Cass, 1989), chap. 5.

25 D. M. Glantz, *After Stalingrad: The Red Army's Winter Offensive, 1942–1943* (Solihull, U.K.: Helion, 2009), p. 391.

26 O. P. Chaney, *Zhukov,* rev. ed. (Norman: University of Oklahoma Press, 1996), p. 237.

27 *Na Priyome u Stalina* (Moscow: Novyi Khronograf, 2008), pp. 396–98.

28 Glantz, *After Stalingrad,* p. 426. This document is one of many by Zhukov cited verbatim by Glantz in this volume. My treatment of Polar Star and Zhukov's role in the operation is based almost wholly on Glantz's book.

29 Zhukov, *Reminiscences,* vol. 2, pp. 150–52.

CHAPTER 9: *NA ZAPAD!*

1 Ella Zhukova, 'Interesy Ottsa', in *Marshal Zhukov: Polkovodets i Chelovek,* vol. 1 (Moscow: APN, 1998), p. 55.

2 Era Zhukova, 'Otets', in ibid., p. 43.

3 Ibid., p. 56.

4 Letters of October 1943 and February 1944, cited by V. Daines, *Zhukov: Rozhdennyi Pobezhdat'* (Moscow: Yauza/Eksmo, 2008), pp. 384–85, 406–407.

5 I. Mastykina, *Zheny i Deti Georgiya Zhukova* (Moscow: Komsomol'skya Pravda, 1996), pp. 86–87. Photographic reproductions of Zhukov's letters to Margarita may be found in *Georgy Zhukov: Al'bom* (Moscow:

Poligrafresursy, 1995). The Douglas referred to by Margarita would have been the version of the American plane manufactured by the Soviets under licence. During the war these planes – designated the Lisunov Li-2 – were converted for military use and equipped with armaments.

6 When preparing the second edition of his memoirs Zhukov wrote several pages thanking various members of his support team. For some reason the acknowledgment pages were not published (RGVA, F. 41107, Op. 1, D.52, Ll. 72–76).

7 Bedov's memoir may be found in his 'Ryadom s Marshalom' and in V. Peskov, 'Govoryat Sputniki Zhukova', both in *Marshal Zhukov: Polkovodets i Chelovek.*

8 A. N. Buchin, *170 000 Kilometrov s G. Zhukovym* (Moscow: Molodaya Gvardiya, 1994), p. 42. This memoir consisted of a series of interviews with N. N. Yakovlev, who published the first serious Russian biography of Zhukov in 1992.

9 B. V. Sokolov, *Georgy Zhukov: Triumf i Padeniya* (Moscow: Ast, 2003), pp. 433–42; 'Zheny i Docheri Marshala Zhukova', *Komsomol'skaya Pravda,* 7 June 1996, 22 August 1996, 30 September 1996. I am grateful to Boris Sokolov for giving me the reference to these interviews by Mastykina, which were reproduced in her *Zheny i Deti Georgiya Zhukova.*

10 *Georgy Zhukov: Stenogramma Oktyabr'skogo (1957g.) Plenuma TsK KPSS i Drugie Dokumenty* (Moscow: Democratiya, 2001), p. 593.

11 R. R. Reese, *Why Stalin's Soldiers Fought* (Lawrence: University Press of Kansas, 2011), pp. 300–301.

12 W. J. Spahr, *Zhukov: The Rise and Fall of a Great Captain* (Novato, Calif: Presidio, 1993), p. 133.

13 Zhukov, *Reminiscences,* vol. 2, pp. 150–52.

14 S. M. Shtemenko, *The Soviet General Staff at War, 1941–1945,* vol. 1 (Moscow: Progress Publishers, 1970), pp. 152–53. See also the documents in 'Podgotovka k Kurskoi Bitve', *Voenno-Istoricheskii Zhurnal,* no. 6, 1983.

15 Zhukov, *Reminiscences,* vol. 2, p. 160. Zhukov dates these discussions 11–12 April but Stalin's appointments diary indicates that the critical meetings with Stalin took place on 16–18 April. See *Na Priyome u Stalina,* pp. 403–404.

16 Ibid., pp. 211, 159. On Antonov, see Richard Woff's essay in H. Shukman (ed.), *Stalin's Generals* (London: Phoenix, 1997). Rokossovsky admired Antonov, too, describing him as 'a master of operational art' but complained that he never pressed an objection with Stalin.

17 Shtemenko, *The Soviet General Staff at War,* vol. 1, p. 90; vol. 2 (Moscow: Progress Publishers, 1985), p. 473.

18 A copy of this order may be found in the Volkogonov Papers, Library of Congress, Manuscript Division.

19 On Soviet plans and preparations see D. M. Glantz and J. M. House, *The Battle of Kursk* (Lawrence: University Press of Kansas, 1999).

20 D. M. Glantz, *Soviet Military Deception in the Second World War* (London: Frank Cass, 1989), pp. 146–82.

21 K. Rokossovsky, *A Soldier's Duty* (Moscow: Progress Publishers, 1970),

p. 202. An expanded version of Rokossovsky's memoirs published in 2002 contained additional material that criticised Stavka's use of representatives such as Zhukov as an unnecessary barrier between Front commanders and Stalin and the General Staff (K. Rokossovsky, *Soldatskii Dolg* [Moscow: Olma-Press, 2002], pp. 265–66). This seems to have been a common, and predictable, complaint by Front commanders, who naturally wanted direct access to the High Command in Moscow. Those like Zhukov and Vasilevsky who served as Stavka representatives defended the system as a necessary link in the chain of command. That seems to have been the view of Stalin and the General Staff as well, since the trend during the war was towards ever more strengthening of the authority of Stavka's representatives in the field.

22 Cited by Daines, *Zhukov,* p. 358.

23 See T. P. Mulligan, 'Spies, Ciphers and "Zitadelle": Intelligence and the Battle of Kursk, 1943', *Journal of Contemporary History,* vol. 22, 1987; and V. Korovin, *Sovetskaya Razvedka i Kontrrazvedka v gody Velikoi Otechestvennoi Voiny* (Moscow: Rus', 2003), pp. 113–22.

24 See 'Podgotovka k Kurskoi Bitve', *Voenno-Istoricheskii Zhurnal,* no. 6, 1983.

25 A. M. Vasilevsky, *A Lifelong Cause* (Moscow: Progress Publishers, 1981), p. 272.

26 Zhukov, *Reminiscences,* vol. 2, p. 182. On Prokhorovka, see further V. Zamulin, *Demolishing the Myth: The Tank Battle at Prokhorovka* (Solihull, U.K.: Helion, 2011).

27 *Main Front: Soviet Leaders Look Back on World War II* (London: Brassey's Defence Publishers, 1987), p. 118.

28 Zhukov, *Reminiscences,* vol. 2, pp. 194, 208.

29 A. Werth, *Russia at War, 1941–1945* (London: Pan, 1965), p. 619.

30 Ibid., pp. 551–52.

31 E. Mawdsley, *Thunder in the East: The Nazi-Soviet War, 1941–1945* (London: Hodder Arnold, 2005), pp. 274–75.

32 Zhukov, *Reminiscences,* p. 213.

33 Rokossovsky, *A Soldier's Life,* p. 211.

34 Zhukov, *Reminiscences,* vol. 2, p. 233.

35 V. Krasnov, *Zhukov: Marshal Velikoi Imperii* (Moscow: Olma-Press, 2000), p. 408.

36 The document may be found in ibid., pp. 409–12.

37 J. Erickson, *The Road to Berlin* (London: Weidenfeld & Nicolson, 1983), p. 141.

38 Zhukov, *Reminiscences,* vol. 2, p. 221.

39 A. Read and D. Fisher, *The Fall of Berlin* (London: Pimlico, 2002), p. 153.

40 The only source on this conference is Zhukov (Zhukov: *Reminiscences,* vol. 2, p. 225–31. Vasilevsky (*A Lifelong Cause,* pp. 307–309) mentions it, too, but he read Zhukov's memoirs before he wrote his own. There is no evidence in Stalin's appointments diary that such a conference took place but given its large size it would not have been held in his office anyway. Zhukov dated the conference mid-December but a detailed chronology of his whereabouts during the war indicates that it must have taken place in

the early part of the month. See S. I. Isaev, 'Vekhi Frontoogo Puti', *Voenno-Istoricheskii Zhurnal,* no. 10, 1991. This is quite a useful document but where there are gaps in the documentation the author accepts Zhukov's memoirs at face value.

41 Zhukov, *Reminiscences,* vol. 2, p. 238.

42 The document is reproduced in Krasnov, *Zhukov,* p. 417.

43 In his memoirs Zhukov cited this second message but not the first and presented the episode as Stalin's rebuke not of him but of Vatutin: Zhukov, *Reminiscences,* vol. 2, pp. 247–49.

44 Ibid., p. 250.

45 Cited by Daines, *Zhukov,* pp. 421–22.

46 Shtemenko, *The Soviet General Staff at War,* vol. 1, chap. 11.

47 Zhukov, *Reminiscences,* vol. 2, p. 257ff.

48 Copy of the order in the Volkogonov Papers in the Library of Congress Manuscripts Division.

49 *Na Priyome u Stalina,* pp. 433–34. According to Shtemenko (vol. 1, p. 238) the meetings with Stalin were preceded by discussions on 22 May and 23 involving the General Staff, Zhukov, Vasilevsky, and various Front commanders.

50 *Russkii Arkhiv: Velikaya Otechestvennaya Voina, 1941–1945,* vol. 16(4), Stavka VGK: Dokumenty i Materialy, 1944–1945 (Moscow: Terra, 1993), docs. 113–16. See also: D. M. Glantz and H. S. Orenstein, *Belorussia 1944: The Soviet General Staff Study* (London: Frank Cass, 2001), pp. 14–28.

51 *Stalin's Correspondence with Churchill, Atlee, Roosevelt and Truman, 1941–1945* (London: Lawrence & Wishart, 1958), doc. 260, p. 215; doc. 274, p. 224.

52 Zhukov, *Reminiscences,* vol. 2, pp. 273–74.

53 *Marshal Zhukov: Polkovodets i Chelovek,* pp. 324–25.

54 An extract from Batov's memoir may be found in S. Bialer, *Stalin and His Generals: Soviet Military Memoirs of World War II* (London: Souvenir Press, 1970), pp. 417–20. When Batov's book was republished in the 1970s these disparaging passages about Zhukov were removed. See also Spahr, *Zukhov: The Rise and Fall of a Great Captain,* p. 149.

55 Zhukov, *Reminiscences,* vol. 2, p. 279.

56 Stavka VGK 1944–1945, docs. 162–63, p. 120.

57 Erickson, *The Road to Berlin,* p. 228.

58 Zhukov, *Reminiscences,* vol. 2, pp. 286–87.

59 Shtemenko, *The Soviet General Staff at War,* vol. 2, pp. 71–81; *Na Priyome u Stalina,* p. 438.

60 *SSSR i Pol'sha, 1941–1945: k Istorii Voennogo Souza* (Moscow: Terra, 1994), doc. 7, p. 201.

61 Ibid., doc. 29, pp. 218–19. A translation of this document may be found in Shtemenko, vol. 2, pp. 93–94.

62 Ibid., doc. 55, p. 245.

63 Ibid., doc. 100, p. 310.

64 On Bagration and the failure to take Warsaw see A. Tucker-Jones, *Stalin's Revenge: Operation Bagration and the Annihilation of Army Group Centre* (Barnsley, U.K.: Pen & Sword, 2009).

65 Werth, *Russia at War*, p. 786.

66 *Stalin's Correspondence with Churchill, Atlee, Roosevelt and Truman*, doc. 321, p. 254; docs. 322–23, pp. 254–55.

67 Shtemenko, vol. 2, pp. 102–104; and A. Chmielarz, 'Warsaw Fought Alone: Reflections on Aid to and the Fall of the 1944 Uprising', *The Polish Review*, vol. 39, no. 4, 1994, p. 421.

68 Stalin's role is explored in detail in G. Roberts, *Stalin's Wars: From World War to Cold War, 1939–1953* (London: Yale University Press, 2006).

69 Zhukov, *Reminiscences*, vol. 2, pp. 301–303.

70 Ibid., p. 310.

71 Ibid., pp. 296–300; *Liberation Mission of the Soviet Armed Forces in the Second World War* (Moscow: Progress Publishers, 1975), pp. 172–82.

72 Stavka VGK 1944–1945, doc. 234, p. 162.

73 *Na Priyome u Stalina*, pp. 443.

74 Stavka VGK 1944–1945, doc. 248, p. 170.

75 Rokossovsky, *A Soldier's Life*, p. 267.

76 Zhukov, *Vospominaniya*, vol. 3, p. 175. These sentences were omitted from the Soviet-era edition of the memoirs.

CHAPTER 10: RED STORM

1 *Na Priyome u Stalina*, p. 443.

2 S. Bialer, *Stalin and His Generals: Soviet Military Memoirs of World War II* (London: Souvenir Press, 1970), p. 467.

3 Stalin described Silesia as 'gold' to Konev and instructed him to take care not to damage its industrial resources too much. I. Konev, *Year of Victory* (Moscow: Progress Publishers, 1969), pp. 5, 67–68.

4 S. M. Shtemenko, *The Soviet General Staff at War, 1941–1945*, 2 vols. (Moscow: Progress Publishers, 1970, 1986). The first volume was originally published in Russian in 1968, the second in 1973.

5 On Shtemenko's wartime career, see G. Jukes, 'Shtemenko', in H. Shukman (ed.), *Stalin's Generals* (London: Phoenix, 2001).

6 Zhukov, *Reminiscences*, vol. 2, p. 319.

7 O. P. Chaney, *Zhukov*, rev. ed. (Norman: University of Oklahoma Press, 1996), p. 297. Chaney points out that when Zhukov was awarded the Order of Lenin on his seventieth birthday in 1966 the citation specifically noted his use of armoured forces during the Vistula-Oder operation.

8 After the war the Vistula-Oder operation was seen by the Soviet General Staff as the model for Blitzkrieg-type offensives: Interview with the chief of the Russian General Staff, *Krasnaya Zvezda*, 7 May, 2005.

9 *Russkii Arkhiv: Velikaya Otechestvennaya Voina, 1941–1945*, vol. 16 (4): Stavka VGK: Dokumenty i Materialy 1944–45 gg (Moscow: Terra, 1993), doc. 40, pp. 326–28.

10 Cited by P. T. Kunitskii, 'Padenie Berlina: Kogda Ona Moglo Sostoyat'sya?', *Voenno-Istoricheskii Zhurnal*, no. 9, 2006.

11 Zhukov, *Reminiscences*, vol. 2, p. 328.

12 'Marshal G. K. Zhukov: Nastuplenie na Berlin Mogu Nachat 19–20.2.45', *Voenno-Istoricheskii Zhurnal*, no. 2, 1995.

13   Kunitskii, 'Padenie Berlina'.

14   Konev, *Year of Victory*, pp. 5ff.

15   On Chuikov, see: R. Woff, 'Chuikov', in Shukman (ed.), *Stalin's Generals*. Chuikov's memoirs in English: *The Beginning of the Road* (London: MacGibbon & Kee, 1963).

16   A translation of Chuikov's article may be found in Bialer, *Stalin and His Generals,* pp. 500–505.

17   Cited by M. I. Golovin, 'Uroki Dvukh Operatsii', *Voenno-Istoricheskii Zhurnal*, no. 1, 1988, p. 25. The date of the conference is derived from Kunitskii, 'Padenie Berlin'.

18   G. Zhukov, 'Na Berlinskom Napravlenii', *Voenno-Istoricheskii Zhurnal,* no. 6, 1965. A translation of this article may be found in H. E. Salisbury (ed.), *Marshal Zhukov's Greatest Battles* (London: Sphere, 1971). Chuikov responded to Zhukov's article in a letter to the editorial board of *Voenno-Istoricheskii Zhurnal* reiterating his view that Berlin could have been taken in February 1945. The journal's editor, N. G. Pavlenko, sent the letter to Zhukov for comment. Zhukov advised against publication because, he said, Chuikov's claims were 'not corroborated by a scientific analysis of the situation at the time'. In August 1965 Pavlenko wrote to Chuikov on behalf of the editorial board rejecting the letter. He pointed out that Zhukov, with Stavka's full support, had striven until mid-February to take Berlin: 'Neither Stavka nor the command of the 1st Belorussian Front refrained from attacking Berlin until 20 February'. RGVA F. 41107, Op. 1, D. 71, LL. 54–74.

19   V. A. Zolotarev and G. N. Sevast'yanov (eds.), *Velikaya Otechestvennaya Voina, 1941–1945*, vol. 3 (Moscow: Nauka, 1999), p. 251.

20   See Kunitskii, 'Padenie Berlina', pp. 5–6.

21   K. Rokossovsky, *A Soldier's Duty* (Moscow: Progress Publishers, 1970), p. 305.

22   I am grateful to Ambassador Beyrle for granting me this interview and for supplying information about his father. Joseph Beyrle's own story may be found at www.506infantry.org/stories/beyrle_his.htm. See also Thomas H. Taylor's account of Beyrle's exploits: *Behind Hitler's Lines* (New York: Ballantine, 2004).

23   F. D. Vorob'ev et al., *Poslednii Shturm (Berlinskaya Operatsiya 1945g)* (Moscow: Voenizdat, 1970), pp. 44–45. See also J. Erickson, 'Poslednii Shturm: The Soviet Drive to Berlin, 1945', in G. Bennett, *The End of the War in Europe 1945* (London: HMSO, 1996), p. 21.

24   Cited by C. Ryan, *The Last Battle* (London: NEL, 1968), p. 142.

25   *Na Priyome u Stalina*, p. 450.

26   The text of Stalin's message is reproduced in O. A. Rzheshevskii, 'Poslednii Shturm: Zhukov ili Konev', *Mir Istorii*, http://gpw.tellur.ru.

27   Konev, *Year of Victory*, p. 79. Konev dates this meeting 1 April but according to Stalin's appointments diary it took place on the 2nd. *Na Priyome u Stalina*, p. 450. Neither Zhukov nor Shtemenko mentions this incident in their memoirs, although the latter does mention the general belief in Stavka that the allies intended to take Berlin before the Red Army.

28 *Na Priyome u Stalina*, p. 450.

29 O. A. Rzheshevsky, 'Vzyat' Berlin! Novye Dokumenty', *Novaya i Noveishaya Istoriya*, no. 4, 1995.

30 Bialer, *Stalin and His Generals*, p. 500.

31 I. S. Konev, *Zapiski Komanduushchego Frontom* (Moscow: Voenizdat, 1981), p. 404.

32 Zhukov, *Vospominaniya*, vol. 3, pp. 225–26. This passage was omitted from Soviet-era editions of Zhukov's memoirs.

33 On the battle for Berlin, see: A. Beevor, *Berlin: The Downfall 1945* (London: Penguin, 2002); A. Read and D. Fisher, *The Fall of Berlin* (London: Pimlico, 2002); Ryan, *The Last Battle;* and T. Le Tissier, *Marshal Zhukov at the Oder* (Stroud, U.K.: Sutton, 2008).

34 Cited by M. Jones, *Total War: From Stalingrad to Berlin* (London: John Murray, 2011), pp. 280–81.

35 Konev, *Year of Victory*, pp. 105–108.

36 J. Erickson, *The Road to Berlin* (London: Weidenfeld & Nicolson, 1983), pp. 571–72.

37 Ibid., p. 578.

38 C. Bellamy, *Absolute War: Soviet Russia in the Second World War* (London: Macmillan, 2007), p. 664.

39 Ibid., p. 586. A copy of the directive may be found in the Volkogonov Papers, Library of Congress, Manuscript Division.

40 Zhukov, *Reminiscences*, vol. 2, p. 395.

41 See L. Bezymenksi, *The Death of Adolf Hitler* (London: Michael Joseph, 1968).

42 Zhukov, *Reminiscences*, vol. 2, p. 401.

43 Zhukov's meetings in Stalin's office in May–June 1945 are recorded in *Na Priyome u Stalina*, pp. 454–57. On Stalin and the Far Eastern War see T. Hasegawa, *Racing the Enemy: Stalin, Truman and the Surrender of Japan* (Cambridge, Mass.: Harvard University Press, 2005), and G. Roberts, *Stalin's Wars: From World War to Cold War, 1939–1953* (London: Yale University Press, 2006), pp. 279–95. There are unconfirmed reports that the invasion and occupation of Hokkaido – the northern Japanese home island – was also under discussion and that Zhukov dismissed the idea as an 'escapade'. See: J. Haslam, *Russia's Cold War* (New Haven, Conn.: Yale University Press, 2011), p. 60.

44 'Press-Konferentsiya u Marshala G. Zhukova', *Pravda*, 10 June 1945. Zhukov was accompanied at the press conference by Deputy Foreign Commissar A. Y. Vyshinsky.

45 A. Werth, *Russia at War, 1941–1945* (London: Pan, 1965), pp. 889–93.

46 Zhukov's timing is about right. On 19 June he attended a military conference in Stalin's office that discussed the Soviet entry into the Far Eastern war, scheduled to begin with an attack on the Japanese in Manchuria in August: *Na Priyome u Stalina*, p. 457.

47 Zhukov, *Reminiscences*, vol. 2, pp. 423–24.

48 W. J. Spahr, *Zhukov, The Rise and Fall of a Great Captain* (Novato, Calif.: Presidio, 1993), pp. 192–93.

49   Ibid., p. 194. Patton was killed in a road accident in December 1945.

50   Zhukov, *Reminiscences,* vol. 2, pp. 442, 449–51.

51   The two classic studies of the Soviet occupation regime in Germany are J. P. Nettl, *The Eastern Zone and Soviet Policy in Germany, 1945–1950* (London: Oxford University Press, 1951), and N. M. Naimark, *The Russians in Germany: A History of the Soviet Zone of Occupation, 1945–1949* (Cambridge, Mass.: Harvard University Press, 1995).

52   B. R. von Oppen, *Documents on Germany Under Occupation, 1945–1954* (London: Oxford University Press, 1955), pp. 29–35.

53   R. Murphy, *Diplomat Among Warriors* (New York: Doubleday, 1964), pp. 258–59.

54   Zhukov, *Vospominaniya,* vol. 3, pp. 317, 350–51.

55   Cited by Chaney, *Zhukov,* p. 347.

56   Eisenhower Papers, Pre-Presidential Principal File, Box 110, File on Joseph Stalin, Deane to Eisenhower, 28 August 1945, Eisenhower Presidential Library, Abilene, Kansas.

57   *Sovetsko-Amerikanskie Otnosheniya, 1939–1945* (Moscow: Materik, 2004), doc. 346.

58   Ibid., doc. 8.

59   Ibid., docs. 104, 107.

60   Spahr, *Zukhov: The Rise and Fall of a Great Captain,* pp. 185–86.

61   G. Zhukov, *Vosominaniya i Razmyshleniya,* vol. 3 (Moscow: APN, 1992), p. 35.

62   G. P. Kynin and J. Laufer (eds.), *SSSR i Germanskii Vopros, 1941–1949,* vol. 2 (Moscow: Mezhdunarodnye Otnosheniya, 2000), doc. 54.

63   'Stenogramma Vystupleniya Glavnonachal'stvuushchego SVAG – Glavnokomanduushchego GSOVG G.K. Zhukova', *Sovetskaya Voennaya Administratsiya v Germanii, 1945–1949* (Moscow: Rosspen, 2005), pp. 90–100.

64   See Naimark, *The Russians in Germany,* chap. 2.

65   *SSSR i Germanskii Vopros,* doc. 42.

66   Naimark, *The Russians in Germany,* p. 77.

67   G. Roberts, *Stalin's Wars: From World War to Cold War, 1939–1953* (London: Yale University Press, 2006), p. 264.

68   'Marshal G. K. Zhukov u Svoikh Izbiratelei', *Pravda,* 28 January 1946.

69   *Georgy Zhukov: Stenogramma Oktyabr'skogo (1957g.) Plenuma TsK KPSS i Drugie Dokumenty* (Moscow: Democratiya, 2001), doc. 1.

CHAPTER 11: EXILED TO THE PROVINCES

1   G. Zhukov, 'Korotke o Staline', *Pravda,* 20 January 1989.

2   *Georgy Zhukov: Stenogramma Oktyabr'skogo (1957g.) Plenuma TsK KPSS i Drugie Dokumenty* (Moscow: Democratiya, 2001), part one, doc. 2 and n. 2, p. 640.

3   Ibid., pp. 586–91.

4   Ibid., doc. 3.

5   See P. Sudoplatov, *Special Tasks: The Memoirs of an Unwanted Witness – A Soviet Spymaster* (London: Warner, 1994), pp. 313–14, 328.

6   See G. Roberts, *Molotov: Stalin's Cold Warrior* (Washington, D.C.: Potomac, 2012), pp. 17–18.

7   See G. Roberts, *Stalin's Wars: From World War to Cold War, 1939–1953* (London: Yale University Press, 2006), chap. 11.

8   *Marshal Zhukov: Polkovodets i Chelovek*, vol. 2 (Moscow: APN, 1988), p. 70.

9   Zhukov, *Vospominaniya*, vol. 3, p. 364; Zhukov, 'Korotke o Staline'.

10 K. Simonov, *Glazami Cheloveka Moego Pokoleniya* (Moscow: APN, 1989), p. 330. This passage was brought to my attention by O. P. Chaney, *Zhukov*, rev. ed. (Norman: University of Oklahoma Press, 1966), pp. 373–74.

11 S. P. Markov, 'Poslevoennye Gody', in *Marshal Zhukov: Polkovodets i Chelovek*, vol. 1 (Moscow: APN, 1988), p. 21.

12 Document in V. Krasnov, *Zhukov: Marshal Velikoi Imperii* (Moscow: Olma-Press, 2000), p. 463.

13 *Georgy Zhukov: Stenogramma Oktyabr'skogo*, part one, docs. 6, 8, n. 11, p. 643. According to Stalin's appointments diary his last meeting with Zhukov was on 29 April 1946. Contrary to some reports, Zhukov did not attend the 1947 Central Committee meeting that excluded him from membership.

14 Ibid., doc. 9, and n. 13, p. 643; W. J. Spahr, *Zhukov: The Rise and Fall of a Great Captain* (Novato, Calif.: Presidio, 1993), pp. 206–207.

15 A. Mirkina, *Vtoraya Pobeda Marshala Zhukova* (Moscow: Vniigmi-Mtsd, 2000), p. 24.

16 Document in Krasnov, *Zhukov*, pp. 467–70.

17 *Georgy Zhukov: Stenogramma Oktyabr'skogo*, pp. 591–93.

18 Ibid., part one, doc. 10.

19 Zhukov, 'Korotke o Staline'.

20 'Pavel Semenovich Rybalko', *Pravda*, 28 August 1948.

21 *Georgy Zhukov: Stenogramma Oktyabr'skogo*, pp. 641–42.

22 *Reabilitatsiya: Kak Eto Bylo*, vol. 1 (Moscow: Materik, 2000), docs. 26–27.

23 'F. I. Tolbukhin', *Pravda*, 19 October 1949.

24 *Bol'shaya Sovetskaya Entsiklopediya*, 2nd ed. (Moscow: Ogiz, 1952), pp. 222–23.

25 Spahr, *Zhukov*, p. 209.

26 Chaney, *Zhukov*, p. 380.

27 *Marshal Zhukov: Polkovodets i Chelovek*, vol. 2, p. 70.

28 I. Mastykina, *Zheny i Deti Georgiya Zhukova* (Moscow: Komsomol'skya Pravda, 1996), pp. 78–79.

29 *Marshal Zhukov: Moskva v Zhizn i Sud'be Polkovodtsa* (Moscow: Glavarkhiv, 2005), pp. 491. The quote is from a 'diary' of Zhukov's in his daughter Maria's possession. The diary appears to be retrospective rather than contemporary and the date of its composition is unknown.

30 Ibid., pp. 493–94.

31 Ibid., pp. 495–503.

32 Mastykina, *Zheny i Deti Georgiya Zhukova*, passim.

33 'Posle Smerti Stalina', *Georgy Zhukov: Stenogramma Oktyabr'skogo*,

pp. 620–39. The original of this document may be found in RGVA, F.41107, Op. 2, D. 1. It consists of an unsigned, undated, and uncorrected typescript. As the editors of this volume say, it appears to have been composed not by Zhukov but by someone else on the basis of conversations with him. The editors date the document c. 1963–1964.

34   'Posle Smerti Stalina', p. 621.

35   'U Groba Velikogo Vozhdya', *Krasnaya Zvezda,* 9 March 1953.

36   'Posle Smerti Stalina', p. 622.

37   Ibid., pp. 623–24. According to Khrushchev, Zhukov entered the room and shouted 'hands up' to Beria. When Beria reached for his briefcase, Khrushchev, fearing there was a gun in it, grabbed his arm. *Khrushchev Remembers* (London: Sphere, 1971), pp. 303–304.

38   Chaney, *Zhukov,* p. 388.

39   This section is based on D. Holloway, *Stalin and the Bomb* (New Haven, Conn.: Yale University Press, 1994), p. 325ff. A few documents relating to the Totskoe test/exercise may be found in the Volkogonov Papers, Library of Congress, Manuscript Division.

40   In the 1980s, some soldiers who had taken part in the exercise claimed their ill health was a result of exposure to radiation. There were also reports of a higher than normal incidence of cancers in the Totskoe region. These claims and reports provided further ammunition for Zhukov's critics. Victor Suvorov, for example, rather distastefully compared 'Zhukov's experiment' at Totskoe with Nazi medical experiments conducted on camp inmates during World War II. More balanced was the view of David Holloway, the leading western expert on the Soviet atomic bomb programme, who pointed out that the Americans had conducted similar exercises and commented: 'It is clear that measures were taken to protect the troops and the villagers; but it is also clear that the High Command took a harsh view of what troops would face on the nuclear battlefield and wanted to create those conditions in the exercise.' Holloway, *Stalin and the Bomb,* p. 328.

CHAPTER 12: MINISTER OF DEFENCE

1   *Prezidium TsK KPSS, 1954–1964,* vol. 1 (Moscow: Rosspen, 2004), p. 40.

2   See G. Roberts, 'Stalin and the Katyn Massacre', in G. Roberts (ed.), *Stalin: His Times and Ours* (Dublin: IAREES, 2005).

3   On Khrushchev: W. Taubman: *Khrushchev: The Man and His Era* (London: Simon & Schuster, 2003).

4   *Khrushchev Remembers* (London: Sphere, 1971), p. 144.

5   Author interview with Era Zhukova, Moscow, April 2010.

6   'Marshal G. K. Zhukov Interviewed by William Randolph Hearst, Jr., J. Kingsbury Smith, and Frank Conniff, 7 February 1955', *New Times,* no. 8, 1955. The interview was published in *Pravda* on 13 February.

7   See M. Evangelista, '*Why Keep Such an Army?'*: *Khrushchev's Troop Reductions,* Cold War International History Project Working Paper No. 19, December 1997.

8 *Khrushchev Remembers: The Last Testament* (London: André Deutsch, 1974), p. 15.
9 'Proposal of the Soviet Government on the Reduction of Armaments, Prohibition of Atomic Weapons, and Elimination of the Threat of Another War', *New Times,* no. 20, pp. 2–6.
10 See G. Roberts, *A Chance for Peace? The Soviet Campaign to End the Cold War, 1953–1955,* Cold War International History Project Working Paper No. 57, December 2008.
11 'Protokol: O Sozdanii O'bedenennu Komandovaniya Vooruzhennyi Sila Gosudarst-uchastnik Dogovora o Druzhbe, Sotrudnichestve i Vzaimoi Pomoshi', Arkhiv Vneshnei Politiki Rossiiskoi Federatsi, F. 6, Op. 14, Pap/4, D. 54, Ll. 68–74.
12 'Russia's Marshal Zhukov', *Time,* 9 May 1955.
13 Bohlen's report to U.S. secretary of state John Foster Dulles, 10 June 1955, Eisenhower Papers, Anne Whitman Files, International Series, Box 49, USSR 1953–55, File 1, Eisenhower Presidential Library, Abilene, Kansas.
14 Cited by O. P. Chaney, *Zhukov,* rev. ed. (Norman: University of Oklahoma Press, 1996), p. 400.
15 Bohlen's record of the two meetings may be found in the Eisenhower Presidential Library: Dulles Papers, General Correspondence and Memoranda Series, Box no. 3, File: Strictly Confidential U-Z (2). Troyanovsky's record: *Georgy Zhukov: Stenogramma Oktyabr'skogo,* part two, docs. 11–12. Archive copies of Troyanovsky's record may be found in Rossiiskii Gosudarstvennyi Arkhiv Noveishei Istorii, F. 5, Op. 30, D. 116. The two sets of minutes do not differ in any significant detail. It was common practice for Soviet and western interpreters to compare notes after the meeting. My summary combines elements of both.
16 O. Troyanovsky, *Cherez Gody i Rasstoyaniya* (Moscow: Vargrius, 1997), p. 191.
17 Cited by Chaney, *Zhukov,* p. 402.
18 A. Gromyko, *Memories* (London: Hutchinson, 1989), pp. 166–67.
19 Troyanovsky, *Cherez Gody i,* pp. 193–94.
20 Ibid.
21 *Prezidium TsK KPSS, 1954–1964,* vol. 1, pp. 41–42; A. Fursenko and T. Naftali, *Khrushchev's Cold War* (New York: Norton, 2006), pp. 28–29.
22 On the Molotov-Khrushchev struggle, see G. Roberts, *Molotov: Stalin's Cold Warrior* (Washington, D.C.: Potomac, 2012).
23 *Khrushchev Remembers,* p. 539.
24 *Georgy Zhukov: Stenogramma Oktyabr'skogo,* p. 124.
25 Ibid., p. 148.
26 Ibid., pp. 126–33; *Reabilitatsiya: Kak Eto Bylo,* vol. 2 (Moscow: Materik, 2003), doc. 8, part 1, doc. 14, part 3.
27 This document, together with a number of related documents, may be found in the Volkogonov Papers, Library of Congress, Manuscript Division.
28 *Sovetskii Souz i Vengerskii Krizis, 1956 goda* (Moscow: Rosspen, 1998),

doc. 83. A number of the documents in this volume may be found in English translation on the website of the Cold War International History Project.

29 Ibid., doc. 82.

30 E. I. Malashenko, 'Osobyi Korpus v Ogne Budapeshta', *Voenno-Istoricheskii Zhurnal*, nos. 10–12, 1993, no. 1, 1994. This is Malashenko's memoir of 1956.

31 See ibid. and *Georgy Zhukov: Stenogramma Oktyabr'skogo,* part two, doc. 39.

32 *Sovetskii Souz i Vengerskii Krizis,* doc. 100.

33 Ibid., doc. 105.

34 Cited by Chaney, *Zhukov,* p. 413.

35 *Sovetskii Souz i Vengerskii Krizis,* doc. 115.

36 Ibid., doc. 125.

37 Ibid., doc. 132.

38 Ibid., docs. 159, 160, 166, 179, 180, 184, 188, 192. Archive copies of these documents may be found in Fund 89: The Soviet Communist Party on Trial, Op. 45, Dd. 26–40.

39 *Georgy Zhukov: Stenogramma Oktyabr'skogo,* part two, doc. 44.

40 On Zhukov's visit to India and Burma: Chaney, *Zhukov,* pp. 417–19; and W. J. Spahr, *Zhukov: The Rise and Fall of a Great Captain* (Novato, Calif.: Presidio, 1993), pp. 228–30.

41 Cited by V. A. Afanas'ev, *Stanovlenie Polkovodcheskogo Iskusstva G. K. Zhukova* (Moscow: Svyatigor, 2006), p. 250.

42 See S. A. Christensen and F. P. Jensen, 'Superpower Under Pressure: The Secret Speech of Minister of Defence Zhukov in East Berlin, March 1957, www.php.isn.ethz.ch/collections/coll_zhukov/zhukov.cfm. The links to the two versions of Zhukov's speech may be found on the same website (Parallel History Project).

43 'Iz Vystupleniya Marshala Zhukova na Nauchnoi Konferentsii Mai 1957g'. I am grateful to Dr. S. A. Christensen for supplying me with a copy of this speech, which comes from the Czech military archives.

44 *Georgy Zhukov: Stenogramma Oktyabr'skogo,* part two, doc. 49.

45 'Posle Smerti Stalina', in ibid., p. 625.

46 Ibid., pp. 628–30.

47 Taubman, *Khrushchev,* pp. 314–20.

48 *Molotov, Malenkov, Kaganovich, 1957: Stenogramma Iun'skogo Plenuma TsK KPSS i Drugie Dokumenty,* Mezhdunarodnyi Fond (Moscow: Demokratiya, 1998), pp. 38–39, 41, 67.

49 *Marshal Zhukov: Moskva v Zhizn i Sud'be Polkovodtsa,* p. 498.

50 'Vystuplenie: Marshala Sovetskogo Souza G. K. Zhukova na Sobranii Partiinogo Aktiva Ministerstva Oborony i Moskovsogo Garnizona 2 Iulya 1957g'. Copy in Volkogonov Papers, Library of Congress, Manuscript Division.

51 'Anti-Party Bloc Fought Exposé of Stalin Cult – Zhukov', *The Current Digest of the Soviet Press,* vol. 9, no. 25, 1957.

52 Spahr, *Zhukov,* pp. 236–37; Fursenko and Naftali, *Khrushchev's Cold*

War, p. 77; *Marshal Zhukov: Moskva v Zhizni i Sud'be Polkovodtsa,*
pp. 373–75.

53 'Posle Smerti Stalina', p. 633.
54 *Georgy Zhukov: Stenogramma Oktyabr'skogo (1957g.),* part four, docs.
    15, 18, 19.
55 Ibid., docs. 12–14.
56 *Prezidium TsK KPSS, 1954–1964,* vol. 1, p. 264. See also Fursenko and
    Naftali, *Khrushchev's Cold War,* p. 153.
57 *Georgy Zhukov: Stenogramma Oktyabr'skogo (1957g.),* part four, docs.
    1–6, 10, 15.
58 Ibid., p. 217.
59 Ibid., docs. 15–16.
60 'Posle Smerti Stalina', p. 635.
61 *Georgy Zhukov: Stenogramma Oktyabr'skogo,* part 5, doc. 19.
62 The source for this quote is Khrushchev's American biographer, William
    Taubman, who commented: 'With friends and colleagues like these, Zhu-
    kov needed no enemies.' Taubman, *Khrushchev,* pp. 362–63.
63 Chaney, *Zhukov,* p. 445.
64 I. S. Konev, 'Sila Sovetskoi Armii i Flota – v Rukovodstve Partii, v Neraz-
    ryvnoi Svyazi s Narodom', *Pravda,* 3 November 1957.
65 'Posle Smerti Stalina', p. 639.
66 *Marshal Zhukov: Polkovodets i Chelovek,* vol. 2 (Moscow: APN, 1988),
    p. 71.
67 *Georgy Zhukov: Stenogramma Oktyabr'skogo (1957g),* pp. 605–11.
68 Ibid., part two, doc. 29. This was the document that Zhukov was most
    attacked for at the October plenum of the Central Committee that re-
    moved him as defence minister and expelled him from the party leader-
    ship. See further: T. J. Colton, 'The Zhukov Affair Reconsidered', *Soviet
    Studies,* vol. 29, April 1977.
69 'Posle Smerti Stalina', p. 632; *Marshal Zhukov: Polkovodets i Chelovek,*
    vol. 2, p. 70.
70 CIA Staff Study: 'Party-Military Relations in the USSR and the Fall of
    Marshal Zhukov, 8 June 1959', p. 42, www.foia.cia.gov. I am grateful to
    Mark Kramer for directing me towards this source.
71 Cited by Chaney, *Zhukov,* p. 464.

CHAPTER 13: FINAL BATTLE

1 K. Simonov, *Glazami Cheloveka Moego Pokoleniya* (Moscow: APN,
   1989), p. 391. This passage was brought to my attention by O. P. Chaney,
   Zhukov, rev. ed. (Norman: University of Oklahoma Press, 1996),
   pp. 464–65.
2 I. Mastykina, *Zheny i Deti Georgiya Zhukova* (Moscow: Komsomol'skya
   Pravda, 1996), pp. 56–57; author interview with Era Zhukov, Moscow,
   April 2010.
3 *Georgy Zhukov: Stenogramma Oktyabr'skogo (1957g.) Plenuma TsK
   KPSS i Drugie Dokumenty* (Moscow: Democratiya, 2001), part five, docs.

37–38; RGVA, F. 41107, Op. 1, D. 73, Ll. 1–2. It was his old adversary, Nikolai Bulganin, who signed the government decree on his retirement conditions – in one of his last acts as prime minister before Khrushchev sacked him in March 1958.

4   P. N. Pospelov (ed.), *Istoriya Velikoi Otechestvennoi Voiny Sovetskogo Souza,* 6 vols. (Moscow: Voenizdat, 1960–1965).

5   *Georgy Zhukov: Stenogramma Oktyabr'skogo,* part five, docs. 39–41 and pp. 611–14. Brezhnev was accompanied by another Presidium member, Z. T. Serduk.

6   See T. J. Colton, 'The Zhukov Affair Reconsidered', *Soviet Studies,* vol. 29, April 1977; P. M. Cocks, 'The Purge of Marshal Zhukov', *Slavic Review,* vol. 22, no. 3, 1963; and M. Gallagher, 'Trends in the Soviet Historiography of the Second World War', in J. Keep (ed.), *Contemporary History in the Soviet Mirror* (New York: Praeger, 1964).

7   See the extracts from the memoirs of Batov, Belov, Biriuzov, Bychevskii, Chuikov, and Rokossovsky in S. Bialer, *Stalin and His Generals: Soviet Military Memoirs of World War II* (London: Souvenir Press, 1970).

8   *Georgy Zhukov: Stenogramma,* part five, doc. 42.

9   D. V. Pavlov, *Leningrad v Blokade* (Moscow: Voenizdat, 1958); A. S. Zav'yalov and T. E. Kalyanin, *Vostochno – Pomeranskaya Operatsiya* (Moscow: Voenizdat, 1960) *Istoriya Velikoi Otechestvennoi Voiny Sovetskogo Souza,* vol. 1, pp. 240, 244; V. D. Sokolovsky (ed.), *Voennaya Strategiya* (Moscow: Voenizdat, 1962); Bialer, *Stalin and His Generals,* p. 25; K. K. Rokossovsky (ed.), *Velikaya Pobeda na Volge* (Moscow: Voenizdat, 1965).

10 A point made by Brian Bond in his review of *Marshal Zhukov's Greatest Battles* in *The Listener,* 31 July 1969. Copy in Zhukov's personal file series: RGVA, F. 41107, Op. 1, D. 85.

11 A. Mirkina, *Vtoraya Pobeda Marshala Zhukova* (Moscow: Vniigmi-Mtsd, 2000), p. 10.

12 *Khrushchev Remembers: The Last Testament* (London: André Deutsch, 1974), pp. 13–14.

13 *Georgy Zhukov: Stenogramma Oktyabr'skogo,* part six, doc. 6.

14 O. P. Chaney, *Zhukov,* rev. ed. (Norman: University of Oklahoma Press, 1996), pp. 468–70.

15 G. A. Kumanev, *Ryadom so Stalinym* (Moscow: Byliia, 1999), pp. 144–48. This book also contains the text of Zhukov's speech to the conference (pp. 160–72).

16 *Marshal Zhukov: Moskva v Zhizni i Sud'be Polkovodtsa* (Moscow: Glavarkhiv, 2005), p. 544.

17 Much documentation may be found in RGVA, F. 41107, Op. 1, D. 54.

18 'Neskol'ko Voprosov iz Sovremennogo Polozheniya', RGVA, F. 41107, Op. 1, D. 78. Ll. 80–82.

19 *Bitva za Moskvu* (Moscow: Moskovskii Rabochii, 1968); *Stalingradskaya Epopeya* (Moscow: Nauka, 1968); *Kurskaya Bitva* (Moscow: Nauk, 1970).

20 RGVA, F. 41107, Op. 1, D. 76, Ll. 2, 31–128.

21   Chaney, *Zhukov,* p. 475.

22   RGVA, F. 41107, Op. 1, D. 79, Ll. 49–50.

23   Mirkina, *Vtoraya Pobeda Marshala Zhukova,* p. 47; *Marshal Zhukov: Moskva v Zhizn i Sud'be Polkovodtsa,* pp. 503–507. This is an extract from Maria's memoirs.

24   *Georgy Zhukov: Stenogramma Oktyabr'skogo,* part six, doc. 5.

25   Mirkina, *Vtoraya Pobeda Marshala Zhukova,* passim. Zhukov's study, including the original desk and other items of furniture, is re-created in the Zhukov Museum. The desk in the museum is covered in red felt rather than the green leather recalled by Mirkina but perhaps Zhukov had it re-covered.

26   Mirkina says the manuscript was delivered in March 1966 but Zhukov in his correspondence referred to autumn as the date of delivery.

27   G. Zhukov, 'Korotke o Staline', *Pravda,* 20 January 1989.

28   A. Samsonov, 'Looking Truth in the Eye', *Moscow News,* no. 18, 1987.

29   *Georgy Zhukov: Stenogramma Oktyabr'skogo,* part 6, doc. 7.

30   N. A. Antipenko, 'My Znali Druga Druga 25 let', in *Marshal Zhukov: Polkovodets i Chelovek,* vol. 1 (Moscow: APN, 1988), p. 324.

31   *Georgy Zhukov: Stenogramma Oktyabr'skogo,* part 6, docs. 3, 4, 9, 18, 19; RGVA, F. 41107, Op. 1, D. 119.

32   *Georgy Zhukov: Stenogramma Oktyabr'skogo,* part 6, docs. 12, 13, 15.

33   Mirkina, *Vtoraya Pobeda Marshala Zhukova,* pp. 53–55.

34   *Georgy Zhukov: Stenogramma Oktyabr'skogo,* part 6, docs. 16–17.

35   Cited by Chaney, *Zhukov,* p. 476 and W. J. Spahr, *Zhukov, The Rise and Fall of a Great Captain* (Novato, Calif.: Presidio, 1993), p. 262.

36   RGVA, F. 41107, Op. 1, D. 54, L. 75.

37   Some examples are reproduced by Mirkina, *Vtoraya Pobeda Marshala Zhukova,* pp. 103–26.

38   Spahr, *Zhukov,* p. 262.

39   A. Vasilevsky, 'Sovetskomu Soldatu Posvyashchaetsya', *Kommunist,* July 1969; A. Beloborodov, 'Polkovodets o Voennykh Sobytiyakh i Ludyakh', *Voenno-Istoricheskii Zhurnal,* no. 11, 1969.

40   Author interview with Era Zhukova, Moscow, April 2010.

41   RGVA, F. 41106, Op. 1, D. 172.

42   *Marshal Zhukov: Moskva v Zhizn i Sud'be Polkovodtsa,* pp. 508–15. This is an extract from Maria's memoirs and contains the correspondence between Zhukov and Galina during their last years.

43   E. Tsvetaev, 'Poslednii Podvig G.K. Zhukova', in S. S. Smirnov et al., *Marshal Zhukov: Kakim My Ego Pomnim* (Moscow: Politizdat, 1988).

44   RGVA F. 41107, Op. 1, D. 54, L. 184; D. 73, L. 113.

45   'Marshal Sovetskogo Souza Georgii Konstantinovich Zhukov', *Pravda,* 20 June 1974.

46   A. Vasilevsky, 'Pamyati Slavnogo Polkovodtsa', *Pravda,* 21 June 1974.

47   'V Poslednii Put': Pokhorony Marshala Sovetskogo Souza G. K. Zhukova', *Pravda,* 22 June 1974.

48   Translation by Geoffrey Roberts.

49   S. Alekseev, *Rasskazy o Marshale Zhukove* (Moscow: Malysh, 1977).

The existence of this book was brought to my attention by the annotated bibliography in V. A. Afanas'ev's invaluable *Stanovlenie Polkovodcheskogo Iskysstva G. K. Zhukova* (Moscow: Svyatigor, 2006).

50 *Marshal Zhukov: Polkovodets i Chelovek*, 2 vols. (Moscow: APN, 1988); *Marshal Zhukov: Kakim My Ego Pomnim* (Moscow: Politizdat, 1989).

51 G. K. Zhukov, *Vospominaniya i Razmyshleniya*, 3 vols., 10th and 11th eds. (Moscow: APN, 1990–1992).

52 Simonov's notes were published in the main Soviet military history journal *Voenno-Istoricheskii Zhurnal*, nos. 6, 7, 9, 10, 12, 1987. The material was reprinted in Simonov, *Glazami Cheloveka Moego Pokoleniya.*

53 N. G. Pavlenko, 'Razmyshleniya o Sud'be Polkovodtsa', *Voenno-Istoricheskii Zhurnal*, nos. 10–12, 1988.

54 *Marshal Zhukov: Polkovodets i Chelovek,* vol. 1, p. 35.

55 *Georgy Zhukov: Stenogramma Oktyabr'skogo (1957g.) Plenuma TsK KPSS i Drugie Dokumenty,* pp. 583–84.

56 N. Yakovlev, *Zhukov* (Moscow: Molodaya Gvardiya, 1992). Yakovlev had earlier published a short biography of Zhukov for young people: *Stranitsy Zhizni Marshala G. K. Zhukova* (Moscow: Detskaya Literatura, 1985). Mention should also be made of a Syrian biography of Zhukov published in Russian in 1991: M. Tlas, *Marshal G. K. Zhukov: Polkovodets, Strateg* (Moscow: Leksika, 1991).

57 See, for example: A. N. Mertsalov and L. A. Mertsalova, *Inoi Zhukov,* Moscow 1996; A. N. Mertsalov, 'G. K. Zhukov v Publikatsiyakh za period s 1996 do 2001gg', *Voenno-Istoricheskii Arkhiv,* nos. 5 and 6, 2001; B. V. Sokolov, *Georgy Zhukov: Triumf i Padeniya* (Moscow: Ast, 2003); and V. M Safir, 'Novye Mify o Velikoi Otechestvennoi Data Izgotovleniya – 2006 god', *Voenno-Istoricheskii Arkhiv,* nos. 9 and 10, 2007.

58 A. Solzhenitsyn, 'Times of Crisis', in his *Apricot Jam and Other Stories* (Edinburgh, U.K.: Canongate Books, 2011).

59 *Marshal Zhukov: Moskva v Zhizn i Sud'be Polkovodtsa,* pp. 490–91.

CHAPTER 14: MARSHAL OF VICTORY

1 G. K. Zhukov, *Reminiscences,* vol. 2, pp. 474–81. See also *The Memoirs of Marshal Zhukov* (London: Jonathan Cape, 1971), pp. 690–92.

2 M. A. Gareev, *Polkovodtsy Pobedy i Ikh Voennoe Nasledie* (Moscow: Isan, 2004), pp. 125–37.

3 On Stalin as supreme commander see G. Roberts, *Stalin's Wars: From World War to Cold War, 1939–1953* (London: Yale University Press, 2006).

4 A good collection for comparison purposes is M. Carver (ed.), *The War Lords: Military Commanders of the Twentieth Century* (Barnsley, U.K.: Pen & Sword, 2005). The collection includes essays on Zhukov and Konev by John Erickson.

BIBLIOGRAPHY

ARCHIVAL SOURCES

Arkhiv Vneshnei Politiki Rossiiskoi Federatsii (AVPRF – Foreign Policy Archive of the Russian Federation)

Eisenhower Papers, Eisenhower Presidential Library, Abilene, Kansas

Fond 89: The Soviet Communist Party on Trial (Hoover Institution Microfilm Collection)

Rossiiskii Gosudarstvennyi Arkhiv Noveishei Istorii (RGANI – Russian State Archive of Recent History)

Rossiiskii Gosudarstvennyi Arkhiv Sotsial'no-Politicheskoi Istorii (RGASPI – Russian State Archive of Social-Political History)

Rossiiskii Gosudarstvennyi Voennyi Arkhiv (RGVA – Russian State Military Archive)

Volkogonov Papers, Library of Congress, Manuscript Division

NEWSPAPERS

The Current Digest of the Soviet Press
Izvestiya
Komsomol'skaya Pravda
Krasnaya Zvezda (Red Star)
Pravda

PUBLISHED DOCUMENTS

1941 god, 2 vols. Moscow: Demokratiya, 1998.

Georgy Zhukov: Stenogramma Oktyabr'skogo (1957g.) Plenuma TsK KPSS i Drugie Dokumenty. Moscow: Democratiya, 2001.

G. K. Zhukov v Bitve pod Moskvoi: Sbornik Dokumentov. Moscow: Mosgorarkhiv, 1994.

G. K. Zhukov v Stalingradskom Bitve: Sbornik Dokumentov. Moscow: Biblioteka, 1996.

Glavnyi Voennyi Sovet RKKA, 1938–1941: Dokumenty i Materialy. Moscow: Rosspen, 2004.

'Kievskaya Nastupatel'naya Operatsiya v Dokumentakh'. *Voenno-Istoricheskii Zhurnal*, no. 11, 1983.

KPSS o Vooruzhennykh Silakh Sovetskogo Souza: Dokumenty, 1917–1968. Moscow: Voenizdat, 1969.

Kurskaya Bitva, 2 vols. Moscow: Olma-Press, 2003.

'Marshal G. K. Zhukov: Nastuplenie na Berlin Mogu Nachat 19–20.2.45'. *Voenno-Istoricheskii Zhurnal*, no. 2, 1995.

Marshal Zhukov: Moskva v Zhizni i Sud'be Polkovodtsa. Moscow: Glavarkhiv, 2005.

Molotov, Malenkov, Kaganovich, 1957: Stenogramma Iun'skogo Plenuma TsK KPSS i Drugie Dokumenty. Moscow: Mezhdunarodnyi Fond 'Demokratiya', 1998.

Organy Gosudarstvennoi Bezopasnosti SSSR v Velikoi Otechestvennoi Voine, vol. 2. Moscow: Rus', 2000.

'Pobeda na Kurskoi Duge'. *Voenno-Istoricheskii Zhurnal*, no. 7, 1983.

'Podgotovka k Kurskoi Bitve'. *Voenno-Istoricheskii Zhurnal*, no. 6, 1983.

Prezidium TsK KPSS, 1954–1964, vols. 1 and 2. Moscow: Rosspen, 2004, 2006.

Reabilitatsiya: Kak Eto Bylo, 2 vols. Moscow: Materik, 2000, 2003.

Reabilitatsiya: Politicheskie Protsessy, 30–50-Kh godov. Moscow: Politizdatel, 1991.

Russkii Arkhiv: Velikaya Otechestvennaya Voina, 1941–1945. Moscow: Terra, 1993–2000.

   Vol. 12 (1) Nakanune Voiny: Materialy Soveshchaniya Vysshego Ru-kovodyashchego Sostava RKKA, 23–31 Dekabrya 1940g

   Vol. 13 (1) Prikazy Narodnogo Komissara Oborony SSSR, 1937–41, Iunya 1941g

   Vol. 13 (2) Prikazy Narodnogo Komissara Oborony SSSR, 22 Iunya 1941g–1942g

   Vol. 13 (3) Prikazy Narodnogo Komissara Oborony SSSR, 1943–1945gg

   Vol. 14 (1) SSSR i Pol'sha, 1941–1945: k Istorii Voennogo Souza

   Vol. 14 (2) Krasnaya Armiya v Stranakh Tsentral'noi, Severnoi Evropy i na Balkanakh: Dokumenty i Materialy, 1944–1945

   Vol. 16 (1) Stavka VGK: Dokumenty i Materialy 1941 god

   Vol. 16 (2) Stavka VGK: Dokumenty i Materialy 1942 god

   Vol. 16 (3) Stavka VGK: Dokumenty i Materialy 1943 god

   Vol. 16 (4) Stavka VGK: Dokumenty i Materialy 1944–1945gg

   Vol. 23 (1) General'nyi Shtab v Gody Velikoi Otechestvennoi Voiny: Dokumenty i Materialy 1941 god

   Vol. 23 (2) General'nyi Shtab v Gody Velikoi Otechestvennoi Voiny: Dokumenty i Materialy 1942 god

   Vol. 23 (3) General'nyi Shtab v Gody Velikoi Otechestvennoi Voiny: Dokumenty i Materialy 1943 god

   Vol. 23 (4) General'nyi Shtab v Gody Velikoi Otechestvennoi Voiny: Dokumenty i Materialy 1944–45gg

Sovetskaya Voennaya Administratsiya v Germanii, 1945–1949, 3 vols. Moscow: Rosspen, 2004–2006.
Sovetskii Souz i Vengerskii Krizis, 1956 goda. Moscow: Rosspen, 1998.
SSSR i Germanskii Vopros, 1941–1949, vol. 2. Moscow: Mezhdunarodnye Otnosheniya, 2000.
Stalingrad, 1942–1943: Stalingradskaya Bitva v Dokumentakh. Moscow: Biblioteka, 1995.
Stalingradskaya Bitva, 2 vols. Moscow: Olma-Press, 2002.
Voennaya Razvedka Informiruet: Dokumenty Razvedypravleniya Krasnoi Armii, 1939–1941. Moscow: Demokratiya, 2008.
von Oppen, B. R. (ed.). *Documents on Germany Under Occupation, 1945–1954*. London: Oxford University Press, 1955.
'*Zimnyaya Voina': Rabota nad Oshibkami, Aprel'–Mai 1940g*. Moscow: Letnii Sad, 2004.

REFERENCE WORKS

Georgy Zhukov: Al'bom. Moscow: Poligrafresursy, 1995.
Isaev, S. I. 'Vekhi Frontovogo Puti'. *Voenno-Istoricheskii Zhurnal*, no. 10, 1991.
Marshal Sovetskogo Souza G. K. Zhukov: Kronika Zhizni. Moscow: Russkaya Kniga, 1998.
Na Priyome u Stalina: Tetradi (Zhurnaly) Zapisei Lits, Prinyatykh I. V. Stalinym (1924–1953). Moscow: Novyi Khronograf, 2008.
Platanov, S. P. (ed.). *Vtoraya Mirovaya Voina, 1939–1945: Al'bom Skhem*. Moscow: Voenizdat, 1958.
Rzheshevsky, O. A. (ed.). *Kto Byl Kto v Velikoi Otechestvennoi Voine, 1941–1945*. Moscow: Respublika, 2000.
Taylor, B. *Barbarossa to Berlin: A Chronology of the Campaigns on the Eastern Front 1941 to 1945*, 2 vols. Staplehurst, U.K.: Spellmount, 2003–2004.
Velikaya Otechestvennaya Voina, 1941–1945gg: Kampanii i Strategicheskie Operatsii v Tsifrakh, 2 vols. Moscow: MVD Rossii/Glavarkhiv Goroda Moskvy, 2010.

MEMOIRS

Aleksandrov, I. G. (ed.), *Marshal Zhukov: Polkovodets i Chelovek*, 2 vols. Moscow: APN, 1988.
Antipenko, N. 'Ot Visly do Odera'. *Voenno-Istoricheskii Zhurnal*, no. 3, 1965.
Bagramyan, I. K. *Tak Shli My k Pobede*. Moscow: Voenizdat, 1988.
Bialer, S. *Stalin and His Generals: Soviet Military Memoirs of World War II*. London: Souvenir Press, 1970.
Buchin, A. N. *170 000 Kilometrov s G. Zhukovym*. Moscow: Molodaya Gvardiya, 1994.
Cassidy, H. C. *Moscow Dateline*. Boston: Houghton Mifflin, 1943.
Chuikov, V. I. *Konets Tret'ego Reikha*. Moscow: Rossiya, 1973.
———. *Ot Stalingrada do Berlina*. Moscow: Voenizdat, 1980.

'G. K. Zhukov: Iz Neopublikovannykh Vospominanii'. *Kommunist,* no. 14, 1988.

Griogorenko, P. G. *Memoirs.* New York: Norton, 1982.

Gromyko, A. *Memories.* London: Hutchinson, 1989.

Khrushchev, Nikita. *Khrushchev Remembers.* London: Sphere, 1971.

——. *Khrushchev Remembers: The Last Testament.* London: André Deutsch, 1974.

Konev, I. *Year of Victory.* Moscow: Progress Publishers, 1969.

——. *Zapiski Komanduushchego Frontom.* Moscow: Voenizdat, 1981.

Kuznetsov, N. G. *Kursom k Pobede.* Moscow: Golos, 2000.

——. *Nakanune.* Moscow: Voenizdat, 1969.

Main Front: Soviet Leaders Look Back on World War II. London: Brassey's Defence Publishers, 1987.

Malashenko, E. I. 'Osobyi Korpus v Ogne Budapeshta'. *Voenno-Istoricheskii Zhurnal,* nos. 10–12, 1993, no. 1, 1994.

Mastykina, I. *Zheny i Deti Georgiya Zhukova.* Moscow: Komsomol'skya Pravda, 1996. Interviews with Zhukov's daughters and others originally published in *Komsomol'skaya Pravda,* 7 June 1996, 22 August 1996, 30 September 1996 and 3 October 1996.

Meretskov, K. A. *Na Sluzhbe Narodu.* Moscow: Politizdat, 1968.

——. *Serving the People.* Moscow: Progress Publishers, 1971.

Mikoyan, A. *Tak Bylo.* Moscow: Vargrius, 1999.

Mirkina, A. *Vtoraya Pobeda Marshala Zhukova.* Moscow: Vniigmi-Mtsd, 2000.

Moskalenko, K. S. *Na Ugo-Zapadnom Napravlenii,* 2nd. ed., 2 vols. Moscow: Nauka, 1975.

Naimark, N. M. *The Russians in Germany: A History of the Soviet Zone of Occupation, 1945–1949.* Cambridge, Mass.: Harvard University Press, 1995.

'Papa Chetverok ne Lyubil. Dnevnik Smotrel Pridirchivo'. *Izvestiya,* December 1, 2006 (Interview with Era and Ella Zhukova).

Rokossovsky, K. *Soldatskii Dolg.* Moscow: Olma-Press, 2002.

——. *A Soldier's Duty.* Moscow: Progress Publishers, 1970.

Samsonov, A. M. (ed.), *9 Maya 1945 goda.* Moscow: Nauka, 1970.

——. *Stalingradskaya Epopeya.* Moscow: Nauka, 1998.

Shtemenko, S. 'Kak Planirovalas' Poslednyaya Kampaniya po Razgromu Gitlerovskoi Germanii'. *Voenno-Istoricheskii Zhurnal,* no. 5, 1965.

——. *The Soviet General Staff at War, 1941–1945,* 2 vols. Moscow: Progress Publishers, 1970, 1986.

Simonov, K. *Glazami Cheloveka Moego Pokoleniya.* Moscow: APN, 1989.

Smirnov, S. S., et al. (eds.). *Marshal Zhukov: Kakim My Ego Pomnim.* Moscow: Politizdat, 1988.

Sudoplatov, P. *Special Tasks: The Memoirs of an Unwanted Witness – A Soviet Spymaster.* London: Warner, 1994.

Troyanovsky, O. *Cherez Gody i Rasstoyaniya.* Moscow: Vargrius, 1997.

Vasilevsky, A. M. *A Lifelong Cause.* Moscow: Progress Publishers, 1981.

Yeremenko, A. I. *Stalingrad.* Moscow: Voenizdat, 1961.

——. *V Nachale Voiny.* Moscow: Ast, 2006.

Zakharov, M. V. *General'nyi Shtab v Predvoennye Gody.* Moscow: Ast, 2005.

Zhukov, G. 'Korotke o Staline'. *Pravda,* 20 January 1989.

————. *Reminiscences and Reflections,* 2 vols. Moscow: Progress Publishers, 1985.

————. *Vospominaniya i Razmyshleniya,* 10th and 11th eds., 3 vols. Moscow: APN, 1992.

Zhukova, M. *Marshal Zhukov – Moi Otets.* Moscow: Sretenskogo Monastyriya, 2005.

SECONDARY STUDIES

Abaturov, V. *1941: Na Zapanom Napravlenii.* Moscow: Yauza-Eksmo, 2007.

Afanas'ev, V. A. *Stanovlenie Polkovodcheskogo Iskusstva G. K. Zhukova.* Moscow: Svyatigor, 2006.

Andy, J. 'Politics and the Soviet Military: Civil-Military Relations in the Soviet Union in the Khrushchev Era, 1953–1964'. U.K.: University of Birmingham, Ph.D. thesis, 2011.

Antonov, V. S. 'Tri Epizoda iz Memuarov Znamenitogo Polkovodtsa'. *Voprosy Istorii,* no. 3, 2003.

Astrakhanskii, V. S. 'Biblioteka G. K. Zhukova', *Arkhivno-Informatsionnyi Bulleten',* no. 13, 1996.

Axell, A. *Marshal Zhukov: The Man Who Beat Hitler.* London: Pearson, 2003.

Beevor, A. *Berlin: The Downfall 1945.* London: Penguin, 2002.

————. *Stalingrad.* London: Penguin, 1999.

Bellamy, C. *Absolute War: Soviet Russia in the Second World War.* London: Macmillan, 2007.

Beshanov, V. *God 1942 – 'Uchebnyi'.* Minsk: Kharvest, 2002.

————. *Leningradskaya Oborona.* Minsk: Kharvest, 2006.

Bezymenski, L. *The Death of Adolf Hitler.* London: Michael Joseph, 1968.

Bitva pod Kurskom. Moscow: Khranitel', 2006.

Bitva za Berlin. Moscow: Ast, 2007.

Bitva za Dnepr, 1943g. Moscow: Khranitel', 2007.

Bitva za Moskvu. Moscow: Moskovskii Pabochii, 1968.

Bitva za Moskvu: Moskovskaya Operatsiya Zapadnogo Fronta, 16 Noyabrya 1941g.–31 Yanvarya 1942g. Moscow: Tranzitkniga, 2006.

Bobylev, P. N. 'K Kakoi Voine Gotovilsya General'nyishtab RKKA v 1941 godu?' *Otechestvennaya Istoriya,* no. 5, 1995.

Boog, H., et al. (eds.). *Germany and the Second World War,* vol. 6. Oxford, U.K.: Clarendon Press, 2001.

Braithwaite, R. *Moscow 1941.* New York: Knopf, 2006.

Bykov, K. *Khar'kovskii 'Kotel' 1942.* Moscow: Yauza-Eksmo, 2007.

Carver, M. (ed.). *The War Lords: Military Commanders of the Twentieth Century.* Barnsley, U.K.: Pen & Sword, 2005.

Chaney, O. P. *Zhukov,* rev. ed. Norman: University of Oklahoma Press, 1996.

Chmielarz, A. 'Warsaw Fought Alone: Reflections on Aid to and the Fall of the 1944 Uprising'. *The Polish Review,* vol. 39, no. 4, 1994.

Christensen, S. A., and F. P. Jensen. 'Superpower Under Pressure: The Secret Speech of Minister of Defence Zhukov in East Berlin, March 1957. www. php. isn.ethz.ch/collections/coll_zhukov.

Chubaryan, A. O., and H. Shukman (eds.). *Stalin and the Soviet-Finnish War, 1939–1940*. London: Frank Cass, 2002.

Cocks, P. M. 'The Purge of Marshal Zhukov'. *Slavic Review*, vol. 22, no. 3, 1963.

Colton, T. J. 'The Zhukov Affair Reconsidered'. *Soviet Studies*, vol. 29, April 1977.

Colvin, J. *Nomonhan*. London: Quartet, 1999.

———. *Zhukov: The Conqueror of Berlin*. London: Weidenfeld & Nicolson, 2004.

Coox, A. D. *Nomonhan: Japan Against Russia, 1939*. Stanford, Calif.: Stanford University Press, 1990.

Craig, W. *Enemy at the Gates*. London: Hodder & Stoughton, 1973.

Daines, V. *Zhukov*. Moscow: Molodaya Gvardia, 2005.

———. *Zhukov: Rozhdennyi Pobezhdat'*. Moscow: Yauza-Eksmo, 2008.

Erickson, J. 'Poslednii Shturm: The Soviet Drive to Berlin, 1945'. In G. Bennett (ed.), *The End of the War in Europe 1945*. London: HMSO, 1996.

———. *The Road to Berlin*. London: Weidenfeld & Nicolson, 1983.

———. *The Road to Stalingrad*. New York: Harper & Row, 1975.

———. *The Soviet High Command: A Military-Political History, 1918–1941*, 3rd ed. London: Frank Cass, 2001.

———. 'Zhukov', in M. Carver (ed.). *The War Lords: Military Commanders of the Twentieth Century*. Barnsley, U.K.: Pen & Sword, 2005.

Evangelista, M. *'Why Keep Such an Army?': Khrushchev's Troop Reductions*. Cold War International History Project Working Paper No. 19, December 1997.

Fainsod, M. *How Russia Is Ruled*. Cambridge, Mass.: Harvard University Press, 1963.

Forster, J. and E. Mawdsley. 'Hitler and Stalin in Perspective: Secret Speeches on the Eve of Barbarossa'. *War in History*, vol. 11, no. 1, 2006.

Fugate, B., and L. Dvoretsky. *Thunder on the Dnepr: Zhukov-Stalin and the Defeat of Hitler's Blitzkrieg*. Novato, Calif.: Presidio, 2001.

Fursenko, A., and T. Naftali. *Khrushchev's Cold War*. New York: Norton, 2006.

Gallagher, M. P. *The Soviet History of World War II: Myths, Memories, Realities*. New York: Praeger, 1963.

———. 'Trends in the Soviet Historiography of the Second World War'. In J. Keep (ed.), *Contemporary History in the Soviet Mirror*. New York: Praeger, 1964.

Gareev, M. A. *Polkovodtsy Pobedy i Ikh Voennoe Nasledie*. Moscow: Isan, 2004.

Garthoff, R. L. (ed.). *Sino-Soviet Military Relations*. New York: Praeger, 1966.

Gerasimova, S. *Rzhev 42: Pozitsionnaya Boinya*. Moscow: Yauza-Eksmo, 2007.

Getty, J. A., and R. T. Manning (eds.). *Stalinist Terror: New Perspectives*. Cambridge, U.K.: Cambridge University Press, 1993.

Getty, J. Arch, and O. V. Naumov (eds.). *The Road to Terror: Stalin and the Self-Destruction of the Bolsheviks, 1932–1939*. New Haven, Conn.: Yale University Press, 1999.

Glantz, D. M. *After Stalingrad: The Red Army's Winter Offensive, 1942–1943*. Solihull, U.K.: Helion, 2009.

———. *Barbarossa: Hitler's Invasion of Russia, 1941*. Stroud, U.K.: Tempus, 2001.

———. *The Battle for Leningrad, 1941–1944*. Lawrence: University Press of Kansas, 2002.

———. *Colossus Reborn: The Red Army at War, 1941–1943*. Lawrence: University Press of Kansas, 2005.

———. *Kharkov 1942: Anatomy of a Military Disaster Through Soviet Eyes*. Shepperton, U.K.: Ian Allan, 1998.

———. *Soviet Military Deception in the Second World War*. London: Frank Cass, 1989.

———. *Stumbling Colossus: The Red Army on the Eve of World War*. Lawrence: University Press of Kansas, 1998.

———. *Zhukov's Greatest Defeat: The Red Army's Epic Disaster in Operation Mars, 1942*. Shepperton, U.K.: Ian Allan, 2000.

Glantz, D. M., and J. M. House. *Armageddon at Stalingrad*. Lawrence: University Press of Kansas, 2009.

———. *The Battle of Kursk*. Lawrence: University Press of Kansas, 1999.

———. *To the Gates of Stalingrad: Soviet-German Combat Operations, April–August 1942*. Lawrence: University Press of Kansas, 2009.

Glantz, D. M., and H. S. Orenstein. *Belorussia 1944: The Soviet General Staff Study*. London: Frank Cass, 2001.

Golovin, M. I. 'Uroki Dvukh Operatsii'. *Voenno-Istoricheskii Zhurnal*, no. 1, 1988.

Gorodetsky, G. *Grand Delusion: Stalin and the German Invasion of Russia*. New Haven, Conn.: Yale University Press, 1999.

Habeck, M. R. *Storm of Steel: The Development of Armour Doctrine in Germany and the Soviet Union, 1919–1939*. Ithaca, N.Y.: Cornell University Press, 2003.

Haslam, J. *The Soviet Union and the Threat from the East, 1933–1941*. London: Macmillan, 1992.

Hayward, J.S.A. *Stopped at Stalingrad: The Luftwaffe and Hitler's Defeat in the East, 1942–1943*. Lawrence: University Press of Kansas, 1998.

Holloway, D. *Stalin and the Bomb*. New Haven, Conn.: Yale University Press, 1994.

Irinarkhov, R. S. *Kievskii Osobyi*. Minsk: Harvest, 2006.

Isaev, A. *Berlin 45-go*. Moscow: Yauza-Eksmo, 2007.

———. *Georgy Zhukov*. Moscow: Yauza-Eksmo, 2006.

———. *Mify i Pravda o Marshale Zhukove*. Moscow: Yauza-Eksmo, 2010.

———. *Nastuplenie Marshala Shaposhnikova*. Moscow: Yauza-Eksmo, 2005.

———. *Stalingrad*. Moscow: Yauza-Eksmo, 2005.

Jones, M. *Stalingrad: How the Red Army Triumphed*. Barnsley, U.K.: Pen & Sword, 2007.

———. *Total War: From Stalingrad to Berlin*. London: John Murray, 2011.

Karpov, V. *Marshal Zhukov*. Moscow: Veche, 1994.

Krasnov, V. *Zhukov: Marshal Velikoi Imperii*. Moscow: Olma-Press, 2000.

Kulikov, V. G. *Tri Marshala Pobedy*. Moscow: RAN, 1999.

Kumanev, G. A. *Ryadom so Stalinym*. Moscow: Byliia, 1999.

———. *Stalingradskaya Bitva*. Moscow: Bimpa, 2007.

Kunitskii, P. T. 'Padenie Berlina: Kogda Ona Moglo Sostoyat'sya?' *Voenno-Istoricheskii Zhurnal*, no. 9, 2006.

Lenson, G. *The Damned Inheritance: The Soviet Union and the Manchurian Crisis*. Tallahassee, Fla.: Diplomatic Press, 1974.

Le Tissier, T. *Marshal Zhukov at the Oder*. Stroud, U.K.: Sutton, 2008.

Lomagin, N. *Neizvestnaya Blokada*, 2 vols. Moscow: Olma-Press, 2002.

Mal'kov, V. 'Pochemu Marshal Zhukov ne Letal v SSha?' *Sputnik*, no. 5, 1994.

Mawdsley, E. 'Crossing the Rubicon: Soviet Plans for Offensive War in 1940–1941'. *International History Review*, December 2003.

———. *December 1941: Twelve Days That Began a World War*. London: Yale University Press, 2011.

———. *Thunder in the East: The Nazi-Soviet War, 1941–1945*. London: Hodder Arnold, 2005.

Mel'nikov, V. *Ikh Poslal na Smert' Zhukov? Gibel' Armii Generala Efremova*. Moscow: Eksmo, 2009.

Mel'tukhov, M. *Upushchennyi Shans Stalina*. Moscow: Veche, 2000.

Mertsalov, A. N. 'G. K. Zhukov v Publikatsiyakh za period s 1996 do 2001gg'. *Voenno-Istoricheskii Arkhiv*, nos. 5 and 6, 2001.

———, and L. A. Mertsalova. *Inoi Zhukov*. Moscow, 1996.

Mulligan, T. P. 'Spies, Ciphers and "Zitadelle": Intelligence and the Battle of Kursk, 1943'. *Journal of Contemporary History*, vol. 22, 1987.

Murphy, R. *Diplomat Among Warriors*. New York: Doubleday, 1964.

Nagorski, A. *The Greatest Battle*. London: Aurum, 2007.

Naumov, V. P. ' "Delo" Marshala G. K. Zhukova, 1957g'. *Novaya i Noveishaya Istoriya*, no. 1, 2001.

Naveh, S. *In Pursuit of Military Excellence: The Evolution of Operational Theory*. London: Frank Cass, 1997.

Nettl, J. P. *The Eastern Zone and Soviet Policy in Germany, 1945–1950*. London: Oxford University Press, 1951.

Operatsiya 'Bagration'. Moscow: Olma-Press, 2004.

Pavlenko, N. G. 'Razmyshleniya o Sud'be Polkovodsta'. *Voenno-Istoricheskii Zhurnal*, nos. 10–12, 1988.

Pavlov, D. V. *Leningrad v Blokade*. Moscow: Voenizdat, 1958.

Pons, S., and A. Romano (eds.). *Russia in the Age of Wars, 1941–1945*. Milan: Feltrinelli, 2000.

Pospelov, P. N. (ed.). *Istoriya Velikoi Otechestvennoi Voiny Sovetskogo Souza*, 6 vols. Moscow: Voenizdat, 1960–1965.

Read, A., and D. Fisher. *The Fall of Berlin*. London: Pimlico, 2002.

Reese, R. R. *Red Commanders: A Social History of the Soviet Army Officer Corps, 1918–1991*. Lawrence: University Press of Kansas, 2005.

———. *Stalin's Reluctant Soldiers: A Social History of the Red Army, 1925–1941*. Lawrence: University Press of Kansas, 1996.

———. *Why Stalin's Soldiers Fought*. Lawrence: University Press of Kansas, 2011.

Roberts, G. *A Chance for Peace? The Soviet Campaign to End the Cold War*,

1953–1955. Cold War International History Project Working Paper No. 57, December 2008.

———. *Molotov: Stalin's Cold Warrior.* Washington, D.C.: Potomac, 2012.

———. *Stalin: His Time and Ours.* Dublin: IAREES, 2005.

———. *Stalin's Wars: From World War to Cold War, 1939–1953.* London: Yale University Press, 2006.

———. *Victory at Stalingrad: The Battle That Changed History.* London: Pearson/Longman, 2002.

Rokossovsky, K. K. (ed.). *Velikaya Pobeda na Volge.* Moscow: Voenizdat, 1965.

Rotundo, L. 'Stalin and the Outbreak of War in 1941'. *Journal of Contemporary History,* vol. 24, 1989.

Rotundo, L. (ed.). *Battle for Stalingrad: The 1943 General Staff Study.* London: Pergamon-Brassey's, 1989.

Runov, V. A. *Zhukov protiv Gal'dera.* Moscow: Yauza-Eksmo, 2010.

Ryan, C. *The Last Battle.* London: NEL, 1968.

Rzheshevsky, O. A. 'Poslednii Shturm: Zhukov ili Konev'. *Mir Istorii,* http:// gpw.tellur.ru.

———. 'Vzyat' Berlin! Novye Dokumenty'. *Novaya i Noveishaya Istoriya,* no. 4, 1995.

Safir, V. M. 'Novye Mify o Velikoi Otechestvennoi'. *Voenno-Istoricheskii Arkhiv,* nos. 9 and 10, 2007.

Salisbury, H. *The 900 Days: The Siege of Leningrad.* New York: Harper & Row, 1969.

Salisbury, H. (ed.). *Marshal Zhukov's Greatest Battles.* London: Sphere, 1971.

Samuelson, L. *Plans for Stalin's War Machine: Tukhachevskii and Military-Economic Planning, 1925–1941.* London: Palgrave, 2000.

Scott, H. Fast, and W. F. Scott (eds.). *The Soviet Art of War.* Boulder, Colo.: Westview, 1982.

Shukman, H. (ed.). *Stalin's Generals.* London: Phoenix, 1997.

Simonov, K. *Tovarishchi po Oruzhiu.* Moscow: Gosudarstvennoe Izdatel'stvo Khudozhestvennoi Literatury, 1961.

Sokolov, B. V. *Georgy Zhukov: Triumf i Padeniya.* Moscow: Ast, 2003.

Sokolovsky, V. D. (ed.). *Voennaya Strategiya.* Moscow: Voenizdat, 1962.

Spahr, W. J. *Stalin's Lieutenants: A Study of Command Under Stress.* Novato, Calif.: Presidio, 1997.

———. *Zhukov: The Rise and Fall of a Great Captain.* Novato, Calif.: Presidio, 1993.

Stalingradskaya Epopeya. Moscow: Nauka, 1968.

Stoecker, S. W. *Forging Stalin's Army: Marshal Tukhachevsky and the Politics of Military Innovation.* Boulder, Colo.: Westview, 1998.

Stone, D. R. *Hammer and Rifle: The Militarization of the Soviet Union, 1926–1933.* Lawrence: University Press of Kansas, 2000.

Stone, D. R. (ed.). *The Soviet Union at War.* Barnsley, U.K.: Pen & Sword, 2011.

Suvorov, V. *Beru Svoi Slova Obratno.* Donetsk: Harvest, 2005.

———. *The Chief Culprit: Stalin's Grand Design to Start World War II.* Annapolis, Md.: Naval Institute Press, 2008.

———. *Icebreaker: Who Started the Second World War.* London: Hamish Hamilton, 1990.

————. *Ten' Pobedy*. Donetsk: Harvest, 2003.

Sverdlov, F. D. *Oshibki G.K. Zhukova (god 1942)*. Moscow: Monolit, 2002.

Taubman, W. *Khrushchev: The Man and His Era*. London: Simon & Schuster, 2003.

Taylor, T. H. *Behind Hitler's Lines*. New York: Ballantine, 2004.

Tlas, Marshal M. *G. K. Zhukov: Polkovodets, Strateg*. Moscow: Leksika, 1991.

Trevor-Roper, H. R. *Hitler's War Directives, 1939–1945*. London: Sidgwick & Jackson, 1964.

Tucker-Jones, A. *Stalin's Revenge: Operation Bagration and the Annihilation of Army Group Centre*. Barnsley, U.K.: Pen & Sword, 2009.

Ustinov, D. F. (ed.). *Istoriya Vtoroi Mirovoi Voiny, 1939–1945*, 12 vols. Moscow: Voenizdat, 1973–1978.

von Hagen, M., *Soldiers in the Proletarian Dictatorship: The Red Army and the Soviet Socialist State, 1917–1930*. Ithaca, N.Y.: Cornell University Press, 1990.

Vorob'ev, F. D., et al. *Poslednii Shturm (Berlinskaya Operatsiya 1945g)*. Moscow: Voenizdat, 1970.

Vorotnikov, M. F. *G. K. Zhukov na Khalkhin-Gole*. Omsk: OKI, 1989.

Weeks, A. L. *Stalin's Other War: Soviet Grand Strategy, 1939–1941*. Lanham, Md.: Rowman & Littlefield, 2002.

Werth, A. *Russia at War, 1941–1945*. London: Pan, 1965.

————. *The Year of Stalingrad*. London: Hamish Hamilton, 1946.

Yakovlev, N. *Zhukov*. Moscow: Molodaya Gvardiya, 1992.

Yarushina, L. V. *Tri Marshala Pobedy*. Moscow: RAN, 1999.

Zamulin, V. *Demolishing the Myth: The Tank Battle at Prokhorovka*. Solihull, U.K.: Helion, 2011.

Zav'yalov, A. S., and T. E. Kalyanin. *Vostochno – Pomeranskaya Operatsiya*. Moscow: Voenizdat, 1960.

Zhuk, U. A. *Neizvestnye Stranitsy Bitvy za Moskvu*. Moscow: Khranitel', 2005.

Zolotarev, V. A., and G. N. Sevast'yanov (eds.). *Velikaya Otechestvennaya Voina, 1941–1945*. 4 vols. Moscow: Nauka, 1998–1999.

INDEX

Page numbers in *italics* refer to maps.

ABOUT THE AUTHOR

GEOFFREY ROBERTS is the author of *Stalin's Wars* and *Victory at Stalingrad*. He is professor and head of the School of History at University College Cork, Ireland. Roberts is a frequent contributor to British, Irish and American newspapers and to popular-history journals and has been a consultant for TV and radio documentaries.